Patsy

Patsy

The Life and Times of Patsy Cline

Margaret Jones

DA CAPO PRESS • NEW YORK

Library of Congress Cataloging-in-Publication Data

Jones, Margaret, 1952–
    Patsy: the life and times of Patsy Cline / Margaret Jones.
        p.   cm.
    Originally published: New York: HarperCollins, c1994.
    Includes bibliographical references, discography, and index.
    ISBN 0-306-80886-2 (alk. paper)
    1. Cline, Patsy, 1932–1963. 2. Country musicians—United States—Biography. I. Title.
[ML420.C57J66   1999]
782.421642′092—dc21
                                                                98-43424
                                                                     CIP

3 4 5 6 7 8 9

First Da Capo Press edition 1999

This Da Capo Press paperback edition of *Patsy* is an unabridged republication of the paperback edition published in New York in 1995, with several minor textual emendations. It is reprinted by arrangement with the author.

Published by Da Capo Press, Inc.
A Member of Perseus Books Group
233 Spring Street, New York, N.Y. 10013

Manufactured in the United States of America

Acknowledgments

A heartfelt thanks to all those whose recollections helped make her real and whose energy nurtured this book: Otto Kitsinger, for reading my manuscript and for help in Nashville along the way; Rick Kot and Jennifer Hull, my editors at HarperCollins; Maureen O'Brien, for giving me the idea to do this book; Don Roy, discomeister extraordinaire; Tom Miller, for technical assistance; my agents, Maureen and Eric Lasher.

Writers who generously shared their notes and their time: Brian Burnes, Joli Jensen, Joe Sasfy, Steven Schmidt, Dale Vinicur, Jonny Whiteside; thanks also to Wolf Bolz, Jay Bruder, Mahli Caron, Paul Kingsbury and Ronnie Pugh at the County Music Foundation, Marion Cox, Bill and Linda Culver, Judith Flannery-Lukas, Rochelle Gazin, Christopher Gibson, Terese Hartman, Janice Head, Gertie Horak, Michael James, Bill Jones, Helen Jones, Marie Jones, Rosemary Jones, Tim Jones, Bob Joseph, Anthony Kar, Sandy LeClerg, Patsy Montana, Bernard Schwartz, Ellen and Michael Shapiro, Claudia Simms, Christian Smith, Thomas Tarleton, Lola Vance, and Elizabeth Whitney.

She has come through in spite of everything—unsubordinated by her material, her early sentimentality, false starts, and bad choices. Her integrity cannot be sufficiently remembered with awards, whether they be Pulitzer Prizes, medals of the American Academy, or honorary degrees. She has made herself the complete mistress of her talent. Her foot is on her native heath and her name is Willa Cather.

—Louise Bogan
New Yorker, August 8, 1931

A lot of fear went through me when Patsy died. It just about killed me. I remember thinking, "What's going to become of me? Who's going to look after me? Who's going to fight for me?" I felt all alone in the world, and I was real scared.

Patsy was my closest girlfriend in life. But she wasn't just my girlfriend. She was my protector. She looked out for me. She taught me how to dress. She taught me how to get on and off the stage, how to wear makeup, how to start a show and how to leave people wanting more at the end. She made sure I had clothes to wear and many times when she bought an outfit for herself, she'd buy one for me just like it. She bought curtains for my house because I was too broke to buy 'em. She promoted me with the radio stations all she could. She'd tell those disk jockeys, "If you want to talk to me, you'll have to talk to both of us." We'd get so silly doing our interviews. I'd love to get ahold of them tapes. They probably erased them the next day.

She used to call me "little gal." I've had close friends in the business, but I think she probably more or less didn't have many close friends. She would tell me things. She'd say, "Take this to your grave." And those things I will take to my grave and things I told her she took to her's. There are some things we'll never know. Maybe I wasn't her best friend, but she was mine. Maybe she saw something of herself in me, 'cause she and I both grew up the hard way, had to be women when we were children, and she was a woman, a wise, older woman, even though she was so young when she died. Whenever there was any problem I would take it to Patsy, and she would pat me on the shoulder and say, "Hey—don't ever let nothin' get you down. You got to run your own life. It's goin' to be all right." And it was. She's the one that gave me enough confidence to know that I could do anything I set out to do. She did, and I did, and I can.

Patsy didn't let nobody tell her what to do. She done what she felt, and if a man got in her way she let 'em know they couldn't stand there. I thought that was good of her. I think that's probably why I started writing like I did. Songs like "Don't Come Home A-Drinkin' with Lovin' on Your Mind," "You Ain't Woman Enough to Take My Man," and "The Pill." I don't think any of them would get anybody worried today, but back then the girls would be too scared or too embarrassed to sing 'em. I was a little braver than most of the others I guess, I was the first one to get my records banned. But every record of mine that was banned became a number one hit.

I think of her all the time. I love her family today just like I did then. I even named one of my twins after her. Since I sing her songs and I hear other people sing her songs, there's hardly a day goes by that I don't think of her. I think about the way she would hold out one arm, real ladylike. When she walked out you noticed her 'cause she knew who she was and what she was doing. And that arm. She always used that arm. It was like a prop. Even on slow songs. That arm could do what most people couldn't do with their whole voice, with their whole body. And she never used any choreography. It was just the voice. I can't imitate her. I started out by imitating Kitty Wells, but there's something about Patsy I can't imitate, and I won't try. To me, Patsy was my best friend and I couldn't imitate her. It would hurt too much. I think she showed the world what music is supposed to sound like. She had a big impact on young and old alike, there was no age barrier. Her music hit all phases of music—pop, rock, country. I'm sure she was one of God's greatest singing angels. There would be no limit to what she'd be doing today if she were still alive and, Lord, I wish she was.

Those days after she died were like a dream, a bad dream. The one thing that kept me going was remembering the last words she spoke to me when I saw her for the last time. She hit me on the bottom and said, "Little gal, it's gonna be you and me, all the way. We're gonna stick together forever." And she meant forever.

Some people don't like me saying it—they think you're crazy—but I believe in ESP and reincarnation and psychic stuff, and I think that those who don't believe it are crazy because reincarnation is the only thing that makes sense to me why we're here on earth. I believe, like the Hindus, that with each lifetime we get to be better people as we try for perfection. Maybe it's because of our past lives together—I do know Patsy and I have a psychic bond. I have dreams about her and sometimes she comes to me. I know that she guides me, and I feel she's here. She can be so funny and so delightful, and she can be so stern when she has to be. Once I was in Vegas, at the Riviera, and when I got to a medley of her songs I lost my voice completely. Here I am, right up on stage, and I'm thinking, "Oh, Patsy, what am I gonna do?" I kind of closed my eyes and opened them up, and you know, you're in a spotlight, looking right into that light. It looked like she was just sitting up above, sitting there, looking at me. There she was, grinning, and sitting with one leg tucked under her, one leg over, and she just kind of had her arms folded around that one leg, and she just smiled at me and I felt her patting me on the shoulder as if to say, "Everything's fine." And I remember thinking I'm so nervous. Then she said, "Now listen—don't let me down. You can do it." And I got through it and I don't even remember singing. So now when I get troubles with my voice or other problems, I say to myself I can get through this because Patsy is here with me. And she is, just like she said she would be.

—LORETTA LYNN

Introduction

In May 1957, Patsy Cline rode through the streets of her hometown of Winchester, Virginia, in the biggest event of the year. Accompanied by the blaring horns and thundering drums of a hundred marching bands, she smiled until her face was sore and waved as thousands of craning spectators lined up ten deep along the parade route. Where Patsy grew up it was every little girl's dream to sit on the top of the back seat of a convertible in a beautiful gown and ride down the streets of Winchester in the Grand Feature Parade of the annual Apple Blossom Festival.

For the last ten years, Patsy had paid her dues, working in virtually every juke joint, club, fire hall, Moose Lodge, park, drive-in theater and county fair in the tristate area, in towns like Brunswick, Barryville, Warrenton, Mount Jackson, Elkton, Front Royal, Martinsburg.

Everywhere she sang, people just loved her to pieces. She'd get up there and by the end of the evening she'd have them "mopping tears," she'd say. But for some damn reason, they never accepted her in Winchester. "I don't know what's wrong with this town," she once complained to a friend. "It's like they don't want a person to make anything of herself." In a way, she was right.

Not that local recognition had eluded Patsy. Small towns are hotbeds of activity. Out of boredom, people get very creative with their spare time. And there was a whirlwind of speculation about Patsy, all of which led to the same conclusion: "She'll never amount to a damn."

At one point, Patsy, decked out in full western regalia, sang between two B movies on the roof of the cement block refreshment stand of Winchester's Royal Drive-In. In the middle of pouring her heart out she was honked at and booed by certain folks in Winchester who sat behind their windshields sucking slushies, impatient for the next flick. Patsy fled into a trailer that was used as an office with the local musicians who backed her. "Why? Why do people in Winchester treat me like this?" she cried angrily. Then she uttered what had become her refrain: "One of these days I'm going to come to Winchester and draw one hell of a crowd. One hell of a crowd!"

Sure enough, through a stunning series of events, Patsy had recently cracked into the big time. It started a few months earlier, in January, when she won Arthur Godfrey's "Talent Scouts," the prime TV variety show with a top ten Nielsen rating and a combined radio-TV audience of 82 million. It was the biggest house Patsy had ever played, and they loved her. The song that launched her, "Walkin' After Midnight," was a hit, topping Jerry Lee Lewis, Bill Haley and the Platters. Godfrey, whose nasal baritone and folksy patter were as familiar as good ole Lipton Tea—one of his favorite sponsors—invited her to be a regular on his show. That week she got more fan mail than Godfrey himself. Godfrey paid her $1000 a week, a hell of a lot more than the $8-a-night gigs she used to work around Winchester.

A reporter from the *Winchester Evening Star* who interviewed her one month before the Apple Blossom fete noted she had just returned from a cross-country tour that took her as far west as Los Angeles. Ed Sullivan was begging for her services, as was Alan Freed, the self-styled "King of Rock and Roll." She had a fan club that kept track of such trivia as her hobbies ("collecting salt and pepper shakers, earrings and pictures") and her favorite foods ("spaghetti and fried chicken"). Best of all, she was finally able to say what she had always, ever since she was a little girl, dreamed of saying to her mama, and she inscribed the words she had mentally rehearsed all those years diagonally across the bottom of a glamorous new publicity photo of her in her large, flowing handwriting: "We finally made it!"

The dark-haired, dark-eyed beauty with softly rounded cheeks and creamy skin, whose picture took up a whole page in the Apple Blossom Festival program book, bore a striking resemblance to Patsy. But it was not Patsy. Not by a long shot. The caption read: "HER MAJESTY QUEEN SHENANDOAH XXX."

"Miss Anne Denise Doughty-Tichborne, 1957 Queen of the Apple Blossoms, is an English 'cousin' from across the seas. The nineteen-year-old daughter of Sir Anthony and Lady Doughty-Tichborne was educated in England, Italy and Spain. . . . Queen Shenandoah XXX who, on her seventeenth birthday, was presented to Her Majesty, Queen Elizabeth II, is talented musically and numbers among her many accomplishments the domestic attributes of cooking and sewing."

★   ★   ★

The credentials of the Apple Blossom queen were unimpeachable. She met the single most important criterion of the committee of Virginia patriarchs who had elected her. She had a pedigree; she was an aristocrat through and through.

In Virginia, nothing could be more important than certified blue blood. Virginia has always had one of the largest and busiest genealogical departments in the country. "There is a deliberate cult of the past rooted in the belief that somewhere in the back of every Virginian's family history is a royal insignia," wrote a correspondent for the *New York Times.*

"You can only understand Virginia in terms of its mythology, for what Virginians *think* they are has a great deal to do with *what* they are, although the two things are not always the same."

"And, to say 'I am a Virginian,' or 'My family, of course, came from Virginia' is to impute a certain modest elegance to one's genes and chromosomes, to suggest the superior quality of character, breeding, and gentility, as well as to fix the physical boundaries of a routine biological fact."

Winchester was sensitive to its royal history. In 1957 the city, whose population numbered 15,000, boasted being "the oldest English Colonial settlement west of the Blue Ridge." The names of the streets celebrated the original patriarchy. "English associations of famed personages, chiefly of British descent." They were a virtual *Who's Who* of generals, admirals, dukes and lords: Washington, Braddock, Boscowan, Loudoun, Cecil, Monmoth, Amherst, Fairfax, Germain, Cameron. If that weren't enough, Winchester also laid claim to General Thomas "Stonewall" Jackson, and Harry Flood Byrd, former U.S. senator, state governor, aristocrat, apple grower, architect of one of the most potent political machines in the country and spearhead of the South's resistance to the 1954 Court-ordered desegregation of public schools.

Not that the majority of Virginia natives were descended from the gentry. Most were of English, German, Scotch-Irish and Dutch working-class stock. Once the settlers checked the native Indian population and drove the French out, they found the gentle Shenandoah, Tidewater and even the rocky Piedmont regions looked like heaven compared to where they'd come from. They modeled the economy of Virginia after the English manorial system. The lesser farmers from the upland regions—even if they were hillbillies—admired the patrician values of the elite, slave-holding planters from the lowlands. Chief among these were chivalry, gentility, independence, property and patrimony. Out of this mishmash came the notion of the Southern "gentleman," embraced even by rednecks. Critical to the equation, however, was the

Southern belle, the lady on the pedestal. She was the ideal: a woman of breeding, beautiful (but unattainable), talented (but not ambitious) and, above all, domestic.

The Apple Blossom Festival was meant to celebrate just such a woman. Which put Patsy on a collision course with Southern Womanhood.

Fruit was big business in the Shenandoah, and Winchester, the county seat, was the "Apple Capital." Jonathans, Pippins, Red Delicious, Golden Delicious, Grimes Golden, Stayman, Yorks and Rambos went through the National Fruit Company's processing plant on the outskirts of town, where both Patsy's mother and grandmother had worked, and ended up on grocery shelves as vinegar, juice, applesauce, cider, apple rings, apple butter.

In 1924, an Apple Blossom Festival that would bring thousands of tourists to town was conceived by a confederation of Virginia orchardists, the biggest of whom was Harry Flood Byrd. The official tag line of the fete, "The bounties of nature are the gifts of God," was eventually supplanted by a less officious slogan: "We want the world to know, the best apples grow in the Shenandoah."

Though hardly the bacchanalia that is New Orleans' Mardi Gras, Winchester's Apple Blossom Festival was nevertheless touted as "The World's Most Famous Springtime Extravaganza." Visitors came from all over the country, and if, like Patsy, you grew up in this part of Virginia, the Apple Blossom Festival was encoded in your genetic structure. For days, before and after the three-day affair, the *Winchester Evening Star* (owned by Harry Flood Byrd) ran banner headlines: "RED CARPET IS OUT FOR QUEEN-ELECT'S ARRIVAL TOMORROW," and "QUEEN SHENANDOAH XXX BEGINS RULE OF APPLE REALM," and "QUEEN LEAVES CITY, ANNUAL RETURN TO NORMAL BEGINS." The hoopla included parades, band concerts, air shows, receptions, fireworks, apple pancake breakfasts, a formal ball for the big shots and a square dance for the working-class folks. An elaborate coronation ritual was staged as an Elizabethan pageant on the steps of Handley High School. Local radio station WINC offered live coverage.

The main event was the Grand Feature Parade. People packed the historic streets to get a glimpse of the parade marshall. In years past, Bing Crosby, Bob Hope and Bert Parks led off. In 1957 it was James Cagney. Close behind Cagney, perched atop a wedding cake of a float, was Queen Shenandoah XXX, with her court of princesses. The *Winchester Evening Star* noted every nuance of the queen's performance, beginning with her dress, "one of the most elegant gowns ever donned by a Festival Queen." It was, of course, white, "made of white lace and tulle over white taffeta, embellished with teardrop pearls and embroidered heavy with pearls and beads around the close, round neckline."

Before the weekend was over, the queen gave a necessarily ladylike statement to the *Star:* "I enjoyed every minute of it, particularly all the dances. Everyone was very sweet to me and it was lovely to ride around as if I really were a Queen. I loved all the children. I enjoyed the pageant so much and thought all the floats were beautiful. I appreciate very much all the work that went into the organization of the festival and I want to thank everyone so much for the good time I had."

Many car lengths behind the Apple Blossom queen, on the heels of American Legion Post 108 Drum and Bugle Corps, Patsy draped across the top of the back seat of a red Oldsmobile convertible decorated with a banner that read, "A WINNER ALL THE WAY." Red, she always said, was the color men liked. Her statement was not covered by the *Star,* and some people in Winchester would say it was not very ladylike.

This was not Patsy's first Apple Blossom parade. Indeed, she had participated the two previous years, each time gussied up in her trademark cowgirl couture—tailored and sequined affairs with colorful appliqués and five-inch fringe shimmying from bosom and hem. She looked good—maybe too damn good, remembered Patsy's girlfriend, Pat Smallwood. For some reason, her name was omitted from the program book. But Patsy never did kowtow to the veneer of the legendary Southern belle with its charades of etiquette and morality: her retort, "The hell with 'em," was Patsy's equivalent of Scarlett O'Hara's "fiddle-dee-dee."

There were various explanations offered for Patsy's ill treatment by her own hometown.

"She sang—but that's all she did," Smallwood said. "But it didn't matter what she done. Back in the fifties, anything a woman did out of the ordinary was a big deal. She wore makeup and tight clothes and that was considered loose. See, the town was sort of jealous because she was a sexy-type lady. She had it. She was built. There weren't any girls around doing what she was doing and none as good as her either. And she wore the cowgirl outfits. She could be very sexy. She was gorgeous. Fantastic figure. Built kind of like Jessica Lange."

"Yeah, they laughed at her," said local musician Johnny Anderson, who'd backed Patsy on numerous occasions and knew her well. "This town's got a lot of funny people. They stay in a clique. If I'm from that side of the tracks, I'm from that side of the tracks, and you're not going to let me forget it. It's as simple as that. There are certain people who have always controlled this town. They control the banks, they control the council, and if you're not one of them the hell with you. You're just a peon, and you'll always be a peon as long as you live. And they won't let you forget it, either. It was always on her mind that she was from Kent Street, the other side of the tracks. She was proud of it, really. See, she was for the underdog."

"It's not what you are, it's who you know and how well respected you are," said another one of Patsy's girlfriends. "She despised that. I would say to her, 'Well, I don't know why you let it bother you.' She would say, 'It doesn't, really.' But deep down you knew it did."

At this year's parade, as a concession to her newfound status as a pop singing sensation, Patsy wore her makeover look: a strapless evening gown, rhinestone earrings and nosebleedingly high heels. It didn't matter—Patsy would always be a cowgirl. Fiercely independent and proud, if provoked she would run off a string of epithets that could make a sailor blush. "Forthright," the *Winchester Evening Star* primly noted.

"Women, in those days, kept their mouths shut," offered Phil Whitney, who managed the local radio station where Patsy made her broadcast debut.

"Know who reminds me of Patsy?" asked musician Mary Klick. "Bette Midler. That same down-to-earthiness."

As the parade rounded the home stretch, Patsy plainly heard the catcalls that came from the crowd. Some of her loyal friends did too. After the parade was over, John Reid searched her out. He found her sitting in her car on a side street all by herself. There wasn't another soul nearby. Even her driver had deserted her, he recalled.

"She looked like someone's stepchild," Reid said. "I felt real sorry for her because cars would come off the parade route and park so that people could stop and talk or gather around, but Patsy was all left out."

Reid had his Polaroid Land Camera, and as Patsy stood in front of her car like it was about to turn into a pumpkin, he snapped a picture. She was still fuming when the shutter clicked. "Sonsabitches," she growled. "I'll show them yet."

Chapter One

*E*LKTON, VIRGINIA, ninety miles southeast of Winchester, is on the banks of the south fork of the Shenandoah River, a great slow river nestled along the rounded slopes of the Blue Ridge Mountains. The Shenandoah Valley, rich with limestone, is green and abundant, making conditions ideal for farming. The mountains were home to the first hillbillies—tough, staunchly independent Scotch-Irish yeomen who came to this country to escape the forces of "civilization" and its taxation, jails, hangmen and debtors' prisons.

Just outside the town of Elkton is a three-story white farmhouse of substantial proportions, an equally solid barn and a smaller house made entirely of limestone. This impressive homestead was built by Solomon Jobe Hensley, Patsy's paternal grandfather. On the property there is a large, simple, vertical stone marker engraved with the name "Solsburg." It is a fitting monument to Sol Hensley, who was proud, plain, proprietary and, like most Hensleys, outspoken.

Hensleys take up four columns in the Elkton telephone book. They were one of the original Virginia families. Sol was one of the original hillbillies—a third-generation Virginian, born on his granddaddy's farm, Hensley Hollow, deep in the heavily wooded Blue Ridge.

Unlike the slave-mongering aristocrats who settled in the Tidewater, sturdy hill folk like the Scotch-English Hensleys believed in work—hard work. Through fortitude and willpower, Sol Hensley expanded his family legacy so that by the beginning of the twentieth century he was paying taxes on a thousand acres of prime Rockingham County farmland distributed over three farms, including the one he was born on up in the hills.

Within his lifetime Sol transformed himself into a country squire. He built his estate, painted the house white, named it Solsburg and wielded enough power to get the name listed on maps of the region. By local standards, he was considered a wealthy fellow. "He believed in making money, believed in helping himself," said old-timer Hobby Robinson, a lifelong Elkton resident.

He was called "the Baron." He was big, arrogant and a son-of-a-bitch to get along with. He distrusted outsiders, which was anyone who wasn't a Hensley. He once had an antique sale at Solsburg and posted his shotgun-toting sons on the property to prevent anyone he didn't know from buying *his* stuff.

"Ever see the TV series 'The High Chaparral'?" asked Robinson. "Leif Erickson reminded me of Sol Hensley. They looked alike, with all that gray hair. The old man rode a horse a lot too, just like Leif Erickson." Sol's wife, Margaret, was as tiny and yielding as Sol was big and demanding. And like many a steel magnolia, she quietly took command of her realm, the home. Together she and Sol further enlarged the Hensley family dynasty. They had four daughters and a son who died in infancy before Samuel Lawrence Hensley, Patsy's father, took his first gulp of air in the big white farmhouse at Solsburg, on August 16, 1889. Two sons and a daughter, for a total of eight children, followed.

The Baron was a firm believer that the father is God's unchallenged patriarch on earth. He demanded submission and deference, was relentlessly critical, meted out punishment freely and expected all of his children to be as proud, aggressive and independent as he was. In most ways they didn't let him down; the Hensleys were regarded as a feisty lot. Sam, the oldest son and first in line to inherit the family dynasty, was the focus of the Baron's assertiveness training. "He was hard on Sam, hard on his whole family, hard on everyone—you betcha. He cracked the whip," Hobby Robinson recollected.

Everyone said Sam took after his father. Once, when Sam was working as a foreman on one of his father's farms, Sol put up the farm against anyone who could cut corn faster than Sam. The contest began in the morning. Sam watched idly, picking his teeth until it became apparent the Baron would loose his wager. At three o'clock Sam picked up his knife. By sundown he was declared the champion corn cutter of Rockingham County.

Sam went as far as the seventh grade, as far as the limited educational system in Elkton would permit. It was more important for a young man growing up in the late nineteenth century to learn a trade. Sam learned blacksmithing, an important vocation in Southern agricultural communities. Turning metal into hot, molten ore somehow seemed to suit his fiery temperament. Later in life, as a master blacksmith, Sam would be employed as a wheelwright, horseshoer, tool maker, quarry man and general mechanic.

"He could take a piece of metal and do anything on the face of the earth with it," recalled Herman "Punk" Longley, Patsy's first cousin. "He could take a piece of heavy equipment he had never seen before in his life and in fifteen minutes he could tear it down and put it back together. He was just gifted that way."

Sam's greatest gift, however, was his singing. All the Hensleys were talented musically. Sam's sisters studied at the nearby Shenandoah Conservatory of Music. His brother Ashby was an accomplished guitarist and pianist who played everything from local country dances to formal parlor affairs. Sam, too, played the piano, but singing was his forte. He had a strong, sweet tenor and clear, almost theatrical diction. He was dramatic. By choice and by temperament he could only be a soloist, and his voice dominated the weekly Hensley family songfests as it did the church choir. While he sang all the popular secular music of the day, he prided himself on his rendition of his favorite hymn, "Life's Railway to Heaven."

But music was not enough of an outlet for Sam's dramatic vocal abilities, which sought expression through language in other ways. He was fascinated by words—specifically, the vernacular. His cursing even upstaged the Baron, an eloquent four-letter man himself. Combined with the one personality trait of Sam's that no one who ever knew him ever forgot—his "ungodly, uncontrollable temper"—Sam was a wonder.

As the son of the relatively well-to-do Baron, Sam was able to indulge his taste for cars, whatever was the biggest at the time. He was, all the women agreed, undeniably handsome, with a mane of fair hair, a strong jawline and dreamy half-lidded eyes. According to one female relative, "You've met men who think they're God's gift to women? He was that type."

Sam was also fond of "putting on the dog." Blacksmithing was grimy, sweaty work, but he would transform himself into a superb figure of the upper class in wing collar, Prince of Wales jacket, linen shirt and a length of gold watch chain cascading across his middle. A cigar sometimes lit, often not, was a permanent fixture on his face.

In 1917, the day after the country entered "the war to end all wars," Sam, in a moment of patriotic fervor, enlisted. PFC Samuel Hensley participated in combat in the Argonne Forest, one of the bloodiest battles of World War I. When he came back, friends and relatives noticed some change in him, a new edge to his temper. Even small matters sent him spiraling off. He also began to go on drinking binges. It was a secret side of his personality—not even all the relatives knew about it.

"He drank a lot of whiskey—moonshine," offered Hobby Robinson. "He was a weekend drinker. Hardworking when he worked. Sam wasn't belligerent at all when he was sober. Happy-go-lucky, in fact. But he could get mean when he was drinking. Hard, very hard. When he was down in the quarry he wouldn't take anything off anybody. We have a lot of mountain people like him here. They don't take any guff. They'll go over 50 percent but they won't go over 70."

Sam married his first wife, Wynona Jones, right around this time. She was a beautiful, dark-haired young woman who had attended Shenandoah Conservatory and shared Sam's love of music. They made a striking couple. Sam was a demanding husband but she seemed to be a balm to his aggressive, forceful personality. In one family photo, in which Sam is dressed to the nines, looking dreamy-eyed at the camera, Wynona's hand rests on his shoulder and their legs brush against one another. Their first child died in infancy. A son, Randolph, was born and then a daughter, Temple Glenn, nicknamed Tempie. At early ages both children were sent to Sally Mann, a local music teacher, for instruction. Wynona was pregnant with a fourth child when she was in a car accident. Both mother and child died. Sam was devastated. Unlike many widowers of that era, he did not remarry promptly to give the children a new mother. Instead, he sent them to live with Sally Mann, unmarried (therefore a "spinster"), who, it was believed, came to Elkton from New York.

It was not certain why he chose Mann for the job that normally went to spinster aunts, except that it was rumored that Sam had an affair with her, and she loved him very much. Sam had agreed to help Mann financially in return for her mothering his son and daughter. But after a few years of dogging him unsuccessfully for support, she gave up and adopted both children. Thereafter, Sam had limited contact with his children. Years later, Randolph Mann's memory of his father was sketchy. He didn't even go to Sam's funeral: "I saw him once, I think, twice. I worked for Bausch and Lomb and happened to be going through the town where he was living. He was getting on in years. I took him to supper. We didn't say much."

While Sam was dealing with the aftermath of his wife's death, his father was experiencing a series of financial crises that ultimately contributed to the disintegration of the Hensley family dynasty. It all started when the Baron "got in a jam" with a fifteen-year-old girl from Elkton.

Sol got caught with his nose dirty and it was the town's biggest scandal. The girl's family extracted a substantial amount of money for Sol's indiscretion.

At the same time Sol was hit by other problems. Southern agriculture was in a decline after the war and was dealt a crippling blow by a severe drought. Then came the stock market crash of 1929. The Depression debilitated the agrarian South. Sol was beset with unsellable goods and mortgage foreclosures. He was forced to sell off his land in bits and chunks. Sam, who turned forty the year the stock market collapsed, saw his patrimony disappear almost overnight. Raised in a culture where the oldest son inherits all, he began his fourth decade in utter disillusionment—bitter and angry at his fate.

All over the South, people who had lived on the land left in the hope of finding work in the cities. Sam joined the wave of Depression-era vagabonds for whom the automobile served as transport to different towns and different states. He worked on farms, on quarries, on the railroad or not at all. Once he worked as a scab at the Ford Rouge Plant in Detroit.

Wherever he went he kept reinventing himself. "He could put on some of the most beautiful put-ons you ever did see," remarked Punk Longley. He would blow into town with his big car, in sartorial splendor, smoking his trademark cigar, looking every inch the Virginia patriarch. The first thing he did was join the local church choir, where his heavenly voice rang out in praise of the Lord. He was very impressive—at least that is probably the effect he had on Hilda Patterson, Patsy's mother.

Hilda hailed from Opequon, an Indian word meaning "pure water." It is a settlement four miles outside of Winchester, known for its prize-winning apples, cultivated by orchardists like the Stecks and the Byrds. Poor and middling farm families like Hilda's were employed by the orchardists during harvest season to pick the apples. Otherwise, they lived off their small subsistence farms.

Hilda Virginia Patterson was born March 9, 1916, the third child born to James Arlington Patterson and Goldie Lavinia Newlin. When Hilda was still a toddler, her father died at age thirty-three, the victim of the deadly flu epidemic of 1918. It was the final tragedy in a series of tragedies; prior to contracting the dreaded disease, he had fallen from a roof and, as a result, had his leg amputated.

Her bad luck forced Goldie to go to work to support herself and her brood. One of those places was the National Fruit Company's processing plant in Winchester, whose labor force consisted mostly of women and children. After several years of extreme hardship, Goldie met and married Frank Allanson.

Frank was a gruff man of few words, who would apply to his family a code of discipline he learned while working as a guard on a prison chain gang. Goldie was remembered as an optimistic soul whose earthy sense of humor and resourcefulness contrasted with her husband's rawness. In addition to the three children from her first marriage, Goldie had five more with Frank.

Goldie was from the tradition of Southern farm women who believed work—hard work—was a point of pride. Like many rural families, the Allansons struggled, especially once the Depression hit. Frank, when he could, got work as a day laborer, while Goldie and the children ran the farm.

As the second oldest girl, Hilda worked beside her mother, helping her juggle the never-ending demands of "women's work": washing, cleaning, tilling the garden, turning the apple churn, sewing, preserving, caring for the young ones, helping to birth the neighbors' children. They also handled "men's work": toting pails of water to and from the house, cutting firewood, planting in the spring and harvesting in the fall. Once children were old enough to lend a hand, they joined in the domestic labor force, becoming adults before they were out of their teens. Goldie, who died from what country folks call "sugar diabetes," was an old woman at her death at age fifty-two.

Hilda was a lovely, dark-haired, fifteen-year-old with deep-set, mystical eyes when she met Sam, who was working at a sand mine in a nearby hamlet. Their marriage took place at the Frederick County Courthouse in Winchester on September 2, 1932.

Six days later, another event occurred that was again duly noted by the Commonwealth of Virginia: the birth of the couple's child, in Winchester Memorial Hospital. She was given the names of both parents: Virginia Patterson Hensley. Their address was listed as Gore, a settlement in the mountains near the West Virginia line, where the red slate and dark shale of the heavily wooded mountains, and the rocky creek that slices through them on its way to the Potomac, are as different from the Shenandoah Valley as the flinty hillfolk are from the gentle lowlanders.

It was literally a "shotgun wedding," according to Punk Longley. Frank Allanson, former prison guard and man-of-few-words, applied the pressure. The irony of the situation didn't escape folks in Elkton: "Like father, like son," it was once again said. Sam, unlike Sol, could not buy his way out of his "jam." It was an inauspicious beginning.

Chapter Two

*I*N 1932, darkness descended on the country with the frightening appearance of bread lines, the closing of banks and hungry-eyed men standing on street corners selling apples. "Brother, Can You Spare a Dime?" was a reality. "Shuffle Off to Buffalo" and "April in Paris," the year's hit songs, expressed the fantasies of a nation reeling in economic collapse. Apple pickers made $1.25 a week.

A few weeks after Virginia's birth, Sam, age forty-three, moved Hilda and the baby back to the family estate, Solsburg, to live. In spite of the circumstances that led to the marriage, Hilda was certainly desperate enough to marry a man old enough to be her father. She probably believed her future as the wife of the scion of the Hensleys was secure, and was willing to make whatever sacrifices were necessary for a bit of that security for herself and her baby. It turned out to be very different from what she expected.

Sol's wife had passed away and that same year the Baron suffered a debilitating stroke. The newlyweds moved in with the incapacitated but still cantankerous old patriarch. Hilda, the woman of the house, was expected to look after him.

Sam's hair-trigger temper could be quite impressive to a sixteen-year-old girl; his demands on her attention were constant. She lived "in constant fear." The baby was her primary source of hope and happiness in a strange new and uncertain world.

Hilda called her Ginny, though relatives and friends from grade-school days remember she was also called Patsy at times, from her middle name, Patterson. But the name Patsy didn't stick until later.

As a child Ginny exhibited a precocity unusual for one so young. Her first exhibition of showmanship occurred when she was four years old: she won a street fair talent contest with a tap dancing performance. Nobody knew where she learned to tap dance, though it was remembered she idolized Shirley Temple and her rendition of "On the Good Ship Lollipop." The prize was a lamp. For a child of four, the real reward, however, was the thrill of making so many people so happy. It was a revelation. She immediately announced to her mother she would be a dancer when she grew up.

Besides being talented, she was intensely loving yet self-contained and strong-willed. "A true Hensley," she was pegged.

"I can see Patsy right now, walking up the street, five or six years old, singing at the top of her voice," Hobby Robinson recalled. "She come in my store with her daddy. I always put shoes on her. He'd say, 'Give her the best you got.' I knew their funds were limited. We called them Mary Janes—black patent leather. That's what she wanted and she insisted on. Just for the heck of it I'd put some other shoe on her and boy, she'd get all over me, she'd really fuss. When her daddy would go to pay for her shoes she'd go up and hug him around the legs. I never saw him show much affection around her, though. She seemed to be a little shy of her daddy. I don't think she was afraid of him. Just a little shy. She wasn't that way with me. She'd give me a rough time. She was outgoing, but with him she held back a little bit. Maybe he fussed at them at home—that's what I think."

The image of a little girl hugging an emotionally unresponsive father who thinks he is giving her what she wants speaks volumes for Ginny's relationship with her father. She grew up in a home environment charged with guilt, shame and fear. While to the outside world Sam could efface a certain charm through his dramatic presence, talent and ability to put on "the most beautiful put-ons you ever did see," the dark side of his personality made life at home hell for Hilda and Ginny. He, like his father, believed a man is the unquestioned authority in his home. He had a demanding personality anyway and wanted complete submission. When factored in with his explosive temper and his binge drinking, he was a time bomb.

Sam and Hilda fought constantly, she, out of fear for herself and her daughter. Punk Longley's description of home life had a ring of the old school about it: "He was in control of his family all right, no question about it. He expected them to do what he thought was right, even when he didn't do it himself. And when he said it, he meant it. He wasn't just talking through his hat. He told them to do something and they wouldn't do it right then and there, well, that would start the fire."

Hilda's sister-in-law, Marie Allanson, was a young newlywed herself at the time: "He was rough-talking. When I first got married he scared me. I was afraid of him. We would usually go over there to eat and he was usually on fairly good behavior those times, but once I went and stayed with them a week and I remember thinking, 'How can Hilda stand it?' "

Hilda left home on a number of occasions. Once Sam, a shotgun in hand, and his brother tracked her down at a Sunday school picnic to order his wife back home. The sight of her emerging from a swimming hole in her bathing suit stilled his trigger finger. "God, ain't she beautiful?" he said.

Even as a young child, Ginny, intensely loving but feisty, felt her mother's fear where her father was concerned and that made her angry. Sam was just as unreasonable in his demands on Ginny as he was on Hilda. As outspoken as any Hensley, she armored herself for battle and entered the fray, whoever was the loudest take all. Between Sam and his daughter, there was no contest. But rather than dull her fighting spirit, the disputes with her father toughened her and established the confidence that stood her in good stead as an adult.

"It was a contest of wills," offered Longley. "Her disposition was his. She would do something to displease him and he would yell at her and then that would start the yelling. He had an unholy temper. She did too. They were born with it. Temperament of the breed, I guess."

When Sam was exploding, anyone in the vicinity would catch the flak. Under the circumstances, Ginny discovered that her natural outspokenness caused problems for her mother. She learned to hold her tongue for her mother's sake.

"When Uncle Sam would clash with either of them, the one would take up for the other. If it was between Uncle Sam and Virginia, Hilda would take up for Virginia, and if it was between Uncle Sam and Hilda, Virginia would take up for Hilda. She'd always take her mother's side. Uncle Sam would stamp and fume and fuss and cuss."

Mother and daughter established the relationship that would last for the rest of their lives. "They were like a wolf pack," observed one family friend. There weren't that many years difference between them, and as Ginny got older, she was the one Hilda turned to for support and advice. They always claimed they were more like sisters than mother and daughter. Ginny was Hilda's proverbial tower of strength. "I was sixteen years old when Patsy was born," she later recalled. "All my life I'd had hand-me-downs, but when she was born, she was mine. We grew up together. We were hungry together."

★   ★   ★

Like all children, Ginny needed to know she was loved. With her mother it was always and forever unconditional. With her father she never quite knew. And, as it would turn out, she took great pains to find out.

As Ginny got older, she metamorphosed into a leggy girl and by early puberty she already had the beginnings of her woman's body. It was probably around this time that Sam noticed her in a new way. As an adult, Patsy broadly alluded to an incestuous relationship with Sam to a handful of friends with whom she felt safe in unloading the secret burden of guilt and shame she bore. Several girlfriends from Winchester, Loretta Lynn, June Carter, songwriters Donn ("Walkin' After Midnight") Hecht and Mae Boren Axton, were among those in whom she confided. Understandably, many of her friends remained guarded discussing the details of a taboo subject that caused Patsy so much pain and confusion, and for which she would extract promises, as she did with Loretta, to "take this to your grave."

"She never mentioned her father to me but she mentioned a relative, somebody in the family," Hecht related. "She was pretty well embarrassed. You knew damn well it was her father because she talked about him a lot in other respects."

"She cried and cried," said Axton, "and I just held her. She felt something was wrong with her."

Sam's relationship with his blooming pubescent daughter was charged with sexual tension, as he was alternately verbally and physically abusive. Patsy would describe how her father "made sexual advances toward her," though avoiding any discussion of the particulars. She alternately loathed and loved him, a common feeling among sexually abused children. Ultimately, she felt that her early experiences had something to do with her inability to establish intimate relationships with her husbands and lovers, a common long-term incest fear that also manifests itself in anxiety, hostility, eating disorders, guilt, shame, sexual dysfunction and a tendency toward revictimization in adult relationships with men—all of which Patsy exhibited later to varying degrees.

Based on what she told Hecht about her "frequent experiences" with her father, Hecht posed her dilemma rhetorically: "If you had your father play around with you, how would you feel about it when you met a nice guy and one thing leads to another and all of a sudden these reflections would cause you problems? If you had frequent experiences with a father, your father turning you on, and you couldn't go to bed with him, why this could be torture."

Many incesters deny they are hurting their children. In their minds they are pleasuring them, helping them attain adulthood, loving them, giving them what they want by responding to their natural human need for love and attention. If the common pattern in incest held in Ginny's case, then she was probably made to feel that she was a lucky little girl, special, or, at the very least, different from the other girls her own age. This "specialness" was to be a secret between father and daughter. She told Loretta, "Take this to your grave."

Said Lynn, "We made a deal—that certain things would remain between her and me. We could just look at each other and we knew what those things were. She told me about when she was little. By the time she was eleven years old she had already lived a woman's life.

"She didn't want to talk about it, and she told me why she didn't. She said, 'He put me through this, through havin' to grow up before my time.' " Here Loretta refers back to her own marriage, at age fourteen, as chronicled in her autobiography *Coal Miner's Daughter:* "I understood very well because when I was fifteen, I was thirty. And when I got to be thirty, I was fifteen. So I understand Patsy very well, even though I wasn't understandin' all she meant very well back then."

The families of incested children, including spouses and even perpetrators, are often drawn into an intricate drama of denial, guilt, shame and secrecy, thus, in a sense, becoming victims too. This contributes to the widespread cultural denial of the reality and the harmfulness of incest, which many believe may have been especially prevalent in the South, which on the one hand was obsessed with sexual repression and, on the other hand, charged with sexual tension. Southern codes of behavior gave white men the greatest latitude in fulfilling their sexual desires. White, married women were duty-bound to keep the family together, at all costs, and at whatever personal sacrifice that might entail. The convoluted family dynamics around incest may seem unfathomable for those unfamiliar with the subject, which the modern recovery movement has in more recent years since shed light on.

Exactly when and how Hilda learned about the goings-on between Sam and Ginny is not clear, any more than the effect that terrible knowledge undoubtedly had on Hilda herself in shaping her incredibly close relationship with her eldest daughter. However, when Hilda spoke at length to veteran Hollywood producer Bernard Schwartz (who had produced *Coal Miner's Daughter* in 1980), in preparation for making his 1985 movie *Sweet Dreams*, which purported to be the story of Patsy Cline, she was quite frank in her description of certain guarded details of Patsy's childhood. Schwartz related how Hilda, shaken but "stoic," opened up the painful subject of Patsy's incestuous relationship with her father, in the conviction that such information was important in understanding her famous, yet often misunderstood daughter, and was thus integral to the development of the biopic. "For me, she was the real hero of the story, this proud, proud woman," Schwartz recalled of his many meetings with Patsy's mom. Schwartz, in turn, promised to depict the relationship between Patsy and her father with discretion. Transcriptions of the many interviews Schwartz conducted with Hilda comprised part of two six-inch, loose-leaf binders of background information that, during the course of screenwriting and production, came to be referred to as "Bernie's Bible."

Actress Jessica Lange agreed to play the part of Patsy in the movie on the strength of an original screenplay written by Robert Getchell, in which the shadowy relationship between Patsy and her father, and the role that alcohol played in the equation, were alluded to in several key scenes. The intention, according to Schwartz, was to describe "the demons she [Patsy] lived with." Scenes were shot, with an actor who played the part of Sam, by the noted British director Karel Reisz (*The French Lieutenant's Woman*), but ended up on the cutting-room floor. Though both Lange and Schwartz wanted the pivotal scenes included, Reisz edited them from the picture because, according to Getchell, they "didn't turn out well." Speculation had it that the real reason they were excluded was because the movie's director was out of his league in handling a dicey subject like incest. Instead, the filmmakers opted for a "love story" in the mode of the 1955 film *Love Me or Leave Me*, the biopic of the life of twenties torch singer Ruth Etting, starring Doris Day and James Cagney.

Another common feature among sexually abused children is mistaking the abnormal for the normal. The parents don't let the child go to other people's houses very much. They don't want anyone to know what's going on. Ginny did not grow up like other kids her age. Because of what was going on at home, there were no picnics, no having friends over. Her mother was her only friend. When she started getting interested in boys, Sam would "embarrass her in front of them," said Marie Allanson. Other relatives also perceived the oddness of the home situation and may have suspected more than they let on. As one of Ginny's uncles put it, "He was strict on her. He didn't let her have too much freedom."

While Ginny was growing up the family moved nineteen times. From school and birth records, a fragmented childhood steeped in a smog of secrecy can be pieced together. She attended first grade in Elkton. She attended second grade at Ann Smith School in nearby Lexington, and at this time her brother Sam Jr.—thereafter known as John—was born. Ginny began third grade at Ann Smith School but withdrew before the end of the year when the family moved again.

Almost halfway into the school year, she was enrolled in the fourth grade at Handley Elementary School in Winchester, in December 1942. Three months later the record shows she withdrew. The advent of World War II created a vast need for swift production and manpower and around this time Sam got a job at the Naval Shipyard in Norfolk.

Ginny's sister, Sylvia Mae, was born in nearby Portsmouth at the time Ginny would have attended sixth grade. In 1945, at age thirteen, Ginny began seventh grade at Middletown Elementary in Frederick County. The following year she repeated seventh grade at Middletown, but once again the family moved, because after three months she withdrew. In November 1947 she enrolled in the eighth grade at Sydney Gore High School in Gore, where the family lived until the following year, and she started ninth grade in Gore. But after six weeks she withdrew, and in December 1948, the record shows she enrolled in Handley High School in Winchester. She dropped out shortly thereafter, but there was no formal withdrawal. She simply never went back to school again.

Under the circumstances, Ginny's scholastic record was lackluster and explains her later insecurities about writing and speaking in front of a microphone. In the eighth grade she earned D-minuses in all her subjects except for a B in the one she knew best—geography.

The effect of all the moving was to ensure silence and secrecy. The family inhabited a series of dilapidated houses. Abandoned farmhouses dotted the Virginia countryside, as rural Southerners left their homes and their hometowns and went to the city in the desperate hope of finding work. The family would move into these big, old, haunted houses, since Sam "was not an apartment man," and it was Hilda's job to make it "normal."

"Hilda painted and papered—she did every house they ever lived in," recalled Marie Allanson. Sam wouldn't have lived in it if she hadn't. She was a worker. She'd get it all painted and fixed up and then he'd move again."

It was important to maintain the appearance of prosperity, of normalcy. Regardless of their financial status, Sam always had to have a big car, the house had to be fixed up "or he wouldn't live in it" and dinner had to be formally served to him by Hilda and Ginny in the dining room.

The Depression shattered the old family structures. On a mass scale it raised fundamental questions about women's relationships with men who could no longer provide for their families in a world of new uncertainties. Many times when there was no food on the table, Hilda went out and got work—"anything and everything." They ate the poor folks' diet of rabbit and squirrel out of necessity. Sam, however, insisted on playing the part of the patriarch, and lived beyond his means.

"He didn't make enough money to pay the rent," said Nellie Patterson, another one of Ginny's aunts on her mother's side. "You don't make your rent, you get put out. You can't have carpeting, and you can't have a big piano and you can't buy a big car unless you have a big-paying job. We always looked up to them because they had everything nice, but they were up to here in owing. They would move sometimes two or three times a year into some big old house that had sat empty. But Hilda was a great artist when it came to making a room quite livable. She'd make slipcovers for the sofa and chairs. She's a good carpenter. She wasn't lazy. She'd work her heart out."

They attended church, both Pentecostal and Baptist—wherever there was a church choir. Sam would occasionally go on a "religious kick," the hypocrisy of which might have seemed obvious to Hilda and to Ginny, whose own relationship with God and church was problematic. Patsy was never religious. "Too many hypocrites go to church," she once told a friend.

But church meant music. As soon as Ginny was old enough she was allowed to sing with her parents in the choir. The Pentecostals, in particular, were a freewheeling denomination active throughout Virginia, and their open-throated gospel singing accompanied by whatever instrument was available was a joyous affair. Ginny loved gospel.

Music gave pleasure and served as a balm to the underside of the Hensley family life. While they were living in Elkton, Ginny was given an old upright piano for her eighth birthday. Her half sister, Tempie, had grown into quite an accomplished "long hair" pianist under the tutelage of her adoptive mother, Sally Mann. Ginny would visit Tempie and beg her to play. Though piano lessons were considered a luxury, Ginny learned to play "by ear" anyway—a demonstration of her innate relative pitch, the ability to name a note or an interval after hearing a given note.

"All you had to do was hum something to Patsy and she could play it on the piano," remembered one relative. "I was surprised she turned out to be a singer and not a pianist. She was terribly talented. It's a shame her dad didn't help her more. He didn't do anything for her. He didn't help any of his children."

Singing, however, became the focus of her ambitions. From a practical standpoint Hilda claimed, "It was the one thing she could do that wasn't going to cost us." Ginny took comfort in the Hensley family songfests, at which "Peace in the Valley" might have been the theme. Sam was the star of the show at the songfests and Ginny might have found her bond with him in their shared talent for music. As a child she could safely channel all her emotions into music. In a family of well-kept secrets, Ginny sought wholeness and comfort in maintaining what for her was the most intimate contact of all, at a distance. Singing was a God-given talent. "You might say it was my return to the living that launched me as a singer," Patsy once told a newspaper reporter. "In early childhood I developed a serious throat infection and my heart stopped beating. I was placed in an oxygen tent and the doctors brought me back to life. I recovered from the illness with a voice that boomed forth like Kate Smith's."

Whether or not Ginny suffered from a bout of rheumatic fever as a child, as was alluded, the comparison to Kate Smith was revealing, as far as an early influence on her singing style. "The first lady of radio," Smith had three shows running in the late thirties and early forties, and was the highest-paid woman in broadcasting during the golden era of radio. Her hearty, "Hello, Everybody" opening salvo was her signature, and she had a big, unaffected way with Broadway show tunes.

Another possible influence was Helen Morgan, the torchy, tear-stained chanteuse famous for her 1927 stage appearance in *Show Boat* as well as both the 1929 silent film and better-known 1936 version. When the 1957 movie *The Helen Morgan Story,* starring Ann Blyth, was made, the album was played in Patsy's home many times. Record producer Owen Bradley recalled that "Patsy loved Helen Morgan. She loved to sing Helen Morgan songs, especially 'Can't Help Lovin' Dat Man of Mine.' We worked on some of those tunes; in fact, we even talked about doing some of that stuff in an album before she died and we worked out the arrangements in my office. I played the piano and she sang."

But the singer who, consciously or not, had the greatest impact, if not on Ginny's sound then on her style, was an Arkansas-born yodeling star she never met who shared her name: Rubye Blevins, better known as Patsy Montana, the yodeling cowgirl.

Montana was the first female country soloist to dress in full cowgirl regalia, complete with fringe, boots, hat and, in one publicity still, a six-shooter. When in 1936 she sold a million copies of "I Want to Be a Cowboy's Sweetheart"—the first million-selling female in country music—it meant that about 90 percent of American households that owned phonographs had purchased her record.

The grim reality of the Depression had a lot to do with Montana's appeal. When people were standing in bread lines, the stereotypical image of a country musician as a coveralled hayseed hit a little too close to home. The cowboy, on the other hand, was a rural image but dignified, independent, strong and romantic.

Throughout Ginny's childhood the cowboy image entered the mainstream via the movies. Gene Autry, America's top western star, made ninety movies between 1935 and 1953. There were other singing cowboys—Tex Ritter, Eddie Dean, Jimmy Wakely, to name a few—but none with the appeal of the "King of the Cowboys," Roy Rogers, and his partner in song and in life, Dale Evans, the "Queen of the Cowgirls."

But while the female lead in most cowboy movies added up to little more than occasionally saying, "He went thataway," Montana's popularity remained high throughout the forties, when she was a fixture on radio barn dances. As a cowgirl, she presented an alternative to the long-suffering wife, dutiful daughter and rube comedienne, the stock female characters of country. She was sassy and independent, on an equal footing with the cowboy who was her buddy, whether a friend or a lover.

Patsy had already adopted something of the cowgirl in a class photo from the seventh grade in which she wears a brightly colored scarf around her neck, tied cowboy style, an accessory she was never without, according to a former classmate. In an early publicity photo at age sixteen, she wears a fringed vest and skirt and cowboy boots.

Radio was standard entertainment during Ginny's youth. Saturday nights she tuned into a magical world inhabited by Cackle Sisters, Gully Jumpers, Fruit Jar Drinkers, Possum Hunters, Cotton Pickers and Fox Hunters. The "Grand Ole Opry" was the granddaddy of the radio barn dances and once a week she eagerly awaited her three-hour experience, along with millions of other Americans within WSM Nashville's 50,000-watt broadcast range.

In the twenties, newly licensed radio stations were desperate for programming. Network feeds and transcription services were still relatively rare, so stations looked for local talent. Outlying rural areas were brimming with musical activity, from sacred harp singers to hot pickers and fiddlers, and oldtime vaudeville acts were always looking for work. A marriage was made, and the barn dance, a country musical variety show, was born.

When Ginny was growing up, radio barn dances were enormously popular, topping popular stars like Al Jolson, Guy Lombardo and Fred Allen in national listener polls. Ginny might have listened to any number of them within broadcast range: WWVA Wheeling, West Virginia, had its "Wheeling Jamboree." WRVA Richmond, Virginia, had its "Old Dominion Barn Dance." WLS Chicago aired its "National Barn Dance," on which Patsy Montana was a fixture. At least a dozen such programs flourished. Even Northerners got in on the craze and for a while WHN New York had a barn dance hosted by a youthful Tex Ritter.

But the "Grand Ole Opry" was in a class by itself. When Patsy tuned in to 650 on the dial, she got hot-blooded hillbilly. The audience could be heard whooping and hollering their approval and encouragement to the succession of string bands, gospel quartets, rubes, hot-picking banjo players, lonesome cowboys, ex-vaudeville comics who made Ginny erupt in a fit of giggles with their horseplay and corny jokes dealing with sex and religion and the colorful announcers who bantered with the radio audience, encouraging them to buy the sponsors' products—Pet Milk, RC Cola, Crazy Water Crystals, Martha White Flour—and to "keep those cards and letters coming." It was downhome and homey. The Opry's cast of wild characters made her feel that being different was something you could be proud of.

Of greatest interest to her were the singers. These weren't the folks who sang in church, or the friends and relatives who stood around the piano at the family songfests singing hymns and sheet music. These singers could present the extremes of emotion, hope, sorrow, pleasure, sex, violence, adventure. They were bigger than life. They were show people.

There was Roy Acuff, the original "King of the Hillbillies" (later renamed the "King of Country Music" when the word *hillbilly* became unfashionable). Acuff and his band, the Smoky Mountain Boys, represented the Appalachian style. There was Texan Ernest Tubb, who represented the western tradition of honky-tonks and roadhouses. His band, the Texas Troubadours, featured the plaintive crying of the steel guitar that Ginny loved so much and the pulsating rhythms of the dance hall. There was Eddy Arnold before he became a famous crooner. There was Texas Ruby, a deep-voiced singer, one of the few women on the show.

Still associated with the Opry in the forties was its progenitor, Judge George D. Hay, the "Solemn Old Judge." It was Hay who gave the Opry its name. It was Hay who sounded the foghorn that opened the show. It was Hay who made the musicians dress in bib overalls and floppy hats and pose for publicity photos in pig pens, corn rows and hay bales. And it was Hay who gave colorful rural names to many of the musicians, who were not farmers but watchmakers, auto repairmen, railroad telegraphers and policemen.

And it was Hay who enjoined the cast to "Keep it down to earth, boys." It was that essential quality of the "Grand Ole Opry" that impressed Ginny's imagination and prompted her to say, at the ripe age of ten, that one day she would be a star of the "Grand Ole Opry."

Chapter Three

IN 1948, the Hensley family moved to Winchester. The city could boast of one radio station, four public schools ("three white, one colored"), two movie theaters plus a drive-in and of course the Apple Blossom Festival. There were other attractions that didn't make the official guidebook, including a dozen or so gin mills on the outskirts of town. Live musical entertainment was a feature at each. Compared to life in Gore, where expressions of culture were limited to the Hebron Baptist Church Choir, Winchester was high cotton.

Ginny started making the rounds. Some of her first real friends date from the time they saw plucky Ginny Hensley standing on some audition line, made up and ready to go on, or hard at work at a local drugstore. She did not spend much time going to the movies, going out for Cokes or pursuing boys. Her show business debut was prompted by what turned out to be Sam's biggest put-on ever.

For a year and a half prior to moving to Winchester, the Hensleys had been living in an old house that had sat empty along upper Back Creek in Gore in the hills near the West Virginia line, miles from the nearest neighbor. In Gore, Sam was considered something of an oddball even by the standards of the hill folks of West Virginia, a state that has prompted many of the myths about hillbillies, moonshine and miscegenation. He was a mystery. He worked at the Unimin sand mine operation, where he'd worked when he first met Hilda. He was a good singer, everyone conceded, and sang in the Hebron Baptist Church Choir occasionally. He had a big dark car and drove like a nut, "used to outrun the cops, scared Virginia so bad she'd get down in the back seat and cover her head," according to her uncle, Charles Spaid.

In the fall of 1948, the Hensleys suddenly moved into a run-down duplex in Winchester, on crowded Kent Street, where Depression-era families came when they left their subsistence farms in the rural areas in the hopes of finding work in the apple factory or the textile mill or the railroad. In gentle Winchester, it was the wrong side of the tracks. "Unless you were compelled to, you wouldn't want to have lived on South Kent back then," said Reverend Nathan Williamson, a local minister, who, years later, conducted Patsy's funeral services. "The people there did not have much of this world's goods." Their neighbors recalled seeing very little of Sam, as though he were coming and going. Then he left, for good. There was rancor on both sides. In later accounts, Sam bitterly laid the blame for the breakup of the family squarely on Hilda. As far as Hilda was concerned, his insults had been unspeakable. His name was rarely mentioned in Ginny's home again. Indeed, in none of Patsy's own accounts of her early childhood did she ever refer to him or to his singing.

After being such a dramatic presence in her life, his disappearance reverberated with equal force. Though she had to symbolically slay him, thus bearing the burden of the family secret, it liberated her, at last, to pursue her passion with complete abandon.

Ginny was not bothered by her new surroundings. To the contrary, her new neighbors were people who had been down on their luck, people who knew hardships, people who had been rejected. They were Ginny's kind of people. Ginny assured her mom that she would help take care of the family financially, shouldering the "father" role as the main breadwinner.

Work was not new to Ginny. Growing up she worked side-by-side with her mother, her "best friend." As a young teenager, when times were rough and there was no food on the table for a family of five, she'd gotten jobs by lying about her age. After she dropped out of Handley High, she took a job at Rockingham Poultry on North Kent Street. The company required that employees be at least eighteen, but Ginny lied about her age and earned her meager paycheck by standing in rubber hip boots, butchering chickens, cutting their necks as they dangled from lines tied to their feet. When the foreman discovered she was only sixteen, he let her go. Ginny cried and told him how desperately the family needed her paycheck. She was allowed to work two more weeks until she found a job as a countergirl at the Greyhound Bus depot.

Finally, Ginny approached Hunter Gaunt who, with his wife, owned a drugstore and soda fountain right around the corner from where the Hensleys lived on Kent Street. The Gaunts liked Ginny and felt sorry for the Hensleys, with no father and having to grow up "the hard way." They gave Ginny, who was such a responsible girl, a job as a clerk and fountain attendant, paying her minimum wage, seventy-five cents an hour, to mix and serve vanilla cokes, lime rickeys and root beer frosties. Even with the singing that she started pursuing with such single-minded intensity, Ginny was a diligent employee. She wore a white uniform, bobby socks and loafers, and she had a certain maturity and sense of style about her that made her stand out from the other girls.

Pat Smallwood vividly recalled the day she met Ginny at Gaunt's: "I had seen her in an amateur contest in town and at the time thought, 'Gosh, she's pretty. I'd like to meet her.' One day I walked into Gaunt's and there she was. I was sitting at one end of one of the little round tables there, having my Coke, and we started talking. I said, 'You're Ginny Hensley, aren't you?' 'Yeah,' she said, '*I'm* Ginny Hensley, *whaaat . . .* ?' I said, 'I thought I was going to meet ya.' She says, 'Well, now ya met me, baby.' She was a wisecracker. I was the giggly type and she was down-to-earth and knew what she wanted out of life. She was only three years older but she knew what she wanted to be and knew how to go about getting it. She liked her job, but she'd say, 'You know, I'm going to be something one of these days. I won't be doing *this* for the rest of my life.' "

WINC broadcast out of its offices in downtown Winchester on a mere 250 watts—barely a blip by today's standards, but in the days of uncluttered airwaves, WINC was the only radio station between Hagerstown, Maryland, and Harrisonburg, Virginia, and could be heard as far away as Charlottesville until programming ended at midnight. At that point, the big 50,000-watt clear channels came bowling through until the morning farm report started the day all over again.

The station's programming mix leaned heavily on the popular music of the day—Bing Crosby, Perry Como and Nat "King" Cole— and carried any of a number of variety and drama series available by transcription. "Morton Downey," "Front Page Drama," "Terry and the Pirates," "Tennessee Ernie Ford and the Pea Pickers" and "Checkerboard Time with Roy Rogers" came to the station on 16-inch ETs— that is, electrical transcriptions. But like radio stations everywhere in the late forties, WINC depended on local talent for much of its programming. Winchester's National Municipal Marching Band was broadcast from WINC's front lawn because the band was too big to squeeze into the studio. There were broadcasts of local dance bands, as well as the Sunday morning devotional program presented by the Winchester Ministerial Association, which served up hymns and homilies.

At WINC, Saturday morning was designated hillbilly music day.

Saddle Pals, Swing Boys, Melody Boys, Playboys, Ramblin' Boys, Buckaroos and Apple Pickers filed in and out of the WINC studio continuously from 9 A.M. until the final notes of "Amazing Grace" signaled the end of the show at noon. Each band was allotted a fifteen- or thirty-minute slot depending on advertisers. Any band that could get a local merchant to pop for $5 for a half-hour of air time was on.

"They brought me the copy to read just before they went on," remembered Phil Whitney, manager, announcer and chief engineer at that time. "A lot of it was scribbled by hand. Half the time the guys would cut a piece of newspaper advertising out and hand it to me to read live over the air. I'd have to hit it cold. I had a problem on the air one time. We called them charcoal grills but the copy said the sponsor had a new shipment of braziers in. Only I accented the second syllable. I finished reading, 'Ours are made out of iron.' You wouldn't believe the calls."

On-air gaffes were standard among the musicians too. Whitney recalled one time when a hillbilly wound up his last tune and reckoned into the microphone as to how it was "time to get outahere," then looked at the big clock on the wall and exclaimed, "I'll be goddamned if it ain't."

It was on one such morning in 1948 that Ginny made her live broadcast debut. For weeks musicians noticed her out in the visitors' room at the station, observing the three-ring circus inside the studio through the big glass partition. Her version of the story ran: "I used to sing or hum along with the recordings I'd hear on the radio. One day I got real brave and walked into the Winchester radio station at the hour a hillbilly band was being featured. I told the leader, 'If you just give me a chance to sing with you, I'll never ask for pay.' "

It was the last time she never asked for pay.

The leader of the band, the Melody Playboys, was "Joltin' " Jim McCoy, who was only a few years older than Ginny, but already a seasoned veteran of the schoolhouse circuit. McCoy grew up in nearby Berkeley Springs, West Virginia, listening to every Ernest Tubb, Vernon Dalhart, Bailes Brothers, Tex Ritter, Spade Cooley and Bob Wills record ever made. He dressed western, à la Tubb, his idol, in tailored western suits, and his act at one point featured a sharpshooter who would shoot pieces of chalk out of his daughters' mouths. McCoy was impressed by Ginny's moxie. He told her, "If you've got enough nerve to stand before that microphone, I've got nerve enough to let you sing."

She had the courage, but according to station manager Whitney, "She wasn't all that great when she started. She gave the appearance of being confident, but she was an anxious gal—she wanted to get on the air real bad. She had visions of her future and that was one of her goals and she was straight ahead about it. She was going to get it one way or another."

Flush with the success of her first foray into the public arena, Ginny had grander aspirations. She became obsessed with ads she'd seen in some pulp fan magazines, "the worst from California—always from out there," said Robert Gaines, Sr., the owner of G&M Music Center. Juxtaposed between promises to ninety-seven-pound weaklings, "New Bodies for Old!" and guarantees to "Starve pimples by removing the oils that pimples 'feed' on" were the dubious ads that promised a "career as a singing star."

G&M Music Center was the oldest and largest music store in Winchester. In the years between World War I and World War II, store owner Gaines dropped his line of player pianos, accordions, pump organs, Norge refrigerators and Speed Queen washers to concentrate on band instruments, especially guitars, as well as phonograph players and 45s. He had a listening booth and a small recording studio that cut aluminum discs from a stylus cutter. Gaines offered the studio as a special service to valued customers, and didn't advertise, but Ginny found out about it. After that, she would show up every Monday morning, like clockwork, her hard-earned money in hand, and insist he record her so she could send away to the places in the ads.

Gaines felt sorry for Ginny, who had had to drop out of school to support her family, and he suspected there had been problems at home. He knew the Hensleys were strapped and thought Ginny was wasting what precious little money she had on the bogus claims of the ads in the tacky magazines. But even after patiently explaining what a scam they were, he found he couldn't say no.

"We tried to discourage her for a long time," Gaines said. "They were just trashy magazines. We tried to tell her what we knew was happening, but she just wouldn't be discouraged. She was so young, so eager and anxious to sing. She had just a natural talent. We had a piano teacher here in town who came to give lessons. At first she sort of made fun of Patsy, said she would never make it. But later on she recognized the quality she had to her voice. Likened her to Bing Crosby in her ability to slide from note to note. Once or twice she even came up here and played a little piano accompaniment for Patsy."

Ralph "Jumbo" Rinker was Ginny's first big crush. A piano player who played strictly in the key of C, his cocktail lounge repertoire included songs like "Smoke Gets in Your Eyes," "Stormy Weather," "I

Only Have Eyes for You," "Begin the Beguine." He played everything from the local country club to the less-than-savory gin mills on the outskirts of town like the Melody Lane, on the West Virginia line, "the kind of place that had a piano and a juke box and a place where some guy might play country music," Rinker recalled. "People would work all week and come Friday night. They'd have beer or whiskey, get drunk, have a big hullabaloo time, fight, go home and think you had a big night."

One evening, sixteen-year-old Ginny and Hilda showed up at the dive on a mission. Jumbo described his first meeting with Ginny: "I started around nine and played 'til about one. When I took a break I was sitting at the bar, with my girl, and Mrs. Hensley came over and said, 'You Jumbo Rinker? I'm Mrs. Hensley and this is my daughter Virginia.' She said, 'Would you do me a favor? Would you play a couple of songs and let Virginia sing? She wants to sing. She's trying to get started in the music business.' I said, 'Sure, be glad to.' Ginny named a few songs, but I didn't know any of them—they were mostly country songs. So she says, 'You pick a song.' I say, 'Nah, you pick a song from my list.' She knew the words to most of the songs I did, so she picked one. 'Want to try that? You have nothing to lose. Everybody's having fun—they won't care. I'll start out and you just jump in.' And she did. And she sang a couple more songs. People liked it. Before she left she asked if she could come back down and sing again. I said, 'Sure,' and she came, I think one or two more times."

Jumbo was eleven years older than Ginny. He had an easy smile and an affable personality. "You're either 'buddy' or 'honey.' " To Ginny he was rather dashing, with a head of thick wavy hair gone prematurely white, and thanks to some wealthy aunt who had a charge account at the finest haberdashery in town, he was well turned out. And he could mix as easily with the bluebloods as he could the rednecks.

But Jumbo also had a wild side that appealed to Ginny. He was a notorious "rounder." He had a pilot's license and wealthy friends with airplanes. He liked to drink, have a good time, drive fast and had a predilection for getting into dazzling wrecks, including a dramatic airplane crash that occurred when he was under the influence: "the only man who ever had a wreck and got all messed up and came out better looking than before he had the wreck," said Rinker's friend, Johnny Anderson.

Ginny immediately caught his eye, too: "She was fully developed and had a nice figure. She made quite an impression on me because I was young and she was young, but I thought she was at least eighteen.

How do you put it? I'm thinking she's a girl, I'm a boy, so if I can make out with her, this is going to be great. Later I got to know her. I found out how old Ginny really was."

But try as she might, Ginny's relationship to Jumbo never blossomed into the smoldering love affair she fantasized about. Jumbo was married to a redheaded hellcat with whom he never did actually settle down. Smitten by his fiery wife, he was unavailable to Ginny for the kind of romance she craved. Jumbo said they were "just friends." Still, to Ginny, it was more.

They started dating. "I'd call Ginny up, 'Whadarya doin'?' 'Nothin'.' I had an old piano and she'd come over and sing, and we'd cut up and have us a real good time. Then we got to smoochin'. We got to be real close buddies. Course I was still madly in love with my wife. But Ginny was filling in the void in my life. And we could relate through our music. She was very kindhearted. Did things for me that were uncalled for. She worked over at Gaunt's Drugstore and made about twelve bucks a week, and she'd buy me a carton of cigarettes and things like that. She shouldn't a done that and I told her, 'Don't do that, please,' but that's the way she was.

"We did everything. Rode motorcycles, flew airplanes. I always had wheels of some kind. And I always had a buck, so we didn't have to worry about something to eat. I had pretty nice clothes because I had a charge account so I could do myself right up. And I was always welcome because people knew me—I was Jumbo. I could play the piano, I was an entertainer, a musician. This was the attraction. So at the tender age of sixteen, she thought she was in love."

Of Winchester's two largest movie theaters, the Capitol was, by far, the more elegant, with a large marquees over imposing double doors, an ornate box office, red plush seats, baroque boxes, a tiered balcony and miles of fly space behind the raked stage. Around the proscenium was a giant mural, "The People of Winchester Appealing to Washington for Protection Against the Indians." It was built for stars like Eddie Cantor, Al Jolson, Ed Wynn, Paul Robeson, Fritz Leiber and Sarah Bernhardt, all of whom at one time graced its stage. Besides screening first-run movies, the Capitol was home to the Winchester Little Theatre's productions and other local highbrow cultural events.

The Palace, despite its name, catered to the common folks. On occasional Saturdays, the Palace hosted "kiddie" amateur shows of the type widespread throughout the forties and fifties that later spawned the television equivalent in Arthur Godfrey's "Talent Scouts" and Ted Mack's "Original Amateur Hour." The format was a movie, followed by the amateur contest, then another movie. The prize money was $5,

$3 and $2 for first, second and third place. The blow-by-blow was carried live by WINC.

Ginny entered and sang "Yankee Doodle Dandy." She wore an Uncle Sam outfit consisting of red-white-and-blue-striped shorts and cutaway jacket, fishnet stockings, high heels, and top hat, and she carried a cane. She always did her own hair and makeup: "She rolled her own hair; she did not go to beauty parlors," Pat Miller pointed out. "She didn't believe in perms; she rolled it. We would go to the movies with her hair in rollers with a scarf tied around her head. She'd put on a little bit of makeup though. Not a whole lot, just enough to make herself look pretty. Yeah, it was considered loose in those days, but she was different. I think she was too much for this town to handle. A lot of women here were jealous of her. But it was singing that was on her mind. Not makeup. Not hair. Not men. She was more interested in singing than anything else in the whole wide world."

Ginny won first prize. The show was judged by Winchester's "Mr. Entertainment," Jack Fretwell, a wholesale beer and wine distributor whose calling was show biz. "She wasn't all that good—she didn't register," Fretwell claimed.

But soon after, Fretwell saw Ginny perform again. The event, held at the Capitol Theatre, was a regional competition for "Original Amateur Hour." The winner of the contest was determined by an audience applause meter. The prize was a trip to New York to compete on national television. Ginny entered and impressed Fretwell with her rendition of a tune from *Show Boat*. First prize went to a ten-year-old black tap-dancing whiz, but this time, Ginny got an honorable mention.

Not long afterward, Fretwell saw Ginny Hensley yet again, at a rehearsal for the annual minstrel show, an important charity event sponsored by the local Jaycees and staged at Handley High for the benefit of the Winchester Memorial Hospital. The show was styled as a vaudeville event, with singing, dancing, skits and comedy routines. Fretwell served as emcee. Rehearsals were held months before the performance. Ginny auditioned and won a spot in the show. Fretwell said she did a solo performance of the song "Oklahoma" and sang and danced in the chorus.

"This time she's more sophisticated," recalled Fretwell. "Plus I can tell by the audience response that she's coming across."

"She could hear something one time and sing it," said John Reid, who also appeared in the minstrel show. "She never needed much rehearsing. Her voice just rolled out of her."

Ginny's voice may have sounded effortless even then, but she was a relentless perfectionist, according to local pianist Nettie Carbaugh, the accompanist for the show. Carbaugh recalled, with ill-concealed exasperation, the demanding young woman who one year sang "Lovesick Blues" in a racy, black satin outfit made by Hilda that featured a skirt slit up the side, black fishnet stockings and high heels: "She wanted to rehearse all the time. She wouldn't appear in public without a rehearsal. She'd come down to my house in Stephens City to rehearse—even when I didn't want her." Carbaugh gave Ginny some advice she apparently took to heart: "I told her, 'Know your key.' Musicians hate it when someone comes to sing and doesn't know what key he sings a song in. I later heard she carried a little black notebook with her with her keys written in it."

After seeing her rapid progress, Jack Fretwell decided to pay a call to 405 South Kent Street. Fretwell had an offer for Ginny he thought she couldn't pass up. The Jack Fretwell Orchestra was the house band at the Yorks Inn, on Route 11 on the outskirts of town. It was owned by Alfred deMazzon, a native of Venice, Italy, who had once managed the posh Carlton Hotel in Washington, D.C. When deMazzon bought the Yorks, he transformed it into a showplace, with a fountain and exotic caged birds in the lobby. When a competitor opened the John Marshall Nightclub in nearby Front Royal, Marshall decided to give deMazzon a run for his money.

He created a sophisticated 1920s ambience reminiscent of New York's finest speakeasies. He'd envisioned fine food, dining and dancing and an orchestra with a girl singer perched on top of the piano à la Helen Morgan. He called Fretwell and offered him a job playing for the Saturday night crowd. Fretwell set about looking for his girl singer.

"She was the only girl around that had any kind of voice at all," Fretwell said. "I thought she'd go over in a nightclub because they're pretty brutal. I went over to her house on Kent Street to talk to her."

Ginny eagerly agreed to the job. "I think she saw it as an opportunity to polish her talent." She fixed her work schedule to accommodate the new development in her career. She would race home from the drugstore, peel out of her uniform, wash and set her hair, which she wore slightly waved over one eye, Veronica Lake style, and iron the costume Hilda had made for her, usually "something showy with pizzazz." Fretwell would come to the house early to rehearse the five or six numbers she would perform later that evening—songs like "Embraceable You," "Time on My Hands," "Stardust" and the song that always brought the club to a standstill: "You Made Me Love You."

"When I went back to her house a lot of times there was a different man with her mother. In the kitchen, they'd be drinking and partying. It wasn't a normal home, let's put it that way. I saw a lot of things that reminded me of my home—I came from a broken home, too. We both had to pull ourselves up by our own boot straps. There's a lot of things you have to do when you don't have a father and I think it showed in her feeling, her delivery.

"The club owner, he was an older man—he was crazy about her. Asked her if she would come earlier and become a cigarette girl. You know—the old, stereotyped cigarette girl? Long black net stockings, short whatever, high heels. She did that in the early part of the evening, before the singing started, kind of a hostess. He just loved her."

Throughout this time, Ginny continued to sing at beer joints and dance halls like Donald Patterson's in downtown Winchester where she was still singing "a little more on the pop modern side, at first," according to local musician Bud Armel. Anyone who bothered her soon discovered that she could hold her own. She had the Hensley gift for words, observed Johnny Anderson, who first met her at this time.

"Patsy knew when to turn it on and when to turn it off. She wasn't dumb. But if you crossed her up she'd tell you off. Oh, I heard her cuss people out, hell yeah. If some guy would come and try to make time with her, she'd tell him to go to hell and get lost. She didn't mess around."

Hilda didn't know for certain if her daughter was destined for immortality, but she did know they would stick together no matter what. They always had. She took in sewing to make ends meet and vowed to help her talented, ambitious daughter with her music any way she could. She could stretch potato sandwiches and pennies to last any distance between where they were and the stage Patsy needed to get to. Many times she drove Ginny herself to and from her singing engagements in their broken-down jalopy of a car. As for Ginny, between her job at Gaunt's and her budding singing career, there was very little time for sleep, let alone the things average teenagers did, but Ginny was exhilarated by the round of activities: "We wouldn't get home until about three o'clock in the morning," she recounted. "A few hours later I was up getting ready to return to work in the drugstore."

Chapter Four

*I*N MAY 1949, a new program debuted on WSM the first Friday of every month: Wally Fowler's "All Night Gospel Sing." It became to gospel music what the "Grand Ole Opry" was to hillbilly music. John Wallace "Wally" Fowler and his Oak Ridge Quartet (the precursor of today's secular-pop Oak Ridge Boys, after forty changes of personnel in as many years) had been heard on the Opry since 1945. The new program established Fowler as the undisputed "Gospel King," and his Oak Ridge Quartet as one of the best-known gospel acts in the business.

Ginny loved gospel music, having grown up on everything from the good old tunes from the Baptist hymnal to the rocking, rolling songs for which the Pentecostals were famous. And she was a big fan of Fowler, one of the new breed of twang-free country singers in the mold of Eddy Arnold, who'd hoisted gospel to a new level of showmanship.

Fowler and his Oak Ridge Quartet had clearly been inspired by black gospel acts, both in style and substance, and Fowler was once a student of "Professor" Lee Roy Abernathy, who wrote the gospel classic, "Ev'rybody's Gonna Have A Wonderful Time Up There," which delivers a gospel lyric as pure boogie. Dressed in black shirts, black cuffed and pleated trousers and white ties, the Oak Ridge Quartet served up such standard Southern white gospel fare as "I've Got Faith," "Jericho Road," and "Have a Little Talk with Jesus" in swinging style. They raised the eyebrows of some of the more staid in the gospel community. "If you deviated from gospel in the South, they'd hang you," pointed out one of the members of the quartet. But four white boys chanting spirituals "the way the coloreds used to do it" proved exciting to Fowler's younger fans. One of these, according to Fowler, was a young, unrecorded Elvis Presley, who came backstage to meet the

Gospel King after one of the group's famous all-night sings in Memphis.

Besides his regular appearances on the Opry, Fowler and the Oak Ridge Quartet played road dates more than two hundred days a year. Fowler booked the dates himself, independently of the Opry's own booking agency, the Artists Service Bureau. To get around the Opry's ban on announcing upcoming dates not arranged through the Artists Service Bureau, Fowler had a ploy, which might very well have been how Ginny heard about his upcoming appearances in Winchester. This probably occurred sometime during the summer of 1949.

"Dear Lord," he might have begun, "please watch over these boys as they travel down the highway to Winchester, Virginia, and please watch over all the people we hope will come out to see our show next Friday night at the Palace Theatre there in Winchester." Fowler, of course, would have embellished with as many cities and itineraries as possible until he was at the point of being yanked offstage by a stage hook.

Fowler had six shows at Winchester's Palace Theatre that day. Ginny knew, from listening to his broadcasts, that Fowler sometimes invited other singers from the gospel firmament to join him on stage for part of the program. She made up her mind to get a spot. She talked her way into the backstage area, whereupon Fowler felt her tugging at his sleeve.

"I turned around and here was this young lady. Oh, no street clothes for that kid. She was dressed just as pretty as you ever seen. She came for the occasion. She knew she was going to get on that stage. I turned to the fellows: 'Hey, fellows, here's a young lady says she can sing.' I felt something about her. I knew she was a little cocky, but I figured she had real self-confidence. So I said, 'So you think you can sing.' She says, 'Yessir, I sure can.' "

Intrigued, Fowler challenged her to prove it on the spot. "She was a very cute girl, a little bit chunky. She had a bubbling, outgoing personality—she's a Virgo, you know." She gave a demonstration of her talent and Fowler was impressed. He'd once passed up an opportunity to manage an unknown Hank Williams. The Gospel King had a real flair for promotion; he was already earning substantial royalties from songs he'd written for Eddy Arnold, including Arnold's "Mommy, Please Stay Home with Me." In addition, he marketed his own label as well as records he'd made for Capitol, his song books, his music publishing company, his printing company and even his own mustard seeds—"Wally Fowler's Mustard Seed," an idea that came to him to plug one of the quartet's popular songs, "Faith as the Grain of a Mustard Seed."

Even in the naming of the Oak Ridge Quartet, Fowler exploited a current event. Oak Ridge, Tennessee, was the secret location for the administration of the Manhattan Project. After the explosions over Japan that ended World War II, the secret was made public to the whole country. According to one WSM announcer, Grant Turner, "The term 'Oak Ridge' was pretty hot. It signified advanced technology, the atom bomb, the Manhattan Project. People had sort of gone nuts about it."

Once Fowler met the stage-struck girl with the surprisingly sophisticated voice, he could smell a discovery in the making. Fowler instinctively knew that nothing warmed the hearts of a small-town crowd faster than breaking out an undiscovered talent. He gave the command: she would perform.

"I asked her if she knew 'I'll Hold You in My Heart,' which I had written for Eddy Arnold. She said, 'Oh yes, I love it. I can do that one.' This girl sang anywhere anybody would let her on stage. That was the story she gave me, and her mother, too, later. She just loved to sing and she wasn't bashful about it either. Any little girl or little boy could come up and say, 'I can sing.' But it was her positive attitude—it's amazing what a positive attitude will do. I wasn't trying to make fun of her when I said, 'Hey, guys, this young lady says she can sing.' And she stayed right on track; she didn't budge. Her eyes were as bright as stars. She just knew she was going to get on that stage, and that was the half of it."

Fowler's hillbilly band, the Georgia Clodhoppers, opened the show. But the folks had come for gospel, and Fowler and his Oak Ridge Quartet wouldn't disappoint them that day. After the Clodhoppers' turn on stage, the Oak Ridge Quartet came out. The group typically opened with "Dese Bones" and continued with a few classic Negro spirituals—then they might launch into standard church material like "Peace in the Valley," followed by a few instrumentals before the show reached its denouement with a thumping, call-and-response delivery of a good old hymn like "How Great Thou Art," with Fowler leading, his warm flexible baritone chanting "the way coloreds used to do it."

Ginny's turn at the microphone probably occurred before the Oak Ridge Quartet took the stage. "She absolutely captivated them," recollected Fowler. "She went off stage with a thunderous applause and had to come back to take a bow. The band wasn't prepared to do another song, but she went on and sang another chorus of 'I'll Hold You in My Heart.' "

"I wish you the best of everything," Fowler told her. "May the greater stars of your destiny always lead you on your highway of happiness; you look so happy tonight, Virginia." Ginny invited the Gospel King home to meet her mother. Fowler politely declined, but later changed his mind: "I thought at the time, 'This little girl is really something—she might have potential to be groomed for bigger and better things.' All the guys in the band—they just flipped over her. I told them, 'Guys—sixteen.' "

After the last show, Fowler went to Kent Street, where he met Ginny's mom, and touted her daughter as a "female Eddy Arnold—you just don't hear them like that too often." Hilda was skeptical until the Gospel King made a surprising proposal that, to Ginny, must have sounded like the answer to her prayers or a line that might have come straight out of a Hollywood movie: "I told them I'd like to arrange for an audition at the Opry. They couldn't believe it—thought I was kidding them. They thought I was just one of the people going through the country acting like a big shot."

For a big shot though, Fowler was good for his word. He called about six weeks later with the good news that an "audition" had indeed been arranged. Fowler's summons was Ginny's call to Mecca. There was no question that she wouldn't go. Unfortunately, there were some logistical obstacles to making the almost 1400-mile round-trip to Nashville: Hilda's car could barely make it to Front Royal and back, and Ginny, of course, had her job, on which her family of four depended. But the Gaunts gave her time off and a family friend agreed to take the whole Hensley family to Nashville. Driving all night long, five to a car, including four-year-old Sylvia and eight-year-old John, they arrived in Nashville tired, cranky and rumpled. At a public rest stop, Ginny promptly climbed on top of a concrete Tennessee Department of Public Works picnic table and fell asleep. Afterward, she washed and dressed in the restroom of an Esso station.

They'd been instructed to be at the Opry to meet Opry general manager Jim Denny at Denny's office on the fifth floor of National Life's building on Seventh Avenue, when he arrived at 9 A.M. sharp. So, early that morning, in anticipation of what she surely believed was a rendezvous with destiny, Ginny and her retinue headed for downtown Nashville.

On the way there, they might have passed the world's most celebrated monument to the triumph of classical art. The Nashville Parthenon is an exact replica of the original Parthenon in Athens, Greece. It was built in 1897 out of plywood and plaster, as part of the Tennessee Centennial Exposition. When the yearlong celebration ended, the idea of a Greek temple became a fixation of Nashville's upper crust, who'd proclaimed their city the "Athens of the South" and wanted a symbol to go along with it. Rather than demolish the temporary temple, the city forefathers set about rebuilding the structure out of materials that would truly stand the test of time. The second Parthenon was completed in 1931.

That was six years after the Nashville-based National Life and Accident Insurance Company founded its own radio station, WSM ("We Shield Millions"), to serve as a sales tool for its agents in the hinterlands, who offered free Opry tickets to induce people to buy the company's low-cost "shield" policies. The company had hired one of the most popular radio announcers of the day, Judge George D. Hay, to preside over the radio show that rubbed some of the snootier residents of Nashville the wrong way. Hay, a former newspaper columnist from Attica, Indiana, had been largely responsible for making the "Grand Ole Opry" one of the most successful live shows on radio. He blew a steamboat whistle, provided corny, irreverent commentary and generally maintained a down-home tone for the rural music format that was being copied by radio stations all over the country.

Prominent Nashvillians (including some of the directors of WSM), who basked in "the glory that was Greece," were irked that this Northerner Hay was getting so much attention for his rube radio show. But it was conceded by the bottom-line-minded insurance executives who ran the station that the company sold insurance policies to millions of working-class, rural Americans who listened to Hay's broadcast. So Hay continued in his slot. It became the most profitable thing WSM ever did.

As the Opry broadcasts became wildly popular, WSM rented a series of bigger venues to accommodate bigger and bigger audiences: first, a small silent movie house, then the Dixie Tabernacle, the War Memorial Auditorium and then, probably sometime in 1943, the former Union Gospel Tabernacle, a brick monolith with massive white-framed arched windows and enough hard wooden pews to accommodate 3482 people. It had been built by Captain Tom Ryman, a turn-of-the-century riverboat captain who ran pleasure boats catering to the hedonistic pastimes of drinking and gambling. Ryman was challenged by one of the great preachers of the day, Sam Jones, to attend a tent revival in an area along lower Broadway. Ryman came, accompanied by his debauched fellow river runners. For his sermon, Jones chose one of the most potent themes in Southern folklore: mother. The message hit Ryman like one of God's own thunderbolts. He immediately renounced his sinful ways and built the preacher a glorious tabernacle right on the spot.

★   ★   ★

Even though it was a Friday when Ginny arrived in downtown Nashville, the countdown until the Opry show the following evening had already begun and Ginny could sense the excitement brewing in the area near the Ryman Auditorium on lower Broadway. People came from all over the country, by every means of locomotion imaginable, to experience the Opry. Linebaugh's bustled with out-of-town hillbillies downing coffee and sugar donuts. Opry fans milled around Ernest Tubb's Record Shop and poked their noses into the dingy hospitality of Mom's, the bar across the alleyway from the Ryman that later would become famous as Tootsie's Orchid Lounge. By Saturday noon, there would be a line in front of the old tabernacle to purchase tickets (sixty cents reserved, thirty cents unreserved). It was rare when the Opry wasn't sold out.

The show ran from 7:30 to midnight. People in the audiences made themselves at home, opening hampers of aromatic fried chicken and country ham they'd brought from home, devouring Moon Pies before they melted and batting the hot, muggy air with little cardboard fans with wooden sticks. Babies cried, kids ran up and down the aisles and hawkers worked the house, selling Opry programs (ten cents) and trinkets marked "Souvenir of the Grand Ole Opry." The audience whooped and yelled out their requests to their favorite artists, who obliged—it was rude not to. Haughtiness did not exist in Hillbilly Heaven.

The chaos out in the house was matched by frenzy on stage and in the wings, as anywhere from 120 to 140 cast members made continuous, fast-paced entrances and exits during each fifteen- and thirty-minute segment. It was like a musical revue and the performers represented a wide range of styles: "It is more than hillbilly. It is valley-billy, river-billy, desert-billy and blues-billy as well," said the late Opry announcer "Cousin" Louie Buck, who described Nashville as the "Broadway of Country Music."

The man who directed the traffic at the Opry was a nonentity to Ginny, who could otherwise tell you the names of all the stars. Jim Denny couldn't sing a note or strum a lick, yet he was one of the most powerful men on the Nashville music scene and was considered the biggest booker of one-night stands in the world.

Denny had started out in the mailroom of National Life and Accident and worked his way up through the filing room, to the accounting department and then to the keypunch room of the actuarial department. In the beginning the Opry was his moonlighting job. He worked as a ticket scalper, then as a bouncer, then as a concession operator. Then in 1946 he secured what was one of the most important behind-the-scenes jobs at the Opry: the head of the Artists Service Bureau. He was made the Opry's full-time general manager in 1951.

Denny was shrewd. The Opry paid artists next to nothing. Having taken the time to get to know the show people, Denny had long realized that the real money was out on the road. When he took over the Artists Service Bureau, which booked Opry stars all over the country, he had the power to hire, fire and put performers on the road in traveling Opry units all over the country, from which he deducted the station's cut and his own. In 1956, when he was abruptly fired by management who didn't cotton to his old-boy network, the powerful Denny claimed: "There were lots of irritations between me and Jack DeWitt, the station president. One factor was that I always used to park my white Cadillac in the station parking lot right next to his little black Chevy."

What Ginny and her mother in all likelihood did not know when they arrived at Denny's office at 9 A.M. sharp was the Opry's "house rule."

"How old is the young lady?" Denny had asked Fowler when he returned to Nashville following the Winchester performance.

"Well, I believe she's only sixteen," Fowler replied.

"We can't handle nothing like that. They got to be eighteen or better."

True enough—the Opry made an appearance of compliance with child labor laws, but the restriction mainly applied to girls. There were many instances of the Opry employing male musicians younger than eighteen. Girl singers were rare and girl soloists were an anomaly. The girls worked with their husbands, like cowgirl Texas Ruby, or Annie Lu, or their families, like the Cackle Sisters or the Poe Sisters. And if they didn't have any family, they invented them, like "Cousin" Rachel Veach, who did a comedy routine with Pete Kirby, who played Dobro in Roy Acuff's band. Kirby had neither blood ties nor legal ties to Veach, but he was billed as her "Bashful Brother" Oswald.

The reality was that if you were a serious female artist you could forget about the center spotlight at the Ryman. It was said that girls would never be stars because the good old boys in the audience with their wives "would get their ears slapped down if they stared at a strange female, much less applauded her." About the only way a woman could get a star billing was if she cultivated a homely image, like Sarah Ophelia Colley, who, as Minnie Pearl, was the Opry's reigning female icon. And Cousin Minnie knew how to play by the rules. A product of a genteel Tennessee family, a finishing school graduate who studied Shakespeare, her "man-hungry" rube comic routine was based on her deliberate cultivation of a sexually nonthreatening image. Her privileged family background, combined with her education, an even bigger handicap by hillbilly standards, meant she had a double taboo, which she artfully downplayed by explaining to the press that she went to college "only for two years. I don't reckon it marked me too much."

Ginny clearly had the deck stacked against her, yet Fowler had made a promise to her mother. So when Denny reminded him of the "house rule," the Gospel King coaxed him into seeing her, "more or less as a favor to me."

Fowler must have known the futility of Ginny's "audition"; in any case, he was on the road when Ginny and her mother arrived at Denny's office. When the general manager appeared after a long wait, he did not take the pains to conceal the fact that Ginny's "audition" was perfunctory. Denny was a short, stocky man who dressed impeccably, if not like a dandy, in brown pin-striped suits. He wore a big diamond horseshoe ring on his pinky finger and a gun at his waistband, having been deputized during his years as a bouncer. He had an easy manner of dealing with show people that belied his gruff voice, and he walked like a bear. Some people felt immediately intimidated upon meeting him. But he quickly took a shine to the irrepressible and guileless Ginny, who in a very grown-up way enthused so infectiously to him about how much the Opry meant to her that Denny soon had a fatherly arm around her shoulder as he walked her around, introducing her to the Opry personalities on the premises. One of these was "Moon" Mullican, the "King of Hillbilly Piano Players," famous for a distinctive honky-tonk style developed in the dance halls around his hometown of Corrigan, Texas. On the spur of the moment, Denny asked Mullican to sit in on the girl's "audition."

She sang and Mullican offered praise. As compliments floated around the room, they were interrupted by an unexpected visitor: Roy Acuff, the King of Country Music. Ginny and Hilda nearly dropped. Acuff was a living legend. During the war years, a G.I. popularity poll ranked him ahead of Frank Sinatra and Bing Crosby. The Japanese paid him the ultimate compliment with a battle cry thought to be the crowning insult: "To hell with Roosevelt, to hell with Babe Ruth, to hell with Roy Acuff!" After the war, Acuff ran for governor of Tennessee. His platform was pure Opry: "I'm not a politician. I'm just a country boy, trying to run things as honest and square as possible." Acuff lost the election but at least he was still king, it was pointed out. If he had won, he'd be just another one of the forty-eight states' governors.

Acuff apparently overheard Ginny's audition; in any case, he invited her to sing on his "Dinner Bell" broadcast later that day. Denny, meanwhile, was stumped about what to do with Ginny. As efficiently as he ran the Opry, he wasn't always a keen judge of talent. One well-known legend offered by Elvis Presley biographer Albert

Goldman has it that Denny supposedly told Presley in the fall of 1954 that he should go back to driving a truck after Presley made his one and only Opry appearance. The incident may have been exaggerated, but Denny was concerned about keeping the Opry performances strictly country.

Denny suggested to Hilda they spend the night in Nashville. His proposal threw her into a quandary: they didn't have enough money for a motel and her friend needed to get back to Winchester. Had Hilda explained her situation to Denny, he might have helped them out. As it was, Hilda decided they should return home. If Ginny was crestfallen to have come so far, so close to her dream come true, only to turn back, she put on a stoic front. Hilda reckoned that if the Opry was really interested in Ginny, they would be in touch.

Weeks, then months, went by, however, and there was no word from Nashville. Hilda no doubt echoed Ginny's feelings when she later said, "They let us down. I guess we expected better treatment than that." At one point they contacted Fowler. He tried his best to explain the Opry's position to them. Fowler referred to his conversation with Denny: "He felt she was a good talent, but she was sixteen." Denny explained to Fowler: "It's just a little too early, Wally, I just can't get involved with her. We got a hard and fast rule around here that they got to be eighteen." Fowler said, "Well, okay, I'm not trying to break your rules, but this girl is *going* to be big."

Fowler explained further: "They wondered why I hadn't tried to do more for her. They couldn't understand what my intentions were. I had expressed such an interest in Virginia. Her mother said, 'Mr. Fowler is either one of the most sincere people or he's the biggest . . . ' "

To make it up to them, Fowler offered to pay for professional publicity photos for Ginny. She and Hilda returned to Nashville a few months later for the portrait session, which Fowler paid for along with a thousand glossies at ten cents each. It may have been during this trip that Ginny was invited to sing a thirty-minute set on Roy Acuff's show at Dunbar Cave, an amusement center complete with hotel, swimming pool, lake and an outdoor stage that Acuff had bought to provide ongoing work for his band, the Smoky Mountain Boys.

Pete Kirby, a.k.a. "Bashful Brother Oswald," vividly remembered teenage Ginny Hensley singing in the park: "I hadn't heard anybody sing like that since we been in the business. She had a different type of voice. Roy must have been impressed to have invited her." Ginny told Kirby that meeting Roy Acuff had been the thrill of her life. He and the others in the band saw Ginny and her mom sleeping in their car in the park. He later learned, "She didn't have any money to pay for a room. They didn't tell anybody that. Probably a pride thing."

Chapter Five

FTER HER EXPERIENCE at the Opry, Ginny began to nurture her dream of becoming a singer—a *country* singer. At first, few people in Winchester who'd seen her perform were aware of the direction her music would take.

"She wasn't country really," noted Jim McCoy of Patsy's early years. "Her love of pop is what made her what she is today. There were very few songs she did that were strictly country, but to be a member of the Opry, which is what she wanted more than anything back then, she knew she had to stay a little country."

"First time I seen her, she was more on the pop-modern side—she wasn't too much country until a few years later," agreed Winchester country musician Bud Armel.

That was about 1952. By then, she'd met bandleader Bill Peer, who played an influential note in her early career. She also started going by the name "Patsy," slang for a victim, a dupe, a sucker, a pushover, a big softie.

Ginny may have first encountered Peer at WINC, where his "Melody Boys" were part of the lineup of talent on hillbilly music day. Peer lived a short distance from Winchester, in Charles Town, West Virginia, with his wife and two children. He was considered a decent musician with a good country band and the gift of gab that makes for a good front man or car salesman—in fact, he worked for the Martinsburg, West Virginia, Buick-Cadillac dealership during the day. But his ace was his job as a country music deejay for WEPM Martinsburg ("Bill's Melody Time"), and he milked his contacts for all they were worth, booking his Melody Boys into hillbilly clubs, fire halls and military bases throughout Virginia, West Virginia, Maryland and Washington, D.C. He had quite a following.

Of all Peer's gigs, however, the plum was the tristate Moose Lodge circuit. In the fifties, after the big bands died out, the Moose Lodges, which cater to local business and civic leaders, still offered live musical entertainment, dining and dancing in a family atmosphere. The Brunswick, Maryland, Moose was a well-known hot spot, and Peer and his band owned the biggest night of the week, Saturday. "He played there for years and years," said Johnny Anderson. "All the bands tried to get him out and undermine him, but they kept on keeping him there. It was his regular Saturday night job, and it was a must."

Brunswick was a working-class town, a railroad town. But because of its close proximity to Washington, D.C., it was able to attract even well-known musicians: the big bands of Paul Whiteman and Tommy Dorsey played the Brunswick Fire Hall in the forties. A block away from the fire hall, the capacious Brunswick Moose Lodge had a large, four-sided bar and a huge wooden dance floor that accommodated several hundred or more members of the Loyal Order of Moose. You had to get there early on Saturday night if you wanted a table. The members came every Saturday night with their wives, dressed to the nines, expecting to be entertained. Peer did not disappoint.

He played the part of a country music meister to the max. Naturally, he dressed the part of a cowboy. "He made the public like him," recalled one musician. "He could talk to an audience and get their attention and you could hear a pin drop."

Peer told Ginny that if she got some country material together he would audition her. And so one Saturday night in 1952 she arrived at the jam-packed Brunswick Moose Hall outfitted in full cowgirl regalia, ready to go on. If Peer was impressed by her style, he was even more impressed by her knock-'em-dead voice.

Earlier in the year, Kitty Wells, a thirty-three-year-old housewife-singer with years of pent-up emotion in her plaintive voice, rocked the world of country music when her recording of "It Wasn't God Who Made Honky-Tonk Angels" became a smash hit. It was the first big record for a woman since Patsy Montana. Wells's achievement was the first challenge to the cave man assumptions about female artists—in a variation on the jealousy theme, the thinking ran that because the market for country music records consisted primarily of women, women would not buy a record made by another woman.

Wesley Rose, son of Fred Rose, co-founder with Roy Acuff of the publishing giant Acuff-Rose, which Wesley took over in 1954, expressed the view of the country music industry: "Kitty sang for housewives *as* a housewife. She related completely to the women who bought the records. She wasn't a sex symbol or anything like that. She was a housewife and that's why she took off. She took the woman's side and she never represented any danger—because she was a housewife, the women never felt she was any danger to them with their husbands."

Ginny liked Wells, but the queen of country music's nasal voice and straitlaced reserve was one hundred degrees from Ginny's own full, rich, pop-singer sound and the sense of pizzazz she brought with it. Peer saw her undeniable talent and potential. He decided it was time to add a girl singer to his act.

As for Ginny, Peer's unqualified interest in her talent and the offer of help that went with it was all she needed to hear. Rather than discourage her, her "failed" Opry audition made her only more determined to achieve her goal and she'd gone about it wholeheartedly. It was said you could prick her bubble a hundred times and it wouldn't burst.

That night, she might have poured her heart out to a very easy-to-talk-to Bill Peer about how she'd won a talent contest at the age of four, her goal of being a star on the "Grand Ole Opry," her performance with Wally Fowler and the encouragement she'd received from some of the biggest names in country music. He offered to take her under his wing, to be her manager even. One of his first suggestions, supposedly, was that she adopt a professional name. Patsy, a good old Irish name, sounded just right for a country girl singer. He told her he would help her polish her act and get a record contract.

Patsy, for all her bravado, knew nothing about how to get started. Peer looked like a godsend. She depended on him and he threw himself into his new role with gusto, exaggerating his own connections in Nashville, particularly those with Ernest Tubb, for whom he had opened on a number of occasions when Tubb played the Charles Town Racetrack.

"Bill was kind of big-mouthed," said Johnny Anderson, who played with Peer in the mid-fifties. "He sold people a hell of a bill of goods. He was a bullshitter, let's face it. Let me tell it like it is."

"He didn't have any connections," agreed Bud Armel, who also played with Peer around this time. "That's one reason why Patsy didn't make any money off her first recordings. He didn't have any connections in Nashville and he didn't know the field, and that's how it was."

Peer threw himself into the Pygmalion role. He set about polishing his "discovery," rehearsing her and helping her create a full-blown country act. Under Peer's tutelage, she quickly blossomed. She "could really put it out to a crowd," observed one Moose Club member. "Usually you've got them up there moaning and groaning and no one cares. But when Patsy got up there, everyone listened."

From the beginning Patsy impressed her bandmates with her diligence and perfectionism, always insisting they have enough rehearsal time. She made up for her lack of experience with sincerity and a sense of professionalism. Not only had she learned her keys, as she'd been told to by piano teacher Nettie Carbaugh, but she had them all written down in a little black book she always carried with her.

She earned eight dollars a night working with the Peer outfit. In the beginning she averaged three gigs a week with them, everything from the respectable Moose Lodges to the really raw country juke joints, the kind with no sign outside that are known only by word of mouth. She quit her job as a soda jerk at Gaunt's in order to go full-time and try to make a go of it.

"She was a nice person to work with," recalled Roy Deyton, one of the Melody Boys. "I never had an ill word with her. We would just listen to her songs and she would say, 'I'd like to do this song, listen to it.' They were top songs of the day and she had already learned them. It didn't take us long to learn them because they weren't all that hard to do. We had a better sound than what most of the local people had. We were a regular country band but we had a little more variety than the average country band. We could play a little smoother style. Patsy would not sit in with just any band. We had the beat and the tempo she wanted. We were probably the first band she ever had that would get behind her and work. We didn't have the attitude that making someone else look good would make us look bad. We just wanted to sound good."

She approached her act with Peer with her usual sense of style. Hilda made her cowgirl outfits, beautifully tailored show costumes with fringe and sequined appliqués and accessorized western-style with real thoughtfulness for detail. She had a fine figure and liked to show it off. Guitarist Deyton recalled how Patsy liked to wear her clothes—tight: "A guitar string had broke and I had to replace it, but hadn't cut the end off it. On some of the finer strings you don't do that until you find out they're going to hold. The stage at Brunswick was such that the drums were in the back, Ray [Roy's twin brother] was sitting right here and I was right behind Patsy, who was up real close to the mike singing, and Bill was right next to her, so we were all pretty close. Patsy had one of these tight outfits on, real tight, fit snug around her body. She was at the mike singing and then she stepped back and then forward, real quick. And I noticed she did that two or three times. She kept moving away from the guitar. Finally, about the middle of the song, she figured out what was getting her and said, 'Roy, damn you! Cut that string!' "

If cowgirl is a spirit, then Patsy seemed born to it. She'd always been outspoken "for a woman": she fine-tuned her "just-one-of-the-boys" demeanor. Patsy loved slang and quickly adopted the country musician's patois. "Hoss," derived from "horse," a form of address used among the boys to indicate that the person being addressed is "one of the boys," was the ultimate stamp of approval. "If she liked you, you were 'hoss,' " said Roy Deyton. It was as simple as that. Her bluffness could also serve as her armor. She was the only woman working with a bunch of men, and frequently in some rough joints. In this world, the masculine talk, the kind of talk she heard growing up around her father, helped her to fit in.

"I never thought about Patsy as a person I would like to go with," Deyton recalled. "We were working together, so I never thought of her that way, even though she was a very attractive woman. We were like her family. She liked us as musicians and she liked us as people, and we spent a lot of time together and so she thought of us as, like, younger brothers."

Patsy treated the bandstand as if it were sacred ground; as its high priestess, she demanded respect. "She did not like for somebody to treat her like dirt. She had her pride and wanted you to respect her," Deyton said. As brash as she often seemed, she was offended by anyone who tried to violate her dignity and she made her feelings clear, deflecting anyone who got fresh with her with the verbal equivalent of a blast from a twenty-two. Patsy could scald the hide off a horse with her salty language.

"We always showed that respect toward her and I guess that's one reason why we always got along," Deyton said. "She was kind of quiet and right courteous to people who admired her and appreciated her music. She was nice to most men if they would treat her likewise. She liked the company of men. She got admired, you know? Some of them would try to buy her drinks to get acquainted, and a lot of times they would get overbearing. They think they're macho and can do anything with any woman they want. Then she'd tell 'em to back off. She would talk with her eyes, get daggers in her eyes—she had those dark, dark eyes. If you respected her, you never had any problems with her, but if you were smart or sarcastic, she would put you in your place. She'd come back at you with whatever was on her mind at the time."

In spite of the family feelings that existed between Patsy and the other Melody Boys, Peer's interest in his discovery was more than just professional. It wouldn't be the first time he'd had an extramarital affair. Deyton described him as a "womanizer": "He couldn't leave women alone. He was always running to other women. He was never satisfied."

Patsy did not have romantic feelings for Peer, who was eleven years her senior, married with two children. She wanted his friendship. She felt she needed his help in order to get the next break. Ultimately, she couldn't refuse him, others reasoned. "He was persistent as hell," observed Johnny Anderson, who knew Peer well and even played in his band for a while. "He wouldn't take 'no' for an answer."

"He kept chasing her and just got to her at a weak moment," confirmed Deyton. "He was a way to catapult her somewhere. We knew she was never serious about Bill. There was something else in her life and it was her desire to do music—she was so determined she would use whatever means were at her disposal at the time to get there. And she wasn't the type to hold back, you know? If someone was willing to offer her help, I guess she was willing to go as far as she had to go, like a lot of girls in the movies. That's the way it was and she just did what she had to do."

For Peer, it was love. He lavished her with gifts—clothes, jewelry—and justified them as a business investment. Deyton estimated that Peer spent the equivalent of $30,000 in today's currency on Patsy. The affair became a popular subject of gossip in Winchester—enough to wreck her "reputation." Her attitude was, "The hell with 'em." Given her ambition and her style, she was perceived as an opportunistic hussy. "On the surface, Patsy acted as though she didn't care what anyone thought of what she was doing. 'It was none of their damn business,' she'd say. She wasn't even attracted to Peer; the affair was what she thought would make *him* happy, a thank-you-for-what-you-are-doing-for-me kind of thing," according to Deyton.

"She never had any real deep feelings for Bill. We joked sometimes and said to her, 'How's things with Bill?' 'Aw, he makes me sick,' she'd say."

On the other hand, she felt guilty about the conflict the scandalous affair had created in her relationship with her mother. Hilda expressed her disapproval of Ginny's activities with Peer by silently boycotting her gigs with Peer's band. "Hilda was from the old school," observed one friend. "You didn't do things like that. And when it did happen, in the fifties, if you were a 'nice girl,' you wouldn't have a reputation for long." For the first time, Ginny couldn't open up completely to her mother. The idea of living a life of dishonesty with Hilda pained her, yet she was going to do what she had to do to make it.

*   *   *

Her solution to the dilemma came on March 7, 1953, when, with no fanfare, Patsy suddenly got married. Had her hometown friends been invited to the out-of-town ceremony, they would have been puzzled: two people could not have seemed more mismatched than the feisty, ambitious cowgirl singer and the short, heavy-set, phlegmatic Gerald Cline.

Cline was a regular at the Brunswick Moose, where Patsy had met him only a few months earlier. The scion of a fairly well off family from Frederick, Maryland, Cline was involved in the family construction business. Though only seven years older than Patsy, he could have passed for her father.

Cline won Patsy over through sheer braggadocio and the kind of joking that put people at ease. He looked to her like a big spender. He would come to Winchester to call on her in his big Buick, generously bearing gifts of groceries and other little luxuries for the Hensley family. Hilda approved of the affable and seemingly well healed Cline, who was devoted to her daughter. Perhaps the match would give Patsy, whose reputation had been tarnished by the Peer affair, some badly needed respectability. For Patsy, Gerald Cline was her ticket out of Winchester; he could financially support her budding career. "She thought she could learn to love him," noted Pat Smallwood.

The couple applied for a marriage license in Frederick, a one-hour drive north of Winchester, and quietly exchanged vows at the Frederick United Church of Christ a few weeks later. It was a simple ceremony with only a few witnesses on hand. It would be Hensley no more. Nothing masks quite so well as a new name. A new name means a new identity with which to face—or avoid facing—the world. Her first husband's name would turn out to be his greatest legacy.

Patsy broke the news to her friends after she'd moved into a modest duplex with Gerald in Frederick, just a short distance from the Cline family home. Everyone was nonplussed. No one had an inkling that "settling down" had been on her mind.

It wasn't. Patsy made it clear she had no intention of becoming a housewife. The affair with Peer was getting out of hand and she hoped that her new marital status would put a damper on Peer's affections, while her well-to-do husband would support her career.

Her idea backfired. Gerald's "wealth" mostly consisted of his expectations of his family's largesse. The reasonableness of such expectations had already been undermined by his prior transgressions against propriety. He married his first wife after getting her pregnant, and after that marriage failed, he was sued for nonpayment of child support. Now he'd married a "show person." It would be a cold day in hell before the Cline patrimony would be passed on to this ne'er-do-well, let alone used to bankroll his flashy wife's singing career. The reality was that he was just on the payroll of Cline Construction Company, and lucky to have that.

In other respects Gerald was good to her. He even bought her a racy new Buick Roadmaster coupe in her favorite colors, red and white. But Patsy couldn't help but notice that Gerald's earthbound physical appearance was matched by an equally wooden disposition. He was, in a word, boring. "Dull-dull was the word," Pat Smallwood said.

"She would go somewhere and come back all enthused and excited and he couldn't care less. She'd come over here to do her washing at her mother's on the weekend and I'd go down and talk to her. And she said, 'Gerald just acts like he couldn't care less whether I make a go or whether I do anything. It's like he's disinterested.' She had a lot of spunk, wanted to get somewhere, and he treated her good, but it was just so boring. He never paid any mind to anything she told him—like he didn't care. He loved her, but he didn't care. He wasn't interested in music. He was interested in taking little clocks and watches and stuff apart."

When friends wondered why she married him, she told them, "I guess I thought I loved him or something, but he's so dull." Yet Patsy seemed resigned to tough out a passionless life with Gerald in exchange for security. According to girlfriend Becky Miller: "I think Patsy would have used anybody to get where she wanted to go because along the way she was used. I know that because I had a discussion about it one night sitting here. I think she felt Bill Peer used her and I'm not so sure about Cline. And I think her family used her. Hilda's attitude was, 'I gave up my youth, the good years I had, to you. Now it's your turn to pay me back.' Patsy and Hilda had no one to turn to except each other and they loved each other. But I do believe that Hilda made Patsy feel like, 'You owe me something.' I'm not saying that's wrong. Hilda was from the old school and back then you took care of each other. That's the way it was."

The onset of the cold war in the fifties created a climate of atomic paranoia. People took comfort in the time-honored American virtues of home, church and community. The work world was a man's world. Women were offered rewards for staying at home and breeding: homes in the suburbs and appliances, and if they were still unhappy, their family doctors supplied them with prescriptions for miltown and Equanil. But sex researcher Alfred Kinsey discovered that there was more slipping and cheating going on than the button-down attitudes of the time might imply. Patsy wasn't doing anything that half of Frederick was doing, noted Roy Deyton.

It became clear to Patsy that she still needed Peer as much as ever. Her affair with him resumed. But even with the pressure of juggling two men, Patsy managed to stay on track with her singing career. "It was always the job. She was always there to work the job first," observed Bud Armel.

Peer was determined to get her a record deal. He began spending more freely on her after receiving a substantial inheritance.

"Now there was a man that really loved her," voiced Pat Smallwood. "He got her a fur stole one day and brought it to my house. I never will forget it. He said, 'When Patsy comes home will you give her this and tell her it's from me?' I said, 'Are you serious?' He said, 'Yes.' She came over to my house that evening and I said, 'Oh, by the way'—I had it hid behind the couch—'there's a gift here for you.' She said, 'Who?' I said, 'There's a card.' She said, 'Why here?' meaning the gift. I said, 'I don't know.' So I drug the box out and she opened it and said, 'Oh my word . . . ' And it was from Bill. She wore that stole for years and years—she loved it. Yeah. He really did care about her."

Backed by the Melody Boys, Patsy cut a demo tape at WINC, which had one of the largest, best-equipped studios in the area. Peer dubbed Patsy "the second-greatest female country singer alive"—an oblique reference to Kitty Wells, the title of whose latest hit sounded like a description of Peer's situation: "Paying for That Back Street Affair."

Chapter Six

*I*N THE FIFTIES, Washington, D.C., had a distinctly Southern feeling. After the war, the population peaked at 800,000, and about half were white Southerners who'd emigrated from rural areas. The corner of 12th and New York Avenue, in downtown D.C., was a kind of hillbilly crossroads. On the one side of the street was the Greyhound Bus terminal and, on the other, the Trailways Depot. Buses caked with the dead insects and road dust of the Maryland, Virginia, Carolina and Tennessee countryside hissed to a stop. Out of their portals stepped country girls fresh out of high school, wearing their going-to-the-city dresses, looking for work as secretaries in the gray government monoliths, and crew-cut boys smelling of Aqua Velva, on leave from nearby Quantico Marine Base, Bolling Air Force Base, Andrews Field and the Norfolk Naval Base, looking for girls. Everyone was looking for action.

Next door to the Trailways, catty-corner to the Greyhound Station, was the Famous, the most popular hillbilly bar in D.C. by virtue of its prime location and the fact that it also offered live music every night of the week. Inside the darkness of the tavern was a large U-shaped bar, mismatched tables and chairs and a raised bandstand over which a sign cautioned rowdies, *"Keep Off the Bandstand—Musicians Only."* A battered old upright piano "looked like a bunch of beavers went in there and ate half the blacks off," said a former member of the Peer band. The people, they didn't know any different. They thought the piano was in fine shape."

D.C.'s strict liquor laws seemed to aim straight at the down-home hillbilly clubs. You couldn't stand up with a mixed drink. You could not get hard liquor at the bar and carry it back to the table—you had to be seated and served by a waitress. You couldn't table hop with drinks—the waitress had to move them for you. Still, the laws didn't prevent patrons from enjoying themselves—thoroughly. Hence the slogan "Every night is Saturday night at the Famous."

The same held true at the many hillbilly dives around D.C.: Harry's Tavern, across the street from the Famous; five doors down was Captain Guy's; and, just a short distance away, the Ozarks, the Rendezvous and the Boondocks. Fanning out from the downtown area like a pinwheel were maybe thirty-odd buckets. Over in Georgetown, a roughneck, working-class neighborhood at one time, before the lawyers and diplomats moved in, was the Shamrock, the Corral, B&J Tavern, the Potomac Tavern and Pete's. Just over the D.C. line were Strick's, the Homestretch Inn, the Quonset Hut, the Village Barn, the Dixie Pig, the Social Circle and Hunter's Lodge. If you were a hillbilly musician living anywhere in the three-state area that bordered D.C., you worked the flourishing club scene there. Everyone knew everyone else, and there was plenty of work, Patsy soon discovered.

With Patsy added to the act, Bill Peer and the Melody Boys were pulling an enthusiastic following everywhere, including the D.C. bar scene. In the beginning, Gerald accompanied Patsy, toting her lyric sheets or microphone stand, sporting his fringed "jingles jacket," similar to Patsy's western-style jacket, his only concession to his marriage to a show person. Patsy, meanwhile, was spending more and more time at her mother's in Winchester; she and Gerald were on-again, off-again.

By 1954 Patsy had developed a country act like nothing anyone had ever seen. She was a star in waiting to be discovered. She started to incorporate a Nudie's-of-Hollywood-meets-Frederick's-of-Hollywood costume in her act. "The Outfit" consisted of a pair of fringed short shorts that emphasized Patsy's bodacious fanny, a fringed décolleté top that bared her midriff, broad wrist cuffs, a dashing white scarf tied flush around her neck and the usual white cowboy boots. It was cowgirl show glitter to the max and it is still remembered for its sheer audacity.

"That outfit was part of her show down there at the Famous, and don't let that name fool you," said Leo Miller, the piano player in the Peer band. "She'd come out there with those shorts on and she'd stand there and shake a little bit. Well, you can imagine—the audience just about jumped through the walls." If anyone heckled her, Patsy let them know where they could go in no uncertain terms. She'd cock her head to the side like she did whenever she meant to emphasize a point and lean into the microphone with some snappy one-liner like, "I thought I left you in the parking lot." She always was a wisecracker.

"The Outfit" caused a considerably bigger squawk at the far more conservative Brunswick Moose. Bill Peer tried to talk Patsy into wearing less shocking attire to their regular gig; the governor of the Moose Lodge was "fit to be tied," recollected Johnny Anderson.

"My brother Charlie was playing with them at the time and he told me, 'Jesus Christ, those people are raising hell about it.' See, those women over there got jealous of Patsy. They were jealous of her anyway. They were older people—you know how Moose Clubs are. And she really shocked 'em. I went over there one night to listen, and man, she was up there, had all that eye makeup on, those goddamn short shorts, the bare midriff and the boots. Whew! It was something. And she was built. Yeah, that's Patsy for you. Even today that'd be kind of risqué. But she didn't care if she shocked 'em. She just wanted people to know, 'This is me, whether you like it or not.' Her attitude was, 'The hell with 'em!' Bill brought her out of that some, but you couldn't tell Patsy much. You'd see her driving around the street in that red and white convertible with the top down, with her hair up in rollers and a red bandanna wrapped around them. She'd see you and stop and yell out, 'Hi, hoss,' or something like that, just rougher than hell. And everybody seen her was jealous because she had that new car and all. 'Oh, Patsy Cline—she'll never amount to a damn'—that's what they used to say about her."

"It wasn't like Patsy was purposely trying to look like a sex bomb," said singer Pete Pike, who also saw Patsy's act in D.C. "It was just a costume to her. I could walk in a dressing room with Patsy and it wouldn't make no difference at all. She'd change clothes right in front of you, just like it was an everyday thing. She wasn't the kind of girl you fall in love with. She was a buddy. She would come to me with some of her problems and I gave her my advice and then she would go and cuss somebody out, you know? She didn't really listen to my advice. She was a tomboy girl."

Lillian Claiborne was an unlikely habituée of the D.C. bar scene. A tall, blond patrician woman in her early fifties, Claiborne discovered Patsy one night at the Famous and was totally taken by her. A local record entrepreneur with a soft spot for the underdog, Claiborne became one of her angels.

Claiborne's neighbors at the Manor Country Club, the estate where she lived in Rockville, Maryland, were the kind of people who joined the DAR or the Junior League. Not Lillian Claiborne. Her regal appearance notwithstanding, she had a feisty streak and a love of down-home music. She was once an amateur singer with classical aspirations, and she both wrote and arranged music. Claiborne started DC Records in 1946 with Haskell Davis, a local music publisher—hence the name of their company as both a statement of location and an acronym for the owners' names. The small, independent label, like so many others that sprouted up in the post–World War II years—known as "mongrels"—specialized in "race" music—R&B—and its white trash counterpart, hillbilly.

Claiborne plumbed D.C.'s formidable pool of black musical talent, producing gospel, blues and R&B acts, putting them out on DC and its subsidiaries, Gamma and Loop. She would not cowtow to the "whites only" dictums of segregation that infused life in D.C. at the time. She sponsored, managed and fraternized with a number of black artists, her foremost protégés being blind bluesman Harmon "Maskman" Bethea and Frank Motley, an R&B act whose band was named the Motley Crew. As a side note, she recorded the young Marvin Gaye when he was singing in a D.C. gospel group.

Hillbilly took up less of Claiborne's time, though she was a familiar face at the dives, where she always seemed to be toting a black briefcase stuffed with music and paperwork. She had a keen eye for talent and produced a number of hillbilly discs noteworthy mostly for the names, including Jimmy Dean and Roy Clark in their first recordings.

The biggest problem facing DC Records, like so many other mongrels, was pressing and distribution. As a result, Claiborne was always looking around to make deals with bigger labels, like Philadelphia-based Gotham, with whom she had an on-again off-again relationship for years. As a result of her deal making, her contacts in the burgeoning independent record industry were quite extensive. So Claiborne, indeed, might have looked to Patsy like the angel she was seeking.

Despite the difference in their social status, Claiborne seemed to be as much of a cowgirl in her own way as Patsy was in hers. Claiborne was a pistol—"one hell of a woman," according to an engineer at one local recording studio. She was honest and open about her interest in Patsy. She plainly felt Patsy was a great artist. Patsy, in turn, had tremendous respect for the unpretentious but regal Claiborne, who told her to call her Lillian. By 1954, Claiborne had a manager's contract with Patsy. According to one witness, she helped Patsy further refine her act and gave her financial support. Claiborne clearly thought Patsy had potential beyond what DC Records could offer, and the record entrepreneur was looking to make a deal with a larger label.

"Mrs. Claiborne believed in her," related Kay Adelman, at whose Washington, D.C., home Lillian and Patsy were frequent visitors. "She'd say, 'This is going to be a great artist some day.' Patsy would have gotten no place without Lillian. She gave her money for her meals, her food, her cabs, her driving expenses. She put her up in hotels—listen, she spent a small fortune on her. She used to tell me all the time, 'My husband is raisin' hell, 'cause I keep on buying all this western stuff for Patsy Cline. Boots, boots, boots, Hats, hats, hats. I don't know what I'm going to do. I got to hide it from my husband.'"

If Patsy was, indeed, under contract with Claiborne, as Adelman insisted, just where Peer fit into the relationship is uncertain. One thing is clear: Patsy had been trying for a while to extricate herself from her entanglement with Peer and Claiborne's appearance in her life came at the right time. Patsy may have been playing both sides against the middle in an effort to get her career going and to get herself out from under Peer's pressuring and the sexual demands he placed on her. As one friend put it, "Patsy was a very plainspoken, sweet person who didn't bullshit people. She was not a con artist of any sort. But Patsy was very capable of telling little white lies if the little white lies would serve to keep from hurting someone, in her opinion."

Through her relationship with Lillian Claiborne, Patsy got to know and work with Ben Adelman, another fixture on the D.C. music scene. Adelman, and not Bill Peer, as one story goes, appears to have been the direct link to Patsy's first recording contract.

The gregarious, redheaded Adelman was a "Jewish feller" who hailed from upstate New York and had fallen in love with country music in the late forties. He was willing to spend a lot of his wife's money just for the fun of being in the ball game. Fortunately, his wife, Kay Adelman, was an heiress and supported his efforts. Adelman was something of a musical whiz; for sixteen years prior to World War II he was a member of the U.S. Navy Band and could play seven instruments. But Adelman's real talent and the focus of his energies was songwriting. His early compositions were in the Tin Pan Alley mold, but when his interests shifted to the booming country and western field, he started writing hillbilly music. His wife claimed he wrote or co-wrote literally thousands of tunes that are registered in the Library of Congress.

In the early fifties, with the advent of new recording technology, it became possible for a small-timer like Adelman to operate a recording studio. He opened a low-budget place on Georgia Avenue called True Tone. It was a tiny one-room facility on the third floor of a row house. "He used to order all this equipment from Germany," said his wife. "When it came in, I am telling you, I wrote checks until I thought I would drop. All kinds of German equipment, and it all came out of what I had. By the time he died, I was broke."

Adelman was enthralled with record making, since recording was chiefly a means to get his songs published and distributed. He did some cutting sessions for Lillian Claiborne, but mostly he worked independently, recording performances of his music by virtually every hillbilly musician of note then working in D.C. and shopping the tapes around to a number of independents, including Syd Nathan's King Records in Cincinnati, for whom Kay Adelman claimed her husband cut some early Hawkshaw Hawkins tapes. Businesswise, it was all done fifties style: "A shake of the hand is good enough for me," he would say. For the more ambitious musicians, recording for Adelman represented a shot at a record contract. Adelman wanted a publisher and hit records. The equation worked for both the artists involved and Adelman for a few years until everyone became the wiser. By then, Adelman had become disheartened after some bad experiences with the record industry and put some of the tracks out himself on his own budget labels, much to the irritation of Jimmy Dean, one of Adelman's earliest protégés, some of whose least memorable performances were released on budget LPs titled *Jimmy Dean and the Town and Country Men* and *Featuring the Country Singing of Jimmy Dean.*

Roy Clark, years before his "Hee Haw" fame, was just another young hillbilly picker when Adelman started recording him. Clark frequented Adelman's a lot in the early fifties.

"All the musicians in Washington played on everybody else's what they called 'sessions'—very loosely put-together things," Clark reminisced. "No one ever got paid. You played on mine, I played on yours. It was a very low-key operation. More than anything, back then, it was to hear yourself on a record, almost like Elvis, when he recorded that song for his mother at Sun. I'm sure in the back of our minds we would have loved to have a hit record, whatever that was. But that was another world to us. It was a place to go, we had a lot of fun and it was very loose. He [Adelman] was a neat little guy. We had a great rapport. We laughed a lot; he liked a good joke and had this great big laugh. If there had been such a thing as a regular studio musician with him, I was it. If I was there he'd say, 'Can you come by tomorrow at two?' and I'd go by—that kind of thing. He was very enthusiastic about everything—almost like a child. He just loved making records. He really got a kick out of it."

There was a constant flow of pickers, fiddlers and singers coming and going from the studio, and "Patsy did not particularly stand out," said musician Wade Holmes, another regular who backed Patsy on the sessions. Indeed, it was a "madhouse." Soundproofing did not exist. Adelman's Magnatone recorder was propped up on a chair. If a streetcar rolled out on the street below, everyone knew it. "Most of the time I was up there, I was either busy working on the equipment—I'm an electrician—or playing behind somebody or arranging something or rewriting something," Holmes recollected. "Somebody was always rewriting a song. They didn't like a line, they'd go in there and two, three of them would get their heads together and change the words around. It was a kind of hassle all the time.

"There was no air conditioning in the summer and no heat in the winter. It was a tiny place; everybody was stepping all over the wires, everybody was breaking the wires, everybody was trying to get their two cents in, and the ones who were the loudest usually got front seat, you know? If you were cutting, sometime it would take ten tries before you got something that sounded halfway decent. Somebody would either talk in the middle of it, somebody would slam a door, the phone would ring and then you'd have to start all over again. We did some pretty good-sounding stuff when everybody got down to the nitty-gritty, though. We had some good musicians. There was no reverb or anything. The main problem in those days was getting treble. But the stuff I cut up there still sounds good today. The bass is a little weak, but in those days you didn't have electric bass. Patsy always sounded good. She had a real feel for singing and she carried her own."

However informal Adelman's "sessions" were, Patsy was earnest in her hopes they would lead to the recording contract that Claiborne promised. Whether as a result of Adelman's influence or Claiborne's, most of the tracks she cut were in more of a pop-country vein, with Adelman's songs "All Because of My Jealous Heart" and "I Can See an Angel" remembered in particular. Frequently, after the cutting sessions, Patsy and Claiborne would stop by the Adelman home in Northwest D.C.

Recalled Kay Adelman: "Patsy looked like she got down once in a while and Lillian used to say, 'Patsy, don't get down in the ditch about this because it takes time to become a star. You have to work a long time; you have to work hard. Look at me—I'm putting all this money in you and my husband's mad as hell because I'm doing it.' Patsy would usually end up saying something like, 'I'm going to keep on recording and trying until I get something.'"

Her break came in the summer of '54, when Bill McCall, president of Pasadena, California–based 4 Star Records, paid a visit to Adelman's studio.

In 1952, Adelman recorded Jimmy Dean and the Texas Wildcats on "Bumming Around." He sent the tape to Bill McCall. McCall liked it, pressed it, and when, by March 1953, the song peaked at number five on *Billboard*'s country and western charts, McCall put Dean under a short-lived contract. After Dean's hit—his only chart hit of the fifties until "Big Bad John"—McCall and Adelman developed a close relationship. "He came to our home many times," said Kay Adelman. Adelman went to California to see McCall three or four times. Each time he went, he crammed his biggest valise full of masters of various artists he'd cut, along with the lead sheets of his songs. McCall promised to send him publishing contracts for the songs in the mail. Adelman waited and waited. They never arrived.

Among the tapes that Adelman took to California were at least a dozen Patsy Cline tracks, which later disappeared from the 4 Star offices in Pasadena and have still not resurfaced. Kay Adelman recalled what happened: "When he started inviting Ben out to California he'd take him to the races and take him to dinner, take him here and take him there. Ben was so happy when he came back. He'd say, 'Well, I'm in real solid with a publisher now. He just treated me royally. All these years of trying—maybe now I'll start getting some hit records.'"

As a result of Adelman's efforts, McCall released his first single on 4 Star and subsequently leased Clark's masters to Decca Records' Coral subsidiary. Clark never did know what the deal was behind his contract. Given Adelman's gullibility, the songwriter undoubtedly got the short end of the stick.

"It was all worked out between Ben and McCall," Clark said. "I met Bill McCall only one time when he came to Washington. It was quite an event because Ben wanted me to come up and meet him. I met him and that was about it. I was very naive and in awe of all these people, especially someone from out in California."

Soon after Patsy signed her 4 Star contract, she and Clark both got wise to McCall's M.O. Clark explained: "McCall would send a demo out to Ben and say, 'Ben, have Roy Clark record this and don't say anything to Jimmy Dean.' In other words, don't use the same musicians on it and don't tell Jimmy that Roy's going to do it. Well, he would say the same thing to Jimmy. Evidently this was a practice of his—he would try to get as many cuts on this record as he could and probably farm them out or go back to getting his airplay royalties.

"I was in the Famous one night and the waitress comes over and says, 'Patsy Cline is on the phone for you.' So I went to the phone and she said, 'Roy, this is Patsy.' You know, she talked just right straight ahead. We said our 'how-are-yous' and then she says, 'Did you record'—and I can't remember the name of the song—"for Ben?' And I said, 'Yes.' I was a little surprised that she even knew it. She said, 'He sent me your demo to learn and wants me to record it.' I'll never forget it because I was sitting in that phone booth, feeling devastated. I thought I was the golden boy and *I* was going to have that record. When I finally got my composure I said, 'Well, I didn't know that,

Patsy, but you go ahead and record it because if you don't somebody else will. She said, 'Well, hoss, somebody else will because I won't. I don't play that game.' That was very early in her career and I was very touched and impressed that she would even call me because my name was not on the record of whatever he gave her to learn, but when she played it she must have recognized me.

"There were a lot of things that happened like that and Ben got to be frustrated after a while. I picked up on the frustration and so I didn't like Bill McCall for what he was telling Ben to do. At times Ben would say, 'Well, I'm just not going to do it.' But whatever the relationship they had, Ben didn't have a whole lot of leeway."

Kay Adelman believed that McCall "stole" many of the songs Ben took out to California, which is not inconsistent with the horror stories other musicians and songwriters told about McCall.

"He came back from California once all depressed," recalled Kay Adelman. I said to him, 'Ben, you act like you don't trust Mr. McCall.' And he said, 'I don't want to talk about it.' I think they did something to him out there."

McCall was a short, dapper Texan with a penchant for hatwear—berets and Stetsons. He had squinty eyes and a face like a road map—the occupational hazards of a career in mining. In the forties, McCall staked claims around Nevada. Rumor had it that he once unsuccessfully sought a mining claim for removing gravel on the Las Vegas strip. But McCall had better luck in his various other mining ventures around the state. His most lucrative claim turned out to be his fluorspar properties.

In the forties, fluorspar was a prime ingredient, along with shellac, in the manufacturing of records. Once shellac rationing ended after World War II, and the recording bans imposed on the industry by the American Federation of Musicians were lifted, years of pent-up creativity found expression on disk. The public's appetite for music of all types was whetted by the ubiquitous sound of radio—the first car radios, clock radios and transistor radios. McCall could see the opportunities for someone with the raw ingredients for making the biscuits from which records were pressed. He reckoned the record industry was the last of the gold mine businesses.

One of his accounts was Pasadena-based 4 Star Records. In 1946, 4 Star, undercapitalized and in poor financial straits, went into receivership. For $5000 McCall acquired controlling interest in the company and began his career as a record executive.

In many ways McCall's acquisition was his biggest gamble ever. Independent labels specializing in the kind of product the major labels would not or could not handle sprang into being and, more often than not, folded overnight. It wasn't the flops that so frequently brought a company to its knees as much as the hits. Many indies usually had no distribution and relied on an independent distributor to act as the wholesaler. A hit record meant that more records had to be pressed, which meant the record company owed the pressing plant. But when the record was distributed, payment was made to the distributor, not the record company. When the record company would go to the distributor to collect, the distributor would hold back. The record company could neither cover its pressing plant bill nor its legal fees if it were to sue the distributor, and so it folded.

McCall knew how to play hardball. Don Pierce, McCall's vice-president until 1952 when he helped found Starday Records, said when it came to business he was as "tough as nails."

"When Bill came in we had about forty or fifty creditors and no money to pay them. When I was in charge, they were calling me on the phone and I was about to have a nervous breakdown trying to get them paid or stalled off. Bill took that over from me and let me go off and handle sales and production-type things. He was an absolute master at working those distributors. He got them to have a creditors' committee, and then through the creditors' committee, he would allocate a certain amount of money every sixty days or so that those various distributors would get a check for $1.50 or $2.35. They saw that this was going on for years and years and years. After we got a hit on 'Deck Of Cards,' he'd call them in one by one and say, 'If you take 15 cents on the dollar, I'll write you a check right now.' And he just about wiped all those creditors out. It was a masterful piece of work."

In the late forties, McCall's lineup of talent included a number of noteworthy country artists: Tex Tyler, Webb Pierce, Hank Locklin, the Wilburn Brothers, Ferlin Husky (who went by the name of Terry Preston) and the Maddox Brothers and Rose, the most popular hillbilly act on the West Coast. Los Angeles–based producer-entrepreneur Cliffie Stone credited McCall for having "terrific ears." But McCall didn't claim to know anything about music. He bragged that he paid his cleaning lady to sort through demos after-hours. If she found something that she liked, she was instructed to set it aside. "I figured a woman who mops floors for a living, who works that hard, if she would spend her hard-earned money on a record because she loved it, then it must be good," McCall once claimed.

Whether the cleaning woman story was legend or fact, McCall's backroom hustling was not atypical of the era—he just brought it to a lower common denominator, according to virtually everyone who had dealings with him.

One of McCall's most nefarious practices was to take a share of the writing credit on songs he'd published. He used a number of pen names, including his wife's maiden name, Ethel Bassey. But his favorite was "W. S. Stevenson"—a lucky combination, he figured, derived from William Shakespeare and Robert Louis Stevenson. Since McCall took a writer's credit on almost several thousand songs, for a brief while "W. S. Stevenson" was thought to be the most prolific writer in the business. One story went that someone in the Hollywood music community wanted to host a tribute dinner for "W. S. Stevenson" at the Hollywood Roosevelt Hotel in recognition of his contributions. After the identity of "Stevenson" was ascertained, the dinner was abruptly canceled.

McCall was canny. In 1947, he was one of the first in the industry to replace breakable shellac with semi-flexible vinylite, the forerunner of the LP. Thanks to a business relationship he'd forged with Syd Nathan's King Records, which had thirty-two branch offices, McCall had great distribution, which he further expanded. In those days nearly every big city had four or five independent record distributors. Each one of those distributors would handle fifteen or twenty independent record labels, one for jazz, three or four for R&B, and so forth. They all needed a supply of country music. Some of the distributors had a 4 Star exclusive, but McCall got around it by putting out some of the same material that was on 4 Star on Gilt Edge, a subsidiary that had been dormant for years until McCall saw the need to revive it. "That way, rather than having thirty-two outlets for country music, we would end up with fifty or sixty outlets," Don Pierce explained.

One of McCall's lucky connections was Harold "Pappy" Daily, a Houston-based coin machine operator and record distributor to the jukebox trade, who operated somewhat in the mode of Ben Adelman. Daily was interested in hillbilly music and had a little studio in Houston. Artists in Texas who didn't have access to New York, L.A. or Nashville would go to Pappy and ask him if he knew how they could make records. He would have them come in and cut. It was all nonunion and he'd pay about five dollars per man per song. He'd make the masters and send them out to 4 Star. Don Pierce, who went into partnership later with Daily to start Starday, explained:

"Pappy would say, 'These guys are very popular down here—they got radio time and they're doing personal appearances and here's some masters on the thing. You can have the record and you can have the songs and you press up a thousand records and send them to me right away and we'll get something going.' That's how he got Webb Pierce—he came down to see him. Hank Locklin did the same thing."

When Pappy Daily realized he was giving McCall the artists, the masters and the publishing rights on the songs, as well as handling promotion and distribution for McCall, and getting nothing in return, he appealed for a more equitable arrangement—to no avail. In 1952, Daily broke off his relationship with McCall and started Starday with Don Pierce, who'd gotten embroiled in a legal dispute with McCall and was ready to quit. Enter Ben Adelman.

Adelman may have met McCall through DC entrepreneur Connie B. Gay, whose protégé at the time was Jimmy Dean, but Syd Nathan could just as easily have served as Adelman's conduit to McCall, since Adelman had been sending songs and tapes to King Records. Around the time they started doing business together, McCall had just experienced a downturn in his luck. It began when the Maddox Brothers and Rose decided to leave the label. The union required one session for every four songs. The Maddoxes would blow into Los Angeles from the road for cutting sessions that lasted all night, for which they did not get paid. They were able to use nonpayment in order to get a release from McCall. Other acts that wanted out of their contracts took the same tack, including Webb Pierce. "He felt that it was a sin to pay anybody, see?" Pierce claimed. "I finally got loose from him. Used my head and got a lawyer. The union called on him for all the back money, and he said, 'I ain't payin' this!' So I says, 'Well, write me a letter of release then,' and he did."

Beset by the mutiny of some of his biggest acts, compounded by union problems, McCall shifted his focus. He turned 4 Star into a glorified lease operation in service to his new interest, publishing.

He had wisely deduced early in the game that the real money was in copyrights. When a song is played on the radio, neither the performer nor the record company receives a royalty, but the publisher does. That makes a hit song something like an annuity, earning money year after year for the copyright holder. McCall would try to get airplay by putting some songs out on long-play, ten-inch "deejay copies," which he sent out to radio stations with a card reminding them to log airplay credits to 4 Star Sales, the name of his publishing company.

McCall bought many of his songs for $25 or $30 apiece from down-and-out writers and affixed his nom de plume, W. S. Stevenson. Sometimes he hired a "staff writer" to doctor them up a bit—Donn ("Walkin' After Midnight") Hecht was one. Hecht claimed he tinkered with many songs from the 4 Star files, including Carl Belew's classic, "Lonely Street."

"He got a lot of stuff from Carl Belew and other writers without having written the song, and BMI was very unhappy about it," offered

Don Pierce. "The thinking was, if you've got the publishing rights, you've got half of it there and you control the whole song. How much more do you have to have?"

To further his share of publisher and writer royalties, McCall introduced restrictive clauses into the contracts of artists stipulating, in effect, that the artists could only record songs to which he had publishing rights and, in most cases, including Patsy's, a writer's credit as well. McCall would then deduct every conceivable expense associated with getting a record made and played, leaving nothing in the end for the artist. After his union problems, McCall learned something about how to make his contracts airtight, leaving no room for an artist to escape.

Singer-songwriter Marvin Rainwater, another Adelman protégé, was one of the many artists who suffered from McCall's practices. Recalled Rainwater: "Through Adelman there we fumbled around and got stuck with one of McCall's civil contracts that lasted forever. It was a union contract so we couldn't break it. Then I got on Arthur Godfrey's 'Talent Scouts' independent of McCall. Started getting recognition. But I was tied to McCall, so I couldn't do anything with my music. I was appearing on the Godfrey show and I didn't want to give any of my material I was doing to McCall because he would just take it and never pay you. He raped everybody. He didn't care. He had a tremendous ear for music, and if he hadn't been so all-fired crooked, he'd a been a wonderful man, because he could talk you into just about anything."

Singer-songwriter Durwood Haddock said, "The only time I ever got any money out of him, I had to call him and make up a story that I'd had a car wreck. I think he felt a little sorry for me, so he did send me a little money. But then when I went for the check, I found that he had deducted $60 for an ad for Carl Smith in *Billboard*. He had recorded 'There She Goes,' and that just rankled me because I didn't want Carl Smith to do the damn song anyhow, and there I was paying for the ad. But I should have known better, because after me and Eddie Miller signed contracts with him he took us out to breakfast and ordered us each a shot of whiskey. I was just a young hillbilly fiddle player and it was the first time I ever drank whiskey. And he lifted his glass and said something I'll never forget: 'Let's have a toast, 'cause this is probably the most you'll ever get out of 4 Star.'"

Patsy may have been warned about McCall. At one point she called the one person she felt would tell her the gospel truth: Wally Fowler. Fowler, as it turned out, had his own horror story. He had signed an exclusive five-year writing contract with 4 Star and was a year and a half into it, with no money to show for it. He too had tried to get out of the contract, and when McCall held him to it, he simply started writing under his wife's name and sent the material to other publishers.

"She was always very ambitious, very eager," Fowler recalled. "She said, 'There's this man out here and he wants to record me. He said he was from 4 Star Records.' Asked if I knew him. I said, 'Patsy, honey, I'm gonna tell you the truth. You know I am for you. I wish you the best in life and everything. Now I'm not trying to point the finger at the man 'cause there's three looking back at me. I'm not going to do that to any human being. But if I were you, I wouldn't sign anything long-term with him. A year at the most.'"

Disregarding Fowler's warning, Patsy affixed her large, schoolgirlish signature to a standard AFM contract, for two years and sixteen sides, on September 30, 1954. She had just turned twenty-two a few weeks earlier.

Buried in the fine print were a few details with far-reaching implications:

She would be paid royalties at the rate of 2.34 percent of the retail price of a record, less than half the going rate at most labels. That meant that if she had a modest hillbilly hit of 25,000, the most she would stand to make after all the standard deductions would be $440. Even more onerous was McCall's usual restriction on material: "The musical compositions to be recorded shall be mutually agreed on between you and us, and each recording shall be subject to our approval as satisfactory, for manufacture and sale."

Finally, there was the option-to-renew clause. Though nothing exists in the way of a paper trail to verify the dates, Patsy probably renewed her contract twice during the next six years. Patsy got paid $50 for each side cut. When she was broke, she would call McCall and ask for an advance against future royalties. McCall would give her money but would require an extension on her contract. Since Patsy had no hits between 1957 and 1961, she very likely felt that she had no choice but to accept McCall's terms. Her situation was not unlike that of T. Texas Tyler, speculated Don Pierce. "Tyler was always dissatisfied, but when he got broke and needed some money, Bill would give him an advance, but made him sign up for a longer period of time. Very likely he gave Patsy advances when she needed them but required extensions on the contract."

If Lillian Claiborne did, indeed, have a contract with Patsy, McCall apparently convinced Claiborne to let go of her hold on Patsy. There may have been a trade-off, whereby in exchange for exclusive rights on Patsy, McCall agreed to do business with Claiborne. This would explain the sudden appearance after September 1954 of a number of Claiborne's R&B acts on 4 Star and Big Town, an R&B subsidiary that

McCall started in 1948. Whatever the deal between them was, however, Claiborne was less than thrilled with the outcome: she was forced to drop her interest in Patsy. Bill Peer's name, not Claiborne's, appears as witness on Patsy's 4 Star contract.

"I saw Lady Claiborne in the studio a couple of times after Patsy left and she was very depressed," recalled Kay Adelman. "And Bill McCall was in the studio at the time. I said, 'Who's in there?' She said, 'Just between you and I, that son of a bitch from California, that's who.' She learned to hate him. She felt he had stolen her artist away from her."

Chapter Seven

*C*ONNIE BARRIOT GAY was fond of saying he "couldn't carry a tune in a bucket." Nevertheless, he had an uncanny sense of timing.

Gay was a true pioneer of the modern country music industry. He saw its entertainment potential for TV and tailored his product for the broadest possible audience. Beginning in the late forties and throughout most of the fifties, Gay consolidated a media empire and supplied it with programming at a time when many television stations were still broadcasting test patterns. Within just a few years Gay took hillbilly music out of the dives and the one-room schoolhouses and staged lavish productions in venues normally reserved for more uptown fare: concert halls, arenas, stadiums. His ultimate goal was network television, and he succeeded, in 1957. When asked to explain how he came by such prescience, Gay would point out that he was the seventh son of a seventh son, signifying supernatural powers.

With all the false starts, Patsy, in her more discouraged moments, thought it would take sleight of hand to launch her. As the fates would have it, in the summer of '54 she came to the attention of the man who came to be known as "country music's media magician."

The National Country Music Championship was held every summer at the Warrenton Fairgrounds in the rolling horse country of Fauquier County, Virginia, a forty-five-minute drive from downtown Washington, D.C. It was a weekend affair that typically drew crowds in the 12,000-plus range. Country music fans would spread blankets on the grass, dive into wicker baskets loaded with fried chicken, biscuits and potato salad and listen to everything from bluegrass to rockabilly. Hot pickers, fiddlers, squeeze-box players and Hank Williams hopefuls would come from all over the Virginia–Maryland–West Virginia–D.C.

quadrant to compete in the big event. Winning the contest meant plenty of bookings throughout the area and widespread exposure through live television and radio appearances—and a shot at a record contract.

Patsy was primed.

She first entered the competition in 1953. Jimmy Dean and the Texas Wildcats were the backup band. Wearing a red and white cowgirl outfit, Patsy belted out her favorite crowd-pleaser, "Bill Bailey, Won't You Please Come Home," a dance hall standard made popular in recordings by dozens of artists from Louis Armstrong to Pearl Bailey. It was the wrong choice of material for a "country-country" crowd. She lost to a dervish of a bluegrass fiddler, Scotty Stoneman, of the D.C.-based Stoneman family, well known in the area.

Marvin Carroll, who played steel guitar for the Texas Wildcats, vividly recalled that day: "She was an unknown—we had never seen her before, and she just stood us on our ears. We could see how great she was. But it wasn't her fault that she lost. 'Bill Bailey' was a good up-tempo song—we played it all the time at dances. But it was a pop song, and a singer against a fiddler in that part of the country? Well, everybody knows that Virginia is bluegrass country."

The following year Patsy entered again, hitting the boards in full western regalia. Backed this time by Bill Peer's band, she won the crowd over with a full-throated, soulful rendition of the 1950 Bob Wills hit, "Faded Love." This time Patsy took the $100 first-prize money. More important, though, she caught the eye of the event's head honcho and emcee—a tall, thin, rather good-looking man with stick-out ears and a woman's name: Connie B. Gay.

In 1986, Gay hyped Patsy as "the greatest female singer in country or pop to ever walk the face of the earth." Yet his first encounter with the unknown girl singer from Winchester was unremarkable, according to Gay: "I had seen her once prior to the contest. I knew Bill Peer—he played dances and shows for me. He brought her over to the radio station [WARL, where Gay deejayed]. And I must say I was not very impressed with her when I first met her because I didn't hear her, so she was just another girl. But once she entered that contest in Warrenton, she walked away with everything, as far as I was concerned."

No wonder Gay was initially underwhelmed. Without a microphone in front of her and the music into which she could pour her heart, Patsy—in contrast to her stage act—seemed tongue-tied. When she was with him, she let Peer do all the talking. "She pretty much let her singing speak for her," recalled Roy Clark, who played with the Texas Wildcats in the early fifties. "In fact, best I can remember, she was kind of shy. She wasn't outgoing at all. Not that she was a wallflower—she would speak if spoken to, and would carry a conversation, but she wouldn't lead one. I got the impression she was just becoming aware of the big world out there and she was cautious about how she was going to fit into it."

Though at this point they'd both been recording in Adelman's studio, Clark didn't actually meet Patsy until shortly after her Warrenton win. Gay arrived at the Famous one night with Patsy who, dressed in just a simple country girl's dress, looked just like the girl next door—until she opened her mouth. Patsy was accompanied by Gerald. Clark thought them an unlikely twosome.

"I have a girl singer who I want you to listen to and tell me what you think, so get her up there," Gay told him.

Clark explained: "Connie was just showing her off. It wasn't like, 'Tell me do you think she's any good?' It was, 'I want you to hear something.' And here comes Patsy. She had on a black dress, her hair done up fifties-style. It was obvious she was a country girl—it was typical of a country girl's going-to-town dress. So I introduced her and brought her up on stage. She told us she was going to do 'I'm Walking the Dog,' a Webb Pierce tune. I think she gave us her key, and she might have given us the tempo, but that was about it. She was so sure of herself; she was so good; her singing was so positive and so powerful that you followed her. It was like we had been rehearsing forever. There was no hesitation—she led you to where she wanted to go and you wanted to go with her. She had this real gutsy sound, such a great communicating voice. I guess she sang like every girl wished she could and probably every man. Well, she literally blew the roof off the place. And I looked down at Connie and all the guys in the band were looking at one another with this 'Goll-ee' look. And Connie, boy, he was just grinning from ear to ear."

Connie B. Gay was one of the most important behind-the-scenes players in country music when he first took Patsy into his stable of performers, where she was showcased on TV as a soloist. His own rags-to-riches story was in the best tradition of country music.

The improbably named locale of Lizard Lick, North Carolina, was Gay's birthplace. One of ten children of poor dirt farmers, he worked his way through the University of North Carolina during the Roosevelt era, financing a degree in agriculture by working various odd jobs, including reading news on the college radio station and managing a college big band. After graduation, Gay hit the road, working for a while as a streetcorner pitchman. His gimmick was to buy pocketknife sharpeners for a nickel each from Gilman Brothers in Chicago. "Sold them for a quarter in hick towns and for fifty cents in sucker towns like Washington."

Gay's admiration for Roosevelt inspired him to go to work for the Farm Security Administration. During the war he worked on the USDA's "National Farm and Home Hour," one of the biggest network shows of its time. Like radio announcers everywhere, Gay was a jack-of-all-trades, handling everything from writing agricultural tidbits for FDR's fireside chats and Victory Garden slogans to fielding phone calls. That is when he discovered the seemingly universal popularity of hillbilly music. It seemed like every time he played some good old down-home music, the switchboard lit up and the cards and letters poured in from all over the country.

It wasn't long before Gay realized that despite its cosmopolitan veneer, the nation's capital was at that time "the biggest city in North Carolina." The residents, half of them transplanted from the hinterlands of the South, brought with them a thirst for the whining of fiddles and the crying of steel guitars and the adenoidal laments of white soul that went unquenched because D.C. did not then have a radio station that catered to hillbillies. So in 1946 Gay approached WARL, then a new, 1000-watt station with a clear signal that reached five states, with a proposal for a thirty-minute country show to the station director, Frank Blair, later of "Today" show fame. In place of a salary Gay agreed to take a cut of the advertising dollars. Blair, dubious, agreed. As Gay noted, "To try [hillbilly music] in a white-collar town, a town of so-called 'intellectuals,' the seat of government, was something entirely different."

He called his new hillbilly show "Let's Be Gay with Connie B. Gay," and it brought the hillbillies in D.C. out of the closet. It soon snowballed into "Town & Country Time," a three-hour musical broadcasting event. Gay put together a hillbilly radio band dubbed the Wheeler Brothers, hired Clyde Moody and the Radio Ranchmen (with guitarist Billy Grammer) as well as regulars Grandpa and Ramona Jones, Hank Penny and the then still unknown Jimmy Dean.

Gay rushed to the U.S. Patent Office to register "Town & Country" as his service mark and became one of the first to coin the term *country music*, in place of the less flattering connotation of *hillbilly*. But to succeed in the postwar years, Gay knew he had to dispel the connotation that it was the music of ignorant, toothless, barefooted, inbred white trash; it had to become smooth, or smoother.

In the late forties, when television came in and everyone predicted radio would die out, Gay started buying up little radio stations all over the country, establishing his Town & Country Network. At the same time he started getting in on television with an experimental country music show that aired on WMAL Channel 7. Within just a couple of years, if you lived anywhere near D.C., you couldn't turn a radio or TV knob without getting "Town & Country."

Gay saw that TV built a demand for live concerts, so he dovetailed his broadcasting ventures with live events featuring big-name talent like Hank Williams, Ray Price and Hank Thompson, and publicized them in the Barnum and Bailey mold ("featuring the most colossal glittering array of hillbilly talent ever witnessed by mortal eyes"). In this regard, Gay might have been inspired by ex-carny man Colonel Tom Parker, who was Eddy Arnold's manager at the time in Arnold's pre-crossover days.

Gay claimed to have struck "a kind of unspoken gentlemen's agreement" with Parker and the other major behind-the-scenes players in country music, mainly Jim Denny of the Opry, along with powerful Nashville promoters Oscar Davis and Joe Frank. The "deal" was to control personal appearances by the top country acts. As head of the Artists Service Bureau, the Opry's in-house booking agency, Denny wielded the most power, dictating where and when Opry stars worked. But Gay, more so than the other three men, grasped the tremendous potential of radio and, more important, television. Their backroom deal gave Gay exclusive access to Opry acts in the mid-Atlantic states, almost like a regional franchise. According to Gay, "This one would work one area and that one would work somewhere else. I got Washington and the Northeast. They thought the East was the short end of the stick, but that was where the money was, in the media. There were big men in the East who understood the media, but they didn't understand my muscle and they left me alone. They could have squashed me like a bug, but to them I was a penny waiting for change."

In 1947, Gay booked the DAR's Constitution Hall for two nights for a package show headlined by Eddy Arnold. The event turned into a twenty-seven-week run that was televised live on the Town & Country Network as "Gay Time." Tickets were considered outrageously expensive—$3 to $6—but Gay believed the steep price would add to the cachet of "country" music, and sure enough, senators and cabinet members attended. *Variety* reviewed: "The audience whooped it up for the boys and lost all semblance of control when Cowboy Roy Copaz [sic], a tenor with a pair of lungs geared for hog-calling, took the stage."

It was too much for the DAR, who booted the hillbillies out of Constitution Hall. Unfazed, Gay moved his shows into the National Guard Armory, the Uline Arena, Turner's Arena (now Capitol Arena),

Griffith Stadium and even the Lincoln Monument, where one concert drew 15,000 people. He ran excursion trains from Washington, Baltimore, New York, Boston and Philadelphia to the Grand Ole Opry. He booked the Wilson Line, which cruised the Potomac River, for his "Hillbilly Midnight Cruises." He staged a "Hillbilly Air Show" that featured wing walkers, sky divers, pickers, fiddlers and yodelers and played to 55,000 people.

Gay made a deal with the Department of Defense to provide them with radio transcriptions for Armed Services recruitment programs, featuring talent from his own stable. He produced tours that played military bases in the Far East, Europe and the Caribbean. As a broadcaster, as well as a supplier of programming to the government, Gay was sensitive to potential conflict-of-interest charges by the FCC if he were to pursue his interest in country music in a more commercial vein. Some believe that is the only reason he stayed out of the record business (although he did have informal dealings with Bill McCall, according to Don Pierce).

In addition to his work as a concert impresario, he continued to produce a morning radio show and a late afternoon TV variety show. His sponsors turned to him when they needed to make a commercial and Gay, in turn, hired his own talent to make jingles. Unlike Nashville, where musicians sold shoes and pumped gas all week for the love of playing—and very little else—Washington, D.C., was one place where there was plenty of work for everybody, as long as you knew Gay.

"Connie ran the town," said singer Dale Turner, one of three girl singers in Gay's employ in 1954. Turner's first recollection of Patsy was during the summer of '54, when she sashayed into Strick's wearing a dazzling red and white cowgirl outfit, which alone was enough to make her stand out. Her entourage included Bill Peer and the band and Gerald. Patsy, going to or coming from another gig, was asked to get up and sing a number.

"We all circulated around D.C.," Turner said. "You went from club to club to see your friends, sing or whatever. Everybody knew everybody but no one had seen her up until then."

Patsy obliged her fans at Strick's with "San Antonio Rose." That and the outfit were etched in Turner's memory: "Once you saw her, you would never, never forget her."

Beginning that summer, Gay frequently booked Patsy as the girl singer with Jimmy Dean and the Texas Wildcats. One early gig was Wednesday nights at Rockwood Hall, a large dance hall just over the D.C. line that played to packed houses during the week; the Brunswick Fire Hall was also remembered. There were countless other dives. Patsy, meanwhile, was still appearing with Bill Peer at the

Brunswick Moose and at Rockwood on Tuesdays, a date also likely to have been arranged through Gay.

Under Gay's tutelage, Dean had learned "a little about timing, about stage presence, about when to go on and when the hell to get off," Gay recollected. With his lanky, clean-cut good looks, affable personality and aw-shucks charm, Dean proved himself to be made-to-order for television in the fifties. Patsy was his perfect female foil. Whereas Dean was a cornflake, Patsy came on like hot salsa. The division of labor was clear: Dean handled the jokes and the patter; she handled the singing. Patsy, according to Dean, "couldn't talk." In fact, she worried every time she stood in front of a microphone that she might say something grammatically incorrect.

"She had a limited command of the vocabulary," Dean said. "Patsy was amateurish on the microphone—except when she sang. People liked to listen to her—you bet they did. She was flashy. She had a wonderful personality, a great grin. She loved to sing and when she sang it was obvious that she was enjoying herself to the fullest and doing exactly what she wanted to do."

Gay was quick to spot what potential a no-pump natural like Patsy held for television: "I looked for three things as far as television was concerned. One, talent. Two, photogenic people or photogenic costumes, movement or action. Sometimes a person was not particularly photogenic or didn't display talent, but it was so damn interesting. I can think of the earlier days of square dancing—square dancing per se got nowhere on TV until clogging came in. And those fast-flying feet and bang-bang of the clogs was a good example. I can think of people who were talented but not photogenic—Patsy Cline was a good example. Patsy was not a beautiful person. Anyone who said Patsy was beautiful is just being nice as a revisionist. Patsy was not beautiful. She was not ugly, but she was not what you now look for when you see Dolly Parton or that type. But Patsy had so damn much talent that she absolutely submerged and overwhelmed and sunk everything else around her. And her talent came to the top on TV."

Patsy was cast as a regular "special guest" on Gay's daily half-hour "Town & Country Time" TV show, broadcast live at 6:30 P.M. out of the WMAL studios on Connecticut Avenue. As the show ended and the sponsor credits rolled ("brought to you by Briggs Ice Cream and Hot Dogs"), Dean and the others, including Patsy if she was booked that night, would pack up their instruments, pack them into their Chevy carryall and hightail it out to some club, fire hall or auditorium where Gay had booked them, where they would play until the wee hours of the morning, before repeating the same routine again the next day. Gay had them working "night and day," according to Marvin

Carroll, including doing commercials for some of Gay's sponsors; Patsy, it was recalled, supplied the vocals for a dry cleaner.

"We was worked to death," Carroll said. "We'd do the TV show, the radio show, and in between all this, within a hundred-mile radius, we was riding back and forth night and day doing personal appearances, radio shows, commercials, everything. I got about $250 a week, which wasn't too good—that was for everything. But I was about twenty-four, twenty-five. I had never done anything like this before and I thought then it was pretty good money."

Dean and the Texas Wildcats, with whom Gay had a management contract, were paid a weekly salary. The entrepreneurial Gay, whom some of the musicians described as a "father figure," installed a slot machine in his office and paid them in rolls of quarters so that they wouldn't blow their hard-earned money in Maryland, where slots were legal. Gay was a tough businessman, but was considered fair by most of the musicians. The other acts were paid on a per diem. Patsy started out at $25 a day and was later raised to $50, probably around the time she started getting records released. It was still a bit more than the other two girl singers associated with the Gay TV show—Turner and singer-guitarist Mary Klick—were getting.

Patsy's new status enabled her to continue to provide financial support for her mother, brother and sister, as well as anyone else who needed help. One day she filled her car with groceries she bought at the local A&P and called Jumbo Rinker to help carry them out to Gore, which had been devastated by a fire that swept through the mountains, burning many poor hill folk out of their homes. "She never lost track of who she was, never," Jumbo recalled. "That's why she could be so honest and there was nothing false about her. She knew who she was."

Those unpretentious qualities endeared her to many other "hosses" she worked with at that time, including Marvin Carroll: "She was such a down-to-earth person. She could sing better than anyone and she never looked down her nose at anyone. She made you feel equal. Course, she had such a hard life. She'd learned from the school of hard knocks. You could tell she had been around. She never talked a lot about it, but I remember once sitting around the Brunswick Fire Hall and she was saying that her father left them and they had nothing and her mother made all her clothes and how she had worked in a drugstore and started out like that. She seemed to appreciate everything that happened to her—even right then—and she wasn't even big yet."

But once Patsy settled into life with the Town & Country TV "family," conflicts with the show's "father figure," Gay, seemed to be inevitable, especially since Patsy was such an iconoclast compared to other girl singers.

"Patsy was different," noted Turner. "She was already competing and she was already fighting for what she wanted. I knew that, but we were just that different. She had to fight harder for what she wanted because she cared more about what she wanted. To me, to be on that show, that was *it*. Patsy got into fights with Connie; I never did. He'd dress me out from time to time, and I might go off and cry, but he always made it up to me; he was always good to me. He was always fair; he always paid me what we agreed to and it was more money than a secretary could make. I was one of the youngest, at twenty-one. I didn't have the responsibilities. Jimmy was married; he had a house and had payments to make. I hadn't gotten to that point. Patsy was helping her family, from what I understand, but they seemed dependent on her because no one else was really working. So I'm sure Patsy had to pull more weight, and she was more grown-up."

Chapter Eight

*A*FTER BILL McCALL signed Patsy to his 4 Star label, he immediately contacted a fellow gambler: Paul Cohen, A&R (artists and repertoire) man for Decca Records from 1945 to 1958.

By 1954, 4 Star was a limited operation. What McCall wanted to obtain, through Cohen, was a lease arrangement with Decca like others Cohen had made with him over the years beginning in the late forties with T. Texas Tyler and, later, Roy Clark. Under their standard deal, Cohen handled the recording of McCall's artist, thereby taking the hassles off McCall's hands. McCall then leased the resulting master to Decca. Decca would press and distribute—in Patsy's case, as with Roy Clark, on its Coral subsidiary. McCall would send out ten-inch deejay promotional copies to generate airplay royalties. McCall could collect publishing and, in many cases, writer's royalties, without having to get involved with musicians and their unions, manufacturing and distribution of the product—in short, everything that was not lucrative for indies.

For Cohen, as for A&R men for the other major labels, the relationship with small record entrepreneurs like McCall was a symbiotic one: the indies ferreted out regionally popular styles and performers that the majors co-opted for the mass market, sometimes effecting change in the artists' sounds and styles as a result. A prime example was when RCA Victor A&R man Steve Sholes purchased Elvis Presley's contract from Sun Records' Sam Phillips; thereafter, with the addition of vocal choruses, heavily electrified guitars and drums, Presley's sound smoothed out sufficiently to appeal to the crossover market and he actually started crooning.

Patsy was not consulted when McCall and Cohen made their backroom deal, the terms of which did not benefit Patsy in the slightest for the entire six years of her 4 Star career. The deal did involve financial gains for both men, however. McCall made it attractive to cut Cohen in.

Cohen was a wheeler-dealer in many respects. He started a dozen or more publishing companies of his own—all named after brands of whiskey. Then he had the chutzpah to open his office two blocks away from Decca, so he would be operating right under their nose. But by holding him to a salary and not permitting the A&R man to participate in record royalties as is done today, Decca had, in effect, created a monster. The label did not make it very attractive for entrepreneurial guys like Cohen to put songs in Decca's own publishing company.

"We had many deals with Paul, and money changed hands," acknowledged former 4 Star VP Don Pierce. "He'd record some of our songs and we made it worthwhile for him. When we had an act that maybe we didn't have the money to pay union scale or they were back East or we wanted to get a Nashville sound—especially once Bill got into the publishing—why he was happy to make this kind of deal with Decca."

In Patsy's case what apparently happened was that Decca gave McCall 5 percent of the royalties; since Patsy's royalties were calculated at only 2.34 percent, he could pocket the difference, minus half a cent to Cohen.

"After I was with Starday I made the same kind of deals with Paul," Pierce noted. "I let Arlie Duff go to Decca after we had 'You All Come' on Starday. The deal Paul made with me was that he would record Arlie and pay us a penny over rights on Decca sales and we would get to publish one side of each record. Now, in the case of Patsy, I'm sure Bill had an exclusive contract on her, but she wasn't much of a songwriter; therefore he probably made a deal where he paid her the regular 4 Star rate and they agreed to do only 4 Star songs, which, you know, that's not too bad a deal for Decca because they got a good artist. Now record companies are handing out 10 percent and 15 percent royalties. In those days, 5 percent was tops and a lot of artists were getting only 2 and 3 percent."

Cohen was one of the original Decca men. He was twenty-seven when his fellow Chicagoan Jack Kapp founded the company in 1934, under the aegis of British Decca. Cohen started out as head of Decca's Cincinnati branch office.

The Kapps loved hillbilly music and were influential in getting Louis Armstrong and Bing Crosby to record hillbilly songs. Dave Kapp, Jack's brother, would barnstorm the South, recording musicians. He hauled his portable rig to Memphis, New Orleans, Dallas, Charlotte and San Antonio. Kapp would hit town, rent two hotel rooms across the hall from one another and then put the word out. Musicians would drive from hundreds of miles away in beat-up jalopies and farm trucks for a chance to make a record. Kapp would set up his all-mechanical recording equipment with wax disks in one room and start cutting. Nothing was electric. He maintained constant speed by using 100-pound weights on plumb lines below the turntables. While Kapp sat in one room, the musicians sat in the room across the hall. One of Kapp's earliest acts was onetime Louisiana governor Jimmie Davis, whose first Decca hit, "Nobody's Darlin' but Mine," was cut when Davis was a clerk in the criminal court in Shreveport.

During the Depression, while the rest of the phonograph industry was in a slump, Decca lowered the price of records from seventy-five cents to thirty-five cents. Hillbilly music, which Decca produced from the very beginning, was a viable product because the costs of recording were so minimal and the artists worked for next to nothing. In the 1940s, while big pop acts like Bing Crosby, Louis Armstrong, the Ink Spots and the Andrews Sisters made Decca the dominant force in the industry, mainstays Ernest Tubb, Red Foley and the Carter Family provided solid financial underpinnings for the company.

In 1945, Cohen was promoted to head of A&R for Decca's country division. Cohen was the logical choice for the job. He loved Southern food, Southern women and Southern music, not necessarily in that order. At the time of his promotion, stars like Foley and Tubb typically recorded in the big northern cities—New York, Chicago, Cincinnati. Cohen figured that once a week, every big name in the hillbilly musical firmament was in Nashville for the Opry. He concluded that all the recording ought to take place in Nashville.

Cohen's timing was fortuitous. Three WSM engineers had just opened the first commercial recording studio in downtown Nashville, in the Tulane Hotel. It was called Castle Studios, after WSM's broadcast handle, "Air Castle of the South." Right away, Castle was booked for everything from R&B and blues sessions to pop dates for the Andrews Sisters and Rosemary Clooney and big band dates for the orchestras of Ray Anthony, Woody Herman and Francis Craig.

Castle's biggest client was Paul Cohen. He would come down to the Athens of the South from New York for three- and four-week periods, "throwing off sparks like crossed electric wires," according to one trade publication account, cutting four or more sessions a day, every day. "You'd be making a record and he'd snap his fingers and tell you how great it was," said producer Owen Bradley. "It maybe wasn't so hot, but damn, you'd think, 'Man, this is a smash.' And when it was, you'd say, 'Damn, he really knows what he's talking about.' He did it often enough."

Nashville was Cohen's "fishing hole," and he galvanized the town, convincing Ernest Tubb to record there; soon all the other acts fell into line. Then the A&R men from the other labels followed his example and set up offices there.

"The King of Nashville," as one industry man put it, was a snazzy dresser who sported a pinky ring. Though "Pauley" was hardly a handsome man, his magnetic, hammy personality, boundless energy and go-to-hell, cowboy approach to the business endeared him to the Nashville *goyim,* including Louisiana-born singer Faron Young, who first started hitting during Cohen's regime.

"Paul was one of the first Jewish guys who actually came in to Nashville, once they saw country music was getting to doing something," observed Young. "Before that, most of the country people wouldn't accept Jewish people. They were too clannish about that. He more or less broke the ice, then the rest of them came in and more or less took over this business. Hell, they own all the labels and every damn thing else now. Them and the Japs."

When Cohen wasn't overseeing a session he'd be gambling at the Automobile Club or entertaining in his suite at the Andrew Jackson Hotel, wining and dining the artists, writers, song pluggers and various other hangers-on, or shacked up somewhere—the women loved him, said his (male) colleagues. "He was a swinging guy," said producer Milton Gabler, head of Decca's pop division. While Cohen was out gallivanting, Gabler, who went to Nashville to record some of his acts, took over for him. It was a boys' club, with boys' games.

"He was a great womanizer, a great dice player," Gabler reminisced. "It was very exciting to watch him play dice. He was a hell of a guy. I once said if I had his epitaph to do it would read, 'All his enemies loved him.' "

Recalled Al Gallico, who headed the Tin Pan Alley publishing firm Shapiro-Bernstein: "I used to take trips with Paul—got to meet a lot of people and got to like the country people, so I started to spend a lot of time with the country part of the music business. It was good because the big band business was going nowhere—it was the end of the band era and it was good I went into country, one of the best moves I ever made. But he was something else, man, Paul, I loved him. He was the greatest, really a man's man, you know? I liked everything he did. He liked to gamble; we gambled together. Yeah, you gotta love Paul. If it wasn't for him there wouldn't have been a Nashville. It was his whole idea."

★   ★   ★

As head of A&R for Decca's country division, Cohen was responsible for a blue chip roster of talent that included the top acts of the time: Ernest Tubb, Red Foley and Webb Pierce (whom he signed after Pierce got free of 4 Star). In 1952, Cohen signed the one and only female star of country to Decca, Kitty Wells, and by 1954 he had two other solo girl singers under contract: Goldie Hill and Wanda Jackson. But any assumption that Cohen was a "woman's producer," someone who promoted women in the business, would be misleading. Kitty Wells was an accident. She was getting ready to retire from show business to tie on an apron in 1952 when she joined Decca. Wells was part of an act with her better-known husband, Johnny Wright, and brother-in-law, Jack Anglin. As Johnny and Jack, the act had a number of hits on Victor. It was really Johnny and Jack that Cohen wanted; "Miss Kitty" was the bait, according to Owen Bradley, the hands-on producer who recorded most of Cohen's acts in the early fifties. Then there was this "answer song."

Answer songs had generally developed as male responses to hit songs by other males, but in 1952 a song was brought to Bradley's attention that was to become the first female answer to a male. The idea was novel enough to launch Wells. After that, female answers became a trend, with songs by Jean Shepard, Goldie Hill and Betty Cody.

Bradley explained: "Paul was very astute at developing relationships and he wanted one with Johnny and Jack. It just so happened that Johnny had this wife who was a singer. And we had this song, 'It Wasn't God Who Made Honky-Tonk Angels,' for a girl—any girl, which some guy had brought by my studio. It was an answer song to 'The Wild Side of Life,' which was a big hit. So that was good enough reason to sign her. It could have been any girl but it turned out to be this girl. All the pieces fit. Paul did things like that—he would have little motives for doing things."

Cohen signed Goldie Hill, "the Golden Hillbilly," in 1952 and she had never sung professionally before in her life, but Hill was also a great beauty, certainly a great asset for a girl singer. After Cohen signed Webb Pierce, Pierce became the hottest artist in country. Hill was a nineteen-year-old IBM operator for the government whose brother fronted Pierce's band. Pierce brought her to Nashville. Said Hill, "Webb said to Paul Cohen, 'I want you to hear this girl sing.' I got up and sang about a verse of one of the two songs I knew and Paul says 'We'll sign her here and record her tomorrow night.'" Hill had country hits for Decca every year beginning in 1953, until she got married in 1957 (to singer Carl Smith) and faded away.

Wanda Jackson, whose recording career never really took off until she switched her label to Capitol in 1956 and changed her style from country to rockabilly, was another fluke. She was a junior in high school in Oklahoma City in 1954 when she was signed by Decca. She told the story: "Hank Thompson heard me on the radio and invited me to sing with his band when he was in town. That led to working with him pretty steady when he was in town. Well, he was trying to get Billy Gray, his front man, a record contract. They had this song, 'You Can't Have My Love'; it was a duet, so he said this would be a natural. I did two songs, demos; Bill did two. He sent them to Paul Cohen and said, 'By the way, if you see fit to sign them both we have this song we feel will be a hit.' We set up a recording session at Decca's studio in Hollywood. Billy and I did the duet, they released it and it hit. I never met Paul Cohen. Decca sent me my record contract in the mail and I signed it on the back of my guitar."

McCall must have been thinking in terms of Patsy's pop potential when he got in touch with Bill Peer and told him to put together a band that could handle pop as well as country material. Cohen was not sufficiently impressed by the Adelman demo tape; a demo session was scheduled at the Decca studios in New York for November 1954. McCall sent Patsy a batch of 4 Star copyrights to learn.

Peer put together a pick-up group, promising them club dates around New York and a chance to be signed by a major label, plus all expenses paid, in exchange for providing backings on the demo session. The band would also play for Patsy's audition for Arthur Godfrey's "Talent Scouts," one of the top-rated prime-time television programs in the fifties.

Compared to all his other efforts on Patsy's behalf, landing the audition date had been a major coup for Peer. In just four years, from 1950 to 1954, television ownership went from just 15 percent of American households to almost 50 percent, and "Talent Scouts" was one of two top-rated programs Arthur Godfrey had in prime time. The other show, "Arthur Godfrey and His Friends," was simulcast on CBS radio. Together Godfrey's hour-and-a-half of prime time reached an estimated 82 million viewers.

"Talent Scouts" featured aspiring professional entertainers who auditioned for the show. Those who made the final cut performed live in front of a CBS studio audience. The winner was chosen by an audience applause meter and usually went on to appear on Godfrey's other shows. If Patsy made it to the final round, she would be in stellar company: Godfrey had already introduced scores of well-known entertainers to the American public through his television and radio shows, including Billie Holiday, Rosemary Clooney, Pat Boone and Tony Bennett.

The five in her group drove from the Apple Capital to the Big Apple in two cars and checked into a suite in the modest Dixie Hotel off Times Square. As usual, Peer took charge. He registered himself and Patsy as "Mr. and Mrs. Bill Peer."

Peer had arranged the Godfrey audition with the help of a New York agent who he had met at a Florida disk jockey convention, Ritchie Lisselli. Lisselli's most important client was pop singer Teresa Brewer, another brash, up-tempo singer somewhat in the mold of Kay Starr. The suite at the Dixie was paid for by Lisselli, who had also arranged a bunch of club dates around Manhattan. Upon their arrival in New York, Lisselli provided the musicians with, according to band member Leo Miller, "every bit of help he could possibly do. Anything we wanted, he was right there. We didn't ask for anything. Matter of fact, it was too much at times for a bunch of country boys."

Patsy spent three days going over the material McCall had given her. Peer took her out shopping for a more sophisticated wardrobe. But the fast pace of New York overwhelmed her. "That place scares me," she admitted. She joined the band for only one of the club dates that had been arranged by Lisselli and otherwise kept a low profile. Leo Miller and John O'Brien, two of the musicians accompanying her on that trip, saw very little of Patsy. The musicians made the rounds of the clubs in ten-gallon hats that Lisselli had purchased for them for the appearances. The clubs were packed with hooting, hollering, foot-stomping New Yorkers who warmly greeted the four boys from "out West." Cowboy music, as country music was called there, was in vogue.

Only two months earlier, *Hayride*, a hillbilly musical revue featuring members of the cast of the Old Dominion Barn Dance out of Richmond, Virginia, debuted at the 48th Street Theatre. Columnist Earl Wilson's review, though generally positive, was peppered with "hillbillyese." Like the ugly American habit of talking louder and slower, as if foreigners exhibit lower IQs instead of a different language, Wilson's prose, like most mainstream journalism in the fifties, was simply patronizing toward the musical genre of poor white folks.

"Us Broadway slickers got to learn another new language—hillbillyese.

'Cause with the hillbillies from Hollywood and Texas and even some from the hills—comin' to the city, we got to know what they're saying. When the new hillbilly op'ry, *Hayride*, opened last night, I hardly knew what a 'squeeze box' or a 'stummick Steinway' was."

As insecure as she was about her own lack of book learning, Patsy was equally touchy about put-downs of hillbillies—her kind of people. A few years later she relished the opportunity to make a dig at Wilson's fellow columnist Dorothy Kilgallen for Kilgallen's more blatant display of intolerance.

Lisselli's solicitude during the New York trip was motivated by his undisguised interest in Patsy. He wanted to manage her. He plainly felt her potential extended beyond that of country girl singer. He dangled the possibility of a part in the movies in front of her and then let her know if she were nice to him, he'd be nice to her. Patsy was repulsed by the unctuous manager and his suggestion, but for the sake of whatever help he might be to her, she kept him at arm's length and hung closer to Peer for support.

At the audition for Godfrey's show at the CBS studios, Patsy seemed to be having a bad day. The pickup band had problems supporting her on "This Ole House," a hit earlier in the year for RCA artist Stuart Hamblen that Rosemary Clooney subsequently turned into a crossover smash, and "Turn the Cards Slowly," a hillbilly boogie offering lines like "Don't you double deal to win my heart." Patsy's performance elicited a perfunctory compliment from "Talent Scouts" producer Janette Davis. Davis, a pop vocalist on Godfrey's show, was the only female producer of a prime-time TV series. In the course of working with amateurs all day long, she had a clipped, no-nonsense manner that made Patsy feel she was getting the brush-off. But what really annoyed Patsy was Davis's implication that she was wasted as a hillbilly singer. In Davis's opinion she had a pop singer's voice. Davis suggested she audition without the country-sounding band that Peer had arranged for her.

"I thought she could handle both pop and country very well," Davis recalled. "There's a certain quality that country singers have that is just inborn, in my estimation, and she had that. But she also could get up there and do a rhythm song or a ballad in the pop field."

Patsy stuck to her guns; she was a hillbilly and proud of it, and she defied anyone to put her down. Before Davis ushered the next contestant in line, she invited Patsy to return the next day for another shot.

The next stop was the Decca studios at the former Pythian Temple on West 57th Street. In addition to the material she had performed at the Godfrey audition, she sang the melodramatic "Three Cigarettes in an Ashtray," a classic of the lover-done-me-wrong genre, and the Irving Berlin chestnut "Always." The demo session did not go any better than the audition. Further aggravated by the presence of Lisselli, who bugged her about the club dates and made her feel like she was being pushed around, Patsy supposedly needed twenty-seven takes on "This Ole House." It was desperately important to her that she get it right. As at Godfrey's studio, there were once again problems with the pickup group, which had limited experience working together. At one point Patsy vented her vexation to the band.

"You're just going to get what you want and the hell with the rest of us," one band member told her. Patsy was ambitious, but she was also loyal to the core. The exchange stung. She may have felt guilty about what she'd been accused of. This may explain why she later claimed she turned down a Godfrey appearance in 1954 because the band was not invited to go on with her. The following day, the band and Lisselli waited for her at CBS for her second try. She stood them up. Related Leo Miller, "We were out in the hall, with Bill. We even carried her music and stuff. We found out Ritchie Lisselli didn't know where she was either. He said. 'Well, I have bad news for you fellas— we don't know where she is. But don't let this stop you—we'll do something with what you're doing. She's not the whole show.' "

The tape that resulted from the New York session did not immediately motivate Cohen to make a deal with McCall. Patsy, disappointed by the glitches in getting her recording career launched, expressed her dissatisfaction with how the session went to members of the Peer band. She complained that she was a country artist, and the tape made her sound like "a little bit of this and a little of that."

"There were a lot of pop singers on the scene at that time that were really good, and I don't think she wanted to compete with any of them in the pop field," said Roy Deyton, for whom Patsy played the demo. "In her mind she was a country-type girl singer, yet she was like us in that she could cross over the line and sing other types of music. But she wanted to get someplace in Nashville, and for that you had to be country."

The following May, Patsy went to a Frederick, Maryland, radio station with Bill Peer and the Melody Boys to have another stab at recording the material she had tried in New York. "We could really cook behind her," Roy Deyton said. "She was really into it. Her attitude was, 'Let's see what kind of damage we can do with this.' I never once heard her complain about the stuff McCall sent her. She had been doing the popular songs that were on the radio, so she was receptive to most of what came in because she wanted to have her own repertoire."

This time the session went down without a hitch. She laid down tracks for "Turn the Cards Slowly," "This Ole House" and "Three Cigarettes in an Ashtray."

Shortly thereafter, she received her summons to go to Nashville to cut her first record. Cohen and McCall had made a deal. By the terms of their arrangement, Cohen agreed to forfeit his right to choose material for Patsy, normally the job of an A&R man. He would endlessly complain to his colleagues at Decca about what a "pain in the ass" McCall was, but a wheeler-dealer like Cohen couldn't pass on the combination of Patsy's extraordinary vocal chemistry, her chutzpah, as well as that great Southern accent—and the financial opportunities that went with the lease arrangement. "We had to take his contract or we wouldn't get his girl," recalled Milt Gabler of the arrangement. "And Paul wanted her. She was terrific. We all loved her."

Chapter Nine

NINETEEN FIFTY-FIVE was the year of love and marriage. Not only was it a hit song of the day but marriage age and divorce rates were at an all-time low. Padded bras and broad, crinoline skirts confined women's bodies and defined maternal potential. *Love Is a Many-Splendored Thing* was one of the top-grossing movies of that year, while benign, all-knowing TV dads in "Father Knows Best" and "Make Room for Daddy" informed people about how happy families looked. Button-down attitudes ensured social acceptance—which put Patsy on a collision course with conventional morality, beginning with her iconoclastic fashion statement.

Her flashy cowgirl outfits, especially the sportier, short-shorts version, weren't calculated to turn her into a sexpot; when Patsy went out on stage she forgot about everything else. She was in a completely different world, the one in which her flame burned hottest in the act of metaphorically making love to as many people as possible in the most powerful way she knew: singing. And visuals were half of it. "She wanted people to know that she was Patsy—this is me, you sons-of-bitches, whether you like it or not—this is me," related Johnny Anderson.

At home, the reviews about Patsy's personal life started to come in. Word about her ongoing affair with Peer while she was married to Gerald was common knowledge. As far as Patsy was concerned, if life with Gerald was like a bad song, then her relationship with Peer was a country ballad of the melodramatic "Three Cigarettes in an Ashtray" sort. A bit of carelessness during the trip to New York came back to haunt her: she left a coat at the Dixie Hotel that was returned to Peer's wife by a thoughtful concierge apologizing to "Mrs. Peer" for the inconvenience. Patsy's reputation was wrecked in Winchester. Rumors spread that she was bedding every man in sight. "I was forbidden to hang out with her because she was lying around in bed with different men," claimed one former neighbor. As usual, it was Patsy's image of a liberated woman that contributed to the myth about her licentiousness.

"The hell with them" was her response to the gossip mongers. Always ready to turn a confrontation into an advantage, Patsy meant to prove to others she was not easily slighted by the furor. The town was full of hypocrites, she claimed. She only put on stage what most people hid, and yes, it might not be "respectable."

But her brazen appearance and cocky retorts were part of the armor that protected the maiden underneath. Patsy was truly a softie, but you had to know her to know what hurt her. And Patsy didn't let many people inside.

Said Pat Smallwood, "She didn't seem to let rumors bother her. She went on. If it bothered her, you rarely saw that side of her. What you saw was that she was happy and carefree and looking for the next day when things are going to get better."

"She never done a damn thing," said Johnny Anderson. "Respected my wife, respected everybody. If she thought it, she said it, but she wasn't laying around like people said she was. That's not so. All the guys in our band—there were six of us—were nice-looking men. Not a one of them had an affair with Patsy, not a one. I know. The only one I know she ever had an affair with was Bill Peer, and Bill worshipped the ground that woman walked on. And she just used him. What the hell—say it like it is. He was soft as hell, anyway: after he got divorced and Patsy dumped him, he went back and married his first wife again."

"She was out there doing it, and there weren't all that many classy women doing it at the time," offered Roy Deyton's wife, Elizabeth, who frequented the clubs in those days. "I guess there were some women who felt nervous when she was around, but she wasn't out to get another woman's husband. She had no problem with men. She had enough attention. She could have had her choice of men. She was very attractive."

According to friends, Gerald knew his wife was still having an affair with Peer, but he overlooked it, and started dating other women himself. Even Patsy had to admit Gerald was good to her in certain ways, as a provider. Still, there was no spark, no chemistry, none of the electricity that she associated with sexual attraction. Whatever was on Patsy's mind was on her lips, and she confided her marital woes—in explicit detail—to her sidemen. They were, after all, fellow "hosses."

"She said she wasn't satisfied, that he didn't please her. We were like a little family circle, and she would come right out and tell us what was bothering her. I think she was fond of my brother Ray and I. She liked us as musicians, she liked us as people, I guess she figured we were too immature at that time to be interesting. I just never thought about her as a person I would like to go with. We were working together, so I never thought of her that way, even though she was a very attractive woman," Roy Deyton recalled.

Problems in Patsy's personal life came to a head in the spring of 1955 when she started waking up in the morning feeling nauseous. A trip to the doctor confirmed the news she least wanted to hear: she was pregnant.

Like most women in the fifties, Patsy was raised believing in the American dream: a husband, children and the proverbial house with a white picket fence. She surprised Roy Deyton one night with her response when he asked her for advice on his love life. He had found the right girl, he told her, and was thinking of marrying her. He figured as ambitious and practical as Patsy was, she would advise him to postpone marriage.

"I knew getting married might interfere with your music career, but you don't meet a good girl very often, maybe once in a lifetime. I asked Patsy, 'I don't want to mess my music up—what do you think?' I guess she wasn't that much older but she was like a big sister to me, and she had been married and through these kinds of things before. We would talk about a lot of things like that. She asked me if I loved her and I told her yes. She looked me square in the eye and said, 'Roy, I'll tell you, hoss: if you got a good one, you'd better hang onto her.'"

Patsy often told her friends she wanted it all. But not the children part, not now. And under the circumstances, there would always be some doubt as to who the father was. She could really start a war if she had the baby.

She confided in a few friends who helped her find a woman in Winchester who would perform an abortion. She paid in twenty-dollar bills. Soon afterward she was back on the bandstand at the Brunswick Moose, which, as usual, was packed for the biggest night of the week. She didn't want to let her fans down. When she kept running to the bathroom, sick, and finally had to be taken home, her friends were told it was a miscarriage.

The first part of 1955 was a period of frustration for Patsy. She felt a lot of turmoil about relationships and it was distracting her from her main objective. There were plenty of men who were attracted to her, but it was not exactly the kind of attention she was seeking. She was trying to be seen as much as possible as a singer and felt as though she was two beats behind where she wanted to be. A phone call from Paul

Cohen made her feel she was back on track: a date was set for her first Nashville recording session on June 1. Patsy liked the energetic, irrepressible Cohen and, like everyone else, found his hammy personality lovable. Cohen expressed his confidence in her talent in his typically ebullient style. Her confidence soared again.

The industrious Peer used the session date as a springboard to create yet another opportunity to put Patsy before the public. The Martinsburg car dealer Peer worked for agreed to sponsor her and the band in Winchester's Apple Blossom parade that spring. It was the height of scandal season and Patsy played the part to the hilt. As proud as a Kentucky Derby champ, Patsy, dressed in a black cowgirl outfit with white fringe, sat on top of the back seat of a black Cadillac Coupe de Ville decorated with a big horseshoe made of crepe-paper flowers hanging from the hood ornament. Peer, his left elbow resting casually on the driver's door, chauffeured her through the streets named after Winchester's historic patriarchy. The posse of Melody Boys rode with her.

"I'll never forget it—I smiled 'til my face was sore," remembered Roy Deyton. "I guess Patsy was at her peak right then, as far as being from there, and it was a big, hometown thing for her. That's when we met her mother. She never came around to any of the jobs. I don't think she thought a whole lot of Bill. I think it had something to do with him being married and all."

"I'm going to send you a girl. This girl is mean as hell; she's hard to get along with."

Patsy's introduction to producer Owen Bradley, he recalled, was not exactly promising.

Word about how "difficult" Patsy had been in New York had filtered down to Bradley, who in 1955 was considered Paul Cohen's heir apparent in Nashville.

Bradley became seriously interested in record making in 1949, when Cohen put him in charge of producing Red Foley's "Chatanooga Shoe Shine Boy," which became a million-seller, solidified Foley's position as a major star (the host of the "Grand Ole Oprys'" Prince Albert segment and later the host of his own network TV show, "Ozark Jubilee") and began Bradley's career as a record producer. Bradley first met Cohen playing on a Foley recording date for Decca. Cohen thought Foley could use some smoothing out. Bradley, a Nashville-born pianist, arranger and big band leader, was the man for the job, Cohen was told.

Prior to that, Bradley was well known and respected in Nashville music circles as the leader of the WSM studio orchestra as well as his own pop combo, the Owen Bradley Quintet. While serving in the U.S. Maritime Service in the San Francisco Bay area during the war, he was a pianist and arranger for orchestra leader Ted Weems, whose vocalist during that era was Perry Como. Bradley's idea of a girl singer was Kay Starr, Jo Stafford or even Dinah Shore, all with whom he worked as a pops man. He cut a few records in the late forties on Coral that were pure pop: "La Vie en Rose," "Blue Eyes Crying in the Rain" and "Blues Stay Away from Me," which despite its pop sound became a country hit.

The advent of the tape recorder and magnetic tape in the late forties opened up a whole new world of special effects and gimmicks compared to the days when an A&R man's job consisted of holding a stopwatch and making sure the turntables were spinning. For Foley's session, Bradley called on some of the experienced radio orchestra men he knew and asked for something that sounded like a shoeshine rag buffing a shoe. Session drummer Farris Coursey, who played in Bradley's band in the forties and followed him uptown in the fifties, came up with just the right popping sound of a shoeshine rag by beating on his right thigh until it became black and blue and he had to switch to his left leg.

But after the song became a smash, Bradley was bitten by the record bug. After that, when Cohen was out wheeling and dealing and gallivanting and couldn't be in Nashville to take charge of the cutting sessions, he turned to Bradley. Cohen wasn't a musician and Bradley was, and an astute one at that. Cohen wisely kept his instructions to his protégé to a minimum and allowed him to work his magic in the studio: "Why don't you go in and do this song and that song, and anything else you want to do," or "Here's three, see if you can find another one," or "Here's one, find three more." Bradley credited his former boss for his early education in how to make a hillbilly record commercial.

"He was not a musician but he had a great sense of rhythm," Bradley said. "I learned from him how to pick songs. There are some people who will analyze a song, but Paul didn't. He just felt them. He'd either say, 'I love it!' or 'I don't like it'—you know, a gut reaction. He had other certain little things that he liked or disliked that rubbed off on me. For instance, he thought vibraphones and accordions were not commercial. Consequently we did not use them. To this day I have a thing about vibraphones and accordions, and I played vibes. It wasn't that he didn't like them—he just didn't think they recorded well, and accordion reminded him of a polka. When he liked something he was very positive and even when a record wasn't that good he was positive. He would always smile and say, 'It's great!'

whereas I might say, 'That's fine,' and not smile. Paul had a great way of making you feel like he liked you, even if he didn't have that much faith in you."

"Someday they'll promote you and I'll want your job," Bradley told Cohen.

In 1952, Bradley and his brother, session player Harold Bradley, pooled their session money, bought equipment and started a film studio on Second Avenue South to make kinescopes of Opry stars for syndication, the same films in which Patsy appeared in the late fifties. "At the time," Owen recalled, "we were trying to keep from getting into the recording business because the people who were running Castle were real good friends." Three years later, Castle was about to close as the Tulane Hotel neared demolition. Bradley and Cohen stood in an alleyway behind an old, wooden-frame, two-story house on 16th Avenue South, which was then a run-down residential neighborhood, now the heart of present-day Music Row. Cohen had threatened to take his business to another town unless there was another recording studio. Bradley's roots were in Nashville and he had no desire to move. Cohen offered to go in on the $7,500 purchase price of the wooden-frame house. He guaranteed Bradley 100 Decca sessions a year if Bradley would turn the place into a state-of-the-art recording facility.

Bradley Film and Recording Studios was born. Owen Bradley installed a little studio in the basement, knocked the first floor out so it had a high ceiling and set up an office on the second floor. He stocked the studio with Ampex 350 tape machines plugged into an Ampex MX-10 mono-mixing board. But Bradley wanted more sound, which meant more bodies, and the studio was too small. So shortly after opening, he created a second, larger studio by adding a military-style Quonset hut and installed a second control room and mixing board. Word spread that the new studio had the greatest acoustics in the world. Right away, "the Quonset Hut," as it was thereafter dubbed— became the headquarters of the nascent recording scene in Nashville.

Patsy arrived on the appointed date with her married man, Bill Peer, and the man she was married to, Gerald. Patsy's reputation for outspokenness had preceded her and Bradley was prepared for the worst— "someone to come in and just beat me to death, tongue-lash me."

He needn't have worried. The hellcat he was expecting was excited but nervous, and not a little intimidated by the cast that had been assembled for her benefit. The cadre of session musicians setting up to go to work for the next three hours were mostly unknown to her, but Bradley wasn't. Though the thirty-nine-year-old producer considered himself an "apprentice" in the recording field, all Patsy knew was that he produced the biggest acts in country music, including Webb Pierce, Kitty Wells and Ernest Tubb. She exhibited her usual reserve around strangers. Bradley saw through it:

"I didn't think she was any different than anybody else who was trying to get started. It's like when you go to a strange doctor, you're kind of uncomfortable. But after you've been a couple of times, then you relax; you can take off your clothes or whatever you have to do, because you've done it before. The same thing was true for Patsy. After a while, she began to feel like, 'Well, that's a familiar face, it's okay for me to undress and be myself.' She was exposing her emotions, and if she was afraid or intimidated by the presence out there of someone who she thought was going to put her down, or didn't like her or thinks she's no good or something, then she might hold back."

Choosing material from the songs McCall had given Patsy had Bradley stymied. The main "problem," ironically, was Patsy's vocal prowess. To Bradley's ear, tuned by years of the big band sound, her full, pop-sounding voice with a big, broad range did not fit with the female standard-bearer, Kitty Wells, whose current hit, "Making Believe," had been recorded only a few months earlier in the very same room where Patsy now stood. Yet because Patsy was going to be released as a country artist, she needed a sound that was compatible with Wells's.

Patsy had a "country head" and a strong personal preference for growling, yodeling and showy, up-tempo endings suited to her big voice—all of which worked well in juke joints and firehalls. She was convinced that these were the very devices that set her apart from singers like Wells or Jean Shepard, and she was right. No one could outyodel or growl like Patsy, who had a growl like a blues singer. And she came to show her stuff. She was proud; she knew what she had.

As usual, Cohen left Bradley to his own devices when it came to producing Patsy, but he did make his preferences clear earlier: yodeling cowgirls were in the same category as accordions and vibes. Yodeling had become the exception, rather the rule, in country records. It represented an earlier, unfashionable hick era, and with the noteworthy exception of Hank Williams's "Lovesick Blues" and Elton Britt, Slim Whitman, Rosalie Allen and Kenny Roberts, who kept yodeling alive in the fifties, most singers and producers had shaken it loose by the late forties. Bradley kept Cohen's preferences in mind. Though she had definite ideas of her own, Patsy came to her first session open to suggestions and wanting to please. "I was trying to please Mr. Cohen, she was trying to please Mr. Cohen and we could do anything we wanted to as long as we recorded 4 Star songs."

According to Bradley, until 1958 Patsy chose the songs she

recorded from batches of material supplied by Bill McCall, and solicited his advice when she was unsure of or unhappy with the material. "She'd just walk in and say, 'These are the songs we're going to do.' That's what we'd do. Then the pickings got worse and worse and she would complain."

The appeal of "A Church, a Courtroom and Then Goodbye" to Patsy was undeniable, given her own predicament. It is a ballad couched in classic Southern iconography that describes a divorce, a matter in the forefront of Patsy's mind. Though mildly provocative, it falls within the bounds of acceptable country music terrain, delicately balancing right and wrong. The marriage ends in divorce, which is bad, but there is remorse, which is good. Guilt prevails. Kitty Wells could have sung it. The tune was written by McCall's best writer, Eddie Miller, who was under an exclusive 4 Star contract. Miller's masterpiece was "Release Me," on which, in 1954, Jimmy Heap, Perk Williams, Ray Price and Kitty Wells all had had country hits.

The other Eddie Miller tune Patsy could relate to was "Hidin' Out," a laconic ballad about an illicit love affair with lyrics that could have been pages torn out of her diary: "We said we wouldn't meet tonight, my dear/But here we are again, hidin' out." She balanced out the two weepers with the upbeat "Honky-Tonk Merry-Go-Round," a western swing number about making the rounds of juke joints, "ridin' high and feelin' low," and "Turn the Cards Slowly," a perky number from the New York session.

It was the standard practice to record four songs in three hours. Patsy would play the demo tapes McCall had given her to give the musicians the chord changes. She would have already studied the demos and come up with her own interpretation, incorporating her own phrasing and tempo. Bradley and the musicians ran through the songs two or three times before the red light went on.

Bradley's only records of the 4 Star years were destroyed in a fire in 1980 and 4 Star logs are no longer available, hence the personnel are not known for certain. But based on interviews of the leading session musicians of the day who played behind Patsy, an accurate or near accurate personnel list was reconstructed for MCA's 1992 commemorative set, *The Patsy Cline Collection*.

On acoustic guitar was twenty-nine-year-old Harold Bradley, who, as one of the very first musicians to make a career out of session work, was to become the most recorded guitarist in history. Harold, like his older brother Owen, was a musical adept. As a teenager he was influenced by modern jazz guitar pioneer Charlie Christian, whose horn-like electric guitar solos in recordings by the Benny Goodman Orchestra were inspired by Lester Young's long solo lines on tenor saxophone.

Indeed, Bradley, who grew up at the Opry and played at the first Castle Studio sessions, would sit backstage with some of the other musicians and jam on jazz tunes like "Body and Soul." He played everything from R&B (on Ivory Joe Hunter dates—the only white musician on the dates) to big band (on recordings of tunes like "Bunny Hop" and "The Hokey Pokey" with the Ray Anthony Orchestra).

Standing next to Bradley, on electric guitar, was big, burly, twenty-six-year-old Grady Martin, another Tennessee-born musician who, like Harold Bradley, made the transition from the Castle Studios downtown to the Bradley Studios uptown. He'd started out as a fiddler, switched to guitar, and was known for his tight, bluesy, hard-driving solos. Among Nashville pickers, singers and producers, Martin was considered the premiere studio musician and, because of his imposing size and laid-back manner, was usually asked to be the session leader.

Rounding out the fraternity woodshedding in the Quonset Hut were drummer Farris Coursey, fiddler Tommy Jackson, Bob Moore on acoustic bass and Don Helms, guitarist for Hank Williams, on steel. Owen Bradley took over piano chores. Bradley's style was considerably smoother than the gritty, honky-tonk style of "King of Hillbilly Piano Players" Moon Mullican. Ernest Tubb would jokingly refer to him as "Half Moon Bradley."

Patsy styled "A Church, a Courtroom and Then Goodbye" with just a trace of a growl to pep up the weeper, closing with a high, fast ending. On "Turn the Cards Slowly" and "Honky-Tonk Merry-Go-Round" she was on more comfortable turf, yodeling and growling up a storm. Bradley would try to discourage her: "I wish you wouldn't do that there, Patsy," was his effort at diplomacy. He tried again and again to impress on her that she didn't need the gimmicks less well endowed hillbilly vocalists of the thirties and forties used.

"I think she felt she had to turn up her energy, and that's the way she would turn it up. But to me it was just like those cowgirls. And I was thinking about what New York was going to say, because I already had two or three of those who had flopped."

"Gabe, I've got a girl here who's coming to Nashville. I'd appreciate it if you could find a place for her on Ernest's "Midnight" show."

Though Patsy's first single would not be released until six weeks later on July 20, Connie B. Gay was not about to miss an opportunity to get some exposure for *his* discovery during the week Patsy was in Nashville to record. Gay had earlier placed a call to Nashville, to Gabe Tucker, who managed, booked and promoted Ernest Tubb.

Tucker was a graduate of the Colonel Tom Parker School of Management. Tucker learned the business side of music in the late forties, barnstorming the country as the Colonel's aide-de-camp when from 1945 to 1953 he managed Eddy Arnold. Tucker's story about how Parker got the official title of "Colonel" from the State of Louisiana typifies the M.O. of many of the music entrepreneurs of the day: "The Colonel is very loyal to the old carnies. When we would hit a town where a carnival was, by God, we went to the carnival. So we was in Baton Rouge, the Colonel says, 'By God, I know a man who works on the Royal American show. I believe I'll call him and get him to come down and eat supper with us.' So we'll call him Graham—he come down and we sat down to eat and talk show business and the Colonel talked a snow job on all this stuff he done since he started managing Eddy Arnold.

"After he left, me and the Colonel went to our room and we was laying on our beds—he was very lonely and wanted me with him everywhere. And he was smoking that little old Tampa cigar like he always smoked and back then I chewed on King Edward cigars. I was spitting in a goddamn coffee can. I knew every goddamn trick he pulled, and I said, 'Tom, goddamn, as much bullshit as you blow, you ought to have a title.' He blowed on that little ole Tampa cigar and he says, 'What kind of title do you think I could get?' And I said, 'Hell, I just thought a you one. You know Governor Jimmie Davis? He's governor of this goddamn state. Graham is on his staff. I'm going to call him and see if he'll make you a Louisiana colonel.' He said, 'Goddamn, that would be strong, wouldn't it?' I said, 'Hell, yes, and I think I can pull it off.' So I picked up the phone and called him at home. I said, 'Tan's gone back to the restaurant, would you do me a big favor? Would you get Governor Jimmie Davis to make him a Louisiana colonel?' He said, 'Hell, it ain't no big deal. Hell yes, I'll do it.'"

As Tubb's manager, Tucker booked all the acts on the "Midnight Jamboree," broadcast from the Ernest Tubb Record Shop following the "Grand Ole Opry." The show was already full for the week that Patsy would be in town.

"I said, 'Goddamn, Connie, I don't know where I can put her on. I'm only supposed to put four guests on the show. Hell, Connie, who is it?' 'Patsy Cline,' he told me. 'She's worked here for me.' I said, 'Can she sing?' And he said, 'Gabe, you'll be surprised.' So I wrote her in.

"Well, she showed up with that old boy who had a little band up in that area and I think she sang with them. On Saturday I would go into my office in time to check all the guests and make sure everything was in order. My office was way in the back. You had to climb over boxes and everything else to get to me and that's the way I liked it. So while the guests rehearsed with the band, I'd be in the back office, and then I'd go up and listen to them to make sure they wouldn't embarrass us on the show that night. While I was in back, Ernest come in and he sit down on my desk and me and him talked a little bit. He's writing his numbers down that he's going to do on the show, when Rusty, who run the band when Ernest wasn't there or I wasn't there, comes back and says, 'Gabe, I believe you ought to come up here and listen to this girl.' I thought, 'Well, hell, Connie wouldn't send me a girl who can't sing.'

"So I went up there and she was on the stage, and he told her to go through her song again. So she did. And goddamn, I listened to that for just a few minutes and I went up there and said, 'Honey, would you go back and sing that song again for me? I want to go up front and listen to it.' She said, 'Yessir.' She got back up there and sang the song again. So after she got through I said, 'Thank you, honey, we'll see you tonight.' But I said, 'Wait just a minute though.'

"I went to the back, where Ernest is. I used to play in Red Foley's band and that Red Foley was a hell of a singer. I always respected his singing. So I said, 'Ernest, there's a girl on the show tonight Connie B. Gay sent down here, and I want you to hear her. Hell, she is a female Red Foley.'"

Tucker's comparison was a high compliment. Foley had been the star of the Prince Albert segment of the "Grand Ole Opry" and in 1954 he began hosting the nationally broadcast, top-rated TV show "Ozark Jubilee." He was a tremendously smooth, versatile artist who could have been a pop star. With his clear, trained-sounding voice Foley could convincingly move from tear-jerking ballads, to boogie, to blues, to spirituals, to jump tunes in one program with ease.

Tucker continued: "He said, 'Oh hell, Gabe, she ain't that good.' I said, 'The hell she ain't. Go up and listen to her.' So Ernest got up, he went up and he said, 'Honey, would you sing that same song that you're going to do on the show tonight? Gabe wants me to listen to it.' And she did, the same damn song. This makes four times she's singing it. And the band, they knew she could sing. So when she got through Ernest said, 'Thank you, honey,' and he come back and I said, 'Whattaya think, Ernest?' And he said, 'Damn, you are right. She *is* a female Red Foley.'"

Though Tubb recognized Patsy's talent early in her career, Tucker disputed one story that Tubb mentored her and helped her pick "A Church, a Courtroom and Then Goodbye" for her first recording session, since Patsy's appearance on "Midnight Jamboree" occurred after her recording session had already taken place. Tucker booked all the Texas Troubadour's appearances and booked Patsy on all the dates she appeared on with Tubb. "Ernest gets credit for all this bullshit for what he done for Patsy. It's very unlikely he helped her pick any songs or did anything for her because if he had a good song, unless it was strictly a girl's song, he ain't going to give it to nobody. He'd do it himself."

Then and there Tucker decided he wanted to manage Patsy. He tried to discuss the idea with her, but Peer kept intruding and Patsy acquiesced, never to know what Tucker had planned for her, so intimidated was she by the situation.

"I got to thinking, this was a rough time for country entertainers—goddamn it was rough. Rock and roll was eating our lunch. So I decided, 'Goddamn, I know what I'll do. I've got Ernest Tubb, Justin Tubb and the Wilburn Brothers,' and I had another boy on the show that I signed up just about the time Patsy came in, Bobby Helms. So I thought, 'As hard as it is to make a living, I'll book Ernest, the Wilburns, Bobby and this girl, Patsy Cline, and have a package. I'll get out there and promote it and book it myself.' So after the show I told her, 'I want you to come back here on Monday morning. I'll be in my office by ten o'clock. I want to talk to you.' She said, 'Yessir.' She was just a little ole country girl, and I liked that because I was born and raised in the hills—I never seen a freight train 'til I was fourteen years old. So you know how country I was, and I appreciated it. But she never would say nothing hardly."

Tucker was informed that Peer and Patsy, who'd underestimated the length of their stay in Nashville, had spent their last dime. That night he called Roy Acuff's brother, Spot Acuff, who managed Dunbar Caves, the King of Country Music's amusement park on the outskirts of Nashville, where Patsy had once sung as a teenager.

"I said, 'Spot, have you got room for another act on the show down at the Cave tomorrow?' He said, 'Hell, Gabe, I'm full.' I said, 'Well, there's a girl and an ole boy here from up there in Virginia and my friend Connie B. Gay asked me to put them on the "Midnight" show. Hell, they're broke and they ain't got no money to get back home. Could you pay them $50 to come down there and have her sing a few songs?' He said, 'Hell, I don't need her, Gabe, but if you want me to, I'll do it.' So I went up immediately and told Patsy. Course, that damn boy Peer, he kept butting in. I couldn't talk to her for him a talking. I said, 'Patsy, tomorrow I just booked you down at Roy Acuff's Dunbar Caves'—I didn't act like I knew they was broke. I said, 'It'll be good exposure for you; a lot of people will get to hear you. But all I could get on such short notice was $50, but at least that'll buy a little gasoline to get you back to Virginia. I want to see you Monday morning in my office.'

"Monday morning, before I got there, old Spot has called my secretary and she said, 'Mr. Tucker, Spot Acuff just called you thirty minutes ago.' And I said, 'Oh my God, what happened?' She said, 'No, he's very happy—he wants to talk to you.' So I called him back and he said, 'Gabe, any time you got any extra talent on the Ernest Tubb show as good as that girl was for $50, call me.' And I felt so relieved. I thought something had happened and he was going to get on me, because everybody wants to get on the manager. I said, 'Well, I'm glad you enjoyed her work but I didn't hesitate in sending her to you because I heard her sing here and I know Connie B. Gay wouldn't put a dud on me.'

"So I hadn't discussed with Ernest or nobody about taking her on as an artist. I just figured I'll build my own damn show with Ernest, the Wilburns and Patsy and put Bobby on, and that would have been a hell of a package. They were all good. So I had made up my mind that I would manage Patsy. So Monday morning, here comes that goddamn man with her. And every time I'd ask her something, hell, he'd answer. I couldn't talk to her. She sat there just like a little kid that's been slapped away from the table. And I thought, 'God, I wouldn't put up with that bastard for two of her,' because I was a nervous wreck anyway with all the people I had to deal with. So I finally ended up, after I tried to go through what I thought we could do—I didn't even get through, I got so disgusted with him. Hell, he started in telling me what to do. I think they were shacked up. I thought, 'If she is going to let somebody like this bastard hang onto her I need her like I need an extra hole in my head.' I couldn't talk to her without him butting in. Finally, I said, 'I got to get to work, Patsy. It's nice to have you on the show. Any time you come to town just let me know if you want to be on Ernest Tubb's "Midnight" show and I'll put you on.'"

Patsy evidently took Tucker up on his offer to help her and on June 26 she returned to Nashville again for a concert under the shadow of the Parthenon, headlined by Tubb. The Centennial Park event played to a crowd of 15,000. Patsy's appearance on the bill was briefly noted by *Billboard:* "Other c.&w. folk on the park program were Cedric Rainwater, comedy musician, and Patsy Kline [*sic*], of Winchester, Va."

That week, on July 1, she made her debut on the Ralston-Purina segment of the "Grand Ole Opry," hosted by Tubb. He gave her a warm Opry welcome, introducing her as "Coral Records' newest star." Her performance of "A Church, a Courtroom and Then Goodbye" did not elicit the kind of response Hank Williams received for his Opry debut, which won him six encores for "Lovesick Blues." But Patsy was required to promote her imminent release at every opportunity, and the weepy pace of "Church" garnered only polite applause. She was disappointed that the response to her performance wasn't so enthusiastic that a return invitation was obvious. Backstage she was greeted by Faron Young, whom she'd first met when Young appeared on a "Connie B. Gay Presents" event in Washington, D.C.

"I remember that night she came off, she started crying," Young said. "I said, 'What's the matter with you, honey?' She said, 'Oh, I got to be on the Opry but I guess that's the end of it and I'll have to go back to Virginia and that'll be the end of it.' So I went and talked to Ernest Tubb about it and Ernest got her and said to her, 'I want you to come down to Memphis day after tomorrow. Me and Faron are playing Memphis, Tennessee, and we'll just feature you on our show.'"

The Memphis show, at a ballpark, drew 10,000 fans. Though Patsy and the loquacious Young eventually broke the ice and became "like brother and sister," she seemed shy on first impression.

"She didn't say much. I guess she thought it was best for her to keep her mouth shut. I said to her, 'You sure sing your ass off, I can tell you that.' She said, 'Well, thank you, Mr. Young. That's so nice for you to say.' I said, 'You will be a big star, just you wait and see.' I'm sure she probably thought, 'Yeah, that's easy for you to say; you're making money and I'm starving to death.'"

"A Church, a Courtroom and Then Goodbye," backed by "Turn the Cards Slowly," was released on July 20. Cohen's decision to release Patsy on Coral, a Decca subsidiary, which lasted for only her first three releases, came at a time when Decca was experimenting with the notion of a country division for Coral. Producer Milt Gabler, who for a time headed the subsidiary for Decca, recalled, "Being a buddy of Paul's, I went down to Nashville and I asked him for help. 'Give me some writers that can give me some songs.' That's when Owen and I became friendly. But when I saw the songs that were coming in through Paul, I said, 'The son-of-a-gun is picking all the cream off himself and giving me his rejects.' "

While Coral was not as prestigious as Decca, Patsy actually had a better chance for airplay on Coral. Decca was notoriously tight allocating promotion money to its country and R&B divisions. But Coral, for a brief period, thrived. According to Gabler, "Our little label was hotter than Decca; we had more hits. The national sales manager of the company didn't want Coral to get too big because Coral was sold by outside distributors; it wasn't sold by the Decca sales department. We wanted to check and see why it was that independent distributors got more action from the disk jockeys than the Decca men did."

The explanation for Coral's success was "pay for play," which came to light in 1959 during the payola scandal. It had been common practice throughout the industry since the thirties to provide incentives to disk jockeys and program directors. McCall did in Patsy's case, at least in the beginning, probably deducting the costs from her income statement. Donn Hecht confirmed McCall's practices: "You know how you get airplay on a record with a new artist? It costs money. You just don't mail a record to a radio station. In those days if they had time slots at a radio station to play four new records a week, they would choose from a stack of that many hundred. So which got the airplay? The ones that took care of the disk jockey. That, purely and simply, was what the business was all about."

McCall's under-the-table incentives accompanied his favorite legitimate promotion medium, the ten-inch, extended-play (EP) dee-jay copy. He typically included new releases from three or four different artists on a record, along with a cover letter and a return postcard asking deejays to list their favorite performer and favorite song.

"We think PATSY CLINE sings better than any female vocalist we have heard," McCall wrote. "Her diction, sense of timing and phrasing are exceptionally good. We hope that you will agree with us and will give her first record a chance to be heard." Along with "A Church, a Courtroom and Then Goodbye," on which McCall, as "W. S. Stevenson," received a writer's credit, the EP included cuts by Rocky Bill Ford ("well known to your listeners for his records, 'Beer Drinking Blues,' 'You Know Doggone Well I Do,' 'Blowing Suds Off My Beer,'" read McCall's letter), the Stewart Family gospel group (their cut on "He'll Do for You" was covered by Patsy the following year) and other little-known acts.

Patsy traveled to the West Coast during the latter half of 1955 following the release, where she was booked into clubs and on television, including the "Hometown Jamboree," broadcast live from the El Monte Legion Stadium on KCOP-TV. West Coast C&W entrepreneur and producer Cliffie Stone produced the show, which produced among its regulars Tennessee Ernie Ford, whom Stone managed, and featured popular West Coast acts like Lefty Frizzell, Hank Thompson and the Maddox Brothers and Rose, as well as Nashville acts coming through town. Stone recalled that Patsy was traveling with Cowboy Copas on a tour at the time. "She was very easy to work with and kept very much to herself. She was not a big mixer—sort of quiet. In fact, she didn't particularly knock me out. She was just okay."

Patsy didn't forget her friends back home while she was on the road. Before she left she asked Winchester girlfriend Pat Smallwood what she wanted from California.

"I said, 'Send me a crate of oranges,' and she did, but it was a little teeny crate of twelve orange gumballs. The tag was bigger than the crate, and it said, 'Here's this crate of oranges I promised you from California.' I kept it on the whatnot shelf for years until it just deteriorated."

*T*HOUGH PATSY'S DEBUT as a record-ing artist caused hardly a ripple and remained stymied for almost two years, she began to develop a following in D.C. and the surrounding area largely as a result of her association with the Hick from Lizard Lick and the exposure he gave her on TV and radio.

In September 1955, Gay made his biggest push yet into live TV, and his plans included Patsy. The program was called "Town & Country Jamboree." It was a Saturday night extravaganza, broadcast from 10 P.M. to 1 A.M. from Turner's Arena, a wrestling arena (owned by Dale Turner's grandfather) that seated 4000. The fifteen-foot-high wrestling ring served as the stage. The show was sponsored by Gun-ther Beer, Otha Williams' Buick and L&M Cigarettes. Like Gay's daily afternoon program, the new show was hosted by Jimmy Dean, accompanied by the Texas Wildcats, along with a cast of thirty musi-cians, dancers, comics and even a ventriloquist. There were three girl singers: Patsy, Dale Turner and Mary Klick, who sang harmony and doubled on guitar.

Though Turner had seen Patsy perform earlier, they did not actu-ally meet until the night of the first broadcast. Patsy walked into the dressing room, thrust her hand toward her new colleague and said brightly, "Hi, I'm Patsy Cline."

The three girl singers who shared the same dressing room were compatible. Everyone felt like they were part of a close-knit TV fam-ily. "The girls" put to rest the long-held notion that women couldn't work around one another because of jealousy. Patsy, in particular, was generous in offering advice—if she liked you.

"We all got along great, without being in each other's hair," said Turner. "Patsy's style was flamboyant; she was a showman, whereas Mary was more demure and I was an ingenue. Back then my role

models were Patti Page, Joni James, Teresa Brewer and Kay Starr—
more so than the country girls, because there were no country girls to
speak of. When Kitty Wells came along we all began to dress more or
less the same way, not consciously trying to copy her—we just all went
to the same style, with the exception of Patsy, who went to the western cowgirl. And her mama made her outfits. Beautiful outfits—ah!—
with fringe this long. She would have looked silly in little fluffy
dresses. She wasn't built that way. It wasn't her style and she had
enough sense of style that she knew what was right for her. All three
of us were built well but different. I was kind of skinny; so was Mary.
Patsy was rounded. She was good-figured; she was full-busted. She
wasn't hippy—she wasn't big the way people think she was. She was
real good-looking, with that good-looking-type figure that did not
look good in pinafores.

"I never had to ask Patsy for advice. She gave it if she cared about
you and it was not a big hassle, and if she didn't care about you, she
would never say a word. Instead of trying to be better than you, she
always tried to help you. She'd tell you the tricks of the trade and she
could be pretty funny about it, too. I was a pretty good singer but I
didn't have any style. She had a punch and a style and a drive. I would
just sing a song like I heard it on the radio, which was fine, but Patsy
would say, 'You've got to let them know when you're ending a song,
Dale.' She'd always put a punch at the end of her songs. She'd either
slow it way down and soften it or get some more volume and take it
up higher. So she taught me that. I didn't play an instrument so I used
to keep time with my hand. Once she said, 'Don't do that. You look
like you're beating eggs, hoss.' "

"Patsy had something about her, and I was not jealous of her, but
envious," Klick offered. "I was shy. I'm sure a lot of times she mistook
it for my being a snob, but it wasn't that. That was just the way I was.
So I used to admire and envy the fact that she could be herself so
openly. There was never any, 'I'm wondering what they're going to say
about me,' like I would be thinking, or 'I wonder if I'm going to do
well,' or 'Gee, I wish . . . ' She had confidence. She was herself. She
knew what she had and at the time I don't think many people recognized it. Looking back now, you can see why her attitude could have
been so sure of herself. I was flattered one time when she called me
and wanted to know if I had a blouse she could borrow because she
was having her picture taken. So she came out to the house and
looked through what I had. Then someone took a picture of my husband and me and my little girl and Patsy, sitting on the front steps of
the house. I sort of had my head down but my eyes were looking
across at Patsy and I was halfway smiling. I remember later when Patsy

saw the picture she said, 'Why are you looking at me like that?' I told her I was sort of smiling at her because she had just said something to my little girl that made me smile when the picture was taken. Looking back, she was probably overly sensitive. I think deep down she would have been hurt if she thought that somebody didn't like her or accept her."

"Town & Country Jamboree" became one of the top-rated shows in the region, as word got around that the place to be on a Saturday night was Turner's Arena. Every Saturday night the wrestling arena drew capacity houses. The musicians, when they weren't on stage, mingled freely with the audience. The cameras caught everything, including the "mistakes." Whenever a scuffle would break out on the floor, the giant, dolly-mounted TV cameras panned from the music to the action. Once, as the entire cast sang "Ridin' Down to Santa Fe," the "Jamboree" theme song, the scaffold under the wrestling ring that served as the stage started to break apart. The cast slowly sank from view, like a country cruise aboard the *Titanic*. Not about to panic before thousands of viewers, everyone kept on singing.

Unlike the other acts, which were all human jukeboxes, Patsy "set the tone of an original artist," mixing her own 4 Star material with classic country tunes and pop standards such as those of her favorite female singers of the time: Kay Starr, Gogi Grant, Charline Arthur, Kitty Wells and Sophie Tucker. She often closed with a spiritual. Patsy burned on every song.

Said Turner: "She would do 'Your Cheatin' Heart' as a torch song, and then turn around and do 'Lovesick Blues' and bring the house down with her yodel on the end. She frequently closed the show with 'Life's Railway to Heaven.' Every song was an epic, even a silly thing like 'I love you honey/I love your money/but most of all I love your automobile.' She did songs you don't hear anymore, strange little songs, and she did them so well. Like 'Waltz of the Wind' or 'The Gods Were Angry with Me for Loving You.' She could do those kinds of ballads, the old-time ones. She was wonderful. She could sing anything. She had a punch to 'Pepper Hot Baby.' It wasn't all country-country back then; we mixed the pop charts and the country charts. We might do 'Teach Me Tonight' and then turn around and do 'Little Red Wagon.' The Patti Page stuff, the Teresa Brewer stuff. Patsy, back then, reminded me a lot of Kay Starr. She had that quality to her voice. But Patsy had even more to her voice, a nuance or something that no one could ever imitate or capture. In my opinion, she is the singer of the century in country music. Or the singer of the century, period."

Steel guitarist Marvin Carroll, whose musical heroes were Bob Wills, particularly Wills's steel player, Leon McAuliff, was a favorite of Patsy's. She affectionately called him "Big Daddy" and often asked him to kick off her numbers. She absolutely loved western swing, which made two of them.

"She knew I loved to play those songs. Patsy would do little fill-ins for the show, and they didn't care what she sang, so she would do the tunes I liked to play, like 'Faded Love' and 'San Antonio Rose,' so I could do the steel part. I'd kind of clown around with them until she'd say, 'Oh, come on, hoss, we're going to do it then, put it on there, let's do it.' And she'd more or less try to star me rather than herself. She'd stand off to the side and just watch me and smile from ear to ear. She enjoyed my playing as much as I enjoyed her singing, and every chance she got she'd let me play. She'd say, 'Hey, hoss, kick it off,' and she always wiggled her right foot when she sang. She had on those cowgirl boots and she'd lean back on the heel and wiggle her toe. She always stayed on top of the beat, and whatever she was singing, she always got it across to you, especially ballads. She could really make you feel a ballad. That was her ace in the hole. You'd get chills. We just loved playing behind her. She was never a stage hog. In fact, she was a humble sort of person in a lot of ways, especially about her talent. You got the impression that she really didn't know how great she was. She would never say she'd done something good enough. It was always, 'Let's do that again.' We'd do it, but I didn't see nothing wrong with the way she done it first. She just wanted to get the best out of herself."

Patsy told friends she was "busier than a cow's tail in fly season." Besides "Town & Country Jamboree" she continued to appear on Gay's daily show and his radio show, as well as making personal appearances around three states, including working with a local hillbilly band, the Kountry Krackers, every Friday night. She was using Kent Street more often than not as her home base, as much for its convenience—it was an hour and a half drive to D.C.—as to get away from Gerald, from whom her emotional estrangement was complete and her boredom total.

As one of Gay's featured artists, she no longer had to depend on Peer. Peer's wife, whose name was also Virginia, had filed for divorce during the summer, citing adultery as cause for the breakup. Peer had been pressuring Patsy for marriage. She was never more ready to break off the one-sided romance. Fortified with newfound self-confidence, in October she told him her decision. Their last gig together was a promotion for the Martinsburg car dealer who employed Peer.

Patsy was fond of Peer, certainly grateful for all his help. Years later, after she moved to Nashville and became a star, she invited him to be a guest in her home—an offer he accepted and they had a friendly visit. But at the time of the breakup, Peer was devastated.

"We were in the Howard Johnson's restaurant one night, having a snack after we had got through playing," said Roy Deyton. "Bill had already left his wife. And he was really broke up, just down to tears. He was so shook up that he didn't want to eat, didn't want to do anything. We sort of sympathized with him, told him he'd have to get over it. It was almost like he lost his will to live. But after a while he finally got over it. Guess he got to a point where he finally had some dignity. He started hanging around with different women, and then his wife took him back and he married her again."

In 1952, Red Foley took the "Grand Ole Opry" to new heights of popularity, as host of the Prince Albert segment, broadcast by WBC. As a result, Opry performers were booked further and further away from Nashville. The PA segment's sponsor, R. J. Reynolds, wanted as much mileage as possible for its advertising dollar, and put pressure on the WSM honchos to do something about publicizing those personal appearances. WSM came up with the idea of inviting deejays from all over the country to come and celebrate the Opry's twenty-ninth birthday. Thirty deejays showed up. The event proved to be a big party, prompting everyone involved to make the Deejay Convention, as it was called then (later renamed the Country Music Festival), an annual schmooze-fest. Liquor and food were provided by Decca Records, Martin Guitars and Acuff-Rose. The official entertainment was provided by the Opry. Thousands converged on Nashville, including every big name and no-name in country music. They took over the Andrew Jackson Hotel and spilled out into the Hermitage Hotel and the Noel Hotel, and all the motels and boarding houses in town. For once, the tightass Opry crowd really let down its hair in public. It didn't matter what happened—if you were country, you were family.

"It was probably the greatest freeloading blast in history," related veteran deejay Hugh Cherry. "There was all the booze, food and poontang that anybody could handle in the three-day period. The chicks would come in from miles around. It was 2500, 3000 people just milling around getting stoned, playing grabby-butt and everyone was dressed to the nines—from the shit-kickers from all the little-bitty towns to the women who got dolled up in the best clothes from the best dress shops in town."

Paul Cohen timed Patsy's second Coral release, "Turn the Cards Slowly" backed with "Hidin' Out," with the 1955 Deejay Convention, held in November, to take advantage of the once-a-year hoot 'n' holler. Virtually every deejay in the country who ever spun a country platter was there to party and, sober or not, conduct interviews with all the established stars as well as the promising new artists. Patsy would get maximum exposure for her debut record.

Prior to the convention, a write-up appeared in *Country Song Roundup*, a popular fanzine that juxtaposed glorified features on the artists with song lyrics and advertisements designed to separate wanna-be stars from their hard-earned money—the very ads that Patsy had responded to as an adolescent. Under the banner "Hillbilly Queens," along with her photo, was text that carefully promoted Patsy as a sweet, pert, God-fearing country girl. It started out: "Fifteen years ago, Virginia Hensley—known to you as Patsy Cline—Coral recording artist, began learning to sing and play the piano in Lexington, Virginia, where she attended school. Later the family moved to Elkton, Virginia, where she started taking piano lessons. When the family moved to Middletown, Virginia, singing at prayer meetings became a part of Patsy's life. Again, she moved—and this was to Winchester, Virginia."

Detailed as the high points of Patsy's budding career were work in the supper clubs around Winchester, Wally Fowler and the Opry audition and Bill Peer and the Melody Boys. The story concluded that Patsy's "prayers were answered in 1954 when Mr. William A. McCall of Pasadena, California, heard Patsy and a contract with Coral Records followed."

Done up in her glitziest and in a mood to party, Patsy, escorted by Gerald, thus keeping up the front of marital propriety, warmly greeted all the "hosses," bouncing from the Connie B. Gay Enterprises hospitality suite to the Decca suite. The high point of the weekend was the "Grand Ole Opry" on Saturday night, where, as a Coral artist, she had backstage access to all her favorite stars.

A few months before Patsy's feature in *Country Song Roundup* appeared, Elvis Presley was highlighted in the same magazine. The article described him as a "Folk Music Fireball," making note of his prodigious, all-American boy appetite ("at one sitting he ate eight Deluxe Cheeseburgers, two Bacon-Lettuce-Tomato sandwhiches [*sic*]—and topped it off with three chocolate milkshakes").

Patsy was a huge fan of Presley, who'd only just burst onto the national charts earlier in the year. He had been featured on "Louisiana Hayride," more or less a farm team for the Opry, and was touring the C&W circuit throughout the South under top-billed acts like Hank Snow and Faron Young.

Colonel Tom Parker, who booked the Carter Family, Minnie

Pearl, and Hank Snow, among others, was told about the ecstatic teenage audiences Presley attracted: "I don't know what the hell he's got but he goddamn sure stirs them up," said Gabe Tucker. "The Colonel says, 'Well, what's his name?' I said, 'Elvis Presley.' He said, 'Hell, I'm working like hell and ain't making no money. I gotta get me some young person that'll draw in the young people. I heard that name but is he any good?' I said, 'I don't know if he's good or not, but I know that people like him.'"

Parker started booking Presley and then took over as his manager. During the summer of 1955, MGM and Columbia made offers on Presley's contract with Sun. Paul Cohen was approached about signing him. Decca was the biggest label, and Cohen's colleague Milt Gabler had signed Bill Haley and His Comets to the label in 1954 after the band scored one hit on the Philadelphia-based indie, Essex. Haley was one of Decca's biggest acts, pop or country. But Cohen balked at the price for Elvis's contract, about $20,000 at that point. "There are eighty-five hundred guys in Nashville who sound just like this fellow," he supposedly said. "They're all the same. You can't understand them."

Connie B. Gay was another entrepreneur who was offered a piece of the Elvis action. The Colonel arrived at WMAL one day shortly after signing a booking arrangement with Elvis and Jamboree Attractions, the Madison, Tennessee, operation he ran with his main client, Hank Snow. "I've got a boy down here who wiggles his hips and everything. Don't sing too much or anything, but I'm going to give you a chance to get a piece of the action," he told Gay. Gay wasn't impressed. "No thanks," he replied. "I've got Dean and his boys. I've got my hands full. I don't need anything like that."

Patsy loved Elvis's image and his power and his music and pasted his picture prominently on the back cover of the scrapbook she kept that tracked her life and her career. "Yeah, she loved him," said Pat Smallwood. "She used to bop and boogie and get down with all his first records." By the time of the convention he had been elected "Most Promising New C&W Artist." Patsy longed to meet him but never did, though his presence was, indeed, palpable at that year's gathering. It would certainly have an impact on the development of Patsy's record career.

Some country music purists at the convention had launched an underground move to boycott Presley and what he represented, which was considered a slap at the revered form of traditional country music, which was simple and heartfelt and "says what you feel." The Nashville offices of *Billboard* had been receiving irate phone calls from Nashville-based country music executives and talent managers who demanded the "hillbilly kid" be removed from the best-selling country charts on the grounds that he was not truly representative of the country field. "He sings nigger music!" exhorted one executive.

By 1955, the buying habits of country fans had drastically changed, with the division between pop records and country becoming increasingly difficult to define. The fact that the country market was surviving to the degree it was could be attributed to the phenomenon of "crossover" records. Bill Haley and His Comets and Elvis Presley represented the youth crossover field, the largest group of record buyers in the country. They were mostly urban teenagers with eighty-nine cents in their pocket for a single and a taste for R&B. Eddy Arnold was an example of the crossover trend in the adult market, which favored the smoothness of the pop vocalists but the "heart" of white soul. For the bookers and promoters of traditional country music talent, like Gabe Tucker, "Rock and roll was eatin' our damn lunch; they damn near put us out of business."

At first the A&R men at the major labels were unconcerned about the new trend. Most of them thought race music and hillbilly music were "corny" and rock and roll was a passing fad, for "morons." "Jungle music . . . The most brutal, ugly, desperate, vicious form of expression it has been my misfortune to hear," Frank Sinatra supposedly opined. "The comic books of music," exhorted producer Mitch ("Sing Along with Mitch") Miller (who produced probably the schlockiest pop covers of country music in the fifties). But by the time of the 1955 Deejay Convention, the major labels were taking the youth market a bit more seriously. Industry-wide, there was a search for Elvis clones and labels encouraged established artists to record teen-appeal music. Marty Robbins did a country version of "That's All Right" and covers of R&B tunes like "Long Tall Sally" and "Maybellene." George Jones recorded "Rock It." Bill Monroe did a speeded-up version of "Blue Moon of Kentucky" after Elvis's cover of Monroe's 1948 original came out—a cover of a cover of his own tune.

The hard-liners' antagonism against rock and roll reached a crescendo at the 1955 convention. There was an "antiprogress attitude of some C&W deejays, who refuse to play anything even faintly tinged with a pop or rhythm and blues flavor, even when recorded by a C&W artist," *Billboard* reported. The same traditionalists balked at the former Tennessee Plowboy, Eddy Arnold, when he altered his simple, unaffected "Cattle Call" into a Hugo Winterhalter–orchestrated pop grooving. Arnold had sold out. The development of cheaper, portable radios, the evolution of tighter and tighter play lists of national top hit songs and TV accounted for the revolution that was shaking up the status quo: "Network TV, which still has relatively few C&W musical shows, has made Southern youngsters more pop-minded . . . and the kids are no longer buying the old-fashioned type of C&W record."

"[D]yed-in-the-wool hillbilly fans are dying off," concluded one A&R man, "and they were never very good record buyers anyway."

If Elvis Presley had thrown the purists at the convention into a tizzy, Connie B. Gay was prepared to meet the challenge head-on. If rock and roll was to become teenage dance music, then country music would be easy listening music for their parents. A few years later he told the *New York Times,* "Hillbilly music was banjos, guitars, fiddles. We've added a sweet touch to it and taken out the twang. You don't get the raucous plink, plank, plunk of a couple of decades ago," dismissing the first thirty years of country music with a "deprecatory wave of the hand."

Gay claimed to have been the first to drop the "W" from "C&W." "If hillbilly music is a Model T and pop music is a Cadillac, then country music would come along about Oldsmobile," he said. As if to "drive" his point home, Gay went into partnership with Gay Strawser Oldsmobile (no relation) of Warrenton, Virginia, to provide the entire "T&CJ" cast with new cars befitting their status as regional celebrities. "We all got them, and we all got them in different colors," Dale Turner recalled. "Connie arranged it all."

By January 1956, "Town & Country Jamboree" was the most popular homegrown musical TV show in the region, with an audience estimated at more than half a million. As one of Gay's featured soloists, Patsy was in the eye of the hurricane and she loved it. She had "divorced" Peer, was separated from Gerald, had two records out and was a TV star. She threw herself into life with gusto. The cover of the New Year's edition of the *Washington Star* "Televue" seemed to say it all: "JIMMY DEAN AND FRIENDS," read the caption. In the photo, Patsy and Dean sit side-by-side in their western duds in the foreground, while the demurely attired Turner and Klick stand behind them. Patsy toots a small toy horn. Even though her voice and charisma were perfect for the media image that Gay was creating for country music, at one point he tried unsuccessfully to soft-pedal her "hard" look, outfitting her in the Doris Day–country-cute mold. But decked out in ruffles and crinolines like the other girl singers, Patsy's soft, sexy curves looked doughy. She asked Dale Turner for her opinion, grumbling that she looked like a "damn butterfly."

"I remember because it was so funny. It didn't last more than two weeks, I can tell you that. She hated it—a pinafore, with a little apron and big wings. It was awful."

★   ★   ★

Patsy launched the new year with her second recording session, January 5. Despite the rumblings at the 1955 Deejay Convention, it was a straight country session, complete with Don Helms (who backed Hank Williams) on steel guitar and Tommy Jackson on fiddle. She chose two more Eddie Miller tunes (on which McCall took writing credits): "I Love You, Honey" and "I Don't Wanta."

It is hard to believe that the sophomoric "I Love You, Honey" was penned by the same person who wrote "Release Me." Miller said, "I Love You, Honey" was the first song he ever wrote; he was fourteen. In spite of the frivolous lyrics, Patsy pulled it off, belting out a Broadway finish.

"Come On In" was pure schmaltz, fifties TV sitcom music. It was one of Patsy's favorite songs and she made it her show opener. The lyrics make her affinity for the tune understandable. It is the essence of the Southern family romance: "If I had one wish I wish I could/Go back to my old neighborhood/Where the good folks they all love you as their own./When I'd go over to my neighbor's house/Knock on the door and they'd all sing out/'Come on in and sit right down and make yourself at home.' " The incongruity of the secrecy, the loneliness and the shame of her youth represented the ultimate in splitting off and repression. She loved good-time music. Singer-writer Tompall Glaser, who as part of the Glaser Brothers backed her when she was still singing it in Vegas years later, said, "I hated it. We didn't like New York coming in and messing with our songs."

"Come On In," backed with "I Love You, Honey," became Patsy's third release on February 5, on Coral. (The only weeper of the session, "I Cried All the Way to the Altar," was never released during her lifetime.) As with her first two singles, the single made a lackluster showing, even though she continued to promote her records on TV and in personal appearances.

Though in Winchester Patsy was something of a pariah, Elkton welcomed her like a prodigal daughter when she returned that spring for a show. "Met a lot of Hensleys I never thought would be alive," she wrote Jumbo Rinker afterward. "When I walked out on stage they were about to tear the building down. First intermission I went to the lobby to sell pictures and autographs. Sold pictures for 25 cents each. Made $25." She added, "When I sang 'Just a Closer Walk with Thee,' that stopped the show. Everybody in that theater was mopping tears."

Patsy had started to date Jumbo again, even though her separation from Gerald was not official. She went to Baltimore to visit him, where he had a job as a lounge player. She was still looking for love. "I got to have *someone* to love," she constantly told her friends. Jumbo had finally gotten a divorce. Since he was a free man, her flame reignited and she wrote him sweetly worded love letters, signing them "with love, Virginia," and showed him other signs of her affection.

"The place I was playing in Baltimore, they had the TV on and she was there singing, and they didn't believe I knew her," Jumbo recalled. "So when I was up to see her, I told her, 'They don't believe I know you. So when you go on Saturday night I'll turn to channel seven and you dedicate a song to me.' She said, 'I'm sorry, Jumbo, I can't do that.' 'Whaddaya mean you can't do that?' 'It's the policy—none of us can do that. It would mess up the program. Everything's been laid out and we gotta do it that way. But I'll tell you what: I can sing 'You Made Me Love You,' and at the end, where the song goes, 'You know you made me love you,' I'll look at the camera and point right at you.'

"So Saturday night the place was packed and we got channel seven on. Everybody's standing around watching. Finally she came on. And she went through her song. And I told them all what she was going to do. And I said, 'If I didn't know her, I wouldn't know what she was going to sing and what she was going to do. She's going to sing 'You know you made me love you,' and when she gets to the point where she sings 'you,' she'll point at the camera. And she did it. They were all flabbergasted; they couldn't believe it."

In March, the *Washington Star* singled Patsy out in a cover story in the Sunday *Star Magazine*. Headlined "Hillbilly with Oomph," the article, peppered with "hillbillyese," described Patsy as "the feminine singing sensation on 'Town & Country Jamboree' ": "Pahdner, there's a purty li'l thrush in a cowgirl outfit (she's more at home in boots than high heels) who's making city slickers pine for country music. In one word, Patsy Cline's brought something new to hillbilly singing—oomph!"

Interviewed for the story, Jimmy Dean succinctly offered, "When she punches out a hot tune, she sings all over," while Gay provided a more detailed analysis of her popularity, with a barely concealed dig at old-style country girl singing as personified by Kitty Wells. Patsy was a sex symbol, as the photo of her in the infamous short shorts that accompanied the text meant to say.

"Patsy has brought a brand of showmanship and rhythm to hillbilly music that's as welcome as a cool country breeze in springtime," Gay expounded. "We call her a country music choreographer. She creates the mood through movements of her hands and body and by the lilt of her voice, reaching way down deep in her soul to bring forth the melody. Most female country music vocalists stand motionless, sing with a monotonous high-pitched nasal twang. Patsy's come up with a throaty style loaded with motion and E-motion."

Despite the star treatment accorded Patsy by Gay in the article, in reality Gay believed, "You couldn't give away a female singer unless she was part of a show. Patsy was a great singer, but she wasn't worth a fart in a whirlwind when it came to drawing people at a school or armory. Dean had the name, but it was really the package show people came for. People bet on 'Connie B. Gay Presents' and I spent more money promoting myself than anyone."

Gay ran his empire "by the Golden Rule and Jeffersonian principles of democracy." He determined who sang the hit songs each week, established guidelines for costume and makeup, and checked the young cast's rambunctious tendencies by establishing an unwritten Town and Country Code of Behavior. "The atmosphere in D.C. was open and freewheeling, much more so than Nashville," said Dale Turner.

Everyone was having affairs, the most well known being that between Dean and Klick. No one bothered you as long as you maintained the wholesome image Gay demanded of his performers. But if anyone transgressed, even slightly, he treated the offender like a child in need of a spanking. Gay impressed onto Jimmy Dean the importance of punctuality, to the point where the bawdy Texan would pontificate to the rest of the cast, "A man's time is his greatest asset." Roy Clark was subsequently fired by Dean over tardiness.

"Connie took care of everything and told you what not to do," confirmed Dale Turner. "I went to a Marine Corps ball and there was a big fight there, and it was not a country music club, some rock and roll club. And he heard about it, and I was told not to go to that type of club again because he knew the image back then in the fifties of being on TV. There weren't that many people on TV; it was fairly new and you were well known if you were. So anything you did was reported. You were just below being a movie star, practically. And there was to be no dating other people on the show. Course, everybody just did what they pleased—they were just more careful about hiding it from him.

"It was like marriage vows were spoken and maybe taken seriously but they didn't bind you in any way. We were having not a loose lifestyle but it was free-spirited. Everybody was from nineteen to twenty-six and no one had settled down. It was the fifties and honky-tonks were fun and weren't sneered at at the time and alcohol wasn't sneered at, and there weren't any drugs so it wasn't mean. Back then D.C. was a wonderful place. You could be downtown at night, sitting in a park at two o'clock in the morning, talking, going to a diner. You never went home after a show. After you got off you went to a diner over in Arlington or somewhere and sat and talked or went out to the clubs and stayed up until daylight. That's the way you lived if you were in the music business, and you'd sleep most of the day. It was fun.

"We didn't tell each other what we were doing. We had our own affairs. At the end of the show I don't know where Mary went; she probably didn't know where I went. I was single, young and I went to the diners with whoever wanted to get together and sat and talked all night. Patsy never went to the diners in the Arlington area. I don't remember her going around at night after the show. We were together during the day, before the show. She would come over to the house, bring her clothes, she would have her hair up and we would ride around with some of our friends, some of the guys in the band. We would go to rehearsal, then go out to get something to eat. As showtime got closer, somebody would pick her up, a musician usually, and after the show she went home to Winchester."

Patsy occasionally clashed with Gay over the control she felt he had on her career. "Other people wanted to book her, and that would be a problem—Connie wanted complete control," related Dale Turner. "If he couldn't control you, he'd let you go." But just as irksome to Patsy was Gay's decision about certain aesthetic matters, such as the pinafore episode and the square dancing segment of the show in which he wanted Patsy to appear. She finally put her cowboy boot–shod foot down.

Patsy, along with Turner and Klick, were expected to join the Paul Jones dancers for a round or two of do-si-dos, which Dean would jauntily oversee as caller. Patsy felt it was beneath her dignity as a solo vocalist and said it made her feel "like a whore." But ultimately she used her boots as a successful excuse for getting an exemption from the proceedings: the other dancers were clomping all over her feet and scuffing her white shit-kickers.

George Hamilton IV joined the "T&CJ" cast during the summer of '56. He had just finished his first year at the University of North Carolina and fancied himself a country singer, but had a surprise first hit with a pop teen ballad, "A Rose and a Baby Ruth," thereby launching his career as a crossover artist. Gay invited him to come to D.C. initially as a replacement for Dean when Dean was booked away. Gay quickly ascertained Hamilton's teen appeal and in 1956 became his manager. As a teen idol Hamilton played the same bill as Buddy Holly or Gene Vincent at the Brooklyn Paramount and on Dick Clark's "American Bandstand" TV show, then would return to D.C. to work the "Town & Country Jamboree" and tour clubs with Dean, Patsy and the Texas Wildcats. His trademark was a blue blazer with "IV" stitched in gold on the breast pocket, the humor of which did not go unnoticed by Patsy: she good-naturedly dubbed him "Number" and kidded him about being a "college boy." Bemused by his bashfulness, she would nudge him in the ribs now and then with some bit of advice like, "Hey, why don't you tell 'em a couple of jokes now and then; they like to feel like you're tryin' to get with 'em," or "Hey, chief, lighten up. You're just out there singin' them songs. You got to crack a few funnies now and then."

Hamilton recalled: "I was a skinny, awkward, nineteen-year-old at that point, didn't have much self-confidence and had never been much of a ladies' man. Patsy had a very forceful personality, was very confident and self-assured. She was not a shrinking violet by any means. She tended to be in charge. She used to tease me a lot about girlfriends or whether or not I had a date. The musicians would usually chitchat with the ladies at the bars and she used to tease me about how she didn't see me dancing with many of the girls at the clubs. I tended to be a wallflower. I think she probably thought of me as kind of wet behind the ears and more than a little bit green. She'd say, 'Hey, Number, did you score tonight?' I'd say, 'Aw, come on, Patsy,' and blush and she'd say, 'Hey, there's a lot of chicks tonight on the prowl and I never see you making time with the ladies.' "

Patsy thought it was strange that anyone who was getting all that "book learning"—Hamilton had transferred to American University—would want to be a hillbilly singer.

Hamilton explained: "The first time I can remember hearing anybody singing 'Life's Railway to Heaven' on stage it was her. It was my granddaddy's favorite song and I loved my granddaddy a lot; he was a railroad man. I hadn't heard anyone sing that song in a long time and I heard her singing it on the "Town & Country Jamboree." I was really impressed by that and was talking to her a little about country gospel music. As far as the college stuff went, she would say, 'I guess it's all right to get your education and have something to fall back on, but you really need to make up your mind what you're going to be and do. If you want to be a country singer, you need to live it. And don't get above your raisin'. These people out here are down-home folks and they don't want anybody highhattin' 'em. They're really not interested in your college degree if you get one. They want you to give 'em some music you like and entertain 'em.' "

Patsy returned to the Quonset Hut on April 22 for her third session. The Elvis juggernaut was sweeping the industry, its raucous energy and lack of remorse running roughshod all over country music's cherished terrain of retribution and guilt. The departure from established tradi-

This hit-or-miss approach to making records sometimes led to heated "discussions" between Patsy and her producer. Patsy wanted and needed hits as badly as Bradley did, and was just as unsure about how to get them, but would fight for what felt right for her. And what got her applause was good-time music—western swing, up-tempo endings, growls and yodeling—all at which she was an absolute master. She would insist on her way, and duked it out like a real Hensley. She was the only artist who could clear a studio out. "We would tremble," remembered Harold Bradley. "I wasn't used to women opening up like that and it offended me. I'm from the old school, you see? Sometimes the first hour of a session nothing happened but these 'discussions.' "

Owen Bradley soon discovered that the best way to handle his cowgirl was to stand firm, but not too firm. You could reason with her but you couldn't drive her an inch. "If she could dominate me, she would," Bradley said, "but I was pretty stubborn too, and if I didn't allow her to do that, she was a pussycat."

At the April session, Patsy proved beyond a doubt she could work on the same side of the fence as the rockabillies. The session started out with "Stop, Look and Listen," a two-and-a-half-minute discourse on rock and roll and the atomic age: "First there was swing, then the bunny hop/Now the rhumba, samba and then the bop/I don't know what's coming next/Think this old world's in a terrible fix."

She did a 180-degree turn back to traditional country with an Eddie Miller tune, "I've Loved and Lost Again," with a slightly risqué lyric that couldn't have been more apropos to Patsy's own life: "To be true to one alone don't seem to matter anymore/They tell you're out of style unless you've had three or four."

"Dear God" described Patsy's own spiritual dilemma through the Southern dichotomy of sin and salvation. Patsy gave it a totally convincing reading: "I go to church on a Sunday, the vows that I make, I break them on Monday/The rest of the week I do as I please, then come Sunday morning I pray on my knees."

"He Will Do for You," another gospel number, rounded out the session. In one four-hour session they'd covered the gamut—rock, country and sacred music. They were aiming all over the place, hoping one would hit.

tion continued to drive the country music establishment berserk. The debate raged almost daily in *Billboard*: "The disk business thrives on excitement. Any new trend in repertoire should be given a fair trial. If it has any merit, it is likely to add to the all-round quality and salability of c.&w. music. To those who would detract or belittle r.&b. as an influence in the country field, let us caution them not to make the same foolish mistake that embarrassed so many music men in the pop field."

". . . Altho [*sic*] the opposition to rock and roll in the country field is still strong in some quarters, the influence of the new material is gaining tremendous headway. An increasing number of artists and labels are latching onto this type of performance."

Elvis was already seven weeks on top of the charts with "Heartbreak Hotel." *Look, Life* and *Newsweek* hailed him ("A Howling Hillbilly Success," "Hillbilly on a Pedestal," "He can't be . . . but he is"). The Elvis phenomenon set off a race in search of "another Elvis Presley." Victor, Presley's new label, came out with "the female Elvis Presley," Janice Martin; Mercury brought out Eddie Bond and Roy Moss; MGM signed Marvin Rainwater. Capitol's A&R chief Ken Nelson brought Gene Vincent and the Blue Caps to Owen Bradley to record "Be-Bop-A-Lula," joking that he was worried he'd be fired for signing a bunch of guys who "looked like they were in the French Navy." At Decca, Paul Cohen signed ten-year-old Brenda Lee, whose first session resulted in "BIGELOW 6-200," one of the finest rockabilly performances of the time. Another Decca experiment in the youth market was nineteen-year-old Buddy Holly. Cohen sent him to Bradley to record and the resulting session was, in Bradley's words, "sort of a disaster." Cohen and Bradley thought he should be recorded country but Holly had a different idea in mind. "We thought he was a real smart aleck kid," Harold Bradley related. "He'd come over and tell us how to play. We didn't know what he was trying to do; we thought he wanted to be country. We all knew how to do that."

Patsy's first three singles had flopped. It was decided to try her out as a rocker. Bradley was groping, trying to come up with the right "formula."

"We were aiming all over the place to make sure we'd hit," he admitted. "She was sort of rejected because of our work with Kitty Wells. That was the criteria—if you were going to be country, you had to go in that direction. Kitty was a true country singer. Patsy had the kind of personality, the kind of thinking that a country act had, but she also had some of the influence of Kay Starr, maybe Jo Stafford. I don't think she sounded like those singers but I think she had listened to them."

Chapter Eleven

*I*F YOU WERE SUPERSTITIOUS, Friday, April 13, 1956, was not a day to turn your bed, begin a voyage, give birth, die or get married. Bad luck or not, it was the day Patsy met Charlie Dick, whose name was as ill-fated as her own.

Charlie was a Winchester neighbor whose background mirrored Patsy's in some very spooky ways. Born two years after Patsy (under the sign of the Twins) on May 24, he, too, was the oldest of three children and, also like her, underwent a major life crisis at the age of fifteen when his father abandoned the family. In Charlie's case, the circumstances were possibly even more traumatic. It wasn't money, they said. Leland Dick, Charlie's father, had a good job as a supervisor at the National Fruit Company. One night, while all three of the Dick boys were upstairs in bed, Leland sat quietly at the kitchen table, pointed the barrel of a .22 flush against his temple and ended his life. Rumor had it he'd been having an affair with a woman in town and had grown despondent following an argument with her earlier that day.

Charlie's mother, Mary, a quiet, heavyset woman who wore thick eyeglasses, carried on as best she could. She raised her three boys on her own, supplementing her monthly social security payments by taking in ironing. But if that weren't enough tragedy for one family, three years before Leland Dick shot himself, Mary Dick gave birth to twin boys, one of whom was severely retarded and needed round-the-clock care. While Leland Dick had a good job, Mary Dick was able to care for the child at home on National Avenue. But two years after her husband's death, Mary had no alternative but to institutionalize him.

Charlie Dick was known as Charles at home and to all his relatives. As a boy he was remembered as likable, outgoing and industrious, with a paper route he attended faithfully. As a teenager, however, his personality became wild. Though the Dick clan were all teetotalers, Charles started drinking at a young age. He dropped out of Handley High in the tenth grade, like Patsy. Not long afterward, he got a job as a linotype operator, a skilled position that required setting the hot metal presses for Harry Byrd's *Winchester Evening Star.*

Somewhere along the line he became known as Charlie; one family source said it was Patsy who first applied the name. "Sober, he was a nice guy," said Johnny Anderson. "He'd do anything for you." In social gatherings with the guys he was "hail fellow well-met, a lot of fun to be around," drinking too much whiskey, getting into fights and car wrecks and otherwise giving meaning to the word *redneck.* When Charlie drank too much, which he usually did when Patsy's friends saw them together, he justified his surname or, as Patsy would say, "Charlie Dick—and he is one."

"He's a Jekyll and Hyde," said Johnny Anderson. He can be a nice guy. But when he gets drunk, he's nasty. He's a bigmouth, a braggart. He knows more than anyone else, I guarantee you. If he gets drunk, you're a son-of-a-bitch and he's a king, man."

Charlie was charming the way an ole boy can be sometimes the night he met Patsy at the Berryville Community Center, where, backed by the Kountry Krackers, she sang every Friday from 9:30 P.M. to 1 A.M. When Charlie asked who she was, he was told she was none other than Patsy Cline, a star on the TV show in Washington, D.C. Cocksure, snapping his gum, he approached her between sets and asked her to dance. Accustomed to come-ons from fans, Patsy assessed him and came back with a ready response, which Charlie later recalled: "I'm not allowed to dance while I'm working." He was smitten. Later that night he saw her dancing with a short, stocky man. "Who is *he*?" he wanted to know. "Oh, that's Gerald Cline—her husband."

A few weeks later Charlie was back at the Berryville Community Center and so was Patsy, this time without a husband in tow. With the rhythmic shuffle of Ray Price on the jukebox, once again he propositioned her for a dance. This time she two-stepped into his arms.

A week later Patsy was out with Jumbo Rinker when, without any preliminaries, she blurted out what had obviously been weighing heavily on her mind:

"I'm going to tell you something you're not going to want to hear."

"What's that?"

"I met a fellow last week and I been going out with him."

"That's your privilege."

Patsy plunged onward: she told him she was in love.

Sol Hensley.
Collection of Herman Longley, Jr.

PFC Sam Hensley, circa 1918.
Collection of Herman Longley, Jr.

Hensley Family, circa 1918. Sam Hensley is seated second from right, second row. Wynona Jones is at the end on his left. Sol Hensley and wife Margaret seated top row center.

Collection of Herman Longley, Jr.

Patsy at about age eight in a family photo. Sam Hensley is seated far right with Sam, Jr. ("John") on his lap. Hilda is seated on grass, far right.
Collection of Nellie Patterson

Seventh grade photo. Ginny is standing center row, third from right.
Collection of Margaret Jones

Ginny, 1948, in her Grant's Drugstore uniform.
Collection of Margaret Jones

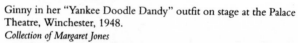

Ginny in her "Yankee Doodle Dandy" outfit on stage at the Palace Theatre, Winchester, 1948.
Collection of Margaret Jones

Contestants for the amateur show at the Palace Theatre, Winchester, 1948.
Ginny is in front row, fourth from right.
Collection of Margaret Jones

Ginny at age 17.
Collection of Margaret Jones

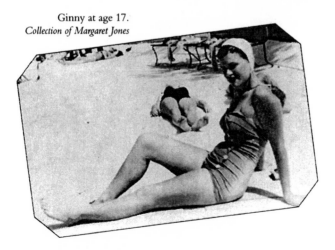

Patsy and Jumbo Rinker, about 1955.
Collection of Margaret Jones

Patsy, Dale Turner, and Mary Klick at Turner's Arena for the *Town &
Country Jamboree*, 1956.
Collection of Dale Turner Westbery

"The girls" posing for *Town & Country Jamboree* sponsor Gunther Beer:
Mary Klick, Patsy, Dale Turner.
Collection of Mary Klick Robinson

Patsy Cline and George Hamilton IV, backstage at Turner's Arena, 1956.
Collection of Herman Longley, Jr.

Sitting on the porch on
South Kent Street, 1956.
Showtime Music Archive

"I hope you're not mad. Hit me like a ton of bricks, Jum. I never thought it was going to happen. I hate to tell you this."

Jumbo was one of those men who never knew what to do when women got emotional. "Ah, Ginny, I want you to tell me. I want you to be real happy."

Patsy could cry easily. She still cared for Jumbo. Could they be friends?

"Don't be like that," he clumsily tried to comfort her. She misinterpreted his reassurances as cavalier: "I thought you cared?" she said between sniffles.

"You know I care for you. As long as we've known each other, what we've been through and the hard times, how can it not be?"

From the beginning, hardly a day went by where Patsy and Charlie didn't either see or talk to each other on the phone. She was intoxicated with love: Charlie was her new man and as such he admired her, protected her, was proud of her and quite literally identified with her. She was a feisty loner, the cowgirl to his outlaw. Describing his attraction, he said, "We were the same kind of person."

Eros, the sexual love of another, the love of somebody who moves you, is invariably a little narcissistic. Patsy, too, was overcome with the magnetic physical attraction of meeting the personification of her animus. She always had a weakness for the underdog and here he was, the town bad boy. "I finally found a man and he's all man," she proudly announced to her friends. The relationship was the perfect setup for the sexual victimization of her youth, and the consequences would be disastrous. "He wasn't my pick of the litter and I didn't see how he'd be hers," said her girlfriend, Patsy Lillis.

"A lot of people didn't like him," observed Pat Smallwood. "He drank a lot. I didn't care for him. He was crude, very crude."

Hilda's dislike of Charlie was instant and instinctive. She worried about Ginny—it was always Ginny she thought about, even before herself. She tried to talk some sense into her daughter but it was useless. She was flying. She was in love with love.

Since Charlie was unwelcome in the Hensley home, Patsy asked one of her pals in Winchester to help her move her belongings out of the home in Frederick and into a trailer she rented in a trailer court outside of Winchester. It was over with Gerald, as far as she was concerned. She was eager to put the disappointments and failure of her marriage behind her.

"She and Gerald decided to agree to disagree in my living room," recalled Punk Longley. "She had a show opening that night and Gerald was driving. They had already been separated, back and forth, back and forth. They came here and stopped. Hilda and Sylvia and John were with them. Hilda and Sylvia and my wife and I were in the kitchen, Gerald and Patsy stayed in the living room, and she got up and she come by me and whispered in my ear, 'Gerald and I want to get a divorce, Punk.' She took it with a grain of salt. I never heard a word from the living room. She said, 'I'm going to see a lawyer the first of the week,' and she did."

Despite his phlegmatic outward appearance, Gerald did not take the divorce with a grain of salt: he was "brokenhearted," one friend said. He'd never known anyone as passionate, as full of fire, as Patsy. After the divorce he started to drink and his weight ballooned. "What do you do when you love a bitch like that?" he wailed. Though nothing was going to get in the way of her and her true love, Patsy felt guilty about her failed first marriage and, as they always did, her emotions found their most sincere form of expression in her music. Recalled Pat Smallwood: "She was singing 'A Church, a Courtroom and Then Goodbye' around that time. That was the one song that was part of her life. It was so sad when she sang that."

Those who knew her insisted that Patsy was not a user. "I'll tell you how Patsy felt," said Becky Miller. " 'I never intentionally started out to hurt anybody. I didn't really think it would matter that much, but it did. And I can't go back and change it, but I can be sorry inside.' That's about the way she would explain something. She really never, ever wanted to hurt anybody. She was a very giving person, let me tell you. She'd give you the clothes off her back. She wasn't stingy. I have to think that maybe this is why she died so soon—because she was so giving. And she had given all her life. And people used her. I think Bill Peer used her, and I'm not too sure about Cline and I think her family used her. But you just get so that you turn the other cheek, and that's what Patsy did, even though she knew."

Through Connie B. Gay's connections Patsy rode in the Apple Blossom Parade once again in May 1956. The grand marshall was Bert Parks, and celebrities like Cyd Charisse, Betty Furness, Mrs. Woodrow Wilson and former Virginia governor Colgate Darden graced the convertibles that preceded the white-gloved and -gowned queen and her court of princesses. Once again, Patsy's name was omitted from the official program book, though she rode on the back of a red and white Oldsmobile convertible draped with a banner that proclaimed, "Town & Country TV Star PATSY CLINE. Courtesy Gay Oldsmobile, Warrenton, Va." This time, Patsy brought her own court: she'd invited her sister Sylvia to ride in the car with her. Afterward, she and Charlie stopped by the Dick home on National Avenue to say hello to Charlie's family. Mel Dick was only nine years old and vividly recalled the day he first met Patsy.

"I had been to the parade and I come running in, and she was sitting at the kitchen table with my mother. Well, I just put on the brakes—it scared me. I thought, 'Here's a cowboy woman sitting in my kitchen—what is this?' She seemed just bigger than life. She had ridden in the parade and she had fringe and she had boots. I never seen anybody like that in my life and I was afraid. She said, 'How are ya,' and she had this big voice. I was startled. She just dominated the room even then. Her family was always loud and boisterous—ours wasn't, except for Charles. You would think Charles belonged to them more than our family. She just took over a room. She was loud and when she walked she knew exactly where she was going; she didn't piddle across the room."

After she met Charlie, a self-acknowledged "partying man," Patsy gave many the impression she was a party girl. Her bravado may have seemed natural but some people saw through the swagger. "She left the impression she was always ready for a good time, but a lot of times people who leave the impression that they're party girls and 'ready to roar,' as Patsy would say, didn't do nearly as much roaring as talking about it," observed George Hamilton.

Patsy's bawdiness was legendary among the "T&CJ" cast. There was the cussing. "She could read you the riot act with an assortment of four-letter words that would curl your hair," Hamilton remarked.

"We were on our way to a date that Connie had arranged in Charlotte and we were all in the same car," recalled Mary Klick. "She had to stop to go to the bathroom, and I guess she was having her period and—you know Patsy—she said, 'Hey, hoss, stop at the next fillin' station, will you? I got to change my firecracker.' She really had a way with words."

"We wouldn't say things in front of Dale that we might say in front of Patsy," said Billy Grammer, then a sideman. "It was no disrespect to Patsy, but Patsy, she'd belt it right back at you."

If Patsy was ticked off, everyone knew it. She liked people who were straight with her. Anything that seemed hypocritical or phony was "B.S." "She didn't like for people to put her on," Hamilton said. "She could smell a line a mile away. Big-talking guys who thought they could sort of bowl her over and make time with her with a big line of gab, she saw through that in a hurry. I often heard her refer to people as 'Chief.' She'd say, 'Hey, chief, who you kiddin'?'"

Patsy got particularly irked if anyone gave her the girl singer treatment, Hamilton noted. "She had a short fuse if a club owner or a dance hall owner would try to get her to go out and dance with the audience or get her to mingle. They expected the girl singers to go out and be nothing more than dime-a-dance girls, and Patsy wouldn't go along with that."

If Patsy was "a pretty bawdy broad at times," as Jimmy Dean offered, on stage she was every inch a diva. It took courage to be Patsy Cline, and she was a queen, but the two aspects of her personality often seemed so incongruous. According to fellow soloist George Hamilton, "She always carried herself like a star. She didn't high-hat me or anybody, but she was not a shrinking violet and there was never any pretense of being sort of shy and retiring like country girls were supposed to be back then. She stood erect, and she had a sort of regal quality, an air of stardom about her. Even way back before she was ever on the Godfrey show she acted like a star, and I don't mean an egomaniac or stuck-up. There was a certain reserve. When you approached her, you had the feeling that you were talking to somebody you'd better respect. And if you didn't, she'd be gone."

Recalled Billy Grammer, "Sing? Good gracious—we didn't have any problem putting our heart in our music because you could get with it when she could get with it. She was easy to work with. She didn't sing like a woman. She belted it like a man. She had that big broadness to her voice. She could flat get with it, and the people out there could sense it—they knew that this wasn't just a little Mickey Mouse feminine voice up there. She always said we made her get with it, and I used to say, 'You don't know, Patsy, the chicken or the egg. We're not saying which came first, but you're the mainstay out here.' She was thankful for the band that we were. And we were good. The boys were homey and down-to-earth and could flat get with it."

Patsy's attraction to a redneck like Charlie seemed a paradox to many. "They didn't look like a match," noted Mary Klick. "I would have expected her to not pick up with anybody after her marriage and that thing with Bill Peer. You would think she would have gone full-fledged for a career and not gotten tangled with anybody, just passed everybody on her way up. She really must have fallen hard for Charlie to stop along the way and give him the time of day."

"She associated with the wrong class of people," observed Johnny Anderson. "You don't pull yourself up associating with Charlie Dick. Now Gerald Cline, she could have. He was in the better class of people, but that didn't suit Patsy. He was too mediocre. She liked Charlie Dick's type. She wanted to live in that class but she didn't want people to put her in that class."

Patsy and Charlie started battling almost immediately, but they didn't let that stop them because they were "so crazy about one another." He accompanied her to Turner's Arena every Saturday night, and was in fine fettle by the time they arrived, having been drinking heavily beforehand. Patsy would drink a little along with him. It "loosened her up," she told friends. Booze brought the fight out in both of them. "Charlie, when he come along, it was a pretty volatile experience," recalled Grammer. "I seen them go at it tooth and nail in the back in the dressing room, and I'm talking fisticuffs."

Patsy was baffled by Charlie's nasty streak, and for the duration of their relationship she would try, unsuccessfully, to control his drinking. At the same time, "She wanted to show him she was just a little bit stronger than he was. Anything he could dish out, she could take," said Patsy Lillis.

"Making up" became just as scorching an affair as their fights, a pattern common in situations where children grow up with attention, love, sex and violence intertwined. Patsy told everyone, "He's my man, and he's *all* man."

Said Pat Smallwood, "I don't think she ever loved anybody like Charlie Dick. I mean, that was a romance. A lot of people didn't like Charlie. He drank a lot. I didn't care for him. I don't think he treated her right. We were at a dance one night at Rockwood Hall. And she worked with the Kountry Krackers that night. And we had been to a store that day and had bought two of those crinolines, you know? To make the skirts stand out. I was sitting at the table and she was singing on stage, and I looked over at the door and here he come in with his pants legs rolled up and her crinoline on and stood in front of the stage with a bottle of beer. I'll never forget it because she was just devastated. He was crude, very crude. He would do a lot of things to embarrass her in public places when she was trying to make a go at it and trying to make a living at it. I seen her give it right back to him; she wasn't afraid of no man; she wasn't afraid of nothing. She'd argue with him; she'd scrap with him. But it still upset her because she loved him."

On June 16 she returned to Nashville to appear as a special guest on the prestigious PA segment of the "Grand Ole Opry." Patsy was introduced by diminutive "Little" Jimmy Dickens whom Patsy, at five foot eight inches in her slanty heeled cowboy boots, towered over. Instead of singing her current release, Patsy revived a sentimental favorite, "A Church, a Courtroom and Then Goodbye," and following a comedy routine by Minnie Pearl, Rod Brasfield and Dickens, she returned to sing the weeper "I've Loved and Lost Again," the forthcoming release. As a concession to the staid Opry, she reworked the lyrics, bringing the numbers down on the bridge; instead of "They say you're out of style unless you've had three or four"—referring to affairs—she substituted, "unless you've had one or more."

Cohen played both sides of the fence in an effort to figure out what niche she fit into. On July 27, he released, "I've Loved and Lost Again," backed with a rocker, "Stop, Look and Listen," on Decca, the label on which she would appear for the duration of her career. Neither side caught on.

That month, at the invitation of host Faron Young, she taped six songs for two 15-minute military recruitment programs for the Navy called "Country Hoedown." The format was long enough for three or four songs, a couple of commercials and some canned dialogue between host and guest. The choice of material was left to the artist and Patsy's choices revealed her own likes: "Turn the Cards Slowly," "Come On In" and "Stop, Look and Listen," on which she playfully goosed Young's band, the Country Deputies, at the tag: "That's what I said boys—stop." She juxtaposed her own material with versions of "Yes, I Know Why," a hit for Webb Pierce earlier that year, Sonny James's hit, "For Rent (One Empty Heart)," and "The Wayward Wind," a smash by one of her favorite pop singers, Gogi Grant. To Young, Patsy seemed unfazed that her recording career hadn't taken off at that point: "Patsy, back then, she was like Elvis Presley. Nobody was going to keep her from making it. She was going to make it. Once people heard her, she was going to be a star and there was no use worrying about it."

By the fall of 1956, she had four singles out and all of them were clunkers. For Bradley, it was a dilemma. Patsy was not commercial for her time. She had "sort of a pop sound" but Kitty Wells was still what everybody thought of when they thought country. As Bradley put it: "How do you make her a successful country singer when you're releasing her songs as country records, not as pop records? If you would have released them as pop records our company would have thrown them in the ash can. They didn't want them. The only way we could get them to put them out was to do country songs. That's not the way it is now, but that's the way it was. So we kept trying to put her in the niche with Kitty Wells and Jean Shepard."

With twelve of the sixteen sides required by her original 4 Star contract completed, Patsy had one more session to prove herself. McCall left no doubt as to the precarious position she was in: "I'm going to lose my financial ass here unless I either come up with a hit for this girl or I dump her," he declared.

Donn Hecht was an L.A.-based lyricist whose musical sensibilities ran to Kay Starr, Pat Boone, the McGuire Sisters and Nat "King" Cole, to whose A&R departments he had been pitching songs without much success. Hecht was counting change to make bus fare in order to get to Hollywood and back to bang on doors and was desperate enough to sign a seven-year contract with McCall, who paid him $600 a month as a staff writer as well as to doctor songs from the 4 Star catalog, for which Hecht received a share in the "W. S. Stevenson" credit. Having some familiarity with legal procedures, Hecht also helped keep McCall within the bounds of legitimacy.

Hecht's first official assignment at 4 Star was to go through demos, pick a star and write a hit. He had already listened to hundreds of mostly hillbilly artists and groups and was beginning to regret his decision to go to work for McCall when McCall played him one of Patsy's demos, claiming, "I have this gut feeling she'll be immortal but I don't know what the hell to do."

"Before the record made ten revolutions I almost fell off my chair," Hecht recalled. He told McCall the "problem" with Patsy was that she was not a country singer. "You've got to have her do pop stuff with a strong blues effect, because when this girl sings, she's crying all the time—you can detect the tears," he said.

In 1954, Hecht and Alan Block, a collaborator on many songs, had written "Walkin' After Midnight," a B-flat blues, with Kay Starr in mind. Hecht pitched Starr's A&R department to no avail. "Nobody wanted a 'Walkin' song," Hecht said. It was languishing when Hecht dug up the lead sheets and, with Patsy's voice still ringing in his ears, he hocked his furniture to pay for a demo session on which he used pop singer Lynn Howard. Hecht played the demo for McCall, who was convinced "Midnight" was a winner. He called Patsy to play it for her over the telephone.

"I stop to see a weeping willow crying on his pillow/Maybe he's crying for me." To Patsy, the lyric didn't have any "balls." She said so to McCall. Patsy insisted on picking her own material and McCall apparently let her, as long as it was 4 Star. But on this song McCall would not take "no" for an answer, and before they concluded the conversation, he proposed that Patsy come out to California, where the discussion over "Midnight" resumed.

Through McCall, Patsy was booked for club appearances and TV shows including "Town Hall Party," a West Coast version of "Town & Country Jamboree." The cast included Tex Ritter, Merle Travis, Wes Tuttle, Eddie Dean and Joe and Rose Lee Maphis, as well as appearances by visiting Nashville artists like Johnny Cash, Hank Snow, George Jones and Carl Perkins. At the 4 Star offices, Patsy was introduced to Hecht. The songwriter recognized her from her previous trip to the West

Coast. She was "[n]ot beautiful, not plain, she walked like a dancer, and something played off her that made her stand out from the crowd."

"Everybody made fun of her," Hecht observed. "She was not a cover girl sexpot. The country people said she didn't sing country music because she didn't sing through her nose, and the pop people felt she was too country to be pop. I once told Patsy, 'You're going to be known as the Hemingway of this business, although you're not a writer, because you're going to have a new style that will completely change the country music field all over the world.' She laughed and said, 'You don't know what the hell you're talking about.'"

Patsy stubbornly refused to budge an inch on "Midnight." "She did not like the song; she did not want to record it because it was not a country song," Hecht recalled. "She had picked everything she had recorded and so far nothing sold. So Bill says, 'Look, we've got to stop this bullshit, Patsy. It's not like I haven't let you do what you wanted to do. It hasn't happened. So let me do something now. It's my money, you know?' We were into the pastry at the time. McCall kept pastries and coffee in the office and she loved that stuff. He said, 'I'll tell you what: I'm going to leave you guys and you can argue with each other, and I'm going to come back and we can talk some more and whatever you decide to do, the hell with it.'

"She could never pronounce my name. I'd say, 'It's like Hector without the O-R.' So when Bill comes back she says, 'I'll tell you what we decided to do, me and Mr. Hector without the O-R: we're going to put out a single, and we're going to put this nothin' pop song on one side and on the other side I get to pick a song that *I* like.' "

McCall bit into a donut. Patsy promised him if she was wrong about "Midnight," she would "never argue about material again."

McCall played the devil's advocate: "What if neither side sells?" Patsy cocked her head to one side like she did whenever she wanted to emphasize something: "You can get yourself another singer."

The next session was scheduled to coincide with WSM's Deejay Convention, held the weekend of November 8, 9 and 10. Patsy had a new cowgirl outfit and a new boyfriend on her arm, and she was ready to roar.

So were the 1800 glib, thirsty deejays who attended, along with a few thousand more singers, writers, managers and industry types. As always, the hospitality suites were stocked with enough booze to float a battleship. The featured speaker, the distinguished, urbane Goddard Lieberson, president of Columbia Records' "Masterworks" division, was a closet hillbilly music fan. He was accompanied by Columbia's A&R boss, Mitch Miller.

Thanks to crossover sales driven by "the younger element," including artists as diverse as Carl Perkins, Bill Haley, Johnny Cash, Marty Robbins, Gene Vincent, Roy Orbison and George Hamilton IV, the industry bragged that 40 percent of sales of all records were "country." Assaying the commercial importance of country music was easier than defining it, however. It could wear a zoot suit, a navy blue blazer, a white sport coat and a pink carnation or Nudie's rhinestone-encrusted Cherokee cowboy suit, as long as it registered in the upper twenty on the Dow Jones ticker of the popular music field. In the old days of country music, once an artist hit, he could ride a ten-, twenty- or thirty-year wave of guaranteed stardom. The development of the chart system and the evolution of Top 40 programming changed all that. The new hit makers might surface for one smash single and disappear, distinguished only as one-hit wonders.

The visiting New York executives played it diplomatically with the country crowd, remembering the Fort Apache stand of the contingent of ornery traditionalists the year before. In his soothing British accent, Goddard Lieberson, taking his cue from the sacred country music terrain, intoned, "All we have to sell is emotion," while Mitch Miller, the schlockmeister of pop who had shepherded country music to artists like Tony Bennett, Jo Stafford and Rosemary Clooney, chimed in, "When a country music song is right, there's no song any stronger. . . . If it has emotional content, it goes and goes until something else comes along."

Despite all this vague "heart" talk, however, nobody really knew what made a hit record in the mid-1950s. Paul Cohen was the first to admit it was a crapshoot. Cohen was even willing to gamble on little eleven-year-old-going-on-thirty-sounding Brenda Lee, whose latest single was "I'm Gonna Lasso Santa Claus."

Patsy brought a batch of 4 Star songs with her to the convention, including "Walkin' After Midnight." A hit was now paramount, and she solicited the advice of a number of people she knew and trusted, including singer-songwriter Marvin Rainwater and his brother Ray Rainwater, a deejay for a Trenton, New Jersey, radio station who also acted as his brother's manager. One-quarter Cherokee, Marvin would appear in a buckskin shirt on a TV set made to look like he was sitting in a canoe. His career as a country-rock act was at its peak, and he'd appeared on "The Ed Sullivan Show," Dick Clark's "American Bandstand" and in Alan Freed's well-publicized extravaganzas at the Brooklyn Paramount.

For Rainwater, it all started with a winning appearance on Arthur Godfrey's "Talent Scouts" in 1955. Godfrey subsequently took a liking to both Rainwater brothers, even flew them in his own private plane to his home in Leesburg, Virginia. Ray, in turn, helped several artists get on Godfrey's show, including Roy Clark, who subsequently tied for a win. Clark wasn't the only Connie B. Gay artist to hit the big time: George Hamilton IV was breaking out as a crossover artist thanks to "A Rose and a Baby Ruth" and an October 1956 appearance on "Talent Scouts." Though Hamilton didn't win, Godfrey regularly booked him anyway on his other prime-time show, "Arthur Godfrey and His Friends."

Patsy was impressed by what an appearance on Godfrey's show could do for her and was convinced that more astute management would help her pull it off after the failed attempt in 1954. At the convention she asked Ray Rainwater for help in picking out songs. Rainwater was booking Bobby Helms and Wanda Jackson in clubs along the Eastern Seaboard, and Patsy asked him if he would manage her.

"Patsy was not always the best judge of a lot of things," Rainwater said. "She could be very contentious—she was hard to help, if you know what I mean. But I wasn't in the agent business; I couldn't make the commitment. I would have lost other people I was working with."

Rainwater did, however, render his opinion about the songs she showed him and, like everyone else she talked to, urged her to record "Walkin' After Midnight." He also introduced her to Mae Boren Axton, who had penned "Heartbreak Hotel" for Elvis Presley. Patsy and Axton became instant friends.

"She badly wanted to record something of mine," Axton recalled. "I told her I didn't think I had anything that would be a hit for her, and I wanted her to have a hit. Later I was sitting in the lobby of the Andrew Jackson with Burt Levy and we were watching these young kids going up and down the elevator with one girl after another, and all those things that young kids do when they suddenly hit. Just watching those kids—one of them had a big hit, the only hit he ever had, and he died in an old hotel room, no money, no anything—Gene Vincent. 'Be-Bop-A-Lula.' And there were several more there like him. George Jones was one of them. He was still hot, but he was drinking a lot. So I said to Burt, 'You know, just look at those kids. They really are on top of the world now. They got a hit; they're making money. Maybe the only hit they'll ever have. Maybe they'll have more and will stay on top. But there are going to be a lot of them who are going to hit the bottom because they're not taking care of business.' One of them I knew had signed with four managers. Each one came up to him and said, 'I'll do this for you . . .' and he'd signed with each one of them.

"I said, 'So I want to know, who's going to pick 'em up? Their wives? Are they going to be there to pick them up; will they care after what they've done? Or will a parent? A friend? Who's going to pick 'em up?' He said, 'You're right, that's exactly the truth. Who's going to pick them up?' I said, 'You know, maybe it'll be you, maybe it'll be me. So when they start down, pick me up on your way down.' Burt said, 'Boy, that's a great idea.' I said, 'That's what I'm going to write for Patsy.'

"We had just had something to eat, and there was a recipe on this menu at the Andrew Jackson. I was there a lot and I was always thinking I was going to get me one of these, so I asked the girl, 'Can I have this?' and she said, 'Sure.' So I had it in my hand, and I just started writing it. By that time, Glen Reeves walked in the lobby and I said, 'Glen, come on, let's go upstairs. I'm writing a hit for Patsy Cline to record.' He said, 'Okay,' and I said to Burt, 'Come on, you can come up with us,' but he didn't go; he went to his room. So Glen and I went up and in a few minutes we had it written. I was writing the words fast as I could. He had the guitar and started putting a tune to it. So I said, 'Glen, she's over there at Owen Bradley's now. I'm going to call over there and tell her you're on the way with the song 'cause I know it's about time for a break. Teach it to her because she may do it today."

"Pick Me Up" was never released during Patsy's lifetime, the likely reason being it was not a 4 Star copyright. Patsy fought to have it released as a single anyway. At one point, Axton received a phone call from Bradley who told her, "Patsy is crying her heart out because she wants us to release 'Pick Me Up' but Mr. McCall won't allow it. Maybe we can work it out with him—she's trying to get away from him—to where it can be the next release." A few years later the song still haunted Patsy; she claimed she sang it for songwriter Harlan Howard, who wrote a 1958 song of the same title. Howard claimed coincidence; Patsy told Axton he got the idea from her performance.

Al Gallico, song plugger for Shapiro-Bernstein, first met Patsy that weekend at the convention. Patsy told him she was desperate for a hit; Gallico had a song: "A Poor Man's Roses (Or a Rich Man's Gold)," which describes a trade-off between a passionless relationship with a monied man versus true love with a poor man—an uncanny description of Patsy's Gerald versus Charlie dilemma. Patsy instantly fell in love with the song, written not by a country tunesmith but by the Tin Pan Alley team of Milton Delugg, a songwriter for Doris Day, and Bob Hilliard, who, among other songs, collaborated on "Be My Life's Companion," a hit for the Mills Brothers. Gallico was a friend of Paul Cohen's and brokered a deal with McCall whereby McCall agreed to let Patsy record the outside copyright, for a "promotional incentive."

When Gallico returned to New York and told Delugg he had a

Patsy Cline record, the songwriter didn't know what to think. He had never head of Patsy "Kline." "It sounded like a girl from the Bronx, you know? I told Al, 'Gee, that's terrific,' not realizing then how terrific it was. But, my God, she sold a couple million of 'A Poor Man's Roses.' And I never got to meet her, never knew her."

Owen Bradley insisted that Patsy had to leave the party at the Andrew Jackson to rehearse "Midnight." Patsy bitched again about the song, but by the time they'd worked out an arrangement in Bradley's office and gone into the studio, the session went like clockwork.

Patsy took "Midnight" at a slower tempo than the more familiar version recorded later in 1961. Bradley and the regular team played it straight country, beginning with steel guitarist Don Helms's opening riff, reminiscent of his work on Hank Williams's records. Patsy, as she did on all her early recordings, stayed right on top of the beat, trying for a driving style but not quite pulling it off. McCall later claimed that the musicians had been bribed into creating a laborious track on "Midnight" so that the other side, "A Poor Man's Roses," would get airplay. "Somebody from Louie Bernstein's office got to this group in Nashville, the musicians, the producer, everybody, and you know what I mean by 'got to them,' " he told Donn Hecht. It was a pretty far-fetched idea. Bradley's reputation for honesty was pristine and Nashville Local 257 was considered one of the most scrupulously run unions in the country.

"The people down here were too honest to even listen to any suggestion like that," replied Helms, who added, "I recorded with the same musicians over and over, and I think if someone had told them to purposely mess up, they'd have told him to go to hell."

The session was memorable for Bradley for different reasons. "We had instructions from Paul to send Bill McCall a copy of everything we did on Patsy Cline. So after we finished making a Patsy Cline record, the engineer picked up a piece of tape and it was a scrap piece, I guess, something he recorded on before—we weren't all that particular back then, and it just so happened it was something we recorded Kitty Wells on. So he transferred these songs onto the tape for Bill McCall. But the spaces in between, instead of cutting out the things in between, he just left blank pieces of that original tape in there. It was a copy and he didn't think he needed to go to all the trouble. Mr. McCall got that tape, he played it and he heard something in there, and it was going backwards, so he turned the tape around and he found that Kitty Wells was singing a song called 'Searching.' And so he claimed that song. The funny thing was that Paul Cohen had already claimed the song for one of his companies. Hell, he sued Paul for that song, but Paul had the contracts."

Following the session, Patsy asked Ray Rainwater to listen to the tapes. Rainwater was impressed with "Midnight" and "Pick Me Up" and offered to set up an audition on "Talent Scouts." Patsy warned him she'd already been turned down by Godfrey, but Rainwater insisted on trying to book her again, telling her, "Timing is everything. Elvis Presley auditioned too and they turned him down."

Back in Winchester, Patsy received some unsettling news. The messenger was her cousin Punk Longley, who went to Kent Street in person to tell the Hensleys that Sam was in a nearby veterans' hospital in Martinsburg and not expected to live long.

"I know you and your daddy didn't get along, Virginia," he told Patsy. "I know you cussed him and he cussed you until hell wouldn't have either of you. But he doesn't have long. He's got one lung; he's got cancer. Is there any way that I can persuade you to go and see him?"

Punk's news stunned her. She was supposed to hate her father but she couldn't—he was her father. She felt guilty: "I shouldn't love him for what he did to me as a child. There must be something wrong with me that I can't hate him." She had not been a nice girl, a good girl. If she was, she would hate her father.

In front of Hilda and the others, Patsy gave Punk a hard time about going to see Sam in the hospital. But in the end, she relented. *Forgiveness* was the word that came up in the course of the family discussion that ensued. Patsy wanted the forgiveness of her whole family for him. His forgiveness would be hers.

Prior to being admitted to the hospital, Sam had been living in a boarding house in Harrisonburg, Virginia, between Elkton and Winchester. He had worked there as a fireman, stoking the elephantine cast iron boilers in the bowels of the old Buckingham Memorial Hospital, raising enough steam to heat the entire building. He had become twisted and bent over, with the perpetual cigar, sometimes lit, more often not, hanging from his mouth. Then came the cancer, which attacked his greatest gift. The angelic, pure, crystal tenor that could sing the praises of the Lord or invoke the Devil himself in a maelstrom of cursing was reduced to choked, hoarse whispers.

"His two brothers and my daddy went to see him one night and they came back all upset," recalled Punk. "They told him they thought he ought to be in a veterans' hospital and he cussed them all out and ran them out on the street. So I said, 'Just keep your shirts on. I'll go talk to him in the morning.' So I went and said, 'Uncle Sam, Ashby, Jim and

Dad all think you ought to be in a hospital. I don't know, and I don't think you do either. Neither of us are medical men. Let's get Dr. Smith up here to examine you. If he says you're fine here, I'll stop by as many times as I can and see that you get anything you need. But if he says you should be in a hospital, I'll put you in a hospital.' Fair enough—you could reason with him but you couldn't drive him an inch.

"Dr. Smith checked him and at ten o'clock he said, 'Have him in Martinsburg at four o'clock this afternoon.' I had a convertible and you couldn't take a sick man in a convertible. So I went to a friend who had a Mercury dealership and said, 'I gotta have a car.' He said, 'I'm going to fix you up right. Take that Continental Lincoln.' He always had to have the biggest automobile at the time, and the day I took him to Martinsburg, the Lincoln was the biggest automobile at that time. I had a pillow so he could sit up and see out. I was going down Route 11 about seventy in that Continental, just floating along, and the only thing he says is, 'Goddamn, this is nice.' "

As his disease progressed, Sam "tried to amend for all the things he had done," said one family member. Though he "was not that much of a talker about his family life, or himself, particularly," in his own way Sam let it be known he wanted a reconciliation with his family, especially Patsy. "He just bragged on about how proud he was of her."

Recalled Punk Longley: "I went to visit him once and he said, 'Punk, I just heard something on the radio that I never thought I'd have a chance to hear in my life. I had the radio on from Waynesboro and I heard Tempie Glen playing the organ at the Presbyterian church there, and when I flipped the station I heard Patsy. I heard them both in five minutes.' "

It had been eight years and another lifetime since Patsy had seen her father. In their lives together he was the center of attention, and now again in death, as the family hovered around his bedside to witness his final drama. Patsy was shocked at the sight of him. Once vital, he had shriveled both physically and vocally, something she had never expected to see.

She communicated her love the only way she could, singing all the old family songs as well as his favorite, "Life's Railway to Heaven." She looked in his eyes for a sign of the words she had never heard, that he loved her. She went to see him several times before he died, on December 11, at the age of sixty-seven—the last of the nineteenth-century men. After the funeral, he was buried among neat rows of headstones of other World War I veterans in National Cemetery in Winchester. Among the relatives who attended, there was a great deal of surprise when Hilda announced that she had arranged for her plot to be next to his.

Chapter Twelve

*P*ATSY WAS SET TO PERFORM on "Town & Country Jamboree" one Saturday night in December 1956, when Dale Turner came running backstage, barely able to suppress her excitement: "It better be a good show tonight because Arthur Godfrey is watching."

Godfrey had been tipped off about Patsy and was tuned in from his home in Leesburg. Ray Rainwater had been good for his word: within a week she had an audition date lined up in New York.

She took Charlie along for company. the corporate atmosphere of CBS studios was a far cry from the downhome setting of Gay's TV broadcasts. Patsy didn't like New York—"that place scares me," she admitted—and Charlie's presence was probably more of a demand on her attention than she expected. She tried to hold her own in the intimidating setting. Executive producer Janette Davis would once again decide her fate. Davis didn't exactly offer her a "Come On In" kind of welcome. the producer sat in a control room with an engineer and a sound man, shooting questions at Patsy, who was in the studio, through a microphone. Patsy sang a few country tunes mixed in with some pop standards. Recalled Davis, "She was rather quiet, not extroverted, in my estimation—laid back. But not when she sang. When she sang it was just terrific. She was really sure of herself."

Patsy was accustomed to the high energy and down-homeness of country audiences. the cold setting of the New York studio, the no-nonsense manner of the producer and the pressure not to make any grammatical errors as she answered questions and thereby risk sounding like an ignorant hillbilly made her feel terribly nervous. She interpreted Davis's response as lukewarm; in effect, "Don't call us—we'll call you." She needn't have worried. Davis was exceedingly impressed with her and claimed there was no question in her mind at the time of the audition that Patsy would not only be invited to appear on the show, but that, "In her case, I knew she was going to win.

"She was just extraordinarily good, a natural. She was a simple girl. When I say 'simple,' I don't mean that critically. It was part of her charm. She didn't look New Yorkish, but neither did I when I came, you know, and maybe that was good. She wasn't tacky. She was neat. I don't think she was beautiful but she had a wonderful sincere look in her face."

The good news was delivered via a telephone call to Patsy's Kent Street address, which notified her of her acceptance and her appearance date: Monday, January 21, at 8:30 P.M. Hilda answered the telephone first, and with the humbling experience of New York still fresh in her mind, Patsy played hard-to-get, telling her mother to make the caller wait before picking up the receiver. She made it seem as though she had better things to do than sit around waiting for a phone call from Arthur Godfrey.

"She called to tell me she didn't want to come [to New York] alone," said Al Gallico. Patsy called Gallico, the one friendly face she knew in New York, to tell him about the booking and to get his help. She wanted to take Hilda and she needed to scrape together some funds for the tickets and a hotel. "She was real country. I said, 'Why don't you take your mother?' She says, 'I haven't got any money. I can't afford it.' I said, 'I'll buy your mother a ticket.' So I bought her mother a ticket and I says, 'Now let me know when you get in town.' I didn't hear from her. So I sent one of my employees over to the Godfrey show. I said, 'Introduce yourself to Patsy Cline and take her to a phone and have her call me.' He did. And so I says, 'Where the hell have you been? I called all over.' She says, 'Well, when we got off the bus at 42nd Street, there's a nice hotel there called the Dixie.' [Patsy was referring to the same place she'd stayed three years earlier with Bill Peer.] I said, 'Get outa that fleatrap. I'll put you in the Essex House.' She says, 'I like it here; it's my kind of people.' She was real country."

"Talent Scouts" had "scouts" introduce the "discoveries" before a live studio audience. the rules excluded family members from this position. Though a family friend offered to be her scout, Patsy was determined that Hilda share in her biggest moment, rules or no rules. She devised a little white lie whereby she would introduce her as "Mrs. Hilda Hensley from Winchester, Virginia—my best friend," which Patsy reasoned wasn't exactly a lie.

Once the contestants were selected, "Talent Scouts" took no chances in leaving the choice of material to the performers. Godfrey had nothing to do with the show or the performers before he went on the air. The decisions were Janette Davis's, and he backed her up. "I knew Arthur so well, so very, very well, and I could talk to him," Davis said. "I would plan the whole thing out because I knew what was good for him." Godfrey had a penchant for people who were naturals, but in many cases that translated to the studied, homogenized "naturalism" of network TV, designed to appeal to the broadest possible audience. Davis saw Patsy as being perfect for the boss, but one in need of the guidance of a network pro. In short, the cowgirl needed her edges smoothed out.

Patsy brought at least a dozen songs with her. Davis, who'd had a minor career as a singer and had been a regular on Godfrey's show before taking over as producer, was not impressed with any of the material. Finally, Patsy produced the lead sheets for the song she least wanted to sing, "Walkin' After Midnight," handed them to the studio pianist and sang a stanza and a chorus. "That's it," Davis's voice echoed through the studio.

"She didn't seem happy about it," Davis recalled. "Not at all. But she was very pleasant. I can understand why, as a singer myself—you have your heart set on doing a certain song and the producer keeps saying, 'Let's hear something else.' But I just knew when she did this song, this was it."

Even Patsy had to now admit there must be something to the song. She called Donn Hecht in Los Angeles afterward to advise him to watch "the tube" on January 21 because she'd be singing his song.

"'You son-of-a-bitch, hoss'—she was laughing. I said, 'Whaddaya mean?'

"'I fought you all the way down the line. I fought Mr. McCall all the way down the line. They've gone through every song I ever sang and recorded and they picked "Walkin' After Midnight." You guys are a bunch of jackasses but you got the people in New York agreeing with you.'"

Hecht added, "One thing about Patsy: she was not a buck-passer. If she had a problem, whether it was a decision that had to do with the music business, recording a song or not recording a song, or some publisher that was on her ass to do something, whether it was Bill McCall or me or anybody else, if there was a disagreement, even slight, she was the kind of person who would go look at herself in the mirror first and ask if she was wrong. If she felt really strongly about it, she would say, 'No, I don't think I'm wrong. I'm going to stand my ground.' But she was not a bitch. She was not the type of person to say, 'Hey, this is what I think and that's it, and I don't give a damn what you think.' She would look at herself first. I admired that very much. Just like songs she was wrong about, that she didn't like and didn't want to record. She'd call me and say, 'You know, I had a feeling I was wrong about that, hoss.' When you're wrong, you're wrong."

Patsy had been amply warned about looking too "countrified." Ray Rainwater met her in New York to help her prepare for the appearance and to pick out a dress. She desperately wanted to win and she had confidence in Rainwater. "I more or less held her by the hand," he said.

Together they combed the shops and Patsy tried on a dozen or more outfits before they settled on a simple, light blue linen sheath with a filigreed boat neckline. "It was a mistake, really, but I insisted on it," Rainwater said. "It was a beautiful dress, but you know how linen is—if you sit down in it you get a mess of wrinkles. She had to stand up all evening. The dress came to just below the knee, with short sleeves and a low neck. It didn't have any embellishments. It was just a beautiful, pretty dress. I'd been told blue is the color for television cameras, and I thought that instead of going out there in something outlandish or something hillbillyish, she should look conservative and elegant, and she did look so elegant in it."

By Monday night, Godfrey had been informed that Mrs. Hilda Hensley of Winchester, Virginia, was none other than Patsy's mom. Patsy's touching little white lie was exactly the kind of thing that endeared her to him. Rather than bawl her out as she feared, he didn't let on, and later milked the story for all its appeal to Middle America. It was those kind of natural moments that made Godfrey's show one of the top-rated TV programs of the fifties.

Bert Farber, who replaced Godfrey's previous bandleader Archie Bleyer in 1954, worked out a pop arrangement for "Midnight" that made the six-piece Godfrey band sound like a small orchestra. After Hilda, visibly uncomfortable, introduced her "discovery," Patsy strolled out to the tape marks on the floor and smiled at Godfrey, who, beaming, looked like Howdy Doody as he stood off to the side of the camera. Then, perfectly self-contained yet dreamy-eyed, she remembered how the railroad tracks looked on the east side of Winchester under the light of the full moon when the scent of apple blossoms floated on the gentle Virginia night air.

In Winchester, TV sets all over town were tuned into the broadcast on January 21, 1957.

"We just knew she was going to win, we just knew—Patsy's got to win this," recalled Pat Smallwood. "She was just thrilled to death. The applause meter went clear to the top; it didn't waver one bit. He [Godfrey] says, 'I believe we have a winner here tonight, Miss Patsy

Cline from Winchester, Virginia.' We just tore the house down where we were watching. She was stunned. But she had a feeling she was going to win."

The camera zoomed in for a closeup of her epiphany. Millions of Americans saw unabashed tears glisten in her dark eyes. Godfrey put a fatherly arm around her, and when the audience calmed down, he asked for an encore. Patsy offered Hank Williams's "Your Cheatin' Heart," eliciting another round of wild applause. Totally in the spirit of the moment, Godfrey made the simple but eloquent observation, "You are the most innocent, the most nervous, most truthful and honest performer I have ever seen. There is surely stardust on you."

"Went on the Godfrey show," she later noted in her date book. "Won."

On the front page of the Tuesday edition of the *Winchester Evening Star* was a small photo of Patsy sandwiched among the full-bore coverage of Ike's second inaugural celebration. The caption above the photo read: "TOPS IN TALENT." The story summarized: "Patsy Cline was first-place winner last night on the 'Arthur Godfrey Talent Scout Show.' She sang 'I Walk Alone At Midnight,' [*sic*] soon to be released by Decca records [*sic*].

"Miss Cline, who has been a constant TV performer with Jimmy Dean and his Texas Wildcats, has made several records.

"She appeared on Mr. Godfrey's morning program today and will appear tomorrow and Thursday also.

"Mr. Godfrey said he was pleased to have a neighbor. Miss Cline's real name is Virginia Helsley [*sic*] and she lives at 608 S. Kent St., with such talent and ability."

The following day, Gerald Cline filed for divorce.

Paul Cohen felt vindicated. His gamble had paid off. While Patsy was in New York he invited her to stop by Decca's offices, this time for the star treatment. Decca was flooded with mail. Its distributors were clamoring for "Walkin' After Midnight" and it looked like the label was in the embarrassing position of having an unreleased hit. If Patsy had smoked cigars, Cohen would have offered her one. "It's a smash," he yelled excitedly, fielding calls from the press and distributors. Cohen was already eager to push her back in the studio. He talked follow-up hit; he talked album. Patsy was giddy with the exhilaration that overnight success brings. The masters from her November session were rushed to the pressing plant and "Walkin' After Midnight" was released February 11, backed by "A Poor Man's Roses (Or a Rich Man's Gold.)"

Once a song is released it is up for grabs by anyone else who wants to record it, as long as the royalties are paid. So it wasn't considered all that unusual, especially given the covering fashion of the time, that Al Gallico hustled an acetate of Patsy's recording of "A Poor Man's Roses" to Patti Page the day after Patsy's "Talent Scouts" appearance. Page obviously listened to Patsy carefully. Her cover version, released hot on the heels of "Midnight," on February 14, aped Patsy's cut, all the way down to the arrangement of guitar, bass and drums. Page had an instant hit. Generally, when a major star covered an unknown, it was the lesser-known performer's version that got buried, but Patsy considered Page's cover a compliment, and while her own recording of "Roses" didn't match the success of Page's, it did chart briefly as a country hit later that summer.

Patsy's hit on "Midnight" triggered its own round of covering activity, with singles by as many as eleven different artists. Most were forgotten. Besides Lynn Howard's demo, released on Accent, there were versions by Eddie Dean on Sage, and a doo-wop version cut by Otis Williams and the Charms on King. Bill McCall supposedly took Patsy's recording, slowed it down to a speed of 33 1/3, pressed about 250 copies, labeled them with the artist's name, "Calvin Coolidge," and mailed them to deejays as a joke, with a cover letter: "This is a hot record and this is the first male vocalist version." But what could have been the most hurtful to Patsy was Pat Boone's cover version for Dot. Donn Hecht had submitted "Midnight" to Boone's label a year before Patsy cut it. Boone passed on it at the time. After Patsy's "Godfrey" appearance (Boone was an earlier Godfrey "discovery"), Dot set in motion a "crash program to complete a Boone cover."

Boone was, according to Hecht, "an uncontested superstar who sold a million or more records on about anything he produced"; hence Hecht's torn feelings. Patsy, he noted, "stood to be mutilated by a release by Pat Boone." The Boone session took place "with full orchestral treatment with Pat Boone 'at his best,' with the statement that 'They think they'll kill her [Patsy] with Pat's version.'" But while Boone's label was getting ready to press, they [his label] got cold feet: Patsy's version had already "gone like a bat out of hell," and it was determined that a Boone release on "Midnight" would, Hecht added, "destroy his image as a never-miss hit maker if he failed to kill her off."

For the duration of the week, Patsy remained in New York to do "Arthur Godfrey and His Friends," and was persuaded to move out of the Dixie Hotel into more uptown accommodations. On the "Friends" program, which was broadcast on radio, Godfrey revealed the truth about Patsy's scout being her mom, then effusively introduced Patsy as "one of the finest country-western-blues singers in the world." Prattle being his forte, Godfrey asked her to what did she attribute her talent. Momentarily caught off-guard as to how to respond to a question about a God-given gift, she hesitated for a beat, then answered with the first thing that came to mind: "Well, I guess, just me." Expecting humility and getting guilelessness instead, Godfrey was now the one to be nonplussed: "Well, don't ever change it," he ad-libbed.

Patsy's first week of performances went without a hitch. "She was kind of the country-girl-coming-to-the-big-city, but it was kind of refreshing," said Louis Nunley of the Anita Kerr Singers, who were appearing on the show that week as well. "I think everybody appreciated it. And she did a good job; she blew them away. It was a very easy show to work. There was an excellent band; they just played everything and played it with the proper feel and all that. And everybody on the show was just plain ordinary people. Nobody on ego trips or anything like that. It was just a very relaxed show, so she fit right in and I think she really enjoyed being there."

Godfrey was particularly fond of "the little people" and unpretentious Patsy was his favorite kind of artist. Godfrey's approach was made-to-order for Middle America. In his nasal baritone he would chuckle, josh with guests and members of the live studio audience, play up bits of "business" and plunk away tunelessly at his ukulele while attempting to sing. Sincere, likable and undeniably talented—but not so full of herself that she would overshadow Godfrey himself, Patsy was perfect for his show, and Godfrey took her under his wing, grooming her to be a regular on his broadcasts.

Godfrey's affection for Patsy might have stemmed from certain similarities in their backgrounds: besides both being from Virginia, both were oldest children, and both lost fathers at relatively young ages—Godfrey's squandered a family fortune and died when he was still a young teenager, leaving the large Godfrey family penniless. Like Patsy, he too had to go to work at age thirteen to support his family. And both of them were straight shooters. In 1953, when Godfrey became annoyed at his most popular singer, the sincere, likable, undeniably talented Julius La Rosa (who was supposedly getting more fan mail than Godfrey himself), he fired him on the air and publicly let his critics know what he thought of them too: "These jerk newspapermen!" and "Muckrakers!" was his description of the fourth estate. "Dope!" was his reference to his rival, Ed Sullivan. "Liar!" was his word for columnist Dorothy Kilgallen.

Godfrey felt that Patsy needed smoothing out, and appointing himself her ad hoc counselor, he didn't hesitate to tell her what to do. Before one of the broadcasts he advised her to shave her legs. As outspoken as even she was, Patsy was astounded at Godfrey's nerve.

"She came back and she was hot about it," recollected Dale Turner about the leg fuzz incident. "But she did it. She had never shaved her legs before. She always wore boots up to here, and then her skirts were to there, with fringe. I never even noticed and we never paid any attention."

"She couldn't understand what made him say something like that," recalled Pat Smallwood. "'He was very blunt,' she said. 'It just came out of the blue.' I said to her, 'Did you get upset?' and she said, 'No, I just thought it was rather rude, in a way, but I'll just shave 'em if it makes him happy.' She was just one of those girls who didn't want to shave right then. It wasn't any great growth or anything; it was no big deal. I guess he just wanted her to look her best and he noticed things like that."

Upon Patsy's return to her hometown, there was some talk of a "Patsy Cline Day," but it never materialized. Other than a dinner sponsored by the local Lions Club in her honor, Patsy's achievement went officially unacknowledged, though her friends turned out to support her. They discovered that up or down, Patsy was always the same down-to-earth gal they'd always known her to be.

"When she did the 'Talent Scouts' show I was sick," remembered girlfriend Patsy Lillis. "As soon as she got back, she come over to my house and brought the demo tapes that she had made while she was there and played those for me. She brought over the Victrola even—at that time that's what they were called. I was still sick. She made that record, 'Walkin' After Midnight,' and I worked at McCrory's five-and-dime and I got her to come down to McCrory's. We had a big sale going on of her record. She come down and autographed the record for us. There were a lot of people there. Big time—that's what I called it."

The world beyond Winchester, however, did take notice of her achievement. Patsy was inundated with phone calls, offers, advice. Bill McCall, Paul Cohen, Arthur Godfrey, Connie B. Gay, friends and acquaintances in the business—suddenly everyone was her best friend and they all had advice. General Artists Corporation, one of the three largest entertainment agencies in the country, proposed handling her bookings. "I'm not making up my mind about anything right now," she told the *Washington Star* on February 9, 1957. "Things are happening so quickly for me, and I'm still in the thinking stage." Among the offers came an opportunity to screen test for a movie. America's film factories were tapping into the youth market, and the studios looked to the plethora of young singing stars for the next James Dean or Marlon Brando. Elvis Presley and Pat Boone were top box office stars and in March Elvis signed a $250,000 contract that paid for Graceland. It was "the biggest deal ever made in Hollywood." But even though Patsy fantasized about the movies, she was apprehensive about what would be expected of her, telling the *Star,* "It would be too much of a headache—I just want to be a singer."

"I think she told me about what part she would be auditioning for," recalled songwriter Mae Axton, who worked as a film publicist. "She was excited, like a little girl. She said, 'Do you think I can do it?' 'You can do anything you want to,' I said, 'but movies are hurry up and wait, so you'd better think about it, but if that's what you want to do, then have a go at it.' Later I asked her about what happened with the movie. She said, 'Well, I'm just too busy.' I don't know if they turned her down or if it was just an excuse."

The obligatory "Grand Ole Opry" guest invitation was extended to country music's new luminary. Now that Patsy had "arrived," Opry management rolled out the red carpet. On February 16, she strode on stage at the Ryman to the beat of thunderous applause. Decca and Shapiro-Bernstein launched a promotional blitz to tout Patsy as a crossover star, beginning with a February 11 "Spotlight" listing in *Billboard:* "Miss Cline, heretofore identified mainly with the country field, makes a strong bid to break pop-wise. Both readings have had strong exposure via thrush's performance of them on Arthur Godfrey's TV airings. The 'Walkin'' side has a fine bluesy flavor and the flip is loaded with reflective sentiment set to a rock and roll pace."

The following week, "Midnight" had caught on in virtually every important market. "Here is the most recent example of a country artist coming into the pop market and cleaning up," *Billboard* noted a week later. "Miss Cline has cracked New York, Philadelphia, Baltimore, Washington and other East Coast cities as well as Southern and Midwestern key markets, where the action is both pop and country and western. It is coming up fast now and should make the charts."

"Walkin' After Midnight" peaked at number 12 on the pop charts on February 23, 1957, and shortly thereafter, on March 2, it became a number 2 country hit. While Patsy was riding high and sorting through her offers, Connie B. Gay's fortunes were also waxing. In March, Gay scored a major coup when his "Town & Country" television format was picked up by CBS. The network was looking for a daily, forty-five-minute live show to replace Will Rogers, Jr.'s "Good Morning!" show. CBS executives had studied the successful ratings for rival ABC's "Ozark Jubilee," the country music showcase hosted by genial crooner Red Foley. The network recognized the potency of

C&W to attract corporate advertisers like Dow Chemical, Bristol Myers, Phillips Petroleum, R. J. Reynolds, RC Cola, Philip Morris, General Motors and Miles Laboratories, all of which were sponsoring country radio and TV programming. While the recording industry waxed on with references to "It says the things we feel" and "It's written solely with the writer's guts" in trying to explain C&W's appeal, the advertising industry got to the bottom line: "People who listen to country music are much more faithful. They buy something because you ask them. They believe."

Gay's competitor for the network slot was the granddaddy of country showcases, the "Grand Ole Opry." An overconfident Opry management, reasoning its roster of talent made it a shoe-in for the spot, put together a hokey production that used two camera angles—medium and close-up. New star Patsy, for whom there was nothing like the Opry, flew to Nashville to appear on the pilot, apparently unaware or unconcerned about the conflict of interest where Gay was concerned.

TV pro Gay, on the other hand, fed one of his live "Town & Country" broadcasts from the WMAL studios over the telephone lines to CBS headquarters. Jimmy Dean, like Arthur Godfrey, George Gobel, Perry Como, Red Foley and other successful musical-variety hosts, came from the just-folks, don't-mind-me school of televisionship so popular during the Cold War years. William Paley, president of CBS, had never been to the Opry and didn't know Roy Acuff from Roy Rogers, but he recognized the made-for-TV cornflake appeal of the fresh-faced Dean, honed to perfection over a period of several years by Gay. Even more important, though, Gay had a proven format on regional TV and an offer CBS ultimately couldn't refuse: he would put up the money for the show "in association with" CBS and handle distribution to all other English-speaking countries, Armed Forces stations and domestic radio audiences. The network awarded Gay a seven-year contract with a liberal out clause to produce the show, which was to be called "The Jimmy Dean Show." Though the show lasted only six months, it was, at that point, one of the largest contracts ever negotiated to supply country entertainment.

According to Gay's account, "I went up to New York City in my tailored cowboy suit and everyone thought I was nuts. But Paley liked what I had to say. More than anything, it was a matter of plain ole salesmanship."

"We were all excited about it when he got the network show for us," said Marvin Carroll. "When he come back from New York, we said, 'Connie, how in the world did you do it?' He says, 'Well, I just walked in that room—it was full of smoke; all those people were sitting around—I didn't know what to say—so I just reached back and got my checkbook and laid it on the table and said, 'Match it.' All of a sudden everybody started talking. They said, 'Who is this man from Virginia with all this money?'"

The show began airing in April. The network sent a production team to Washington, D.C., to oversee rehearsals. Gay figured Patsy had deserted him to do the Opry pilot. But according to her cousin Punk Longley, she intended to do Gay's audition show as well, but illness, brought about by overwork, forced her to cancel at the last minute. It was too late. Gay was galled.

"Virginia had laryngitis. I know she did because I talked to her on the telephone and she said, 'Punk, I've got to try to make the show but I don't know whether I can make it or not. I just can't hardly sing.' She sounded exactly like her daddy did when he had the cancer in his lung. I said, 'Well, Virginia, if you're too sick to go, I'd just call in and tell them I just can't do it.' She said, 'Well, Punk, I've got to.' I said, 'Well, they can't expect you to get up there and sing when you can't sing. Unless you want to pantomime it. That's the only thing you can do.' She said, 'Well, I don't know if I can do that or not.' I think she did that a time or two later, 'cause she was all the time losing her voice. She strained it too darn much. Strained it no end. By the weather and everything else. If she was supposed to sing, she sang."

Once Gay received the network's nod, he held that Patsy was axed from the lineup by CBS because she showed up for rehearsals late, "with alcohol on her breath."

"Patsy was a difficult person," Gay said. "Everybody had a hard time with her professionally—her not showing up on time, bending the elbow too much, and, well, I could go on and on about her ways."

Gay's comments regarding Patsy's unprofessional behavior are specious given the recollections of her fellow "T&CJ" cast members. Patsy was no teetotaler, but she lived by the show biz cliché, "The show must go on," and the idea that she was a beer guzzler was pure myth.

"We played a lot of beer joints and honky-tonks and dance halls and I never saw her inebriated," said George Hamilton. "She was always professional. Patsy could take a drink with the best of us; she could hold her liquor, as they say. But I never can remember ever seeing her mess up a show or miss one. I never even saw her drunk. I've heard these horror stories about Hank Williams, but I never saw that kind of thing in Patsy. Probably what Connie was alluding to in a vague way about her not showing up—he maintained that Patsy had agreed to be on his audition for the network television show and she didn't show. I think something happened to her where she couldn't get there, but Connie didn't accept her excuse. And so Patsy said, 'To hell with you.' In Connie's view, Patsy let him down on that audition. But anytime we played clubs or dances around Washington, she was sober and on time.

"Everything's subjective. In Connie's view, what we think of as a women's lib, independent streak, that could be 'difficult,' because he was the boss, he was the manager, he demanded complete loyalty and Patsy didn't tow the line. Patsy had a hit record, was making great strides and she would have been a great asset to that television show and Connie knew it. When she didn't make the audition he really felt let down and was afraid he was going to lose out. It was a blow to him because he was counting on her as ammunition, but he ended up getting it anyway."

If anyone was experiencing problems with alcohol, it was Gay. While his success was trumpeted in *Broadcasting* magazine ("What the House of Morgan is to Wall Street, the General Motors Building to the auto industry and Onassis' yacht to international shipping, Connie B. Gay's $11,800 limousine is to the cult of country music"), his personal life was in a shambles. His marriage was in ruins as a result of his own rampant alcoholism.

"All my life I had been a good drinker, from college on, a hell of a drinker, never had any problems with the stuff, but one day I just found I was allergic to it," he later recalled. "It made me sick and the sicker I got the more I drank. Never got falling-down drunk on the street, never got arrested, didn't lose any money from it, just became a drunk."

In mid-March, Gay ran a full-page ad in the *Music Reporter* that glaringly omitted any mention of Patsy: "For Jimmy Dean, George Hamilton IV, Buck Ryan, Herb Jones, Marvin Carroll, Mary Klick, Alex Houston, Billie [*sic*] Grammer, Smitty Irvin, Billie Graves, Dick Flood and Dale Turner, may I add another million thanks."

Dean took a dig at Patsy too. He and Patsy normally had a congenial relationship and several years later they patched up their differences "fine and dandy." But Dean, according to Mary Klick, "had this little sarcastic streak once in a while," and when Patsy missed the network tryout he was unforgiving. On a subsequent "Town & Country Jamboree" broadcast, borrowing from Mae Axton's tune "Pick Me Up," Dean peevishly exclaimed, "Patsy Cline is not here tonight. My advice to you, Patsy, is you better be good to us on your way up 'cause you're gonna need us on your way down." Even Gay had to admit Dean's comments were uncalled for: "It was backstage talk on TV and it was unprofessional," he told interviewer Joe Sasfy in 1986.

Tensions had been building between Patsy and Gay even before the network tryout. According to "Town & Country Jamboree" cast members, Gay was threatened that Godfrey was vying for her talent and he interpreted her desire to do what she wanted to do as being "difficult." "Connie wanted complete control," said Dale Turner. "If he couldn't, he'd let you go. And I knew he let her go before that early morning network show started. He replaced Patsy with a girl whose husband was a producer in New York—not a country singer, slicker. I think they were looking for something more uptown. And yet Patsy was going to be a star anyway."

Several "Town & Country Jamboree" cast members knew that Gay had been pressuring her for a contract similar to the exclusive management deals he had with Jimmy Dean and George Hamilton. Meanwhile, Godfrey, too, was proposing a contract and in one newspaper story she said he was "advising her on her career." Inundated with offers, Patsy was reluctant to make any firm commitments about her future. Besides, she was wary of Gay's terms, as she was of Godfrey's. She now considered herself a player in the big leagues, and the old authoritarian platitudes carried no favor with her. In her passionate concern for truth, she was not quite so ready as her peers, Dean and Hamilton, to accept discrepancies between the ideal and actual practices.

"He [Gay] wanted to manage her; he gave her a deal for 50 percent," she told Marvin Carroll. "But she didn't think that was good. She told him she didn't want that. Connie came over to WTOP once—she was doing a show over there—and he approached her on the subject and she came out of there and told us she told Connie he could go take a flying . . . in other words, he could keep it. Patsy was real plain-spoken. She told him what to do with it."

Throughout 1957, Godfrey invited Patsy to sing on his Wednesday night show at three-month intervals. Her powerhouse vocals, naturalness in front of a television camera and country-fresh personality won over TV audiences and Godfrey wanted to add Patsy to his repertory company of clean-cut "little Godfreys," like the McGuire Sisters (who worked on Godfrey's show from 1952 to 1957), Carmel Quinn (1954–1957), Julius La Rosa (1952–1953) and Pat Boone (1955–1957). A man who wouldn't take on a sponsor unless he could authentically endorse its product, Godfrey was a zealot when it came to loyalty from his cast. For this reason he liked the country people.

"He treated me great," Marvin Rainwater said. "All those people he had trouble with, from my viewpoint, was because they were cheating on him. He would pay everybody a tremendous amount of money for singing one song a day and had them sign an exclusive where they wouldn't work anywhere else in case he needed them.

Well, they would slip off and all of a sudden he'd need them and they'd be gone. The McGuire Sisters would go off to Chicago and work a big nightclub and pick up five grand for one night, see? And that's what those people were doing. Godfrey, he didn't tell the world what they did. He just gave them six months' pay and let them go. And then they started screeching and screaming about getting fired."

Patsy didn't want Godfrey's restrictions placed on her. When he learned that she was scheduled to appear on "The Ed Sullivan Show" on April 7, he blocked the appearance. The dour-faced, kidney-clutching Sullivan, like Godfrey a no-talent with a penchant for locating genuinely gifted people, was a prime-time competitor of Godfrey's for hot new musical artists. Sullivan had hustled Elvis Presley, previously rejected by "Talent Scouts," for three shows in 1956, including the famous waist-up appearance. To make Sullivan's "r-r-really big shew" was to make headlines and Godfrey had no intention of letting his rival steal his discovery away from him. From Africa, where he was vacationing when the news of the booking reached him, he issued his edict via Bill McCall. Patsy was undoubtedly disappointed; she told the *Winchester Evening Star* that she "hopes to get everything ironed out after Arthur Godfrey returns from Africa."

Chapter Thirteen

*W*ITH "WALKIN' After Midnight," Patsy finally realized her dream of having a hit, and it reverberated in every fiber of her body. This one piece of plastic was everything she ever wanted—status, financial security, love. Patsy just wanted to enjoy her hit forever. She was "outselling the Platters, Jerry [Lee] Lewis and Bill Haley," according to Paul Cohen. Instead of savoring the moment she'd always dreamed of, the pressure was on for the expected follow-up hit.

Patsy traveled to the West Coast in mid-March for a string of club and TV appearances, including "Town Hall Party" and "The Bob Crosby Show," a daytime musical-variety show hosted by singer-bandleader Crosby, the younger brother of Bing. Crosby's orchestra, the Bobcats, backed Patsy on a pop version of "Walkin' After Midnight" and Crosby paid her biggest fee to date, $1500 for three appearances. She did two episodes of "Western Ranch Party," a syndicated series of half-hour shows filmed at the Art Linkletter Theatre on Vine Street in Hollywood, for Columbia Screen Gems for distribution by Armed Forces Radio and Television. The regular cast included many of the same performers from "Town Hall Party" and Patsy's fellow guest artists for the two episodes were Jimmy Wakely, Hank Penny, Bobby Helms and Johnny Cash. Patsy lip-synched a country version of "Midnight" on one episode and did "I've Loved and Lost Again" on another. Her performance on both episodes made her attraction to the movies apparent: she was an enactor of songs, and she worked with the camera effectively, her gestures and body language minimal, her eyes saying it all.

Patsy did not experience that "Come On In" feeling with the West Coast artists. What her "Town & Country" co-stars considered "regal" was often interpreted as haughtiness. "To be very candid, she was a very unlikable person," observed Wesley Tuttle, music coordinator for the "Ranch Party" series. "Course we were busy. It was all business. She came in, did her stint but wasn't interested in being too friendly with anybody. She was very aloof, cold, no warmth—that type of thing. She had that very superior, very cut-and-dry attitude. Course she was very professional and just fantastic when she sang. Evidently in her younger years she had a pretty rough time. She was just constantly on her guard. I guess she had just decided she would never let her guard down."

She could be "difficult" in other ways. Ray Rainwater booked her around this time for a series of club dates in Connecticut, New Jersey, New York and Pennsylvania. Patsy never did feel comfortable in the big, northeastern cities, especially New York. Though she was "totally professional" behind the microphone, she had come to entertain the folks and was disappointed when turnout at the clubs was low. She griped about it in her typically blunt style. "She was very contentious to get along with—she ranked up there with Bobby Helms," recalled Rainwater.

"They stayed away in droves. She would play to empty houses. That upset her. Some people draw and some people don't, and she didn't. She would complain loudly and in the presence of a lot of other people, and it just didn't go over, you know? If you got a complaint, call somebody down and say, 'Look, I got a complaint here,' instead of airing it publicly. She would raise her voice and complain about things. It would be embarrassing to me to be there and be considered with her."

While Patsy was on the West Coast, the owner of a motel where she was staying in Pasadena presented her with song lyrics that had been penned by a cousin in northern California. Mary Lu Jeans was a poet whose work had been published in *McCall's, Good Housekeeping* and the *Saturday Evening Post,* and she'd recently taken up songwriting with a co-writer, Charlotte White. Patsy was struck by one of their collaborations, "A Stranger in My Arms": "Every story has an ending/This is where our story ends/Please don't hurt me by pretending/For lovers never can be friends."

The song hadn't been set to music. Words are a singer's medium, as much as the notes, and for this reason Patsy had always been compelled to write. Since many other singers wrote their own material, she figured she ought to be able to as well. But whereas dirty jokes or cussing were a more natural form of wordplay, she was intimidated by the written word.

"She used to talk about writing in a negative sort of way," recalled Mae Axton. "She'd say, 'You know, I wish I could write'—that kind of thing. I told her, 'You can—just try it.' She was very insecure about writing, but she wanted to do it. She'd say, 'Well, what do you write about? How do you know when it's good?' I said, 'Well, there are people who get up in the morning and write all day, but I can't do that and I don't think they're the best songs. Something has to happen that I see or hear about and it's an inspirational thing—something touches me. Then I have to write about it.' She said, 'Well I have a lot of things that happen like that.' I said, 'Well, then, write about 'em.' But then, after that, that was about all she said about it."

Since Patsy could play "by ear," she decided to put "A Stranger in My Arms" to music herself. She told the *Winchester Evening Star* it was "the first time ever" she had composed music. The result was a slow pop ballad on which, consciously or not, she may have been inspired by "Some Enchanted Evening," from the 1949 Broadway musical *South Pacific*. She called Paul Cohen and sang the song to him over the phone. No doubt pleased by Patsy's interest in songwriting and impressed by her first effort, Cohen praised her efforts. When McCall tried to register it with BMI, he was informed there was a copyright infringement on the first six notes of "Some Enchanted Evening." Patsy badly wanted to record it, so McCall circumvented the problem by registering the song with Chappel Music, the copyright holder on "Some Enchanted Evening." McCall couldn't take credit as publisher, but he would milk the song for writing royalties by affixing his wife's name, Ethel Bassey, on the song for a third, giving Patsy a third and Jeans/White a third.

Once she discovered McCall had laid claim to the song falsely, Patsy was indignant. "We got one statement from Chappel," Jeans recalled. "They paid $1800 in advance royalties. Charlotte and I each got $300, Bill McCall got $600 and Patsy got $600. Patsy had just sung 'Walkin' After Midnight' on the Godfrey show and she was going to use the song on Godfrey's show, but when she found out McCall put his wife's name on the song, she was very angry. She felt the song had been stolen by him, which it had. Patsy made the statement later on that she wouldn't push it because of what he'd done."

Around the same time she was working on "Stranger," Patsy got back in touch with Lillian Claiborne, whose talent for songwriting and arranging she'd greatly admired. Claiborne encouraged Patsy and offered her a song, "Don't Ever Leave Me," that had been recorded as an R&B number by Claiborne's main act, saxophonist Frank Motley and the Motley Crew, with vocals supplied by female vocalist "Angel Face." The song had been released on McCall's Big Town subsidiary in 1954, probably as part of the deal between Claiborne and McCall over Patsy's contract. Since McCall owned the publishing rights to "Don't

Ever Leave Me," Patsy was free to record the tune. She and Claiborne worked out their own arrangement for Patsy, who opted to give it the red hot mama treatment—Kate Smith meets Pearl Bailey. McCall gave Patsy a third writing credit, a third to Claiborne and a third to the writer, Jimmy Crawford.

In April, Patsy toured Florida, Georgia and South Carolina with singers Ferlin Husky and Faron Young. Young, nicknamed "the Young Sheriff" after his appearance in the film *Hidden Guns* in 1956, recalled Patsy's efforts at songwriting: "We used to get in the car and she'd say, 'Com'ere, listen to this here, Sheriff,' and she'd sing it just to get your opinion on it. We'd get a guitar and give her a chord. She'd tell us it was something she was working on; maybe she'd just be starting it. Hank Williams, he was the same—he'd get you off and sing you a tune, and use you as a barometer, see if you liked the song, and if you did he'd record it. I think I told her she ought to record her songs. I'd say, 'That's a good tune; you just got to finish it. You need a little better hook line on it; you kind of make 'Moon' and 'June' and 'spoon' rhyme—you'd better get those corny-ass words out of there.' But I don't think Patsy was destined to be no great songwriter. She was a singer."

In the latter part of March, Patsy made a swing through the Midwest, playing teen-pop sock hops one day and country dates the next, and, like her "Town & Country Jamboree" co-star George Hamilton, experiencing the schizophrenic life of a crossover artist. She told the *Winchester Evening Star* she "plans to stick with western and semi-popular music, [and] says she doesn't wear her fancy western duds on the big shows. However, the smaller shows seem to like the costumes better."

In Dubuque, Iowa, she appeared with Tony Pastor's band, with whom Rosemary Clooney and her sister Betty sang in the forties before Rosemary's solo career was launched. In Des Moines she appeared on a program headlined by Webb Pierce for a sold-out performance at the Des Moines Auditorium. After the concert, upon learning that fourteen-year-old Shirley Nelson, who had a ticket to the show, couldn't hear her sing because she'd been rushed to the hospital for emergency surgery, Patsy called a taxi to take her to the hospital. A wire service photo of Patsy at the girl's bedside appeared subsequently.

"Patsy had the flu; she was pumped full of antibiotics," recalled Donn Hecht, whom Patsy called after the show. "She was so tired when I spoke to her on the phone. I said, 'For Christ sake, if you keep this shit up you're going to be dead.' She said, 'Well, I know I'm going to die anyway—we're all going to die. But that girl loves me.' Here she'd just finished that show, she's sick, tired, and she's dragging her ass all over the place, but there was a seat in the house that was vacant, somebody who didn't hear her sing. She was told the girl was taken to the hospital. She said, 'What hospital? I'll go and sing for her.' That was Patsy—she had to extend that love to everybody, even if there was one empty seat in the house, she wondered what happened."

McCall deducted every conceivable expense and calculated them against Patsy's royalties—things she thought were being provided by the record company: taxis, telephone calls, postage stamps, room service, and, in all likelihood, Patsy's share of the office pastries, along with all the common costs associated with recording, promotion and manufacturing—including the same high "breakage" percentages calculated before virtually unbreakable vinyl 45s came out, when records were 78s made out of shellac and often broke during shipment. Every six months she received a statement in the mail, which she tore open, excited to see how much money she'd made. The statement was impossible to read without a law degree, and the bottom line was always that rather than the record company owing her money for her hit, she owed 4 Star.

Instead of being flush, or even semi-well-off, she constantly found herself in the position of having to ask McCall for an advance on the next record. Patsy was caught in a vicious cycle: McCall knew she was always broke, even after "Midnight." He would agree to an advance, provided she agreed to an extension on her contract. Like many country artists, Patsy didn't know enough to get herself a lawyer until it was too late, and she didn't have a manager. McCall claimed that he was acting in her best interests and she believed him (thereby giving meaning to the word *patsy*)—until she realized she was being duped. Her lifetime royalties on "Walkin' After Midnight" were less than $900. Some stories had it that McCall, for a period of time, even managed her road money and took part of that.

Still, she was earning substantially more than the $8-a-night gigs she used to play with Bill Peer. Godfrey paid her $1000 a week, while pop dates fetched as much as $700. Patsy finally had a chance to give instead of take. She loved nothing more than helping those who were down on their luck, as she had been all her life. Her first impulse was always toward Hilda. She inscribed a new publicity photo of herself with her head tilted, wearing her "Walkin' After Midnight" dress, to her mother: "We finally made it!" The *Winchester Evening Star* noted, "Patsy Cline expressed the desire to thank all the people for their telegrams, letters and phone calls, and said that she would never forget those who gave her moral support when she needed it most."

With her road earnings she rented a comfortable brick house for the Hensley family a few doors from their old home on Kent Street. No more peeling wallpaper, flaking linoleum and dirty coal stove. Some people couldn't understand why Patsy didn't move the family off Kent Street entirely into a middle-class neighborhood, but "Patsy was Patsy," said Johnny Anderson.

"She never upgraded herself any. Why the hell didn't she go up on Stewart Street? She could have afforded it. That was Patsy. That's where she wanted to be and that's where she stayed."

In addition to the house, Patsy paid for her brother John to come to California with her so she could help him launch a singing career. John, it seemed, had inherited the Hensley talent for music. McCall told Patsy her brother was "very promising and had a good voice."

"She never had anything, you know?" offered Jumbo Rinker. "When she got back from 'The Bob Crosby Show' she called me up and said, 'Come on over. I have something to tell you.' So I say, 'Okay,' and I hurry over. So she gets her pocketbook out and she put about $2500 there on the table. And she said, 'What do you think of *that*?' So I said, 'Well, I'll probably tune in on the radio and find out that the bank's been robbed and somebody'll be knocking on that door in a minute.' She laughed. She said, 'I got fifteen hundred for two shows one one day and one the next.' That was clear, after all the agents and stuff. But she saved every nickel she could because she was trying to help her mother and herself, you know? There were hundreds and fifties there and everything. Spread it out all over there on the tablecloth, old, white tablecloth with flowers embroidered here and there and holes in it.

"She said, 'Take what you want.' 'Ahhh, you'd better not say that,' I says. She says, 'Take what you want. I know you don't have anything and I saved up a few bucks; that's what it's here for.' I says, 'Okay, if you insist.' So I started picking up all these bills, picked up about six or seven of them. She said, 'You satisfied? That all you want? I can always make another trip.' I laughed. But she was serious about it. She said, '*Take* it.' I could have picked up about six, seven hundred dollars, and I picked up the bills one at a time and she didn't say a word. I thought she would stop me. She took the money that was left on the table and put it back in her pocketbook. She meant for me to take that money. And when I gave it all back to her, she was kinda hurt."

Patsy met comedienne June Carter of the Carter Family on a plane from New York to Nashville. Their friendship was close from the start. For Patsy, June was a haven. When Patsy was confused, she went to June's Nashville home to "run and hide" from whatever or whoever was bothering her. As a member of the Carter Family, June was a seasoned pro of both television and stage, but it was June's spirituality in which Patsy sought the greatest comfort.

When they first met, June was in a major life transition of her own. Her marriage to singer Carl Smith, then one of Columbia's hot Opry acts, was on the rocks. June had her comedy act and was appearing on network TV and doing commercials. She started attending drama school in New York, living in New York, but also going home to her fifteen-acre farm in Nashville quite often. "I'd done a lot of television, a lot of comedy out of New York, working out of Hollywood as well," June said. "That's one reason it was easy for me to get work. I didn't have big tunes, but I could draw a lot of people. I was a lot more established."

Other than relying on Bill McCall and Arthur Godfrey for "advice," Patsy still had no management, and the money she expected to receive from her hit record hadn't materialized. She was "trying to get something going in Nashville, but she was broke; she didn't have any money or anything," June remembered. "I took Patsy home with me because I had a big house in Nashville, and even though I was living in New York City, I was coming home quite often. She was making the rounds to see what she could get. We had a lot of fun. We laughed a lot, talked a lot. We'd stay up all night long and talk a lot of times about a lot of things."

Patsy told June she was excited about her newfound public acceptance yet anxious about what the next step would be. There were too many people telling her what to do, and her time no longer felt like her own. She didn't like the business side of singing; she just wanted to do her job in front of the microphone and leave the decisions to others. She wanted someone she could lean on.

She almost had that feeling with Charlie. That he loved her there was no doubt, and sober, he could be a real Southern charmer. He doted on her. She loved him passionately. But when he drank she felt as if his whole personality changed. He was insanely jealous, interpreting her natural friendliness and down-to-earth cowgirl stylings for flirtatiousness and worse. He'd call her a whore, she'd yell back and the battle lines were drawn in a replay of her youth. "He wouldn't quit drinking and he'd party and had a couple of girls in his life besides Patsy," said Patsy Lillis. "He would do a lot of things to embarrass her in public places when she was trying to make a go at it. There were times when she would have dates to perform and there was an argument and he would whip her around the face. But she never took too many of them because she'd fight back. She got tired of it, though. I think she prayed to give it up."

If jealousy, as social scientists maintain, is a consequence not of low self-esteem but of an imbalance of power in a relationship, then each of them felt as though the other had the upper hand. Patsy couldn't control either Charlie's drinking or his womanizing. "Patsy was awfully jealous. That's how I know she loved him dearly, because if you don't care, you're not jealous," Lillis said.

"She wasn't sneaky," said George Hamilton. "I can't picture her sneaking around on Charlie. I read somewhere where Elizabeth Taylor said she fell in love a lot but always married her lovers. Some people don't bother; they just have affairs. Patsy struck me as the kind of person if she'd get fed up with somebody she'd dump 'em and go with whoever she loved. I think she was too big a woman to just want to play sneaky games. I think her one great passion was Charlie Dick. I think he was probably a thorn in her side too. They say opposites attract. Sometimes it's better if one is passive and the other dominant. I think they were both dominant. It sure seemed like a roller-coaster ride but the times they were happy it was beautiful. My impression was that they were a country version of Richard Burton and Liz Taylor."

In Charlie, Patsy met her shadow side, and she was frightened, at times, by the darkness of the image. Other than the feeling that she was very much in love with him, she was often so angry at him that she didn't know what to do. She couldn't understand why he acted the way he did.

"She was going through a lot of different problems," said June Carter. "I was a very spiritual person and she used to call me if she would get mixed up and not know whether she was coming or going about this or that, or if she and Charlie had been fighting. And she used to say to me the same thing, over and over—'June, please—pray for me. I don't have the strength to pray for myself.' At any rate, I spent a lot of time talking for hours on the phone or in person. It would have been times she was a little mixed up in her life."

June was one in a small cadre of intimates in whom Patsy confided her fears and secrets. Once a friendship was established, Patsy, unwilling or unable to let down her guard to reveal her vulnerabilities, sought comfort in maintaining intimate contact from afar. The telephone was her medium for doing this, and her closest friends came to expect desperate calls from her at odd hours.

"I was used to hearing from her in the middle of the night," June offered. "We would talk for two, three hours on the phone. She would just like to get it out, sometimes from the road. She'd call me at home or she'd try to find me." Patsy divulged her darkest secrets to June, including her experiences with her father. To June, the problems she experienced with Charlie were inextricably linked to Patsy's past:

"Anybody who suffers abuse of any kind, I mean, if women take abuse, it usually goes back to childhood in some way, because they go through this thing of thinking they deserve to be abused. She had a lot of guilt in her life that she dealt with. I think that's one of the reasons why she talked to me for so long."

Donn Hecht was another confidante, a "secret person she could talk to, someone who wasn't in the mainstream of her life." He received many phone calls from Patsy over the seven-year period he knew her, and at times when she was in California, he observed her making similar calls to others in Virginia and Tennessee. They might be planned but more often than not they were spontaneous, when she was in some sort of emotional turmoil. Though she might try to make the conversation sound casual, there was always an underlying feeling of urgency. One minute she might ask about something as trivial as how you glue wallpaper around the bathtub without the steam from the shower peeling it off, and in the next breath she'd say, "What's an alcoholic? Someone who drinks every day or someone who every so often gets falling-down drunk?" Or "Are you supposed to enjoy sex all the time?"

Patsy told Hecht she was haunted by her sexual problems. She indicated she thought it was her fault whenever things went wrong and expressed guilt and shame. The secret relationship with her father came up in the course of their conversations. Hecht offered her view in his analysis: "If you had frequent experiences with a father—your father playing around with you, turning you on, why this can be torture. It's like you think you're going to have a love affair with somebody and the guy turns you on physically, gets you excited and then you can't do anything. And you don't know why. And it suddenly dawns on you, 'I couldn't go to bed with my father, naturally, and that was my first sexual experience.' You realize that's the reason you can't go all the way with someone you want to do it with because how can you enjoy something you feel guilty about."

In April, Charlie received his summons from Uncle Sam. He was sent to Fort Benning, Georgia, for basic training and later stationed at Fort Bragg, North Carolina, where, as a linotype operator, he was assigned to the First L&L, for loudspeakers and leaflets, responsible for churning out Cold War propaganda. Patsy was at June's farm in Nashville when she learned of Charlie's induction into the Army. "She threw a fit," June recalled. "She cried and carried on. She was really upset about him going."

Her divorce from Gerald was final and in the spring of 1957 Patsy was free to become engaged to the man she loved. They set a wedding date of September 15. Said Patsy Lillis: "Whoever made that song 'Gone'? Ferlin Husky? Well, every time they played that song, she'd cry."

She told the *Winchester Evening Star* she would stay home for the Apple Blossom gala in May. Like a debutante with a long line of beaus, Patsy added, "It meant rearranging my schedule."

As Decca's top crossover artist, it was determined that her follow-up session would be held in New York. The dates were April 24 and 25, 1957. Paul Cohen was the likely producer. McCall was also present at the session. Owen Bradley was not informed of the change of recording venues until it was too late. Patsy was his artist, and working on the follow-up to the hit he'd helped create was a point of pride. "At the time you sort of felt a little slighted by it," Bradley admitted, adding, "It might have been to please Mr. Godfrey." Since Godfrey was, at this point, "advising her on her career," according to an interview Patsy gave the *Winchester Evening Star*, Bradley's hypothesis was probably correct.

Over the two-day period she cut eight songs for the forthcoming album, most of which represented a 180-degree turnaround from her earlier hillbilly efforts. Included were "A Stranger in My Arms" and "Don't Ever Leave Me." "Today, Tomorrow and Forever" is a midtempo ballad with a beat similar to "Walkin' After Midnight." "Fingerprints" is a ballad penned by Donn Hecht from the Hallmark Card school of sentiment: "I feel the fingerprints/That you left on my heart."

On day two the Anita Kerr Singers were brought in for added sweetening. Since their own victory on "Talent Scouts" the previous year, the Nashville-based Kerrs had become regulars on Godfrey's show. Their session work in New York most likely dovetailed with their TV work that week.

"Try Again," a cocktail lounge blues with a world-weary sophistication, expressed the theme of the session. "Too Many Secrets," an uptempo number with a hint of R&B, employed a call-and-response effect with a brass section. "Then You'll Know" really showed Patsy's ability to do jazz-oriented material and revealed touches of her later recorded work.

The results of the New York session were apparently disappointing; Decca did not immediately release a single. The following month, on May 23, Patsy was back in the Quonset Hut, and Bradley was back in charge. Both felt the pressure to come up with the next hit record. "We were both trying to please New York," Bradley said. "We were on the same team, but we didn't always agree on how to get there. We hoped they liked what we did because if they didn't they might drop us both. That was the crux of it. It wasn't that they didn't love her—they did, and they were very good to me too. But we both knew in the back of our minds that if we pleased them, they would maybe work on it harder, because if you don't get past that hurdle, you've had it."

When Cohen used the Anita Kerr Singers as backup vocalists at the New York sessions he was following a trend that had been started by Bradley and Chet Atkins, Bradley's counterpart at RCA Victor. In an effort to revive the popularity of country music in the wake of rock and roll, the A&R men had been experimenting with a number of ideas, including the use of vocal choruses, overlaying country singers and country songs with the full, lush sounds more typical of pop music. The idea was to create a vocal cushion under the singer.

By 1957, the Kerrs and the Jordanaires, the all-male quartet that backed the post–Sun Records' Elvis on his RCA recordings, were on eight of every top ten country records cut on any given week in Nashville. The two groups were working eighteen hours a day. They were so busy they would show up for a session rarely knowing beforehand whom they would be backing. Recalled Kerr member Louis Nunley: "We just showed up. Sometimes they'd say we're working with Patsy or we're working with whoever, you know. And sometimes they wouldn't tell us who we'd be working with; they would call up and say, 'Are you available at two?' and you'd say, 'No, two I'm working. How about six?' And they'd say, 'Okay, we'll move the session to six.' So we'd show up at RCA or wherever and it'd be sort of a surprise to see who was there."

Noticeably absent from Patsy's May date were any fiddlers or steel guitar players, who were unemployed in vast numbers in the postrock Nashville. The whole town had gone electric. Guitarists, especially the new breed of innovative studio players who were into jazz experimentation, were working the same round-the-clock schedules as the two principal vocal groups in town. The guitar triumvirate of Grady Martin, Harold Bradley and Hank "Sugarfoot" Garland had house accounts with the record companies whereby those players handled all the labels' dates.

Martin, Bradley and Garland were widely regarded as the tightest unit in the record industry. The casual atmosphere of the Nashville studios, in contrast to New York or even L.A., made for a creative environment in which everyone contributed ideas. "In the beginning, Grady and Hank and I were competitive; we were bumping into each other pretty well," recalled Harold Bradley. "We got to be pretty good thieves of each other's stuff. But then, after we defined our territories, we all became friends and then we found it was more helpful to share what we knew. Grady was an excellent leader, but everybody runs out of gas. After coming up with two or three good intros or whatever, I might ask, 'What's up next?' and he'd turn around and say, 'Anybody got anything in mind?' We were always free to put whatever we thought was a really good musical idea in. And we all thought we were arrangers. Grady was the filter. If he liked it, he'd say, 'Great, let's go ahead and use it,' and if he didn't like it, 'No, next song, maybe we'll use it.'"

It was Garland's first Patsy Cline session. Like Patsy, he was an anomaly in wider musical circles: a brilliant jazz guitarist who worked country sessions. "The jazz circles were laughing at him, but flipping over what he was playing," said bassist Bob Moore, also present at Patsy's date. Garland earned his nickname from a 1949 recording of "Sugarfoot Rag," which he'd conceived as a finger exercise; Red Foley immediately recorded a vocal cover version that featured Garland on guitar, for which he later received label credit. By 1957, Garland was playing behind everyone, from Elvis Presley to Patti Page.

In terms of material, this would be Patsy's single most versatile session to date, one that proved her ability as a song stylist and set her apart from every other girl singer in Nashville. The songs covered the map: pop, torch, novelty, blues and jazz. With all the parts going down live and no overdubbing, concentration was very focused and there was an excitement in the studio on which Patsy thrived. Unlike New York, she could get down with the Nashville cats.

She started out with a lofty rendition of a secular gospel number, "That Wonderful Someone," with the Kerrs oohing and aahing in the background. Patsy gave the hard-edged "In Care of the Blues" her red hot mama treatment, complete with growls and a near-yodel at the finale. Bradley tried to tell her such vocal tricks weren't necessary on a recording, but it was often an uphill battle: "There's a lot more energy in growling, yodeling and whatnot," said Bradley, who never saw her live act other than one- or two-song appearances on the Opry. "I would think that if you're doing a live performance and you feel like you're not really getting over with the audience, then you turn it up a notch. It's like turning up the volume on your hi-fi. So you turn it up a notch and look around and see if everybody's listening, and if they're not then you growl a little or yodel or whatever, to get 'em smiling. I think that's what it was with her."

She growled voraciously on "Hungry for Love," on which even the relatively benign Kerrs sounded aggressive. "I Can't Forget" suggested some of her later "hurtin'" material and Hank Garland came up with a jazzy riff that counterpointed Patsy's vocal. Bradley did a pop remake of "I Don't Wanta," originally recorded as a straight country number in her second session; the insipid lyrics and the Kerrs' relentless do-wop-a-doing were redeemed only by Garland's sweet, jazzy break, and Patsy was clearly ignited by his virtuosic playing.

McCall sat in on the date, to the annoyance of everyone in the studio. Bradley was still quietly fuming that Patsy's last session had been taken out of his hands. And Patsy couldn't figure out why she had a smash hit and was stone broke. McCall badgered Bradley over an additional two songs he wanted recorded beyond the standard four. He insisted they were owed him because two of his songs had been screwed up at Patsy's recent New York session. Bradley remained composed until McCall started in on him about a technical problem. That did it. The usually tactful Bradley, who ran the busiest independent recording operation in Nashville, evicted McCall. It was the last time the two of them ever met at a Patsy Cline session.

"We had this technical problem that we were working on, and Mr. McCall was testy, and he really got me irritated," recalled Bradley. "He had a lot of money on that song. He blamed us; he was so intolerant, I thought. Here he'd tried doing it somewhere else and he wasn't successful—which didn't make us that damn happy, if you want to know the truth. Then he was finding fault because we had a little technical problem and he wasn't being charged anything for it. I had a little room where I took him. I knew a bishop in the Catholic Church one time who'd once said something about 'giving a man a little sermon.' That session was a disaster. I don't think he ever came back again. In fact, I think that was part of my 'sermon.' "

But McCall insisted on having the last word. After he returned to Pasadena and the masters of the session were sent to him, he fired off a letter to Bradley. In it he told the producer he refused to pay for all four of the Anita Kerr Singers because he could only hear three voices.

Five days later, Decca released two sides aimed at Patsy's pop fans: "Today, Tomorrow and Forever," backed by "Try Again," from the April session. "Patsy sends a couple straight down the line for all fans—a strong beat in the background accents the power of these sides," ran the ad copy. Her photo was prominently displayed above both Bill Haley and His Comets and Brenda Lee. "Plenty of action due here," the ad predicted.

Chapter Fourteen

FOLLOWING HER MAY SESSION Patsy returned to Winchester to celebrate Charlie's birthday, then hit the road for a dizzying round of one-nighters that had her packing two wardrobes, one for her country dates, the other for pop.

Patsy met Brenda Lee on a tour through the Southwest during the summer of 1957. It was the only time the two of them ever worked a show together, but it was a formative experience for Brenda, who was only twelve years old. As he had been doing with Patsy, Bradley had been experimenting with a pop sound for the husky-voiced child singer with a woman's voice. After Brenda's rockabilly success with "BIGELOW 6-200," Milt Gabler briefly took over on a January 1957 session that resulted in "One Step at a Time," a minor crossover hit for Brenda that year. A week after Patsy's April 1957 session, Brenda was back in Bradley's studio to record her next crossover hit, "Dynamite," which resulted in her stage billing during the tour with Patsy as "Little Miss Dynamite." But Bradley had not yet achieved the transformation that would later lead to Brenda's full-fledged pop stardom, and even though she'd already made appearances on "The Ed Sullivan Show" and "The Perry Como Show," Brenda was still basically a country act whose calling card was "Jambalaya."

In Texas, Brenda and her mother were stranded after a promoter absconded with her money. Patsy came to the rescue. She put them up in her motel room, took them back to Nashville in her car, an old, white Cadillac, gave them money and advised them to "always make sure you get your money before the show and in cash no matter what." When Brenda congratulated Patsy on her success on "Midnight," Patsy's reply was, "Well, thank you, but damn it, it ain't doing me no good. I'm not making anything off of it."

Patsy probably saw a lot of herself in Brenda. Brenda's father died in a tragic accident when she was eight, forcing her mother to work sixteen-hour days in a cotton mill. Little Brenda helped to support her large family by singing in country shows. Despite Brenda's youth and her diminutive stature, Patsy treated her like an adult and Brenda was grateful and flattered.

"She would talk to me about show business, about women and the kind of tough row they had to hoe. She would tell me things like we had to stay in there and fight for the things we believe in and don't give up, because we can do it. I don't think she was necessarily a women's libber—maybe she was, I don't know. But I think she just believed so much in herself and what she was doing and in what women could do in this business.

"I think she had to grow up fast. I think that's one of the reasons why people thought of her as never being young, because maybe she never was. She had to grow up a whole lot before she grew up. That's sad, in a way. I missed my childhood too. She was like a big sister to me. I'd tell her whatever problems I was having, boyfriend problems or whatever, and she'd give me advice and was just great. I just loved her. She was always kinda looking out for folks, and if she could help you she would, no matter what her station in life was at the time, and she helped a lot of people that way. I certainly thought an awful lot of her, and at the time that's what struck me the most about her—not what she was doing professionally because I didn't really know the scope of it. I just knew she held out a helping hand and became my friend when I needed one."

On July 26, 1957, following a ten-day package tour with Ray Price, Ferlin Husky, Faron Young, Hank Thompson and Johnny Cash, Patsy appeared on Alan Freed's short-lived TV show, "The Big Beat," which aired on ABC. Promoter, deejay, songwriter and "personality," Freed had his name constantly in the trade and popular press for his productions of wild stage shows at the Brooklyn and New York Paramounts featuring Fats Domino, Chuck Berry, Little Richard, Frankie Lymon, Bill Haley, Buddy Holly, the Everly Brothers and Jerry Lee Lewis. Patsy appeared on a program that also featured Fats Domino, Clyde McPhatter, Dale Hawkins, Marvin Rainwater and Jimmy "C." Newman, a country singer who was enjoying pop success with "A Fallen Star." She took her fourteen-year-old sister, Sylvia, and Dale Turner along for company, paying the way for both of them.

"That was the first time I ever rode a train in my life," Sylvia recalled. "After the show was over, I sat on a piano bench with Fats

Domino. He made a G clef by using a pencil on a gold-plated piano wire. I never told a soul. I didn't think they'd believe me."

"She didn't act excited; she didn't bubble about it," Turner recalled of Patsy's appearance on Freed's show. "She wanted somebody to be there, I guess on her side. She might have been a little nervous. I don't remember exactly where we stayed but it was interesting to me because it looked to me like one of those film noir movies of New York on the seedy side of town. I liked it. We were probably only there a day and a half or two days. I ran off with one of the agents who'd booked her and she went to rehearsal and I didn't go to rehearsal with her. She got a little hot about that. She was mad, you know—'I brought you here to be company for me and you're running around'—that kind of thing. But that's the kind of relationship we had, and we could talk to each other like that."

For Freed's show, Patsy dressed "pop," in a blue chiffon, off-the-shoulder dress with a full, cocktail-length skirt. She lip-synched "Walkin' After Midnight" on a set made to look like a footbridge. Turner recalled: "Somewhere in the course of the song she had to walk up a set of stairs, it seemed about eight or ten feet high. I couldn't have done it. I'd have fallen. She went up about ten steps, then there was a platform up there that was about six feet long where she stopped for a little while and then that many steps down. What amazed me was that it was so high. But she looked beautiful and did a great job."

Patsy turned around and put on her country clothes for an appearance August 10 on "Country Music Jubilee" (the former "Ozark Jubilee" was renamed in 1957 after it went from a local to a network show), probably her third on that show. "Jubilee," which at one point aired opposite the top-rated Jackie Gleason and Perry Como shows, was seen by an audience estimated at 50 million and its ratings topped "Disneyland," "Lassie" and "The Ed Sullivan Show." The program's success was attributed to the charm of Red Foley, a "barnyard Bing Crosby" who emceed the proceedings, sang and played guitar, recited Edgar Guest–type poems and occasionally exclaimed, "Well, bless your heart" and "That just shows to go ya." Patsy's co-stars were Sonny James, Bobby Lord and Uncle Cyp and Aunt Sap, whose comedy routine involved an elderly married couple who traded off ancient jokes. The program was sponsored by Dickies Slacktime Casual Clothes and Dentine.

Foley began his introduction: "We seem to be getting some real good reaction from you folks lately on the way we've been having both a boy *and a girl* guest each week. And the young lady who has come to visit us this week is the one who made such a hit with her song 'Walkin' After Midnight.' Here with a brand-new tune, 'Three Cigarettes in an Ashtray," is pretty Patsy Cline."

While Foley sat in a café set looking on, Patsy lip-synched the song that would be released two days later (backed by "A Stranger in My Arms.") In spite of the exposure she was getting on national TV and through personal appearances, there was still no chart action.

"Virginia Hensley Cline Wed to Charles Dick on Sunday," ran the announcement in the *Winchester Evening Star.* For Patsy, 1957 was a year of milestones: the death of her father, her first hit record, divorce and now marriage.

True love, like the stardom she'd sought ever since she was a child, had always seemed to elude her. Now that she'd achieved her primary goal by getting her hit record, she was determined to have everything else that went with it.

Offered Patsy Lillis, "That was the whole thing with her—she thought that was it, she wanted it all: the marriage, the roses, the house with the white picket fence, the babies. She thought she ought to have all that stuff, besides her records."

The ceremony was held in the sturdy little brick house on Kent Street. Aunts, uncles, cousins, Winchester friends, many of her musician pals from the D.C. scene, about seventy people in all, gathered to witness the nuptials.

"It was the only time Patsy ever went against her mother," said Lillis, her bridesmaid.

Patsy handled all the details of the wedding. "Everything had to be just so." Glamorous it was not: the reception was given by Hilda at the Mountainside Inn, otherwise known as Burt's Club, a roadhouse on the outskirts of Winchester, the kind Patsy used to sing in when she first started out.

"The bride's attendants . . . wore dresses of dark blue cotton and silk with blue hats, white accessories and white carnations," the newspaper noted. It was the first time they had ever worn high heels and they stumbled around all day, laughing at their own clumsiness.

"Given in marriage by her brother, Sam L. Hensley, Mrs. Dick wore a light blue knit, two-piece dress, white hat and matching accessories. Her only ornaments were pearl earrings."

Charlie held a cigarette between his index and second fingers the entire day except at the moment he stubbed it out when the Reverend S. J. Goode of the Winchester Christian Church joined them as man and wife. A photographer snapped a picture of the newlyweds coming down the front steps of the house, hand-in-hand.

The day turned out warmer than expected. Patsy changed into a cocktail dress with a chiffon skirt and a high, velveteen bodice and the plastic high-heeled mules she loved and had worn on "Talent Scouts." A handmade banner hung from the wall behind the banquet table: "Welcome Patsy—Here's to the star that likes to shine, Winchester's own Patsy Cline."

Charlie's younger brother, Mel, vividly recollected the romance of the day: "That day was just wonderful. They had two big bowls of punch for each family. Hers was mixed and my family's was not mixed 'cause my aunts said we can't go if you're going to have liquor there. My family don't drink, not a drop, no one, except for Charles. It was their family that had the punch spiked. They had these two big bowls. I had this aunt who looked just like a stovepipe. Stern. She got the bowls mixed up and she turned to my other aunt and said, 'Pauline, come have this punch. It's quite good.' She got quite tipsy.

"It was probably one of the nicest times she and Charlie were together. It seemed like there was always a little tension between them, but that day was just wonderful. Now they had a million problems and they would argue and you would think they were just going to half kill each other, verbally. Then they'd get over it and laugh. Remember in the movie—my sister-in-law said her favorite scene in the movie was when he came home and he was late and they tore the whole room up and he says, 'Now do you want to go in another room and tear that up?' It was her favorite scene. If anything was perfect in that whole movie that had to be that scene."

"It was the greatest day of her life," agreed Lillis. "She was happy, happy, happy. Patsy loved Charlie with all her heart and soul, even though she knew he wasn't right for her, deep down."

There was no mention of "Patsy Cline" in the newspaper account of the wedding. As if to hide under her new identity, it was Virginia Dick, all the way. The story concluded, "Mrs. Dick attended Gore School and Handley High School and is a professional entertainer. She plans to continue with her singing career."

The lifeblood of Fayetteville, North Carolina, was nearby Fort Bragg, as the preponderance of auto body shops, gun shops, furniture rental stores and bars would suggest. Patsy was not exactly thrilled to leave Winchester, the place she called home. After the wedding, she and Charlie found their first home together amid the homogeneous track housing built to accommodate servicemen and their families off-base. In October she returned to New York to do the Godfrey show again. Godfrey congratulated her and asked if she was happy, to which she replied, "just as happy as if I had good sense."

"Walkin' After Midnight" garnered a handful of awards for Patsy at the 1957 Deejay Convention, held the weekend of November 15 and 16: she took home *Billboard*'s "Most Promising Country & Western Female Artist," *Country and Western Jamboree*'s "Best New Female Singer of 1957" and *Music Vendor*'s "Greatest Achievement in Records."

Patsy wore a glamorous satin sheath dress, high heels and swept-back hairdo à la Ava Gardner to the proceedings. Her industry friends were perplexed by the skinny soldier she introduced to everyone as her new husband. Said one Opry star, "When I met Charlie at the Opry that weekend, I wondered if ole Patsy had a bag over her head. I couldn't stand him. I don't know what on earth attracted her to him."

Though Patsy could look as glamorous as any Hollywood siren, she had a ready answer for Alan Block, co-writer of "Walkin' After Midnight," when he queried her, "Do you like my song now?"

"Man, you just don't understand," she told him. "I'm just an ole hillbilly. I ain't used to singing semi-classical music." Either Patsy was pulling his leg, or she was downplaying having "gone pop," which country purists considered tantamount to heresy. How else to account for her not telling him she'd indeed sung "semi-classical" music when she was just starting out?

In December, Patsy learned she was pregnant. The news came as a surprise but she quickly accepted the idea of starting a family. It was part of her dream that she shared with American women everywhere in the fifties. She simply had to be happy. She felt guilty about having "messed up" her first marriage, and in spite of the naysayers, she was determined to make her marriage to Charlie work. Now that they were expecting, she hoped he would "settle down."

Charlie was elated by the news. Music was her first love, the only way she could give her heart completely. But the biological fact of pregnancy bonded her to him in a way that the music could not, and for the first time his need to bond completely and merge with her was gratified. He encouraged her to stay at home and be a housewife and let him be the breadwinner. She acquiesced. She was so tired, so very tired from the whirlwind. It seemed there was never a time when she wasn't working and fighting to make something of her life. She couldn't even remember being a child. She just wanted to be "normal."

"I heard from her two times that year [1958]," Donn Hecht recollected. "She told me once she had gone to work for somebody in a variety store down there where she was living. I said, 'You're kidding? What in the hell are you doing working in a variety store?' She just said she needed to relax; she needed to get away from 'all this shit,' she said. She didn't like to cuss over the phone. She would cuss like a sailor in person but she didn't like to cuss over the phone; she felt very self-conscious about it. 'It's like things are creeping in on me and I just want to lay low. I just want to sit down and I want to work around the corner and come home and be normal.' I felt so goddamn sorry for her. It seemed like if somebody would have offered her a thousand dollars a week to sing, she'd of turned it down. She did say she was having a problem, however. She said she was sick. She didn't mention that she was pregnant, but I got the feeling she was, and she wasn't looking forward to it, because if she was happy about it, wouldn't she have said something like, 'Hey, Donn, I'm expecting, and I feel so damn good about it!'?"

She returned to Nashville on December 13 to record her fourth session of the year—twice as many as in previous years. Patsy had a genius for creating her own songs out of others' material and so she chose her numbers carefully. The lyrics of a song are the most important thing a singer has to work with and she had an attitude toward her songs that was comparable to a great actress toward her lines, movements and gestures. She was able to deliver even the most appalling lyrics with conviction.

She fairly attacked the aptly titled "Stop the World (And Let Me Off)," her voice breaking at the outset and sobbing along the way: "Oh stop the world and let me off/I'm tired of going round and round." Bradley might have wished for more restraint on "Walking Dreams"; Patsy growled her way through the song, fighting to keep her vocal above the Kerrs' intrusive background bopping. She found poignancy in Donn Hecht's lyrical pop ballad "Cry Not for Me": "Cry not for me, my love/When I am far away/There's nothing more to say/Cry not for me." The joy of her first pregnancy tempered by the sad memories of her own missed childhood, she delivered "If I Could See the World (Through the Eyes of a Child)" as fervently as if it were a prayer: "If I could see the world through the eyes of a child/What a wonderful world this would be/There'd be no trouble and no strife, just a big happy life/With a bluebird in every tree." Bradley made an exception to one of Paul Cohen's rules and played vibraphone. (Commercial or not, the cut was released later that year).

The following day Patsy guested on the "Grand Ole Opry." She was introduced by Ray Price, who quipped, "We're always glad to have you with us. I want to ask you a favor."

"Well, you just name it," she bantered along.

"'Walkin' After Midnight.'"

"It's a date, boy."

★   ★   ★

When on January 13, 1958, the *Music Reporter* announced that Patsy would be managed by Nashville talent manager Xavier "X" Cosse, it was the formalization of a relationship that had been developing over the previous year. Cosse had been booking Patsy on an ad hoc basis throughout 1957, including most of her Arthur Godfrey appearances, the most recent being a five-day stint during the first part of the new year. Cosse had a solid reputation, having originally been a booker of Broadway plays and ice shows. His clients included Boots Randolph, Chet Atkins, Floyd Cramer and Ferlin Husky, who had gone from being a country novelty act (as Simon Crum, his comedic persona) to a pop crossover star under Cosse's management. His biggest client, however, was his wife, gospel singer Martha Carson, a big-voiced singer whom Patsy greatly admired, who was at the peak of her career.

Far away from Nashville, Patsy felt relatively secure in her state of "semi-retirement," knowing that Cosse would not let her be forgotten. So the news that he would have to drop her must have shaken her. Shortly after the announcement appeared, Carson signed an important contract with General Artists in New York; the agency had plans to fashion her into a café society singer and book her in elite supper clubs in New York and Chicago. Even though time would prove it was a bad decision, Carson and her husband decided to move to New York. Cosse informed all his acts, including Patsy, that it would be best if they got Nashville-based representation.

Cosse's last booking for her was for an April 27 appearance on "Arthur Godfrey and His Friends," her last appearance on Godfrey's show. Cosse had been the buffer between Patsy and Godfrey's production staff, with whom she apparently experienced occasional conflicts of a musical nature. How the split came about is not certain; Dale Turner, with whom Patsy stayed in touch during this time, speculated that the parting came down to Godfrey's inability to "control" her.

"I don't know if she had a hard time getting along with [Godfrey's] management because she had to do what she wanted to do, or if it was problems with the band or what. When you start moving around and working with bands that don't know your stuff, well it can be upsetting, and she was a perfectionist."

Bradley scheduled Patsy's only session of 1958 for February 13. She cut six songs instead of the usual four, combining pop, country and blues. Once again Bradley had hired the ubiquitous Anita Kerr Singers to give four of the six tracks the easy listening touch that was the hallmark of the seminal Nashville Sound.

The pickings included "Just Out of Reach (Of My Two Open Arms)" (covered by Perry Como in 1976—his only country hit); the

Ben Adelman composition "I Can See an Angel"; a pop remake of "Come On In," to which Bradley added a brass section; and "Let the Teardrops Fall," the only strictly country tune of the batch, which Patsy belted, to mixed effect. After the Kerrs left the studio, work resumed on "Never No More," one of her best 4 Star tracks, written by "Walkin' After Midnight" collaborators Donn Hecht and Alan Block and Block's wife, Rita Ross. Bradley encouraged Patsy in giving it a bluesy reading, and instead of going up at the ending as she was prone to do, she finished in a low register. On "If I Could Only Stay Asleep" Bradley achieved the same torchy effect that would emerge in her later style.

Decca continued to release Patsy's singles throughout 1958: on June 2, "Come On In"/"Let the Teardrops Fall"; on August 18, "I Can See an Angel"/"Never No More"; on September 9, "If I Could See the World (Through the Eyes of a Child)"/"Just Out of Reach"; on December 15, "Dear God"/"He Will Do for You." There was no chart action. Patsy was a cold artist.

On February 21 she appeared on the "Country Music Jubilee," and in March, three months pregnant, she was booked on a ten-day tour of military bases in Hawaii on a package headlined by Faron Young and Ferlin Husky that included Jerry ("When You're Hot, You're Hot") Reed before any of his hits. Announcement of the tour appeared in *Billboard,* along with the news that in April she would do a ten-day tour of the Midwest booked by Kansas City promoter Hap Peebles. Young paid Patsy's plane ticket to Hawaii plus "maybe a couple a hundred bucks a day. She wasn't that big; she just wanted to come. We all did—God, we'd never been there before." Patsy was so impressed by the beauty of the islands that she sent flowers back to her mother along with a note: "You've got to see this."

"I remember at one base we were playing she was talking about how much help Arthur Godfrey had been to her," Young recollected. She said, 'I played with Arthur Godfrey for about a year and a half.' All them marines started laughing; they took it the wrong way. She come off that stage crying. She said, 'Them son-of-a-bitches.' I said, 'Oh, Patsy, they're just a bunch of kids—they don't mean nothing by it.' She said, 'Yeah, but they know I didn't mean it like that. Why would they act like I was saying something like that?' It really upset her. But she got hard; she learned the ropes. Later, she got to the point where she would have made a joke out of them laughing at her. She would have said, 'Well, I guess you all took that the wrong way. Only me and Arthur Godfrey will know.' "

In July, Patsy resurfaced again from semi-retirement when Elkton celebrated its Golden Jubilee and Patsy was asked to be the grand marshall in the town parade. Patsy was tickled by the invitation and by the fact that Elkton considered her its most famous native daughter. Eight months pregnant, she rode on top of a convertible wearing a flowered summer dress with shoulder straps, a fitted, empire bodice and very full skirt. Hobby Robinson, whose avocation was photography, was shooting from the top of Kick Sandridge's filling station, along the parade route. Robinson vividly recalled that day: "I talked to her right before the parade. I told her, 'Patsy, I'm not going to take your picture because you're so big. I'm going to wait until after you have the baby.' So when she went by in the parade and I was standing on top of the filling station, she yelled out my name anyway and threw up her hand and gave me a big wave, so I snapped the picture."

Two weeks before the baby was due, Patsy moved back to Winchester in order to have Hilda there for the big moment, as she always had been. The birth took place on August 25, at Winchester Memorial Hospital, the same hospital where Patsy had taken her first breath twenty-six years earlier. Friends claimed that Charlie was out partying the night she had the baby. The child, a girl, was named Julia Simadore Dick. Patsy got the unusual middle name from the 1949 Cecil B. DeMille movie, *Samson and Delilah,* starring Hedy Lamarr and Victor Mature. Simadore was Delilah's sister.

"I'd had a daughter named Seymour and Patsy always loved that name," recalled Patsy Lillis, who visited her best friend on Kent Street the day she got out of the hospital.

"She was all right, you know, wondering what she was going to do, how she was going to manage. She didn't talk about singing. She didn't think she was going anywhere."

"It may have been a lost year but it was one of her best years," offered Mae Axton. "In spite of the fact that it cut her off from working, she felt, 'I am really a woman now. I have my own piece of me.' "

Chapter Fifteen

URING THE PERIOD immediately following the birth of her daughter, Patsy became completely absorbed in the responsibilities of motherhood. After Julie's birth she remained in Winchester where Hilda helped care for the little one. Charlie gave up their house in Fayetteville and moved onto the base for the remainder of his Army stint. Patsy was only too happy to return to Winchester; she hated life in Fayetteville, where, far from her music and her friends, her marital problems took center stage. She told several girlfriends that Charlie was slapping her around while she was pregnant.

"It wasn't a happy time for her," said Pat Smallwood. "She was constantly running back home here, to her mother. He just wouldn't quit drinking and he'd party and the girls in his life—he had a couple girls besides Patsy."

Though she was very happy with the baby and "so proud I could shout her name from the rooftops," in her heart Patsy never really wanted to stop singing; she'd only done it to please Charlie. Her comment to Brenda Lee, "I don't miss the rat race a bit. Well, maybe a little," was an understatement; by the end of 1958, Patsy desperately missed the one thing that gave her complete fulfillment. Staying at home all day "is driving me crazy," she confessed to Patsy Lillis. "I guess I'm just not cut out to be a housewife."

It wasn't too long after Julie's birth that she decided to make a full-fledged comeback. While she was pregnant she quit smoking cigarettes, a habit she'd taken up after meeting Charlie. She had gained almost thirty pounds, which made her look fat. She went on a strict diet. With Hilda's help she got her cowgirl layouts together. Out of the limelight for almost a year, and almost two years since her last hit,

Patsy was a cold artist, and she resolved to make her way back doing the one thing she knew best—straight country.

Some significant developments had taken place in Nashville during Patsy's hiatus that would ultimately pave the way for the transformation of her sound and her style—indeed, that of country music itself.

One of the most important changes occurred in April 1958, when Owen Bradley realized the prediction he had made to Paul Cohen almost ten years earlier. Cohen's flamboyant, seat-of-the-pants style of doing business had put him at odds with the more conservative regime that had taken over Decca. After Jack Kapp's death, there was a power struggle within the company in the early 1950s. Dave Kapp was forced out and Milton Rachmil, originally an accountant for Decca, took over. Rachmil eventually became one of the most powerful men in the entertainment industry.

The Decca honchos frowned on Cohen's often brazen behavior, especially his private music publishing ventures, which were considered a conflict of interest with Decca's operations. "The bosses," as Bradley referred to them, kept Cohen on as long as he got hits for them. But as country music airplay dropped off and Cohen's gambling debts mounted throughout the fifties, and the statements came into his office and he couldn't pay, "He got jammed up and it began to reflect badly on the company," said Milt Gabler. Cohen was given a choice: "Either give up the publishing business and stay an A&R man or go your own way." Cohen flipped them all off and started his own, short-lived Nashville-based label, Todd. But before he cleared his desk at Decca he asked Bradley, "Do you still want my job?"

In certain odd respects, Bradley's promotion to A&R chief for Decca's country division was serendipitous. Sales of hard country records were at an all-time low and in early 1958 the Country Music Disc Jockey Association disbanded. A *Billboard* headline sounded the death knell for country music as it had existed up until the fifties: "RCA'S SHOLES PUTS 'OLD' C&W IN CRYPT."

Elvis Presley's A&R man elaborated: "The little red schoolhouse is no more. It has been replaced by the big rural school centers and when the kids began to cross geographical boundaries, they also began to cross musical boundaries. Television, too, has had its impact; musical tastes have been broadened, perhaps not for the better, but that's the way it is." Bradley, a pops man, was well placed in the new country music environment, which was trying to recapture a share of the market in the aftermath of rock and roll.

For a brief period of time in the mid-1950s it was said that rock and roll was invigorating country. Gene Vincent, Jerry Lee Lewis and other rockers had dual hits on both the country and pop charts, while Elvis's first eleven hits for Victor, between 1956 and 1958, were all big country hits. But by 1958, country music radio had become completely entrenched, and anything that sounded as though it had been made with the teen market in mind was rejected. Even the invincible Elvis's country music action dropped off after "Hard Headed Woman" entered the charts in June 1958, and he stayed off the country charts through the sixties and into the seventies. The same thing happened to other artists who strayed too far from traditional country; the Everly Brothers' country hits dropped off in 1959, after, "('Til) I Kissed You." Buddy Holly had no country hits at all, and neither did Roy Orbison, until 1980. Brenda Lee, a self-proclaimed country artist, had virtually nothing going country (except for "One Step at a Time," which charted briefly in 1957) at a time when she had nineteen hits in the Top 20.

Something had to be done to revitalize the country music market. In 1958 country music's "media magician," Connie B. Gay, came to Nashville in his chauffeured limousine, wearing his derby and Chesterfield coat, and helped found the Country Music Association. The new organization enacted a study to see how country music could adapt to the new commercial radio-record environment as more and more stations made the switch to Top 40 formats. More than anything, country music craved middle-class respectability. Bradley was the man to give it that through the experimenting that would result in the Nashville Sound, with Patsy as its greatest exponent.

When Patsy arrived at the Quonset Hut on January 8, 1959, almost a year had passed since she had worked with Bradley. In spite of the prevailing mood in Nashville for country music to become commercially viable in the new record-radio environment, Nashville sessions, unlike New York or even L.A., remained loose, relaxed affairs. Bradley, unlike Paul Cohen, was a musician and so everybody at his sessions was speaking the same language. The same was true at Chet Atkins's studio at RCA. As a result, the late fifties studio scene was very creative.

"It wasn't just Owen," said pianist Floyd Cramer, who had become an integral part of the "A Team" of session players on hand that, in Patsy's case, also included Harold Bradley, Grady Martin and Hank Garland on guitar, Bob Moore on acoustic bass and Murrey "Buddy" Harman on drums.

"Other producers here, too, who were very knowledgeable about what they wanted to hear, let the musicians contribute. You would suggest certain things on certain songs—do this here, do this here, and here, stop here. They would let us make up the arrangement as we'd go along. We'd arrive at the studio and we wouldn't know what we were going to record. Most of the time they just played a little demo tape or the artist would sing to us and we'd jot down the chord symbols or the notes or just remember it in our heads, and worked out a routine from there. The rhythm section would have chord sheets. There might be an intro where there was a piano part written out, just a lick. Those were some basic road maps we'd get occasionally.

"Once we got the routine and the key, finding which key was best for the artist to sing in, then we'd start to rehearse, whether it was Patsy or whoever. All artists have their thoughts about tempo and all that stuff so they had their input. If there were changes it would either come from Patsy, from Owen in the control room, who could hear everything, or it could be one of the musicians—'we want to change this lick or this chord.' That's the way it went, and it all went down at the same time, because we were recording on three track and on three track you did everything live and there was no going back and fixing it. If it's done right, everyone contributes."

Bradley had a surprise in store for Patsy. Instead of the Anita Kerr Singers, which he preferred for Brenda Lee's records, he'd hired the Jordanaires, whose low chords and soft, spiritual sound counterpointed Patsy's vocal power and broad range. The combination also set her apart from the sound he was developing for Brenda.

In 1954 the Jordanaires did a show with Eddy Arnold in Memphis. The quartet sang "Peace in the Valley," "Just a Closer Walk with Thee" and several other spirituals. Elvis Presley was in the audience and came backstage to meet the group. Jordanaire Ray Walker related the story: "He stuttered a little bit and he said, 'Ahh . . . Ah'm goin' to have a recordin' contract some day and when Ah do would you sing with me?' Gordon [Stoker] told him, 'Yeah, sure,' then he just forgot about the name. Then in 1955 here comes Elvis Presley with his Sun records. I was a disk jockey at the time. That winter when 'Blue Suede Shoes' and all that came out on Sun even the name Elvis Presley did not sound like Vic Damone and all that. Whoever heard of a name like this? And with a middle name like Aaron? You got to be kidding. The deejays were all saying nobody with a name like this is going to get any airplay. Then in January 1956 Elvis came to RCA Victor and asked Chet Atkins for the Jordanaires."

When Elvis started using the Jordanaires on all his smoothed-out records, soon everybody wanted background voices. "We were in the studios all the time," Walker recalled. "One week—128 hours. Sometimes we'd come in at 9:45 A.M., go through the material and start the sessions. We'd have a lunch and supper break and wouldn't be out 'til five or six the next morning. Maybe seven. And then we'd be back again at ten the same morning." Patsy might have been pleased that Bradley was bringing in the same group of guys who backed "*the* hoss," the ultimate compliment she paid Presley. But instead, her reaction was immediate and vehement: "I don't want no four male voices covering me up!"

If Patsy thought the Kerrs—two men and two women—had been intrusive, she figured four guys would sound even louder. "It's not that she didn't like us. She knew us, knew our work and respected us. I guess she just thought we'd be oohing and aahing all over her and all we did was fills with her," said Walker.

But Bradley's conceptualization of a vocal cushion had evolved during the past few years of experimentation and he insisted that the Jordanaires would be just perfect: "You just leave it to me," he reassured her. "My job," he said, "was to keep them out of the way and I think we did a pretty good job."

With her career in a slump after she thought she had it made, Patsy was depressed and frustrated when she arrived for her first session of the year. "She was heartbroken to a certain extent and you could see it on her face," recalled Stoker. "She didn't intend to damage her singing, but that's what happens sometimes when you take time out."

"She'd come off 'Walkin' After Midnight' and had a two-and-a-half-million-seller and she didn't have a dime to show for it," added Ray Walker. "We'd even heard that she was fool enough to send her label her road money and let them manage it, and they took all of that."

Despite Patsy's predilection for the vocal tricks of a roadhouse singer, Bradley had always felt she was a no-gimmick singer. And the lifeblood of a singer is good songs. He and Patsy combed through the 4 Star catalog together. By 1959, most of the material Patsy brought to the session was substandard, according to Bradley. There was nothing either of them could do about it until her contract ran out, and the extensions on her original contract tied her to McCall through part of 1960. Patsy could refuse to cut and ride the contract out, but then she wouldn't get the $50 per side that McCall gave her per session. And Patsy was always stone broke. There was another factor: at this point she was worried that no other label would pick her up.

"Prior to 1958 Mr. Cohen had practically everything to say about what we did," said Bradley. "I helped a great deal. I don't recall looking for material for Patsy. She'd just walk in and say, 'These are the songs we're going to do.' That's what we'd do. Then the pickings got worse and worse and she would complain. After April of '58 I started having a little something to say about it. Up until then it wasn't my business. The only thing I was supposed to do was make the session. Don't make waves. After '58 we started looking for material, both of us. We went through the 4 Star catalog, all the way back, looking for stuff."

Patsy's anxiety over the pitiful state of her career was reflected by the lack of jazzy freedom she employed in the period following her "Walkin' After Midnight" success. Rhythm was her most dependable weapon against the blues, and her lead stuck tenaciously to the beat on "I'm Moving Along," a light, mid-tempo shuffle, and the pop ballad "I'm Blue Again." "Love, Love, Love Me, Honey, Do" had Patsy building to a climax on an ascending riff and was the kind of vehicle that displayed her roadhouse skills. After three and a half hours, Bradley called it a day. "Before, we always tried if we were cutting for Decca to get four songs in three hours or you were a traitor; they'd practically line you up and shoot you," Harold Bradley offered. "But Owen didn't care about that. He wanted to get quality songs. If it took one session to get one, and get it exactly right, that was fine with him."

The following day Patsy took three hours to cut two numbers. On "Yes, I Understand" Bradley used the same double tracking technique popularized by Patti Page, whereby Patsy overdubbed her own harmony on top of her lead vocal. "Gotta Lot of Rhythm in My Soul" would top any rocking performance of the day and she embellished with playful growls and yelps. She'd obviously been listening to a lot of pop radio during her year of "semi-retirement" and she hadn't lost her chops. Her initial fear about the all-male vocal backings vanished after the playbacks. According to Gordon Stoker, "After the first session we did with her, she liked what we did so well that she said she wanted us on everything."

Patsy's decision to revive her sagging career meant she had to endure a slow and arduous round of dues-paying, made even more painful and lonely by the fact that she was trying to live out her duties as a wife and mother while trying to appear as glamorous as a million-seller. Her breakthrough into the pop market two years earlier represented the ultimate goal of any Southern white singer in the fifties, but the business was so volatile that many singers who'd managed to crack the pop field, only to disappear overnight, eventually tried to retreat to the more predictable, albeit less lucrative, country field. The country music establishment exacted a penalty for going pop and "getting all high and mighty." The price was having to hit the road for relentless weeks on end, playing second-rate clubs all over the South, serving as the opening act for some other country artist who'd maybe never had a million-seller in his life. Only after enduring this for months or maybe even years would you be accepted back into the fold.

Patsy was undaunted. At least she was back singing for the folks. She called on everyone she knew and put the word out that she was back in circulation and looking for gigs. Her main source of work during this time was Don Owens, a Washington, D.C., country deejay who'd followed in the footsteps of Connie B. Gay.

Even if she hadn't burnt her bridges where Gay was concerned, Gay was fast fading out of the business by 1959, having had to face his own alcoholism and divorce, not to mention the upheavals within the country music industry. He was rich, and while he still had the opportunity to quit while he was on top, he sold his property rights in Jimmy Dean to CBS in 1958 after an acrimonious parting of the ways.

Just as Patsy did two years earlier when Gay offered her a contract for 50 percent, Dean eventually claimed that Gay exploited him "an awful lot." Gay saw it otherwise: "When I started getting out of the business in the late fifties I gave every one of my musicians their contracts back except Dean. Shortly after Dean went national on CBS, he hit me with a short, greasy lawyer up in New York City who tried to weasel Dean out of his contract with me. I was hurt that Dean didn't come to me, so I just held the contract. Finally, I let him buy it back. That made him madder than anything in his life. He thought I should have treated him the same as the rest. But the rest didn't piss on me. They shook my hand."

With Gay out of the scene, the multitalented Owens moved in to fill the void. Owens started out in broadcasting in the early fifties on various D.C. stations and the million-watt border radio station XERF in Del Rio, Texas. His forte was his encyclopedic knowledge of country music. A songwriter (he penned "Cold Dark Waters" for Porter Wagoner in 1962) and a performer as well, Owens (who died tragically in a car crash a month after Patsy's death) was considered one of the top ten country music deejays in the country with a penchant for hard country.

At WARL, Connie B. Gay put him on the air and relied on his knowledge of country music. Gay, in turn, passed along a few of the tricks of urban radio salesmanship to Owens. When Gay started to recede from producing live country music shows, Owens picked up the slack. By late 1957 he had branched into television as well, with a local program broadcast live from the Hotel Raleigh in downtown D.C. called "Don Owens' Jamboree." At the same time he bought an interest in a small record label that specialized in bluegrass, and began managing and booking a handful of local artists, including Luke Gordon, Vernon Taylor, the Stonemans and, beginning in late 1958, Patsy.

Patsy knew Owens from the time she first started working for Connie B. Gay, and he was one of many music people who came to her wedding in 1957. Though Owens lacked the capital that Gay wielded, and could only pay his headliners scale, he was the main booker of talent in the region at the time Patsy contacted him. Owens was surprised when Patsy came knocking at his door. He figured she'd gone on to grander things. He assured her he'd have no problem finding work for her. She signed a booking contract with him in the little trailer that served as his office in suburban Washington, D.C. All Owens could get for her was $50 a night. She accepted. She blamed McCall for her predicament, complaining that he was "the worst skunk that ever lived," always adding, "I got me a hit record and I ain't never made a cent from it." The business end of music always confounded Patsy, who was suspicious of contracts anyway. Despite their friendship, before signing with Don Owens, she asked Vernon Taylor, a local version of Ricky Nelson, if Owens "could be trusted."

"I told her he could be trusted," Taylor said. Don could only do so much for her or anyone for that matter. He had a day job as a disk jockey and didn't really have great financial backing."

True to his word, Owens immediately lined up dates for her at places like Glen Echo Amusement Park, Watermelon Park and the Rockville Carnival. At an April 19 performance for the opening of the New River Ranch in Rising Sun, Maryland, she was billed as "Patsy Cline and Hank Rector and the Rambling Rangers." She worked a number of dates with Vernon Taylor as well, including one memorable date at the Rockville Theatre on which, in the absence of a country band, she was backed by three black blues musicians on guitar, sax and drums.

"It really stirred her soul to be back working," Taylor reminisced. "She worked hard. She did a couple of shows that night. She was doing a strictly country act and I was doing country and rockabilly and whatever I could throw in. The weird thing about it though was that the show wasn't going well for her at all. She talked to the audience and in so many words said, 'I know this ain't working well but we're doing the best we can and it's really hard because we don't have what we need to work with—we don't have a country music band.' Then in a very complimentary way she gave the show back to me, and she was already a bigger star than I had ever been. I think she pulled those people's heartstrings, because when she came back and did a second show for the same audience, everybody's spirits were up and it went quite well and we all had a good time. You still worked the audience in those days and she was good at that."

★   ★   ★

Charlie was discharged from the Army one month early, in February, and was back at his old job at the *Winchester Star,* drinking and hell-raising in his off hours. They'd settled into a $30-a-month rental on Valley View Road on the outskirts of Winchester. Marvin Carroll hired Patsy to do a Halloween gig at Fernwood Farms in Norfolk. Charlie met her there. Recalled Carroll, "I had to make him behave himself a little bit because he was upsetting her between shows, flirting around with women and drinking. It was making her mad, like it always did. They had a rocky relationship."

The up-and-down marriage took its toll. Patsy's weight seesawed; she started smoking again, though she was always careful to put the cigarette down if someone was taking pictures. Her old friends noticed she was drinking more than in the past. "Patsy never drank that much before Charlie came along," observed Johnny Anderson, who worked with her sporadically during this time.

"She got someone to book her into a country fair outside of Philadelphia but she didn't have a band so she called me and a few other guys to go up there and back her up. There were about three thousand people there. Patsy was the star. See, these fairs used to be a big thing. Christ, we played them all—Boonsboro, Sharpsburg, every place. Man, that was the big thing for a country band. So we drove up to Philly in her convertible. My wife and kids and Patsy and I went in her car and Gene and John went in their own car. She made fried chicken and everything; she was really excited. Charlie went with us. That's when he showed his ass up there and walked up and down in front of the stage, cussin' her and callin' her a whore and a bitch and everything else.

"Yeah, he got drunk and walked up in front of the bandstand just hollerin' at her and cursin' the hell out of her the whole time she was doing that job. And she done a hell of a job. Hell, he'd go off and get drunk by himself. When it was over, this booking agent was waiting backstage for her. I think Patsy got paid $300. She gave us $50 apiece and he wanted 25 percent of the take of whatever she got. I don't think she got more than $50 for the whole damn thing. She was crying and carrying on. I said, 'Hell, Patsy, you can take my share.' She said, 'Hell no, hoss, you earned it.' She was really broke up over the damn thing."

Singer-songwriter Buzz Busby, well known in bluegrass circles, worked with Patsy on one date that coincided with his birthday, two days before hers. In the middle of his set, as a surprise, she walked onstage with a birthday cake she'd made herself, singing "Happy Birthday." After the gig, Patsy told him her problems.

"I just happened to walk by her after the show was over and everyone had cleared out. She was sitting there putting makeup on then, as a matter of fact. She called me over and said, 'Buzz, my husband drinks a lot'—which I already knew. Charlie was there and he was drinking pretty heavy. She said, 'The only problem is when he gets to drinking he gets mean and takes it out on me.' "

Busby continued: "I like Charlie very much. Me and him was drinking together so you know we was buddies. I felt sorry for Charlie for this reason: she went up and did all the performing and he had to take care of the baby. To me that just didn't seem right. I'm old-fashioned. I'm used to women taking care of babies. I don't guess anything was wrong with it but it just looked like Charlie felt out of place. It didn't feel comfortable. I guarantee you he felt uncomfortable. It was obvious to me. I'm sure he felt kind of put out about a lot of things and it might have been his cause for drinking as much as he did."

Discouraged in her career, she was equally disillusioned in her marriage. Charlie expected his wife to mother him and wait on him. Nothing could be more calculated to drive Patsy into a near homicidal rage; she wanted a mate as a devoted lover and companion-in-arms. Instead she got a wiseass kid who retreated into booze and extramarital affairs. She took her own uncertainties and secret vulnerabilities out on her mate, sparring with him and despising him because he wasn't as tough as she was. Patsy took pride in her ability to stand up for herself. "She gave as good as she got," declared Patsy Lillis.

"One time when they were living in Winchester they were arguing and fussing and fighting and I happened to be there and she wanted me to call the law," Lillis said. And I said, 'I can't call the law.' She said, 'Call the law.' And I said, 'I can't do that.' Had I called the law she'd a gone right down and gotten him out. So there's no sense in wasting money because at that time they really didn't have much of it."

Roy Deyton went to see Patsy's show at the Gaithersburg, Maryland, Agricultural Center in the fall of 1959. Deyton, who was used to the smart, no-nonsense cowgirl who could stand up to roadhouse roughnecks, was shocked; he'd never seen her break down and cry before that night.

"[It] went from bad to worse as the night wore on. Charlie got to drinking more and more. They came with another girl from Winchester and he was dancing with her a whole lot; he was plastered and Patsy was embarrassed about it. I could never figure out how she could be married to Charlie Dick, how they could be compatible. I only saw her with him that one time and he was drunk as a skunk. He poured a drink all over her outfit and he had her in tears. I had never seen Patsy broken. I really felt sorry for her. She came up on stage and still had tears in her eyes and she was trying to get herself in shape to sing. She got through her singing but you could tell she was still upset. When she saw me and my wife together she said, 'You two still hanging in there?' It was like she envied us."

In the Quonset Hut on Friday, July 3, 1959, with the Jordanaires and other members of the A Team, Patsy was in tears. The problem, once again, was material. Recalled Bradley, "We just couldn't find anything and I said, 'Well, why don't we just not do anything.' And she started crying and said she needed money—she could get some money for recording. That doesn't sound like a tough old girl, does it? So I said maybe we could do a couple of PD [public domain] songs."

Bradley's rationale for the suggestion was based on the assumption that McCall would claim an arrangement on the PD songs. Patsy chose two Hensley family favorites: "Just a Closer Walk with Thee" (often thought to be PD but actually written by Thomas A. Dorsey) and "Life's Railway to Heaven."

A number of country artists had recorded sacred music to great commercial success, so Patsy's choices were not unreasonable. Elvis Presley sang "Peace in the Valley" on "The Ed Sullivan Show" in 1957, and subsequently recorded it with the Jordanaires. Presley's version, which charted pop, was inspired by Red Foley's 1951 version, which became the first million-selling gospel song, said to be so stirring that when Foley performed it at the Show Boat in Las Vegas he brought the casino to a standstill. Even the croupiers were crying. Foley's previous hit with a gospel number was a 1950 recording of "Just a Closer Walk with Thee," on which he was backed by the Jordanaires. Patsy, like Foley, had an ability to interject herself so strongly into a song that she and her audience would be overcome, hence part of the basis for the comparison.

"She liked the comparison to him—she thought it was a compliment—but she didn't like it," remarked Jordanaire Ray Walker. "Nobody would want to be categorized. It's like an actor—when you get categorized you can't get another part. She was flattered but she didn't believe it. I remember that remark because she had that depth of emotion. But she had to have her own emotion. She would purposely try to stay away from being like a female Red Foley."

Patsy did just the two numbers, for which the Jordanaires, who worked out their own arrangements on all sessions, did an original arrangement different from the Foley version to set hers apart. Just as Bradley figured, McCall took a cut for arrangements. Walker noted that he and the other members of the quartet didn't get paid for the session until eight months later. "We were supposed to get paid in thirty days—4 Star wasn't paying anybody. They had their hooks into her, and she was stone broke."

Chapter Sixteen

RANDY HUGHES, age thirty-one, a junior talent manager who worked for Hubert Long, one of the top three managers in Nashville, was looking for clients. Patsy was looking for management. The two of them met sometime around September 1959. "This gal sings her butt off," he'd been told. In Virginia one weekend, he had a chance to hear her sing, and she was everything he'd been told.

"Like any other person trying to get into that stage of the game, what really makes you a great booker is to have great artists," said Kathy Hughes, Randy's wife at that time. "I think he had his eyes open and was listening to try to find the better people to bring in to Nashville. He came home and said, 'I have heard the greatest girl singer that will ever live'—those were his words. I can remember them as well as if it was yesterday. I was very intrigued to meet this gal if Randy was that crazy about her. And, of course, when I heard her sing, there was no doubt in my mind that Patsy was awesome."

Within the close-knit Nashville music fraternity, Ramsey "Randy" Dorris Hughes, a good old boy who hailed from Gum, Tennessee, was considered a better businessman than a musician, though he did, most reckoned, play a credible slap hole guitar, which substituted for drums at the Opry, where he played most Saturday nights.

In the case of males, the Opry often made exceptions to its "house rule," and Hughes had been playing the Opry since the age of fifteen, as well as working the road as a sideman for the Carter Family, Martha Carson, George Morgan and Moon Mullican. In 1954 he began fronting Lloyd "Cowboy" Copas's outfit. Copas's daughter, Kathaloma, was part of the band. The two of them fell in love and married, and when she became pregnant in 1955, she did what most women did back then—she hung up her cowboy boots and her tambourine in order to raise a family.

On the basis of such hits as "Filipino Baby," "The Tennessee Waltz" and "Signed, Sealed and Delivered," Copas had at one time been a genuine star who got equal billing with Hank Williams. But like many of the old-timers, Copas became a victim of rock and roll. Though still popular in concert, Copas, by the mid-1950s, had lost his touch for hits. Like other desperate artists, he made a brief stab at the youth market on the Dot label. Nothing came of his fleeting foray into rock and roll. He was, after all, a forty-something country singer whose heyday had passed. He was reduced to playing second-rate joints as a supporting act by the time Hughes came along. Hughes vowed that his life would be different from his father-in-law's.

Monday through Friday, Hughes dressed in a dark, conservative suit, white dress shirt and tie, tie clip and a plain white handkerchief tucked into his breast pocket, the attire of a stockbroker. "Randy was an entrepreneur; he liked to do many things. He thought about the future and he was going to get his fingers in as many pies around here as he possibly could," Kathy Hughes said.

He worked for Jack M. Bass and Sons, a local brokerage, ran his own small insurance company on the side and had a hand in a few other small business ventures. But in the country music industry of the fifties, the future was in the burgeoning field of management, especially in the newer type of country music that was emerging out of the experimentation on Music Row.

Hughes connected with Hubert Long, through his friendship with Ferlin Husky, whose band he'd fronted. A former protégé of Colonel Tom Parker, Long's clients included Husky, Faron Young and Hank Snow, the only country acts finding steady work during the rock and roll juggernaut. Long took Hughes on as an aide, and with his natural entrepreneurial instincts, he quickly demonstrated a knack for the business side of music.

Patsy was impressed by Hughes, who was entirely sympathetic about her 4 Star plight and promised to get her out of the mess. Hughes's respect for Patsy's talent bolstered her self-confidence just when she needed that kind of encouragement. She was receptive to his offer to take her on as a client and she liked him as a person. He had one of those quiet, laid-back personalities that's easy for women to like and he impressed Patsy with his head for business, an area so elusive to her. Hughes was the kind of man she could lean on. He told her if she'd move to Nashville he'd have her working as much as she wanted to.

★　　★　　★

While Charlie was in the Army, he and Patsy got an allotment check of $137 a month. After his discharge, the monthly checks, by the grace of a government accounting error, continued to be mailed out—seven in all. They spent the first check, after which Patsy, who knew damn well it was a mistake and feared U.S. government agents would come after them for the money, insisted they hold the checks. Then Patsy decided that the move to Nashville could no longer be postponed. To finance the move, they ran to the bank and cashed their stash, loaded up their belongings and headed South. In Nashville they found a tiny house on Marthona Drive in the Nashville suburb of Madison, where a lot of country entertainers lived. Patsy hoped that the change in scenery and her fortunes, as she fully expected, would bring about a healing in her relationship with Charlie. "We haven't had a fuss since we've been here," she wrote home a few weeks after the move. "He brings me breakfast in bed, but Lord help the kitchen."

Joining the Opry had been a primary factor in Patsy's decision to move to Nashville. Her big crossover hit certainly would have satisfied the Opry's qualifications, even though it had been two years. Opry membership had always been one of her dreams, and like her theme song, "Come On In," she expected an invitation to be extended upon her arrival in Nashville. But no one bothered to ask her. While blatantly forthright in other respects, she kept quiet about the oversight, even though immediately after moving to Nashville she started appearing at the Ryman every Saturday night as a regular guest artist, for the standard fee of $25 a night.

"I remember the first time I met Patsy at the Opry," said singer Margie Bowes, who was married to Doyle Wilburn of the Wilburn Brothers, a former 4 Star act that had gone to Decca in 1955. Bowes had one modest hit on the country charts on the small Hickory label, "Poor Old Heartsick Me," in the beginning of 1959 and thereafter had been made a member of the Opry, so Patsy's expectations were not unfounded.

"She was going to go on right after me. She was guesting. You know how Patsy talked—I used to call her potty mouth. But she was a sweetheart. I was singing, and the Jordanaires were singing with me, and when I finished and walked backstage I saw her standing there and I knew who she was because I remember when she was on Arthur Godfrey.

"I could tell that she was nervous. And I heard her say to one of the Jordanaires, 'You mean I gotta follow that bitch? That girl can *sing!*' But oh, she could sing. Later on I used to go to the studio, to her sessions, to hear her. Her and Owen used to fight. But he knew how to get it out of her. He knew how to bring the soul out of Patsy like nobody else. Once she stopped in the middle of a song and she didn't say, 'Let's modulate'; she said, 'Let's homogenize this song.' Owen said, 'What the hell are you saying?' I liked to die. I'd cry just listening to her sing. He said, 'You mean modulate?' She said, 'Why hell yes, whatever you do to go up.'"

As he'd promised her, Randy put Patsy on the road. She worked as a girl singer for such headliners as Faron Young, Ferlin Husky, Marty Robbins and Jim Reeves, as well as on many of the big package shows featuring Opry acts.

Nowadays musicians tour in customized buses made to accommodate life on the road, but in the fifties everyone traveled in Cadillacs or Chryslers, often in caravans. Patsy usually rode with whomever she was touring. The road was punishing, or as Barbara Mandrell, whose career dated back to Patsy's era, put it, "The road is tough, but the road is a piece of cake now compared to what it was before we had buses."

The road meant long hours, five or six to a car, overnight jumps of four, five hundred miles over two-lane blacktop, cheap motels, bad meals, no privacy and none of the familiar comforts of home. Patsy would get up at 4:30 A.M. one day and at noon the next. Ribald jokes and a bottle helped make it tolerable. Patsy was a real trooper. You could tell a dirty joke around her and she might even one-up you. You could take a drink around her and she'd not only join you, she might pour you one herself out of the Listerine bottle she used as a flask. In the makeshift, cramped dressing rooms that she often had to share with "the hosses," Patsy would un-self-consciously peel down to her slip in front of the boys while she ironed a costume. In a crowded restaurant her distinctive laugh was like a honing device.

"You could travel with her very comfortably, like with five guys in a car together, six with her," recalled Porter Wagoner, with whom Patsy rode that summer in his ultimate hillbilly driving machine, a 1957 Eldorado, with a lipstick, a vanity case and four gold cups on its dashboard. "She never used to complain about anything. You didn't have to worry if a word slipped out of your mouth, something you'd say in front of the guys; you didn't have to worry about offending her. With some of the girl singers, if you said 'shit' in front of them they would say you didn't respect 'em. Things slip out occasionally when you're traveling with guys, then all of a sudden you have a girl with you for ten, twenty days. So she understood that completely. I'd never traveled with anybody in my career who was more of a trooper, who was just one of the guys, who fit into the situation better than Patsy did."

Patsy was an old hand at handling herself in compromising situations. She deflected her male road buddies' come-ons and casual assumptions of road sex like a good ole girl. Ten-day, two-week tours were hard enough, but girl singers who worked with the Nashville musicians had to deal with additional road pressures, explained Dale Turner: "You weren't traveling with any other women, so you'd better get along with those guys," said Turner, who moved to Nashville with her husband not long after Patsy did.

"It was really hard for me once I moved to Nashville because I had been protected in D.C. I didn't get any protection down here at all. They were all after you, all over you, but don't you dare go with any of them because then you're pegged. And not just the stars—the sidemen too. I didn't know how to handle it. I wasn't exposed to it up in D.C. If I wanted to be with someone up there, I could be with someone without a big battle all the time. It was a mutual thing. It wasn't this constant barrage. Whew! Every place. You couldn't get any rest. I went out on the road with Faron and he wouldn't let me sleep because I wouldn't sleep with him. I tried to crawl into one of the beds and I got jerked out of the bed. I think I sat up for twenty-four hours. I was married then, so I finally called Ken because I didn't know how to handle it. I said, 'I'm going to sleep with Faron. I mean, just sleep with him in the bed, because I'm tired and I can't keep my eyes open anymore.' Then I just talked his ear off and threw him out of bed about six times and then we got along fine.

"But that's the battle it was. And I wasn't the pro Patsy was. I'm sure Patsy would have gotten off the bus. That's what I should have done, but I didn't know how to get off the bus in the middle of nowhere. Patsy, she told me about it. She said, 'Hoss, I told Sheriff he had to keep his hands to himself.' She had to fight Porter; Porter's a ladies' man. And Ferlin—Ferlin was a ladies' man also back then. They were all married but there was that double standard, and I'm not trying to talk bad about them because they weren't doing anything that the guy working at the machine shop didn't do. In the fifties it was like marriage vows were spoken and maybe taken seriously but they didn't bind you in any way."

Young worked extensively with Patsy between 1959 and 1961, before her fees got to the point where he couldn't afford to carry her.

"You didn't have to worry about cussin' around her or raisin' hell or tellin' a dirty joke because she'd do the same thing with you," he offered. "That's one of the reasons I thought so much of her. You didn't have that whining and bullshit, like some of them girl singers. Once she got to working on the road, she was the real Patsy; she didn't hide anything back. She'd joke and could be like an ole mama hen to you. If I'd say, 'Come on, let's stop and eat,' she'd say, 'We ate about thirty minutes ago, you little bastard, and you were sleeping. Now you can just starve for a while.' "

Patsy's trip down the comeback trail was one of the darkest periods of her life. The pay was minimal; she earned from $50 to $200 a day during 1959 and 1960. There was no money to show for her hit record. She had to leave her young daughter with Charlie and the babysitters while she hit the road for weeks. Her relationship with Charlie, always rocky, got worse. She was terribly insecure—more than she let on. She would take a few nips before a show to calm herself down. The nipping occasionally got out of hand. Patsy's vulnerability surprised many artists who were in awe of her talent. But she felt she had to be a total entertainer—as though singing weren't enough. She often underestimated her impact on audiences. According to Jordanaire Ray Walker, "She was klutzy at some of her performances. For a long time she was a better recording artist than a performer."

Margie Bowes recalled: "One time we did a Hap Peebles tour. It was a big show—Ray Price, Faron Young, myself—about ten, twelve artists. That was back when Patsy used to drink. She was kind of tipsy and went out one night and the audience wasn't responding the way she wanted them to, so she said, 'Ole PC's finished,' and walked off stage. She didn't sing but two songs. She figured they didn't like her, but they did."

"We were all great comedians," said Marvin Rainwater. "We'd go out on the stage and make everybody scream and holler and laugh. Autry Inman—he was a writer, wrote all kinds of songs for Carl Smith; he was a great comedian and so were most of the other guys on the tours. We'd get out there and just knock them out with jokes. Come Patsy's time to go on, she was so nervous because she'd see what we were doing, making everybody laugh, and she'd go out there and try to tell jokes. Well, she's not a comedian. Matter of fact, the jokes were terrible. I don't know where she even got them. They didn't go over. That would make her totally upset. She drank every once in a while and she'd hit the bottle because she wanted to do the same thing that everybody else was doing, and that made it worse. And the problem just kept getting worse instead of better, so she'd try even harder.

"One night we got together with her, several of us, and said, 'Look, Patsy, we don't want to tell you what to do or how to run your business or anything but we think you need some advice here 'cause you're doing something wrong.' Naturally she said, 'What's that?' And we said, 'You shouldn't be telling jokes.' And she said, 'Well, why not? You guys tell 'em.' We said, 'That's our business. That's because we're not that good; we're telling jokes to make up for it, but you're the queen and you should go out there with pure dignity and not even expose yourself to a joke that might go flat, and you can sing all night and never have that problem. We think you should stick strictly to singing because we're out there just knocked out by your singing, and then when you tell a joke and it goes flat, we feel terrible while we're watching you and the audience feels the same way.' Well, she listened to us. And it made a big difference. All of a sudden she did what she was supposed to do—go out there and just act dignified and sing. And my God, she just destroyed them."

During the interminable days on the road, Patsy tried to put a Band-Aid on her essential loneliness, and both Porter Wagoner and Faron Young claimed brief road flings with her. But Patsy, both said, was like a sister. It was the kind of thing, Young said, "you could laugh about in the morning." According to Wagoner, "It made a few lonely nights out there on the dismal road more bearable."

But Patsy was hardly the libertine she had often been depicted as. The vacuum in her life she was trying to fill was a psycho-spiritual one; her need for love and affection was a craving frozen in her past.

"People sometimes think that if you know a woman very well and a woman knows a man very well that they're having sex," said Donn Hecht. "Patsy wasn't a sexpot. One time we were both very tired and we checked into this motel and they didn't have any adjoining rooms and she said, 'Hey, hoss, we're both grown people. Get us a room with twin beds.' And we spent the night in the same room and we had breakfast the next morning. But when you check into a hotel with somebody they think you're having an orgy. These jackasses who weren't within four blocks of Patsy at any one time who claim that their relationship was much more, they're trying to cop part of the lady's spotlight. They're trying to put some spice in her life that never really existed."

June Carter said she and Patsy did many shows together (outside of their "Johnny Cash Show" appearances in 1962–1963), as well as TV and radio, beginning in 1959. Often it was just the two of them. June would do her comedy routine, then turn the show over to Patsy, who "just sang like Patsy." She typically opened with a bright, up-tempo number like "Come On In," then segued to her standard repertoire, a mix of her own recordings, some pop-country standards and western swing. Then June would join her on stage for a finale.

"Sometimes we'd sing old Carter Family songs if she knew 'em, or if it was something that she knew that I knew. I'd sing with her. I'd sing harmony or she'd sing harmony with me. We might be picking up a band where they had a little club or something, a house band. And we would maybe have to woodshed 'em a little bit, but I played

banjo and guitar and autoharp and Patsy didn't play. So I had a little
system I'd worked out with the band, so even if they didn't know her
tunes I could tell 'em where to go to. But most of them knew what
she was singing.

"Patsy knew she was different from the other girl singers. She
didn't care about any of them; she wouldn't give you ten cents for
them. She used to tell me, 'Look, we don't step on each other's toes.' I
did my funny things and we sung together or I'd do the harmony part,
whatever. I wasn't in any kind of competition with her as a singer
because I wasn't what I consider a great singer. I would draw people
from the fact that I was a comedienne. But the two of us could do a
whole show and we did, many times."

Patsy's attitude toward at least one other girl singer was revealed in
an anecdote about a 1959 club appearance where Rose Maddox was a
featured attraction. Maddox's Capitol and Columbia releases never
achieved the pop success that Patsy did. But even with one smash hit
to her credit, Patsy was at a disadvantage the night she was booked into
the Wheel Club in Oceanside, California. Oceanside was a Marine
town, where Maddox's music had been a staple since the late forties.
The local crowd considered Maddox the ultimate hillbilly boogie
queen, whereas Patsy was thought to be more on the pop side. When
Maddox showed up that night and got up and started clapping her
hands and singing "Sally Let Your Bangs Hang Down," everyone went
wild and started yelling, "We Want Rose Maddox."

Maddox clearly was not one of Patsy's fans as she recalled the incident to biographer Jonny Whiteside: "She [Patsy] had been on and
performed and was settin' at the bar, drinkin' beer. Ever'body was hollerin' for me to get up there so I sang a couple of numbers. A friend of
mine was standin' back there and Patsy turned to her and said, 'If I got
up there and shook like she does, why I'd be as popular as she is!' and
my friend told me what she had said. I do not get up there and shake;
my body keeps time with my singin', is all I do. And that did not set
well with me, hearing that she had said that about me."

In Dallas to do the "Big D Jamboree," Patsy found herself in much
more congenial company with one of her favorite girl singers, Charline Arthur. Arthur had a high-voltage cowgirl act that rivaled any of
the rockers of the era. Though Arthur never had a hit record, Patsy's
liking of her was understandable: they were two of a kind. A native of
Henrietta, Texas, Arthur was three years older within a day. She had a
big, earthy, soulful voice, wore pants on stage when it was unheard of
and her deep voice made many who hadn't seen her think she was a
man. There was nothing cute or coy about her stage act, to which

Patsy might have added one of her favorite descriptives, "ballsy." Arthur claimed, "I was the first to break out of the Kitty Wells stereotype and boogie-woogie. I was shakin' that thing on stage long before Elvis even thought about it. I worked harder on stage than he ever worked and he was not even heard of at the time."

According to Arthur's sister Dorothy Ethridge, Arthur spoke fondly and admiringly of Patsy. She claimed to have played big sister to her, coaching Patsy on her breathing, diction and bandstand presence. They both had headstrong personalities. Arthur had an unhappy relationship with her record company, RCA, and she leveled criticism at her A&R man, Chet Atkins, who she said didn't "have the right substance for my vocal style." She told Patsy she would not have a manager because "they stole you blind," and related how, when Colonel Tom Parker offered to manage her in the early fifties, she informed him, "There's no son-of-a-bitch going to tell me when to go to sleep and get up and take 50 percent."

Patsy revealed Arthur's influence when she showed up one night at the Opry in a costume that went over famously on the road, but was met with mixed reviews at the considerably more tightass Opry. The centerpiece of the outfit was a pair of tight lamé pants, which she wore western-style with all the appropriate rodeo accessories. Just like a champion barrel racer, Patsy wanted to look pretty under the lights. Such style, which was probably more typical of West Coast acts, earned her the reputation of being the resident sex symbol at the Opry. It was the tightness of her clothes, not the baring of skin, that raised eyebrows. She wore her clothes tight around the hips and bust, and went in for flashy fabrics. But on this occasion it was the pants that caused the flap that ensued. It was another one of the house rules that girl singers weren't allowed to wear pants on the Opry (though Ferlin Husky got away with wearing a nearly identical pair of pants). Officials told Patsy she would have to change her costume before she went on. She did. But she was none too happy about it, and let everyone within earshot know.

"It just wasn't the thing of the Opry for a woman to go on in slacks; it just wasn't done," remembered Ray Walker. "She knew that, but she knew a lot of things she didn't want to go along with. But Patsy was just a star waiting to be discovered. She never had anything but a star attitude and she knew what she could do and what got her applause on stage."

Patsy's experiences on the road toughened her. Yet she didn't fool everyone; more than a few people sensed the maiden beneath the armor. "She'd call you 'hoss'; everybody was 'hoss,'" said Margie

Bowes. "I don't care if you're male or female, you were 'hoss,' or she'd call you by your last name. She always called me 'Bowes.' She never called me 'Margie.'

"She put them walls up around her so people couldn't see inside, so she couldn't get hurt. I knew her life had to be hard because she covered up a lot. Patsy didn't open up to people. She'd tell you stuff about how the record's doing or talk about other people she liked, but she never bared her soul. She just couldn't do that. I always wished I could have talked to her. I mean, really, really talked to her. I don't know a person on the face of the earth she completely opened up to."

It was common knowledge in the women's dressing room at the Opry, which was merely the women's restroom with a wire strung across for show clothes, that "you don't mess with the Cline because she'll flat get you cold." She despised gossip—especially if it was about herself. "She didn't talk much about herself," said friend Joyce Jackson, secretary to singer Jim Reeves, who said she and Patsy did most of their "chit-chatting" in the dressing room. "The one thing she always told me was never pay attention to what anybody said about her, because most of the time what anybody was saying wouldn't be the real truth anyway. She'd say, 'If I don't say it, don't believe it.' "

She could party hard with Charlie, party man par excellence. Hearing her unmistakable laugh meant "the Cline," as she so often referred to herself, was back in town. Patsy made like she was always ready to party. But the laugh, for all its boisterousness, contained a sob.

"She loved dirty jokes and she was always telling some kind of joke," said Buddy Killen, a sideman and song plugger for Tree Publishing. "She could get serious with you about whatever you wanted to talk about but she really loved to laugh. If you were in a room just loaded with people, you would hear her laughter above the whole thing. She laughed real loud and laughed a lot."

Amphetamines were, at the time, considered a medically sound treatment for both obesity and depression. The drug works by speeding up the metabolism, hence its street name, "speed"—a way of life for many Nashvilleans in the music business.

Landon B. Snapp was Nashville's infamous version of Dr. Feelgood. Obesity and depression were his specialties. He prescribed from his East Nashville office, and the casualness with which he prescribed speed undercut any notion that his sole concern was his patients' well-being, as evidenced by his conviction, in the 1970s, and sentence of three years in federal prison. It was said, perhaps in jest, that Snapp was once given an award inscribed "Special Songwriters' Award for Helping Co-write More Hits Than Anyone in Nashville."

Snapp wasn't the only Nashville doctor handing out scrips for amphetamines. "Seems like everyone was taking them," said one singer-songwriter. Regardless of who was supplying her, Patsy took her share of pills, "Not to get high, to make the miles," observed one road buddy. Amphetamines probably saved a lot of road musicians from falling asleep at the wheel while trying to make the next gig. But in addition to having to withstand the rigors of the road, Patsy had a real problem with her weight after the birth of Julie, and diet pills were considered an acceptable way to lose weight—fast. She loved country cooking, and was a good cook herself. She cycled in and out of being fat.

"When she wanted a piece of cake, she wanted the whole cake, and I'm sure booze and pills she'd do the same way," offered Margie Bowes. "Her weight was up and down a lot. I knew she was depressed. I went through enough rough times myself to recognize it. But when she hit that stage—I mean, she'd be sitting backstage and you'd think, 'Oh boy, this is going to be bad.' But she hit that stage and, oh man, she was great."

"She'd go on eating binges, then she'd get on a diet," recalled Faron Young. "I'd seen her one time and her damn waist looked like it was twenty inches and the next time it would look like thirty inches. I'd laugh at her and say, 'Man, that ass of yours is getting wider and wider.' She'd say, 'You must like my ass, you little bastard—you keep looking at it and talking about it.' I'd say, 'Well, I do. You got a pretty ass, but right now it's too big. Why don't you get back to where you used to be?' And she'd say, 'Why you little son-of-a-bitch, I can put it on and I can lose it too.' She'd go on one of them crash diets.

"But Patsy was no big drinker or dope head. I'm sure Patsy took her diet pills and stuff, I think most of the girls did. I never took those pills. I'd go to sleep. Hell, there's always five or six of us in a car; one of those sons-a-bitches can stay awake for an hour and drive and then let somebody else drive. And you always had two or three musicians that took 'em anyway. Sons-a-bitches that had the most pills would do the most driving because they didn't want to sleep. I'd see musicians—we'd go out and work for seven, eight days on a tour—then have a day off to rest. Those sons-a-bitches would take pills and stay up that day, too."

June Carter claimed that it was Patsy who introduced her to the benefits and the side effects of speed. At a show they were doing at a racetrack in Philadelphia, Mississippi, they saw a horse collapse and die. Both of them were crying. Patsy reached into her purse and pulled out a green speckled capsule that she said would help calm her friend's nerves. "It isn't much more than an aspirin," she told June. June stayed wired for three days.

"I called her up and said, 'What in the world did you give me? It almost killed me, I can't get to sleep.' And she laughed and laughed. She thought it was the funniest thing. She said, 'Good Lord, that's nothing.' But to her it was just second nature. I know she could stay up like mad and I couldn't."

It might have been on the same tour that Patsy was involved in an auto accident, the details of which remain sketchy (Charlie was unaware of any such accident), but was apparently serious enough to send Patsy to the hospital. "Her mother called and said that Patsy was in a hospital somewhere down in Mississippi," said former WINC station manager Phil Whitney. "She said she was in a terrible car accident. She said she was in bad shape and it could have killed her."

Patsy's reputation within music circles as a bawdy iconoclast aside, she continued to be promoted as a sweet, pert, even demure country girl singer—the only kind of girl singer that could find acceptance in the country music establishment of the fifties. In 1959 promotional ad copy that appeared in *Cowboy Songs* described her as a "god-fearing religious girl who is thankful for all the goodness in her life. There isn't a malicious bone in her body. Patsy is the kind of girl who will go out of her way (no matter how far) to help someone who needs her help. Yes, Patsy Cline is a credit to the music business and a boon to all who love listening to good music." *Trail,* a magazine financed by Marvin Rainwater and run by his brother, Ray, carried a 1958 feature on Patsy's wardrobe, which might have been done as a favor to help keep Patsy's name before the public during her maternity hiatus. The story described her jewelry as being "of the sparkly type," but "in excellent taste because she doesn't 'overdress' with it." She was also said to "limit her use of rouge, powder and eye makeup, because she has a very lovely complexion, and looks always as though she'd just come back from a morning walk in the cool spring air."

Patsy was booked regularly on the "Ozark Jubilee," which was known as "Jubilee U.S.A." in 1959 to September 1960 (when the show was canceled because ABC determined that host Red Foley could no longer convincingly play the part of emcee because he had been indicted for tax fraud and was about to stand trial). In one appearance on November 7, 1959, she sang "Walkin' After Midnight" and "Come On In," and duetted with substitute host Slim Wilson on "Let's Go to Church." The dialogue was canned ("Hello, you big ole slick, slim, sycamore sapling," Patsy quipped to Wilson) and the sets hokey, but the show provided her with an opportunity to choose her own material for a national audience. Patsy would typically do a solo performance, and would usually duet with one of her co-stars or host Foley. On December 12 she sang her current single, "Got a Lot of Rhythm in My Soul" and "Lovesick Blues," which she would record the following month, and dueted with Ferlin Husky on "Let It Snow, Let It Snow" and with Foley on "Walking in a Winter Wonderland." On June 4, 1960, she was back in Springfield, Missouri, to do the show again, soloing on "Lovesick Blues" and "How Can I Face Tomorrow" (which was released the following month), duetting with Cowboy Copas on "I'm Hogtied over You" and singing "Reuben, Reuben" with Eddy Arnold and June Valli.

During the same period Patsy did probably a dozen episodes of *Community Jamboree* and *Country Style,* fifteen-minute military recruitment kinescopes shot at the Bradley Studios (the Bradleys had gotten into films in the early fifties when they first opened the Quonset Hut and kinescopes remained part of the business through the fifties and early sixties). The low-budget films represent country music at its lowest denominator, but the footage is noteworthy for the material Patsy sang, the choice of which was left up to her: Roger Miller's "When Your House Is Not a Home"; Neal Sedaka and Howard Greenfield's "Stupid Cupid," a 1958 hit for Connie Francis; "Crazy Dreams," her final 4 Star release; and "Loose Talk," a 1955 Carl Smith hit.

Patsy's bitterness over her 4 Star deal prompted Randy Hughes to obtain an accounting of her financial status from Bill McCall. McCall would not yield to Hughes's efforts to get a satisfactory explanation, and Hughes finally advised her to ride out the contract until its expiration, probably sometime in the summer of 1960. Two singles were released in 1959 and, without any promotion by either 4 Star or Decca, both went unnoticed: "Yes, I Understand" backed by "Cry Not For Me," on February 23, and "Gotta Lot of Rhythm in My Soul" backed by "I'm Blue Again," on July 20.

Patsy's final 4 Star session took place on January 27, 1960. In a departure from the pop-country terrain he'd been exploring, Owen Bradley planned it as a straight country date, probably as a concession to Patsy, who by now was totally depressed over the complete failure of her recording career after "Midnight." Since going electric, Bradley hadn't used steel guitar and fiddle on a Cline recording since the "Midnight" session. For the last 4 Star tracks he brought in steel player Jimmy Day, one of Ray Price's Cherokee Cowboys, while Grady Martin doubled on electric guitar and fiddle, his original instrument. The balance of the A Team lineup included pianist Floyd Cramer, bass player Bob Moore and drummer Buddy Harmon. The Jordanaires were not hired for the date.

For the second time, probably to appease her, Patsy was allowed to record an outside copyright; "Lovesick Blues" was clearly her choice. Patsy's cover of the Tin Pan Alley song, which had become a country standard, had a lengthy history. Hank Williams's 1949 version was the most famous; others included Emmett Miller in 1928, Rex Griffin in 1939 and Sonny James in 1957. The other three songs on the session all carried the "W. S. Stevenson" imprimatur: "How Can I Face Tomorrow," "Crazy Dreams" and "There He Goes," a feminization of Eddie Miller–Durwood Haddock's "There She Goes," a shuffle recorded by Carl Smith in 1955 and covered by a half-dozen unknowns on McCall's roster. Patsy did a bluesy version of the tune; it was, according to Bradley, a harbinger of her future style on "I Fall to Pieces," prompting Bradley to comment, "We almost had something going on that one."

Throughout the session her voice was smoother and more expressive than at any other time in her recording career, and she was less tied to the beat, particularly on "There He Goes." It may have been the lowest point in Patsy's recording career, but it was the vocal style Bradley had been trying to achieve for almost six years.

On March 7, "Lovesick Blues" backed by "How Can I Face Tomorrow" was released. On August 1, Patsy's final 4 Star recording was released, "Crazy Dreams" backed by "There He Goes." Writer Durwood Haddock stopped by the 4 Star offices in Pasadena to pick up copies of "There He Goes" to plug to deejays in the Southwest. At that point everyone connected with the label had written her off. Haddock said McCall's engineer, Ellery Hearn, told him, "Bless her heart, poor Patsy, it don't look like we're ever going to get a hit with her."

Patsy had been humbled and all but broken-spirited by her six-year 4 Star ordeal. At the Opry on January 9, she hesitatingly approached general manager Ott Devine with a subject that had long been on her mind: "Mr. Devine, do you think I could ever become a member of the 'Grand Ole Opry'?" Devine replied, "Patsy, if that's all you want, you are on the Opry." With none of the fanfare she might have expected, the dream of a lifetime was realized in Devine's casual response. The following month her new status was noted on a crib sheet by WSM's publicity department. Along with a listing of her career high points was Patsy's disillusioned-sounding comment, "I don't want to get rich . . . just live good."

*P*ATSY'S FINANCIAL SITUATION remained fairly bleak. Charlie earned $110 a week as a linotype operator at the Curley Printing Company. Patsy advised her family that if they wanted to reach her, to leave a message at WSM. In May she and Charlie still didn't have a telephone because, "They want $50 and I just can't put that kind of money out right now," she wrote.

In April 1960 she learned she was pregnant. She asked Randy Hughes to keep her working as much as possible; they needed the money. In early May she packed her bags for another round of dates: Abilene, Texas, and Springfield, Missouri, followed by forty-two days straight in California. "We are hoping to get home the month of June," she wrote home. "The car is in real bad shape; it needs work."

"She came backstage at the Opry one night when she was pregnant and she was furious," recalled singer Jean Shepard, who at that point had recently married singer Hawkshaw Hawkins and was expecting their first child. "She was mad at Charlie about it. I said, 'It takes two to tango, Patsy.' She was showing real good, and she wanted me to help her get into this old-fashioned waist cincher with laces. I said, 'Patsy, I can't set you up in that. I can't. It'll hurt the baby.' And she said she didn't care; she didn't want to look like she was pregnant. She said, 'Okay, Shepard, you got your damn reasons and that's fine.' So there was a black lady who worked backstage there who used to help her get laced into it. I wouldn't help her at all."

Shepard's rejoinder belied her own strong feelings about maternity and careers at that time: "It's not that she didn't want the baby. She just didn't want it at that time. Maybe she thought that the bookers wouldn't book her, but all you had to do was call them and say, 'Hey, I'm going to take about four, five months off—I'm going to have a baby.' In four or five months I don't think your career can want that much."

Patsy's ambivalence about pregnancy was exacerbated by her rocky marriage to Charlie. Charlie was having his own affairs and it really made Patsy feel angry and insecure. She complained, "That goddamn applause don't help you any when you're laying in that bed at night being totally ignored."

At one point she hired a stripteaser for a birthday party in Charlie's honor. She would have done anything to ignite the passion they had in the very beginning. Now the only fire was verbal. She couldn't stand it that Charlie had left her out in the cold. She complained that she had to hide her road money from him so that he wouldn't spend it on booze. Then in the summer of 1960, he was laid up at home for several months with a broken pelvic bone as a result of a car wreck, which made him even more dependent on her.

Patsy feared intimacy, yet much as she feared it, she wanted it. And it was the last thing she was likely to get from "good-time Charlie," as she bitingly referred to him at times. When Margie Bowes asked her why she didn't try talking to him about her needs, Patsy's curt reply was, "He just don't get it." She continued to take her frustrations out on him, sparring with him, despising him, yet refusing to leave him. "Charlie was madly in love with her and insanely jealous," said Donn Hecht. "It didn't make sense. Here was a guy who would screw anything that walked and yet if somebody looked at her more than two seconds he would make an ass of himself. He was famous for that."

Patsy would show up at sessions with bruises on her face and a flippant explanation. According to Ray Walker, "One time she came in with a black eye. She had sunglasses on. We didn't say anything about it because she'd always say something first, and she said, 'I asked Charlie something and he answered me.' That's all she said."

Recalled Margie Bowes, "I asked her one time, 'Why do you take that? Do you like that kind of treatment?' She said, 'I can hand it back.' She didn't want to talk about it. I asked Charlie once. He said, 'We don't do it in front of the kids,' which is a bunch of baloney. I think sometimes when you start out like that you do it because someone's hurting you and the anger makes you do it. But then it gets to the point where you just don't care anymore.

"I think she really loved old Charlie in a way. I really believe she did. But I'm not sure if they opened up. That generation didn't. He's the type who just cuts up all the time. I've never known him to be too serious. I never saw them touch. Kissing, hugging, holding hands— never. You know when you're around somebody a lot, sooner or later you're going to see them touch. But I never saw them touch. Isn't that strange? Because Charlie loved her—I don't think he knew how much until she was gone. And when I used to see her, I remember her hugging me. She'd walk over and say, 'Hey, Bowes,' and hug me, but entertainers do that a lot anyway. I don't know that Patsy was ever real close to anybody."

By the latter part of 1960 it was widely rumored that Patsy and her manager were having an affair. What started out as a strictly professional relationship had always been charged by an undercurrent of attraction that took the form of joking and bantering. Patsy wasn't exactly looking for an affair. She wanted Charlie to be her man.

"She wasn't on the prowl looking for nothing," observed Faron Young. "She had more people sharpshooting at her than a Japanese airplane, putting the make on her. Somebody was always shooting at Patsy and Patsy could always handle it. She'd laugh. A woman don't have to get mad to tell you to go screw off. She'd say, 'Hey, cool it, you crazy bastard. You ain't gettin' none of me, so just cool it.' You knew where you stood with her. Patsy didn't have to go looking for nothing; she had all she needed offered to her."

There was no doubt that Hughes was genuinely interested in her talent. And Patsy honestly felt he could help her go places. Unlike Charlie, who, said Young, was "like a big ole kid—she had to take care of him," in Hughes Patsy finally found a man she could really lean on. "She could depend on Randy where she couldn't on Charlie because Charlie was a drinker and a hell-raiser," added Young. "Now she had Randy who carried the load for her, just like Tammy Wynette with Jones—she always had to take care of Jones."

Hughes, in turn, became very protective of Patsy in some very personal ways. At first he didn't want the affair, just as she didn't. He once made the comment to the effect that he would not put the crucial part of his male anatomy in the till. He was married to Copas's daughter, was a devoted family man and was booking and managing Copas, putting Patsy on the road with him. But when Patsy was desperate after one of her fights with Charlie, she would call Randy in the middle of the night. Randy was her knight in shining armor—he didn't want her hurt.

Kathy Hughes didn't know of any affair, but she could understand the attraction. "Charlie, God bless him—he's a lovable person, but he was also a hell-raiser at the time." She explained: "Charlie is just one of those guys. He has a charm, but he just doesn't use good judgment. And Patsy, listen, she did her share too. But when they would have their fights, Patsy would call in the middle of the night. I seen Randy get up a couple of times and go out there. I tried to put myself in Patsy's place. Yes, I would admire my husband too if I were married to this guy who was drunk all the time. Randy was a stable force in her life. He was someone who could give her advice, who she could trust. Patsy's father was an abuser; so she had no stable men in her life. So here was a man who was stable. I'd probably go for him too."

Mae Axton knew about the affair. Patsy, Axton said, would feel "kind of guilty, but not too bad, if she could make somebody happy and it would make her happy. She had sometimes different thoughts than most of us."

"Randy, he was kind of a cute guy, but was married to Kathy, such a sweet wife. She was the daughter of a good friend of mine, Cowboy Copas. He worshiped the daughter and I think he maybe suspected. One time he said to me, 'I am so lucky to have a daughter like Kathy. I just hope she never gets hurt.' "

Patsy was in California in July when she had a near miscarriage. After a two-day hospital stay, she was back in the club that night. "I have to stay in bed all day, lay down while in the car and between shows, or the doctor says I'll be back in there and they won't be able to save it the next time, so I'm really listening to him," she wrote home.

She had a premonition she might lose the baby. She told Donn Hecht she frequently experienced moments of clairvoyance. She called them "hunches."

"[W]e both discussed 'hunches' that became realities," Hecht said. "And I told her that it was a fact that many people had what I called 'perceptive intuition,' and that I confessed we had this in common, and that rather than wonder about it, it should be used as a blessing, and that she should never go against strong feelings of impending disaster."

When Patsy's 4 Star contract expired that summer, Owen Bradley was certain she would want to go with another label, given her bitterness over the previous six years under the lease arrangement to Decca. There were no solid offers, though at a benefit at the Carousel Club in Nashville, Chet Atkins suggested that she'd be welcome at RCA. But Patsy actually feared no label, including Decca, would pick her up. In spite of the problems, she figured Decca was family, and she trusted Bradley. Her car was about to be repossessed when she approached Bradley's assistant, Harry Silverstein, hoping that they would bail her out.

"Patsy's contract with 4 Star was running out," Bradley recalled. "We had a very dry spell—'Walkin' After Midnight' and nothing else. I thought she would go with Columbia or RCA or somebody because

I figured she blamed us. One day I was working with somebody and Harry came down to the studio and he said that Patsy was on the phone a few minutes ago and she wanted a $1000 advance and she would sign with us. I said, 'Really?' and he said, 'Yeah.' I said I would have to call New York, and I did. I was really shocked because I thought she was disgusted with the whole thing and no one would have blamed her if she had been, because we were still doing all those same bunch of songs and not much had happened. So I called New York and they said, 'Oh, that's great.' Bradley signed her to a three-year contract with a two-year option. He could finally exercise the A&R man's creative control over her material. Now all he needed were the right songs.

Nineteen sixty was a turning point in country music. Judge George D. Hay, the progenitor of the Opry, whose dictum was to "keep it down to earth," might have been perturbed at the presence of electric guitars, drums and spotlights on stage at the Ryman. The changes reflected what was happening uptown, at the confluence of recording studios, record company offices, talent agencies and music publishers, where there was a serious hick purge going on.

The number of full-time country music radio stations had dropped to eighty-one. The market for hard country, the music of "a hillbilly, ridge-runner, Okie or any of the not-so-complimentary identifications," according to the station manager of one Pomona, California, radio station, had virtually disappeared in direct proportion to the explosion in the youth pop market in the 1950s.

To a young singer, even to a self-described hillbilly like Patsy, success was no longer measured in terms of a full house in every theater in every small town across America or even an appearance on the "Grand Ole Opry," but by record sales in the millions and appearances on "The Ed Sullivan Show." The new country singers were smooth—Marty Robbins, Jim Reeves, Don Gibson, Sonny James. Even Elvis Presley had affected a crooner style in songs like "Are You Lonesome Tonight?"

The new, uptown direction of country music got a boost when the payola hearings set off a crisis in the music industry beginning in 1959. Rumors of payola spread and the scandal reached a boiling point in 1960 when Alan Freed, "The King of Rock and Roll," was dethroned and America's favorite deejay, Dick Clark, was summoned to the witness stand. At that point, radio programmers began to play it safe, shifting from Top 40, kiddie pop to adult-oriented formats for a "fresher image." The newly formed Country Music Association set about a promotional blitz to sell programmers on the idea that the mass market was ready for the Nashville Sound. Nobody quite knew what it was ("an indefinable, almost mystic element," according to *McCall's*). It sure as hell was easier to say what it wasn't. It eschewed the corn, the twang, the nasal singing, the yodeling, the weepy sound of the steel guitar and the whine of the fiddle—in other words, just about everything that made country music country.

The popular media pointed out that the new breed of smooth country singers weren't ignorant, inbred ridge-runners: they were *stylists*. "Most are from the South and have a natural understanding of country music; but experience on tour, the normal processes of education and just plain intelligence have made them singers-of-the-world, sophisticated enough to recognize that apparent lack of sophistication is half the charm of country music and musicians," noted *McCall's*. Hell, they even knew how to dress. As one singer's agent put it: "My boys can sing in dungarees at the Opry but they'll be just as comfortable in a tuxedo if they have to sing in Vegas."

Owen Bradley, with Chet Atkins the architect of the Nashville Sound, as it was being tagged as early as 1960, maintained that his experimentation of the fifties was not an attempt to "go pop," but simply an effort to come up with hit records to please "the bosses." If having six violins and a full horn section and a chorus to back up a singer on a recording of a pop song was the way to achieve it, so be it. In March 1959, Bradley hired a string section consisting of musicians from the Nashville Symphony to work on a Brenda Lee date—the first time Bradley had ever used strings on a Nashville session. The song, "I'm Sorry," set Brenda's sound, a crying style against a full orchestral backdrop, that he would subsequently use to even greater effect with Patsy. Overnight Brenda became an international singing star. Not long afterward, the term "Nashville Sound" started cropping up in the lexicon of the popular media. By the end of 1960, 45 percent of all hit records were cut in Nashville.

Key to the creation of the Nashville Sound was the A Team. Bradley claimed the mythic "sound" was really just "a way of doing things." Musicians like Hank Garland, Grady Martin, Harold Bradley, Bob Moore, Buddy Harmon, Floyd Cramer, Ray Edenton and Hargus "Pig" Robbins played on virtually every session in Nashville because they worked together efficiently and thus helped keep studio costs down. The result was a spontaneous, loose, jazzy feeling to the sessions in Nashville. "We would go to the West Coast and you'd let a guitar player out there take a ride and it was almost like work shoes," recalled Jordanaire Ray Walker. "It was good, but hard. You take Sugarfoot Garland, Grady Martin, Harold Bradley, and you would just set a clock by them. They all knew each other and they all had that wonderful, nonintrusive way of playing. It was great."

Owen Bradley saw his job as being a "referee" between the performer, songwriter and the session musicians. Bradley's studio provided an inventive setting where serendipitous happenings resulted in new sounds and styles. Fuzztone, a kind of roaring, melodic snore, came about on a July 1960 Marty Robbins session for "Don't Worry." Grady Martin was playing his six-string Danelectro bass when a preamp on the mixing board went bad. Don Law, Robbins's A&R man, thought it was a great commercial sound and kept it. Though Bradley replaced the preamp, the broken one was brought back whenever anyone wanted the sound. Finally it died completely, and when people would come in and ask for "the fuzz," and the engineer would reply that the equipment wouldn't work anymore, they'd complain, "You're only savin' it for Owen's Decca records."

Recalled Floyd Cramer: "Grady played gut string guitar on 'El Paso,' that Spanish thing that's behind Marty Robbins. Then he'd turn around and play the blues—whatever it called for is what the guys would adapt to. There were times I played a metal sound, like on 'Big Bad John,' where it sounds like someone beating on an anvil. We hung up a coat hanger on a coat rack and hung a big metal rod from a boom mike and I hit it with a hammer—I didn't even play piano on 'Big Bad John,' just that backbeat. Buddy Harmon would put wax paper on top of a snare case and get that real tinny, high-pitched thing, and play it with a brush. He'd play anything—the wall—if it worked, if it was different, if it was good."

To keep their chops, musicians like Garland, Cramer, Moore, Harmon, Chet Atkins and saxophonist Boots Randolph jammed at the Carousel Club downtown, in Printer's Alley, and what they played, more often than not, was jazz. Producer George Wein was blown away by what he heard and booked some of the Carousel Club musicians for the 1960 Newport Jazz Festival (which ended up being canceled when rowdy teenagers stormed the festival, but an album was released anyway, *After the Riot at Newport*). Then in August 1960 Hank Garland recorded a straight jazz album. John Hammond wrote the liner notes: "We should not be too surprised when a Country and Western star steps right into the forefront of jazz stars, for Hank Garland isn't the first country boy to make it big in the jazz world. But Hank is the first to do it without leaving Nashville."

If you were a songwriter, in 1960, Nashville was the market. When almost half of all hit records were made in Nashville, a songwriter could score a bonanza with one million-selling crossover hit. Writers were arriving by the broken-down carful. They stayed at "Mom" Upchurch's, a boarding house in East Nashville where you could get a room for Depression-era rates, or for $25 a week they might have stayed at Dunn's Trailer Court, which some believe was the inspiration for Roger Miller's line in "King of the Road": "Trailers for sale or rent."

Harlan Howard, who would pen some of the greatest hits of Patsy's career, was among the wave of creative immigrants who came to Nashville in 1960 via L.A., where he moved in 1955 from Detroit, where he grew up, by way of Kentucky, where he was born (on the same day as Patsy in 1929). In California he was driving a forklift for a book bindery in Huntington Park, making $200 a week—"$225 if I worked overtime"—writing songs on the side and mailing them to Nashville. The biggest royalty he'd ever received was for $27.

Then in 1958, he had his first hit record, "Pick Me Up on Your Way Down," the same title as the Mae Axton tune that Patsy once claimed she'd sung for Howard on the West Coast. Afterward, Ray Price, then one of country's biggest stars, called Howard at the factory, looking for songs. Howard sent him "Heartaches by the Number," Price recorded it and it hit country. But then Mitch Miller gave it to Guy Mitchell to cover and it hit pop. "When I heard Mitchell's record, I felt bad," Howard recalled. "When I wrote the song, it was such a soulful thing. . . . Then Mitchell comes out whistling, ukuleles. I thought he ruined my song—except Mitchell's damn thing sold about a million records."

"Heartaches" was followed by "Mommy for a Day," a 1959 hit for Kitty Wells. Suddenly Howard had "big money"—$100,000. He went and "did the typical hillbilly thing" and bought a brand-new, white-on-white Cadillac Coupe de Ville; then he and his wife, singer Jan Howard, drove to Nashville. They bought a four-bedroom house in suburban Madison for $35,000 and had enough left over to live "real good" for three years without having to work hard.

Howard realized he could make some real money doing this. He went into a writing frenzy, turning out fifteen, sixteen songs every two weeks, then going into a studio with a pickup band or just a guitar to demo his output in one three-hour marathon. "I had just come off a forklift in a factory less than a year before and I didn't want to go back there. I didn't really know what was commercial—what the world wanted and what they didn't. All I knew were stories—little titles, little melodies. It's like a baseball player who bats three hundred—that means 70 percent of the time he doesn't connect. Yet he might be a Hall of Famer."

Howard and other writers who arrived in Nashville around the same time, including Hank Cochran, Willie Nelson, Mel Tillis, Wayne Walker and Roger Miller, would get together in somebody's room for a "guitar pulling," showcasing their latest creative efforts.

"You might say it's like a bunch of Old West gunfighters coming together to see who is best," said Willie Nelson. "Only instead of slapping their holsters and coming up with six-guns blazing, they unsnap their guitar cases and come up singing."

The same writers all pitched their songs to the A&R men and became fixtures at the studios, running back and forth across the street, from the Quonset Hut to the RCA Studios, to catch every session on which they had a song. In the spirit of gunfighters, writers wanted to be there when their song came up to see who would be the victor.

Howard explained: "At the session they played back our songs. That's when you really needed to be there because the best song would stand out like a sore thumb. You'd know if your song was going to be a single or not. It would be, 'Who's going to get Jim Reeves' next record or the next Patsy Cline?' See, the hard part was already done— you'd already beat out dozens of songs, so you'd won as far as that was concerned. And you knew that somewhere along the way your song would appear on an album. Then afterward you'd all go out and have a beer, because somebody always won that round.

"I wrote a lot more songs than Hank did or Willie, plus I was writing for two or three different publishers at the time and they weren't. I was pitching to Owen Bradley and Chet Atkins and all these other producers. And I would take a tape of all these new songs and I enjoyed that. It was like it never broke my heart when they turned me down. I knew they were good songs. And I knew if they didn't record them, somebody else would. I couldn't wait to play a new song to them.

"Owen became like a father figure to me. He would go to the mat for you sometimes, but he wasn't always totally kind to me. I remember one time I was playing him a song. He'd have his glasses down on his nose, studying the lyrics as the song played. We went along like that and got about halfway through the song and he pushes the 'off' button and turns and says to me, 'Harlan, what's *he* doin' here?' Another guy had appeared in the song. I thought I'd been clever, you know? I had this boy-girl thing going along and all of a sudden I'd bring in this outsider. I thought I'd have this song going along and then I thought I'd make it turn left, and Owen'll like it. He said, 'Get him outa here.' It was like he wasn't necessary. I had a perfectly good love song going without this guy. I have no idea what the song was. Out of respect I changed the song. I don't remember if it ever got recorded; all I know was that I learned a lot. Owen was real wise. Why have three people unless the story is about a triangle. In other words, the less characters, the better. That was the lesson. Don't put him in the song unless he belongs there. Keep it simple."

The watering hole favored by writers and Opry stars was Tootsie's Orchid Lounge, located across the alley from the backstage door of the Ryman. Tootsie's got its name from Hattie Louise "Tootsie" Bess, who would extend credit to broke pickers and songwriters and eject rowdy patrons with the aid of a long hat pin. The Elia Kazan movie *Wild River,* starring Montgomery Clift and Lee Remick, helped fund the purchase of the bar, which was known as "Mom's" until 1958. Tootsie's husband, Big Jeff Bess, was a character actor who specialized in playing the heavy. With the money he made from throwing Montgomery Clift in a river and beating him up, he bought a bunch of clubs around Nashville, including the dark little dive behind the Ryman. Through their network of lounges, especially Tootsie's, the Besses gave unknown singers and pickers and songwriters like Roger Miller and Willie Nelson an opportunity to show their stuff, which might lead to an exclusive writing contract, road gig or even a recording contract.

It was mainly a guy's world in there, and mainly songwriters and musicians. The musicians would jam in the back room. Tootsie wouldn't let anyone else back there but music people, so it was like their own little world. On weekends, she would open it up to everyone on the Opry. There was no stage—it was strictly tables and chairs and one little bar in the midsection. As many people stood up as were seated and not nearly as many stars as it was rumored. Not even the ones who drank would come over for fear of the publicity. But artists like Faron Young, Jim Reeves, Ray Price, the ones who really enjoyed a good, cold beer between performances, would come over. Patsy would sit at one of the eight or nine little tables in the back that were pushed up close to the autograph-covered walls of Tootsie's while a congenial Opry crowd congregated around the bar in the center. It was one of Charlie's favorite haunts, and he might be there with her.

Patsy liked writers and hung out with them more than the average Opry star. There were two shows at the Opry, so between shows the singers and sidemen would have an hour and a half or maybe two hours to kill. You could only chew the fat behind the stage for so long, so they would walk over to Tootsie's for thirty minutes, an hour, grab a beer, talk and kid one another and maybe run out back, across the alley, to the nearby back door of the Ryman, to run over a tune with the band before they'd go on for their second show.

Howard recalled: "That's where Hank and Willie and I and Roger

Miller and all the songwriters, we'd be over there, and Patsy would seek us out. And it was quite normal to see her sitting around with four or five songwriters having a beer. Hank had a good sense of humor and was a good storyteller, and so was Roger Miller. She loved jokes. And boy, she'd laugh and slap that big ole thigh. She really had a great laugh. She kind of liked the smutty jokes. She was really kind of like a good ole girl. I don't remember her telling jokes. It was more like little quips. She had a good sense of humor. She was fun to be around, she was comfortable, you could cuss, it wasn't so much like being restricted. She was just a fun music person."

Patsy had always been attracted to writers, perhaps because she was so ambivalent about writing herself—wanting the words to express her heart yet feeling inadequate to what seemed to her such a daunting task. She was forever looking to meet writers who could express the way she felt. As a result, she became close with several writers. Donn Hecht and Eddie Miller were her pals on the West Coast. Hank Cochran, who shared her appreciation of amphetamines, was her main writer-friend in Nashville. When she liked a writer, she would frequently champion his work. In fact, one of Pasty's problems, according to Harlan Howard, was that "she loved us so much she might take some old dog [of a song] in there to Owen that really wasn't of the quality she needed."

Nashville-based singer-songwriter Teddy Wilburn said Patsy once begged him for a song he'd written on the road while taking "old yellers," the nickname for a form of amphetamine that was all the rage in Nashville in the fifties. The Wilburn Brothers were performing near Winchester in 1959, and Patsy and Charlie went to see the show. Patsy was quite fond of Teddy Wilburn, whom she would frequently call, usually with music-related frustrations while she was under contract with 4 Star, the Wilburns' former label. After the show, Patsy insisted the Wilburns come home with her and Charlie. "I've got a big old ham in the oven and I've been cooking all day and you've gotta come out, you've just gotta," she said.

After dinner, while sitting around talking and having drinks, Teddy Wilburn produced the lead sheets for "Dakota Lil," a ballad of the Old West that expressed the cowgirl mythology that held such potency for Patsy: "I wore my guns so proudly/I'd kill for just a thrill/No man could ever back me down/Not me, Dakota Lil." She took it to Owen Bradley, who said absolutely not. Wilburn later offered that "it was probably a good thing she didn't do it because it might not have done her any good.

Patsy basically showed this rough, tough individual, and yet inside, she was putty," Wilburn observed. "She told me that she cried because she wanted to do the song, that she begged Owen Bradley. She wanted to do it so badly."

Patsy's first Decca session was scheduled for November 16. Liberated from her 4 Star straitjacket at long last, she and Bradley were free to pick any song they wanted, or if one of them didn't want it, then songs they were willing to do as a "compromise." Patsy eagerly began scouring for her idea of a hit song.

"Back then, it was customary to write alone," said Harlan Howard. "Hank wrote alone and I did, Roger Miller did and Willie did. We just assumed that's what you did. But Hank came over to the house one day and I was using this garage as my escape place to write. Hank said, 'I got this idea.' He had the first couple of lines of a song. He said I want you to help me. Anyhow, Hank and I wrote this song, actually, half of it. Back then they liked records to be two-and-a-half minutes long. Not four, two-and-a-half, so disk jockeys could get their commercials in—disk jockeys used to talk a lot back then. They wanted short records, so you had to write a volume, an epic, in two and a half minutes. I got to timing the song with my watch and it wasn't very long. I thought, 'Well, we could go back and do that little bridge section again.' I was into it, plus it was Hank's idea in the first place and I thought I'd just tinker around, see if I can make it a little longer, maybe write a second bridge or something.

"Anyhow, I got to writing, and I wrote the second half of the song, which was 'I Fall to Pieces.' And I think the next morning I took it out to Pamper, the little publishing company where Hank worked as a song plugger. Hank liked what I added to it. We were doing demo sessions with bands in little studios about every two weeks then, so not long afterward we went in there with about twelve, fifteen songs. We did these bunches of songs when I was married to Jan [Howard]. She'd sing the girl's songs. So we had her sing 'I Fall to Pieces' on the demo. We didn't necessarily think it was a girl's song, but she just sang a lot better than Hank and I did.

"Right after that, I was out at Pamper and Owen Bradley called. He and Hank talked almost every day. Between Hank and Willie and I, we were getting a lot of records of different songs, each doing our own thing for this one little company. I remember sitting there, and Owen evidently asked Hank, 'You guys got any new songs out there in the office?' He was kind of bird-dogging us, because we were fresh blood and we had some fresh ideas. Hank said, 'Yeah, we've got this little ballad, Harlan and I, called 'I Fall to Pieces.' He said it could be a guy's song or a girl's song. He said it was 'ambidextrous.' Owen evidently said, 'Well, bring it down.'"

* * *

Upon hearing Jan Howard's demo of "I Fall to Pieces," Bradley was convinced that it was a hit. He took it to singer Roy Drusky, who he was grooming as Decca's answer to smooth "Gentleman Jim" Reeves. Bradley believed Drusky's mellow baritone was ideal for his lush production, and "I Fall to Pieces" the perfect vehicle. Drusky disagreed. He told Bradley it was a girl's song: "You don't hear a man saying, 'I fall to pieces.' " Bradley was a little ticked. He took the song to several other artists, including Brenda Lee, but no one wanted to do it. By the time he offered it to Patsy, as far as she was concerned it had a bad reputation. All the big names had already turned it down and she didn't want a dud. She wanted a hit and her first time out on the new Decca deal she wanted to swing. And the sorrowful "I Fall to Pieces" definitely did not swing.

Bradley was flexible. He suggested yet another one of his song trade-offs with Patsy, a "compromise": record "Pieces," and she could choose whatever song she liked.

Patsy was a Hensley: you could reason with her but you couldn't drive her an inch. She recognized that Bradley was fair, and she loved that about him. He was one of the "hosses." She agreed to the compromise.

Jan Howard loved her husband's song and wanted to do it for her label, Challenge Records. But she had to take a back seat to give the song a chance with the big pop labels. It was Howard, who has a pop-sounding voice herself, who came up with the song that ended up on the B side of "Pieces."

By then the two women had a closeness in which Patsy felt comfortable sharing her problems, vulnerabilities and secrets. Their initial meeting got off to what could have been a disastrous beginning when Patsy thought she was dealing with a high-hatter and lit into Jan accordingly. The encounter turned into just the kind of sparring match that Patsy savored, as Jan related: "I had been a fan of Patsy's when I lived in California, before I ever started singing. I loved her voice. When we moved to Nashville and I joined the Opry, I really was looking forward to meeting her, but at the time I was very shy about going up and introducing myself. I was shy around everyone then, and she intimidated me. She kind of commanded a room. Her presence was incredible. When she walked in a room, you knew right away Patsy was there. It wasn't that she intended to do that—that's just the way she was. It's called charisma, and she had it.

"If she liked you, she loved you; she was a very loving person, and a giving person—there wasn't a selfish bone in her body. Or she hated you, one or the other. And you knew it, either way. She was not phony and not two-faced about it. Whatever she had to say, she'd say it to your face. She really loved life and lived life, every minute of it. I especially remember her laugh: it was huge. When she laughed, she really laughed. She didn't just smile and let it go politely. It just rolled out of her.

"So when I started doing the Opry, I'd usually just do my spot, change clothes and leave. But if she was on or someone I really wanted to hear, I'd hang around long enough to hear them. That's what happened this time. I stayed to hear Patsy sing, but I had never met Patsy. I remember what she wore: a cowgirl outfit with fringe and boots. I think the boots were white. So when she finished singing I stood at the side of the stage and then I went back to the restroom to change clothes. As I was changing she walked in and she just stood there and looked at me with her hand on her hip and her head kind of cocked to the side. I was confused. I didn't know what she was doing there like that.

"Her first words were, 'You're a conceited little son-of-a-bitch.' I was floored. I said, 'What?' She said, 'You just waltz in here and do your bit and waltz out and you don't say hello or kiss my ass or nothin' else to no damn body.'

"I said, 'Now wait just a damn minute.' About that time my Irish and Indian temper got up. 'Where I'm from, it's the people that live in a town that make the newcomer feel welcome, and ain't nobody made me feel welcome in this damn town.' "

At that, Patsy was floored. She couldn't believe what she'd just heard—both the content and the delivery, from someone she'd pegged as another stuck-up girl singer. Patsy wasn't afraid of admitting when she was wrong. Her face melted into a big smile, and then she erupted in a big, robust laugh: "You're all right, honey. Anybody that'll stand up to the Cline is all right. We're going to be good friends."

Jan had been given "Lovin' in Vain," an exuberant number by singer-songwriter Freddie Hart that she wanted to record but her A&R man told her no. Jan was upset that she was being disallowed the song, but she promised Hart she'd get him a record. Then she took it to Patsy, who was delighted with it. Bright and sassy, "Lovin' in Vain" was the perfect red hot mama vehicle. She took it with her to the session.

The date got off to a bad start. Bradley had an arrangement of "I Fall to Pieces" that she hated. They'd disappeared into his second-floor office, and when they finally emerged, Ray Walker said, "You could tell she hadn't been eating ice cream and singing 'Happy Birthday.' " Even though Hank Cochran was her good buddy, Patsy had doubts about "Pieces" and she was diplomatic—for Patsy—but firm: "It's a pretty song but it's not for me."

Bradley's own sensibilities had been honed through some of his recent success with the crying style of Brenda Lee, who had a run of monster hits for two years with "Fool Number One," "Dum Dum," "You Can Depend on Me," "Emotions," "I Want to Be Wanted" and "I'm Sorry." What Bradley had in mind for Patsy was a midnight kind of arrangement for Cochran and Howard's simple, soulful lyrics. To the basic A Team configuration—his brother Harold, Martin, Moore, Cramer and Harmon, plus the Jordanaires—he brought in Jimmy Day on steel guitar. Randy Hughes strapped on his acoustic guitar, and Bradley turned his mike down. Hughes was there for Patsy's sake. Bradley appreciated it and it meant a little extra session money for her manager.

Patsy's specific objection to Bradley's arrangement was the ending. Bradley thought Patsy's gutsy voice would do it justice as a slow, forlorn ballad. As usual when she was feeling insecure, she wanted to give it some oomph.

"All she knew was 'Start that guitar and let me sing,' and she'd sing swing," said Walker. "In fact, she didn't understand anything but western swing. She wouldn't cut a ballad. She didn't want to cut 'I Fall to Pieces' because she was afraid of it.

"Finally she agreed to do the song, and when she came down to the session, you could tell she'd been through it with him, because Owen will stand his ground, too. He had to let her know, 'I'm responsible for you, this label is responsible for you and we want this song recorded.' She agreed to it if she could do that ending. He said, 'Patsy, no. It doesn't fit.' She said, 'Well, if I cut it, that's the way it's going to be.' "

The 4:4 shuffle, pure Ray Price and Buck Owens, was the going thing in Nashville and Bradley thought it had been "done to death." He asked for something different from the rhythm section but all the other basic combinations "just lay there and bled," said Harold Bradley. Producer Bradley conceded it had to be the shuffle then.

Hank Garland came up with a tolling bell-like lick on the opening that was totally different and hip. "It was one of the first tremolos out of a guitar I ever heard," remembered Harlan Howard. "It was kind of a new thing, sort of delayed, and I think he was the only one in town at the moment who could play that. And they sneaked in a country shuffle, like a walking bass, which really made it throb. They were all so delighted with it."

The shuffle beat reined Patsy in and contained her; it left her with no alternative but to explore the interior of the song, and she styled it, pausing, breathing, caressing the lyrics. The Jordanaires stayed out of her way with their subtle, low, almost gospellike musical fills. They were on the first run-through of the song, and when she got to the tag, she went up an octave and actually started singing a little faster.

"We had just taken the chords down so we were waiting to see how she would end it, and when she tagged it with that hillbilly swing, we just stopped," remembered Ray Walker. "My face just blanched. She came over to me and said, 'What's the matter? Didn't you like that ending?' I said, 'Well, do you want me to say?' She said, 'Yeah, tell me.' I said, 'We've never heard anything like this. You had us in the palm of your hand when you were singing those beautiful low notes. Then all of a sudden you start *this*. It doesn't fit anything in the song. You lost me.'

"She said, 'Well, that's what Owen said.' I said, 'Patsy, listen to Owen. Owen *knows* what it takes to make a song right. You listen to Owen.' She said, 'Well, swing's always been good to me and I'm just afraid to get away from it and I guess I just feel like I have to have a little touch of it in everything I do.' I said, 'Not in this one. You'll kill it. If you do anything on that tag, go on down deeper. *Nobody* sounds like that.'

"So from there she recorded it again and got deeper and deeper into the meaning of the song. And when she got through we said, 'That's got to be a record.' We went in and listened to the playbacks with her. Most of the time the musicians, after they're done playing, they'll get up and get a cup of coffee or go to the bathroom or go have a smoke, but we would listen to the playback with her and encourage her because we liked her and she liked that. She studied that thing, and when she heard herself, she couldn't believe it. She didn't even think it sounded like her. One time she made the remark, 'I like that even if it wasn't me.' What she meant was if another girl sang it. I think she was real fearful of the world it could open up to her, or that it wouldn't sell, because all she'd known was honky-tonks."

Patsy picked up the tempo on "Shoes," another shuffle from the pen of Hank Cochran, based on an idea provided by Velma Smith, who played rhythm guitar on Don Gibson's sessions and was married to Pamper Music president Hal Smith. "Lovin' in Vain" was the compromise song. A fourth tune, Cochran's "Perfect Example of a Fool," was planned but Patsy lost the demo. Three songs in three hours.

Afterward, Patsy called Jan Howard, for whom she wanted to play back the session. "She didn't like 'I Fall to Pieces' at first," Howard related. "I don't know if she ever really liked it. When she played me that session, she played 'Lovin' in Vain.' That was what she liked and that was what she was singing on the personal appearances. Then one day when she was over at the house she told me, 'Well, I got to learn that damn song ['I Fall to Pieces']. I'm getting requests for it, and I guess I got to learn it."

On January 21, Patsy played the Opry. In the wee hours of the following morning she started going into labor. Charlie had been out all night, "havin' him a ball." He related the story himself on a 1989 video on Patsy's life, *The Real Patsy Cline:* "I got home—it might have been six o'clock—no big deal. And I went on in and went to bed. But then about seven o'clock—I'm not sure about the time—very shortly after I got to bed, Patsy went in and tried to wake me up. Said she had to go to the hospital. Had labor pains. I said, 'Yeah, uh huh.' In my mind I was just thinking she was just trying to get me up because she was mad because I'd been out all night."

Patsy got neighbor Joyce Blair, who helped babysit little Julie when Patsy was away on the road, to take her to St. Thomas Hospital. The following morning Patsy gave birth to a son, named Allen Randolph. Charlie claimed the child was named after Patsy's stepbrother. But Randolph Mann had no knowledge that he had a namesake, making Kathy Hughes's claim that the child was named after her husband more likely.

Decca released "I Fall to Pieces" backed by "Lovin' in Vain" nine days later. Patsy was scared that the disk might not make it and was strapped for funds, with a new mouth to feed. She couldn't afford to waste any time. Within a few weeks after giving birth she was back on the road, while Joyce Blair took care of her babies. She wrote to Jim McCoy in Winchester, telling him, "I want to come home, but I don't have the money. I wonder if you could get us a gig?" McCoy booked the Winchester Drive-In and called the Melody Playboys.

"I asked the boys, 'She really wants to come home and don't have enough money to make the journey. Will you guys work for nothing?' They'd been off from playing for a year and wanted to get back to playing anyway, so they said, 'Yeah.' So the same guy who was in charge of the Winchester Drive-In had a theater out in Charles Town, so we booked that one too, so I was able to get her $150 for both gigs, and boy, she thought that was something."

McCoy placed an ad in the *Winchester Evening Star:*

On Stage—In Person
Winchester's Only
PATSY CLINE
Singing Her Latest Decca Hit Recording
"I FALL TO PIECES"

Patsy and the band got on top of the concession stand between features, *King of the Wild Stallions* ("the gun-hot death on Wild Horse Mesa!") and *Young Jesse James*. Patsy, naturally, dressed in her usual western get-up.

According to McCoy, "Here's Patsy singing, and the women—it was never the men, that's one thing I want to clarify—the women started blowing the horns and booing her. Now she already started to get a name for herself; I guess she was working the Opry then. Here's these women booing and carrying on. Now how do you feel? Here's a girl singing her heart out, has already made it and you got these idiots out there making fun of her and booing her. She started crying so bad. This guy, the manager, he had a trailer that he used as an office. We just took her over there, and I'll never forget it: she said, 'Why do people in Winchester treat me like this?' "

Patsy's new record received no fanfare from Decca's publicity mill. Decca, like all the other major labels during this uncertain time for country music, did not put nearly the kind of muscle into the promotion of country acts as it did the big pop acts, and what promotion they did get came out of the New York publicity office, which tended to regard country as corny anyway. As the head of A&R, Bradley received a salary, could not participate in record royalties, couldn't sign contracts or otherwise control the purse strings and had to go to Decca in New York for approval for just about everything. And still he thought they treated him "real well."

"After Paul left, I felt all alone in the world," Bradley recalled. Fortunately, they sent him a young, handsome go-getter from the Cincinnati branch, Harry Silverstein, to serve as his assistant, handle promotion and, a bit later, help produce some of Decca's bluegrass acts. Silverstein saved the day more than once.

"Harry was very good," Bradley offered. "What he would do is connive to get New York to do things, try to make them think that things were happening when sometimes they weren't, to get them to do something about it. He caused a lot of records to happen that would not have happened if he had not known how to manipulate them and get a little chart action going. And Harry was a master at that. He knew how to call attention to these records. Hell, 'Little Bitty Tear'—Burl Ives started that record out on the coast—they didn't know they had it. All the promotion was being done in New York and then they put Harry on it and he ran promotion out of Nashville—but we had no authority to spend a nickel. We had no budgets or anything. We had to do everything through New York. So he had to manipulate to convince them. If he didn't, he'd be fired."

Little publishing companies like Pamper Music, on the other hand, had much to gain if one of their songs hit. If "I Fall to Pieces" charted pop, it could literally make the company. "Decca had Kitty Wells, the number one country artist, and Brenda Lee, a real big pop artist, so they didn't care, you know?" explained Hank Cochran. "Owen was sold on Patsy and so was Pamper. The song meant a lot more to us. So we just worked and slaved and finally brought it home."

Of the dozens of music publishers in Nashville in 1960, Pamper, Acuff-Rose and Cedarwood, the firm founded by former Opry manager Jim Denny, were the only companies in Nashville employing independent promotion men to plug records. The early "hit men" traveled the back roads with a trunkful of 45s, stopping at radio stations along the way. They lived out of their suitcases, stayed at cheap motels or slept in the back of their cars, and endured all the other inconveniences of the road often just for the love of the business and about $100 a week plus expenses.

Pat Nelson was one of two such promoters working for Pamper. Five times married and divorced, Nelson was "a jolly little fat man who liked everybody and everybody liked him." Nelson's tastes were a hodgepodge; they ran to Tex Williams, Ray Price and singer-songwriter Jackie DeShannon. He also really liked Patsy. And when he liked an artist, he would eat ketchup soup on the road if it meant bringing in a hit. His territory was the Midwest, his home base, Columbus, Ohio.

Stubby Stubbyfield, a promotion man who handled the Pamper account in the Southwest, explained how he and Nelson worked: "Back then we were working pop stations and country stations too. There was a line, but a lot of the country stuff got played on pop stations back then. Pat spent a lot of time on 'I Fall to Pieces.' From Columbus, to Cleveland, Detroit, Minneapolis, Chicago, he kept working that market. But he worked more than just radio stations. He worked one-stops and wholesale, retail, all kinds of outlets. I think that's why he got that record over."

In April 1961, largely on the basis of sales orders, "Pieces" made a modest debut on the *Billboard* country charts, though it still wasn't receiving that much airplay. Nelson continued to plug away. At one point he received an order for five thousand records from a Columbus department store, so he was able to convince deejays to give it some pop airplay around Ohio. Nelson and Hank Cochran were encouraged by the scintilla of action, and Cochran managed to convince Hal Smith to let Nelson stay on the job. Patsy went on the road with Nelson to do sock hops around Ohio.

"We just believed it was there and kept on working on it, 'cause it would crop up in certain areas and just get unbelievably hot, and then it would do it in another area," Cochran said. "We worked on it for six months. Nowadays, there'd be no way in hell you could do that. If a record ain't happening in a matter of weeks, well, you'd better start on something else."

Harlan Howard remembered the promotional effort that went into "Pieces": "I was standing out in front of the little garage behind Pamper, which was my studio, and Hal Smith was talking to Hank. He said, 'We're spending a fortune on this thing. I think it's done all it's going to do. I'm fixin' to get off of it and pull the guy off and get him onto something else.' Hank said, 'Don't give up yet, Hal. The song keeps wanting to be a pop hit here and there.' So he persuaded Hal Smith to stay on with this record. And one of these guys who'd been hired to work these songs took Patsy up there and they did all these teenage sock hops. It wasn't country promotion. All I know is when they come back from this promotion tour, all of a sudden Patsy was breaking out in Ohio, Illinois, Detroit, throughout the heartland of America. And all of a sudden she had this big pop hit."

On May 22, "Pieces" debuted on the pop charts and began a slow but steady climb upward. By August 7, it hit number 1 country and continued the drive up pop until September 12, when it peaked at number 12—"the slowest record going up and the slowest coming down" that anyone in Nashville could recall.

In April, when "Pieces" first appeared on the pop charts, Patsy dropped in on Bradley at the Quonset Hut. He was able to wrangle a small advance for her out of New York. The loan company was breathing down her neck. They wanted her refrigerator, her furniture, her car. She came dancing out of Bradley's office that day, jubilant. In the studio downstairs she ran into the Jordanaires.

"She came in that studio and her eyes were just shining, and she said, 'Ray, honey'—'cause I was the first one she saw. And then she looked around and said, 'Boys, those bastards can't take my refrigerator now. They'll never get my car now. I paid cash for 'em and they're mine and I'm a-keepin' 'em.' I said, 'Well, where'd you get the money?' She said, 'Owen gave it to me, 'cause, baby, they tell me I got one hell of a hit record.' She was just tickled to death. She had enough to pay for her stuff and had a little left over to spend. She couldn't believe it."

By the end of May, "Pieces" was the number 1 record at Decca and was hitting number 1 pop in Nashville. As though it was her first hit record, Patsy said she was "nearly up on the moon and didn't need a rocket." Interviewed on the radio, she said, "This is my second hit record now and I never thought I'd be able to get the first one, let alone the second one."

After "Pieces" started making noise in the spring, Patsy stayed on the road virtually nonstop, promoting the record. She was doing it for her "babies," she said. She missed them desperately, but now that it looked like her career had regained momentum, she was determined to go as far as it would take her. She wanted to give her children the home she never had.

For the second time in her career, Patsy was cast as a crossover act, mixing country stops with pop. One day it might be an appearance on "Jubilee U.S.A." (the former "Ozark Jubilee"), the next day, a sock hop. She was jubilant over her hard-won success.

One afternoon she showed up at the Pamper offices with tokens of her appreciation. She gave Cochran a silver and onyx ring and a money clip, which she pressed into the palm of Cochran's hand saying, "Here, just carry some of that money you're going to be making on 'I Fall to Pieces.' " It was inscribed "To Hank for 'I Fall to Pieces,' Love Patsy." For Howard, she had a silver I.D. bracelet inscribed "Harlan, thanks for the hit. Patsy." Patsy's own feelings toward Howard may have been less magnanimous at one point in the past. She told Donn Hecht that during the dry period after "Walkin' After Midnight," when she was desperately seeking some powerhouse material, Howard turned her down, supposedly saying, "I don't work with amateur singers." She told Hecht, "I all but kissed his ass to have him give me songs, but he don't want a 'nobody' recording his songs." But Howard was impressed with Patsy, not only for the great job she did on "Pieces," but for the fact that she was thoughtful enough to thank him so effusively.

"I thought, 'Wow, this is nice—singers give writers presents when they write 'em a hit,' " recalled Howard. "Thirty years later this is the only present a singer ever gave me except for a great recording."

She continued to express her gratitude in public and private settings. When she was up, everyone had to be up with her. Pat Nelson attended one impromptu celebration at her house. During the party Patsy stood up, looked around the room and pronounced, "I want everybody at this party to realize that if it wasn't for this man here," gesturing at Pat Nelson who was sitting on the couch, "I wouldn't be where I am today."

Singer Rusty York ("Sugaree," his 1959 hit), who was at that party, recalled how Charlie came up to him and asked if he'd ever tried saki. When York said he hadn't, Charlie offered him some. "I don't remember any booze at the party, so Charlie went in the kitchen and he was rattling around, getting this saki for me, and Patsy came in and knocked the bottle out of his hand and said, 'I warned you not to drink anymore.' He said, 'I'm not drinking. I swear I'm not.' But she didn't believe him, and jumped on his case real bad, because evidently he had drinking problems."

"She was out on the road doing dates, when I received a letter from her in the mail one day," recalled Charlie Lamb, who published the *Music Reporter*. "Patsy was very, very sincere. It said, 'Dear Charlie: Will you please draw up a small ad. I can't afford much, but draw up a small ad, and thank the disk jockeys and the radio stations for playing my record. You know how to do it. Draw it up and I'll pay you when I come home. Patsy.' "

The ad read, "I've tried and I've tried, but I haven't yet found a way to thank so many wonderful people for so much. Thank you and bless you all. Gratefully, Patsy Cline."

Back home in Winchester at the end of May to attend her sister Sylvia's high school graduation—the first one in her family to graduate from high school—Patsy learned there was a move afoot to declare a "Patsy Cline Day." "Ain't that a kick in the head?" she quipped. The hometown salute never happened. During the trip, she showed up at McCrory's Five and Dime with her hair in rollers tied up with a bright red scarf, ruby red lipstick, dark shades and skintight capri pants, "the tighter the better," said Patsy Lillis, who clerked there.

"She said, 'I got me my first royalty check.' I said, 'You did?' She said, 'Yeah.' I said, 'What are you going to do?' She said, 'I'm going to buy my mom a new stove and refrigerator.' And she did. That's the kind of person she was. She never went anyplace that she didn't bring me something. I don't care where. One time I had an abscessed tooth, and she wanted me to go someplace with her, and I said, 'I can't go. I got to go to the dentist.' She said, 'I'll take you to the dentist, then we're going.' And she did. And she even paid to have my tooth fixed. And she wasn't making that much money. No indeed. But anything, anytime that you needed her, she was there."

Chapter Eighteen

WHEN "I FALL TO PIECES" started making noise in the spring of 1961, Patsy started making plans. She wanted to take care of everybody. She was able to get herself out of hock, send money home, buy her mother a new gold Cadillac and make a down payment on a modest house in the 5000 block of Hillhurst Drive in Madison, on which she also handled all the payments. In April she made a swing through California, where she told Donn Hecht she'd had another one of her "hunches" that she might be involved in an accident. Hecht advised her, "If your hunch is that strong, you ought to stay away from driving on long trips or being with anybody else on long trips, keep the booze out of the car, don't let people drive who are drinking and try not to cover too much territory. You can't lock yourself up in the house, but just make yourself constantly aware that maybe somebody upstairs is trying to tell you something, you know?"

She used to say to June Carter, "I'm not going to live to be an old woman."

"'Well, I'm not either, so let's just give it a good, hard lick while we're here.' And we'd just laugh about it," Carter said.

Acting on her ill-boded feelings, she wrote out a will by hand while en route, on Delta Air Lines stationery. Dated April 22, and witnessed by Mrs. Rubye C. LaBat, Patsy's only will clearly lacked the input of legal counsel, but did make her feelings about Charlie, who, at one point during one of their public spats declared she was his "meal ticket," abundantly clear:

TO WHOM IT MAY CONCERN:

I, Virginia Hensley Dick (known in my profession as singer Patsy Cline), being of a sound mind and body, leave (and it is my wish) to Hilda Virginia Hensley my mother, my children Julia Simadore Dick and Allen Randolph Dick to be cared for and raised to the best of her ability until they are eighteen years of age. If in this time Hilda V. Hensley would pass away, my wish is that my sister, Sylvia Mae Hensley, take care and raise my children as if they were her own.

Also to Hilda V. Hensley I leave all money which is in my possession at the time of my death or any income to follow coming from my work or record recordings in any way. I leave this to Hilda V. Hensley to use in any way to benefit and educate my children Julia and Allen Dick, as she sees fit. I, Virginia H. Dick, having royalties of 5 percent from each recording sold of the said recording company to whom I'm contracted with at the time of my death or any royalties paid to me thereafter, I wish the money to go to the care and education of Julia S. and Allen R. Dick.

Their father Charles Allen Dick being also of sound mind and body and good income, can visit, help in raising, clothing and educating the children Julia & Allen Dick, in any way but I, the wife of Charles A. Dick, wish that the children *remain* [emphasis hers] in the home of my mother Hilda V. Hensley or Sylvia Mae Hensley until they themselves can choose otherwise. If my home in which I reside is paid for or if the insurance finishes paying the home in full at the time of my death, I Virginia H. Dick leave this home to my children Julia S. and Allen R. Dick.

My personal insurance on myself is to be used to put me away and to be put in a savings account by my husband Charles A. Dick in Winchester, Virginia, to be used for the education of Julia and Allen Dick.

My awards of which I received for my work as a singer and all pictures, I leave to my daughter Julia and son Allen Dick.

My western designed costumes I leave to Julia and Allen Dick.

The children [sic] bedroom furniture is to be theirs [sic]. One oil painting of myself I leave to my mother, Hilda V. Hensley, until her death and then to be passed on to Julia and Allen Dick. My diamond ring to my daughter Julia Dick. To Samuel L. Hensley, Jr., my brother, I leave one blond bedroom suit [sic] and one Polaroid camera and table model television set. To Sylvia Mae Hensley I leave all my jewelry and one black bedroom suit [sic].

To my mother Hilda V. Hensley I leave all clothes, a dinette set, a Kenmore kitchen stove, Kenmore washer, and refridgerator [sic]. Also to Hilda V. Hensley I leave all dishes and kitchen wares.

To my husband Charles A. Dick I leave my western designed den furniture, a hi-fi stereo record player and radio, records and albums and tape recorder and blond floor model television set.

To my husband I leave whatever make car we have at the time of my death.

Whatever household property I may purchase between now and my death I leave to my mother Hilda V. Hensley.

I wish to be put away in a white western dress I designed with my daughter's little gold cross necklace and my sons [sic] small white testament in my hands and to be buried in the resting place of my husbands [sic] choice, and my wedding band on.

I, Virginia Hensley Dick (Patsy Cline) wrote this myself on April 22nd, 1961.

Virginia H. Dick

Patsy left Charlie at home and took her babies with her to Winchester at the end of May. Following her visit, she returned to Nashville accompanied by the whole gang: her mother, sister and brother. She planned to spend some time at home with them before heading back out on the road for a round of dates.

June 14 was a rainy day in Nashville. Patsy got John to drive her to a nearby shopping center to buy buttons, ribbons and thread to mend one of her costumes. It was just after 4:30 P.M. when they headed home in a driving storm on a two-lane road. As they rounded a hill, the driver of an oncoming car pulled out and gunned ahead to pass another vehicle. In the split seconds that followed, her "hunch" became an awful reality.

The impact killed the thirty-two-year-old passenger of the other car and her six-year-old son, while the driver was admitted to Madison Hospital in fair condition. Patsy was catapulted through the windshield and over the hood of the car, while John suffered "a 3 in. deep hole punched in his brest-bone [sic] and cracked his front ribs. . . . " She lay at the side of the road, bleeding heavily. When the ambulances arrived she was conscious but in shock and, unaware of the extent of her own injuries, insisted that she could wait while they took care of the others.

Patsy was admitted to Madison Hospital in critical condition, her scalp nearly peeled off. According to Dr. Hillis Evans, the admitting physician, she was "a gory mess." A deep gash dissected her face beginning at the hairline on the right side, through the right eyebrow, a quarter inch from the eye, across the bridge of her nose, through the left eyebrow and curved up to her hairline on the left side. Her hip was dislocated, her wrist broken and she'd lost a great deal of blood. According to Dr. Evans, she was "almost hopeless at first glance."

"They thought I was gone twice during the sewing up and had to give me 3 pts. of blood," Patsy later wrote Jim McCoy from her hospital bed. "Saw the other lady die," she added.

★　　★　　★

Mae Axton vividly recalled the accident that nearly took Patsy's life: "I was on a rock and roll tour that had started out in Florida and went to Montgomery and Birmingham—I was doing a story on it for the magazine I was writing for at the time. When I got to Birmingham there was this message for me to call Charlie. I called, and he said, 'Mae, Patsy has had a wreck, and she keeps calling for you, though she's unconscious. The doctor said, 'Whoever she is, let's get her here.' Could you come?' Charlie was crying. I said I will be there on the next plane. He said, 'Have someone call us and I'll meet you at the airport.' Teddy Wilburn and Charlie, I believe Teddy, was with him. I got the first flight out and they met me, and rushed me straight to the hospital.

"When I went in, her head was all swollen, she was all black and blue, and her forehead, it had fallen down, the whole forehead, skin and all. She looked unreal. I just sat down by her bed immediately. Charlie sat over there with me. I said, 'Honey, I'm here.' I kept talking to her all night long, 'cause it was late when I got there. She was unconscious, but I kept talking, and I did not stop. I told her I loved her, told her things we'd shared, how I felt about her and Charlie, talked to her about different people, just talked. I said, 'Now I can't do all the talking. You're going to have to wake up.' Later that night the doctor came by and said, 'We nearly lost her.' Finally she opened her eyes, not real wide, because she was swollen, and she smiled, and Charlie started crying, and she said, 'Hello, Mae. I knew you'd come.' A little after that the doctor came in and she said hello to him and said, 'This is my friend, Mae.' He said, 'Yes, I met her.' She said, 'I knew she'd come.' "

While Patsy was still in a postaccident haze, neighbor Joyce Blair, to whom Patsy had entrusted the care of her babies whenever she was on the road, came to see her. Patsy grasped her hand and whispered, "Blair, Jesus has been in my room. He has taken my hand and told me that, 'No, not now. I have other things for you to do.' "

In the days and weeks following the accident, Patsy was attended nearly every day by Reverend Jay Alford, pastor of the First Assembly Church of God in her parish in Madison. One day after the Pentecostal minister started to leave after completing his visit, she asked him to pray with her about her spiritual need. "As I prayed with her, she suddenly began to pray fervently and to weep," Alford recalled. "The presence of the Lord Jesus Christ had entered the room in a very special way. If I live to be one hundred years of age, I will never forget the words she spoke to me after we finished praying. She said, 'Brother Alford, all my life I have been reaching for God and today I touched him.' "

Singer Billy Walker described the spiritual rebirth in Patsy following her near-death experience. Walker had known Patsy since 1956, from a guest appearance on "Town & Country Jamboree," and they were both managed by Randy Hughes. Walker was one of the "hosses," and when he heard about Patsy's accident over the radio, he was one of many music buddies who rushed to the hospital to keep a vigil.

"They still had her in the emergency room. Man, her scalp was just about peeled off of her head. So we hung around there for a while and they operated on her and we came back later on. Lot of people don't believe in the power of prayer but we were praying for the woman. She just about died. Afterward we went up to her hospital room lots of times and had prayer with her. She definitely changed. Patsy was kind of a bawdy gal, kind of raw-talking. But she had a heart of gold, and if she was your friend, she loved you dearly. She had a few choice words that she used often that made her seem a little harsh, but she was a very tender-hearted person. But after that accident, she mellowed. She was more grateful for life. She was more tolerant of people. She was a calmer person. She just changed. She didn't ever cuss as much as she did."

When she realized she was alive, Patsy made a covenant with the Lord. She said she wasn't afraid of going, but she had a lot of things to do; if she could be free to do them, her attitude, spiritually, would be dramatically changed for the rest of her life. Part of her bargain with the Lord was that she would renew her efforts to try to make her marriage with Charlie work, "for the sake of the kids."

Hilda and Sylvia stayed on in Nashville to look after Patsy and the kids, while John returned to Winchester after his two-week stay. As Patsy regained her strength, she held court from her bedside, entertaining visitors with jokes about her horrendous appearance and filling the corridors of the hushed-up hospital with her robust laughter. Bruised and bored, at one point she suggested bringing a WSM microphone to her bedside so she could sing for the folks. She made jokes about the bland, vegetarian diet she was being fed by the Seventh Day Adventists who ran the hospital. Homesick, she told her sister she'd die for some meat. Sylvia smuggled in cheeseburgers and fries, to Patsy's delight, while Hilda brought comfort to her hurting daughter in the form of fried chicken salad with boiled dressing and homemade ham biscuits, and sat on the bed watching Ginny eat every last morsel, giving thanks for her broad smile and healthy appetite.

If the hit record hadn't made Patsy an overnight name, then the timing of the accident did. Once it became clear she was out of danger, deejays all over the country jumped on the possibilities for irony inherent in the title of "I Fall to Pieces," by now in heavy rotation. Cards, letters, telegrams and flowers from fans, record executives and deejays from all over the country poured into the hospital, where she shared her semi-private room with an elderly woman who, she observed, seemed to be in worse shape than she was. Never totally realizing she was so loved, she was deeply touched by the expressions of support. Even with an arm and a leg in traction, she pledged, "I'm going to answer every one of them," and she did. Once the doctors put her right arm in a splint, she started writing, with apologies for her penmanship. Patsy was especially touched by the fact that so many Opry members had rallied around her. It was "Come On In" for her—the country music family at its best. "No one knows the strength, faith and encouragement and good feeling they've given me, to know so many wished me well," she wrote.

"I got flowers from Brenda Lee, Faron Young, WSM, Jan Howard, Bill Anderson, June Carter, the Carter Family, Roy Acuff, Webb Pierce and Tex Ritter and I don't know all. Even Skeeter D. and Ralph. Ha!" The latter reference was to Ralph Emery and his wife, Skeeter Davis. Patsy didn't think a whole lot of WSM's Emery, already one of the most powerful deejays in Nashville, with an ego, many said, to match; rumor around Nashville had it that he played favorites with Davis's records on WSM, but Patsy simply didn't like what she perceived as his obsequious attitude, especially toward the people he considered big stars.

Throughout her ordeal Patsy's attitude was, "They can't keep this ole Virginia gal down." The more pragmatic aspects of the accident didn't escape her attention, either: "I'll get enough out of this to buy a Cadillac, another home, and pay every penny I owe to anyone and have money in the bank, but this sure is a rough way of getting it."

The accident brought out the best in Charlie, who attended to her faithfully during her five-week hospital stay. While "I Fall to Pieces" was making her, once again, an "overnight" sensation all over the country, he brought a radio into the hospital so she could tune in and enjoy hearing her hit song being played on stations across the broadcast band.

She never missed the Opry. One night after the broadcast, as she listened to Ernest Tubb's "Midnight Jamboree," Tubb introduced an awkward girl singer with a Kentucky accent as thick as blackstrap molasses. Though twenty-six-year-old Loretta Lynn had a modest country hit with a song she'd written, "I'm a Honky-Tonk Girl," on the Zero label, she was an unknown to Patsy.

Loretta had only just arrived in Nashville with husband Mooney Lynn, from Custer, Washington. She was a housewife and mother of four while Mooney struggled to support the family with his job at a filling station. She'd been singing for only six months, mostly in juke joints and grange halls around Custer, before she cut her first record. Shortly afterward, Loretta and Mooney traveled to Nashville in their beat-up 1955 Ford, living in their car and stopping at radio stations along the way to give disk jockeys a copy of Loretta's record. In Nashville, Loretta stopped by the publishing and talent offices run by the Wilburn Brothers. After some debate as to whether or not Loretta sounded too much like Kitty Wells, Doyle Wilburn signed her to the Wil-Helm Agency.

Loretta made a demo of Kathryn Fulton's "Fool Number One." Doyle Wilburn took it to Owen Bradley, who because of his work with Brenda Lee, Kitty Wells, Patsy and other "girls" was considered something of a woman's producer. Bradley was enthusiastic about what he heard, but not the way Wilburn hoped he'd be.

"Man, that's a hit song," Bradley told him. "I want it for Brenda Lee."

"Hell, I want this girl here who's singing it to have a record contract," Doyle insisted.

"She's too damn country, Doyle," was Bradley's response.

"If you want that song for Brenda Lee, you give me a contract for Loretta Lynn."

Bradley considered the proposal: "You work with her and get all that Uncle Remus talk out of her, and we'll talk about it, Doyle."

At that point Teddy Wilburn set about doing a Pygmalion number on Loretta, trying to smooth her out much the same way Godfrey had tried to smooth Patsy out. He met with limited success. Vocally, Loretta owed more to Kitty Wells than Patsy, and she was so green it was sometimes embarrassing to watch.

"I remember the first time Loretta went out to sing at the Opry in high heels," said Margie Bowes. "She didn't know how to walk in them. Finally she just kicked them off because she couldn't even stand still in them, let alone cross the stage."

As Patsy lay in her hospital bed listening to the radio, Loretta, wearing a Patsy-inspired western outfit with fringe and boots, took the stage at the Ernest Tubb Record Shop. After singing "I'm a Honky-Tonk Girl," she introduced her next number: "I want to sing this song for Patsy Cline. She's in the hospital. I love her and I just love her singin' and I want to sing one of her songs." While Mooney held *Country Song Roundup,* which had published the lyrics to "I Fall to Pieces," Loretta sang the country version of Patsy's big crossover hit in her little-girl voice tinged with Butcher Holler, Kentucky.

Patsy was deeply touched by Loretta's thoughtfulness and her heartfelt performance. She sent Charlie out to fetch her. Charlie left immediately, went backstage at the Ernest Tubb Record Shop and found the skinny little coal miner's daughter, decked out in a cowgirl outfit. By now Loretta was wondering if she'd made a mistake by singing Patsy's current hit, which just wasn't done. She worried that she might have offended Patsy. But Charlie told her Patsy wanted to thank her. The next morning, Loretta came to call.

"I walked in and her leg was in the air, her one arm was up, her face was covered with bandages except for one eye and down from this eye rolled a big tear. And here was Patsy Cline. I looked at her and she looked at me and she said, 'I want to thank you for singin' my song.' I said, 'Patsy, maybe I shoulda not sung your song.' And she said, 'Honey, it's all right with me.' "

Patsy was released from the hospital on July 17. She went home in a wheelchair, which she needed for the first few weeks she was at home. Some surgery had been done on her during the hospital stay to trim the emergency room sewing-up, but she still had a grotesque, racheted and bruised wound dissecting her face. She wasn't allowed to wear any makeup, which made her feel all the more self-conscious about her ghastly appearance. She was scheduled for plastic surgery for three months later.

That week she made her first Opry appearance since her return to the living. She still couldn't sing, but she was wheeled onstage in her wheelchair to a standing ovation. Weeks of speculation as to whether or not she would ever sing again were laid to rest when Patsy promised her fans she'd be back soon to sing them her hit song. She felt surrounded by love. Her voice deep with emotion, she fervently expressed her thanks for the more than two thousand cards and letters she received and the love of her friends standing off in the wings. "The greatest gift I think you folks could have given me was the encouragement you gave me right at the very time when I needed you the most; you came through with the flyingest colors. I just want to say that you'll never know how happy you made this ole country gal."

When she made her first singing return to the Opry, it was on crutches. Some well-meaning jokesters kidded her about her "sympathy sticks," trying to elicit a spark of the wisecracker they knew. Patsy, hypersensitive and hurting more than she let on, didn't appreciate the joke. She still couldn't believe she had a hit record, after all the blood, sweat and tears, and no one truly realized how insecure and tenuous she felt about having "arrived"—for the second time.

Patsy's first dates, working with Leon McAuliff, were scheduled for Tulsa and Enid, Oklahoma, on July 29 and 30. Randy Hughes told bookers that they could not work her for over six days at a stretch. She needed somebody to accompany her on the road, since she would be on the crutches until the end of the year. Charlie volunteered. He took a leave of absence from his job at the Curley Printing Company to travel with her.

A few months after the accident, Patsy was off the road long enough to do something she'd promised herself she'd do while she was in the hospital. Dressed in a white shirtwaist dress, she joined Wally Fowler at the Ryman for his "All Night Gospel Sing." Patsy sang a few of her favorite gospel numbers, including "Just a Closer Walk with Thee" (released posthumously on the Kapp label two years after her death, this version was recorded by Paul Cohen, who once claimed he'd always wanted to do a gospel album with Patsy), backed by the Oak Ridge Quartet, then joined Fowler onstage for a duet on "In the Garden." The two of them spent all evening talking and reminiscing, and Fowler was amazed when Patsy gave him her testimony in the course of the most profound conversation he'd ever had with her.

"That was the most time I ever spent with Patsy Cline. We talked about everything. She told me she was brought up in some churches. She was very well acquainted with Assembly of God churches, Church of the Nazarene and whatever, but she had gotten away. I'm a Baptist myself, and the way we were taught, the way to go to heaven is to accept Jesus Christ. You accept the Lord and publicly acknowledge him. And if you tell one person, give your testimony to somebody, that's a public announcement that you've accepted the Lord. Country music people say, 'I got it together with the Lord,' and that's what she said. When she was in the hospital there, after the accident, her pastor came out and she told me she renewed her faith and everything. I spoke with her about some of her verbiage. She would use foul language. It was never gross, just foul, and she said, 'Verbiage? What's that?' I said, 'The way you handle words.'

"She told me she had a real awakening, an awareness that life is real and death is for certain, so it did concern all of us to get it together with the Lord. She asked me if I had and I said I put mine together when I was fourteen and a half years old. I told her how the preacher came down, he preached, I believed. I accepted Jesus, and I went out and became a choir director and sang hymns to Jesus in B-flat in a little church in Rome, Georgia. And if I could learn to sing, then anybody could, 'cause I couldn't sing. I just had the desire. I told her I learned that anybody can do anything they want to if they try and put enough into it. And we kinda talked along those lines.

"I said, 'What are your goals, Patsy?' She told me, 'Wally, to be the best damndest singer that ever walked on the face of the earth, and go just as far as it'll take me.' And I said, 'Honey, you're already that. You were that the first time that you opened your mouth and I heard you over there in Winchester.'"

Chapter Nineteen

B
Y AUGUST 12, 1961—almost eight months after its release—"I Fall to Pieces" was a solid pop success: number 12 on the *Billboard* pop charts and a number 1 country hit. During her months of recuperation while her record steadily climbed, Patsy was understandably not available for publicity photographs for the follow-up single and the album that were being planned by Decca.

Single 45s were considered the medium of teenagers. LPs were considered an adult medium, if not an urban adult medium. Patsy was so good, went the thinking, that she appealed to *angst*-ridden teenage girls *and* their parents. She was country and pop.

As soon as possible she was wanted back in the Quonset Hut. Word went out to all the songwriters from Owen Bradley: "Bring me some more songs for Patsy." In response, all the hot young writers were standing in line outside the producer's door. Recalled Harlan Howard: "She was selling a lot more records than most people in Nashville, except for Brenda Lee and Roy Orbison. The rules were to bring her things where she wasn't married, and no children, songs that were supposedly aimed at her market, things that sixteen-, seventeen-, eighteen-year-old girls could relate to. You got to pick out somebody, and they kind of picked out teenage girls, because a lot of them were at her shows."

Among the songwriters, Willie Nelson came out the winner in the next round. Willie had moved to Nashville around the same time that Patsy had, and under similar financial constraints.

"I knew Willie in Texas," said Patsy's pal Billy ("The Tall Texan") Walker. "I was working the "Ozark Jubilee" in '59 and he'd come up there from Fort Worth to try to get something going over there. I was trying to help him, but he wouldn't stay around long enough and went back to Fort Worth. Then I went back to Fort Worth, looking for him. He wrote a song that I cut that year called 'The Storm Within My Heart,' which wound up a country hit. I made a deal to come to the 'Grand Ole Opry' starting the first day of 1960. I come here, we was doing live radio back then, and he come in the old hotel where we all hung around 'til airtime. I said, 'What in the world are you doing here?' He said, 'Ain't nobody buying no songs in Texas.' I said, 'Where are you staying?' He said, 'Out there in that '50 model Buick.' An old gray Buick. I said, 'Get your gear and come on out to the house.' He stayed out there with me for about three months. I helped him get his wife and kids up here and try to get some stuff going."

Willie was practically penniless, and offered to sell Walker a bunch of songs at bargain prices, including "Funny How Time Slips Away," "Night Life" and "Crazy." "I wouldn't let him do it 'cause I did that one time in my career and it cost me a lot of money and I was real sorry. I said, 'We'll get you some money from somewhere.' "

Walker tried to pitch some of Willie's material himself but nobody in Nashville knew what to do with his stuff. Willie, like Patsy, was an anomaly. "I enjoyed fooling around with the phrasing, but it made my sound noncommercial for all those Nashville ears who were listening for the same old stuff and misunderstood anything original," Willie said. "If a song had more than three chords in it there was a good chance it wouldn't ever be called country, and there was no way you could make a record that wasn't called country in Nashville at that time. I had problems immediately with my song 'Crazy' because it had four or five chords in it. Not that 'Crazy' is real complicated, it just wasn't your basic three-chord country hillbilly song."

"I took Willie around to Starday Records, trying to get him a writing contract," Walker continued. "Starday was a big country label back then, and I took Willie over there and introduced him to Don Pierce [the former 4 Star executive, at that point president of Starday]. I said, 'This kid's a good songwriter.' He said, 'What kind of songs does he write?' We were in the studio and I had the guy turn on the machine and I did the first demo on 'Crazy,' just me and my guitar. Don said, 'Man, that song sounds like a piece of shit.' I said, 'You can't be serious?' He said, 'That ain't really good and country.' "

Willie had connected with Hank Cochran, and for $50 a week had been hired as an in-house writer for Pamper Music. In early 1961, Faron Young sold two million copies of a tune Willie wrote, "Hello Walls." Around the same time, Billy Walker came out with "Funny How Time Slips Away," which hit a respectable number 23 country (but didn't go pop until November 1961, after Chet Atkins gave it the

Nashville Sound treatment on a Jimmy Elledge cover). Suddenly Willie had his first royalty checks. He thought he was, in his own words, "the greatest songwriter on earth." While Willie was out on the road playing bass for Ray Price, Hank Cochran pitched his songs for him. Cochran took "Crazy" to Owen Bradley.

Walker recalled: "Hank called me up and said, 'Well, you've already got one song of Willie's.' He and Patsy were thick and he wanted 'Crazy' for Patsy. He said. 'I'll find you another song,' which he did, and it sold a million records for me, called 'Charlie's Shoes.' I agreed to let my hold on 'Crazy' go because Willie needed the money. I knew that I already had one good song of his and none of us knew that 'Crazy' was going to be that big a standard. But then, we didn't know that 'Funny How Time Slips Away' was going to be, either."

In 1953, while working part-time for a small music publisher, Randy Hughes discovered a song that he subsequently took to the Davis Sisters, Skeeter and Betty Jack (who were not related). They recorded the song "I Forgot More Than You'll Ever Know," and it became a big hit. But Betty Jack didn't live long enough to enjoy her success. She was killed in a car crash that seriously injured Skeeter, sidelining her career for a number of years. But the tragedy didn't dull people's appreciation of Randy's talent, and some thought he had a knack for putting singers together with hit songs.

Patsy had strong likes and dislikes of songs, but once she had her mind made up, she would aways consult with her manager. Her feeling was that she'd spent almost four years with nothing happening, and ever since Randy came along, things had been happening.

Patsy and Charlie and a few friends gathered at the Hughes's home that night Willie arrived, crew-cut and clean-shaven, to play his demo of "Crazy." One story goes that Patsy did not initially like "Crazy." But Hank Cochran, who first took "Crazy" to her, and Owen Bradley, recalled, "She loved it." If anything, it might have been Willie's singing that was an irritant to her. Charlie had gotten his hands on one of Willie's demos, not necessarily "Crazy," and kept her awake all night long after an Opry performance, playing the recording at top volume over and over, driving her nuts.

"She fell in love with the song—we all did; it was just gorgeous," recalled Kathy Hughes. Willie took it in stride. Ever since "Walkin' After Midnight," which hit when he was a deejay in Vancouver, he had thought Patsy was "the greatest singer in the world." But having the first big crossover female act in Nashville cutting his tune was just part of being "the greatest songwriter on earth." Today her recording of "Crazy" remains his favorite.

* * *

With "Pieces," Patsy cracked the Midwest and parts of the Eastern Seaboard, but she still hadn't swept what New York–based record executives considered the key pop market—New York. They wanted more sophisticated material from the girl singer who reminded at least one Decca executive of chanteuse Helen Morgan. That meant pop songs, even standards. It was Owen Bradley's job to make Patsy all things to all people.

"I was talking to the people from New York, following orders," Bradley related. "They said when you make an album try to make it so it will last at least ten years. Okay, if you do that, you can't just do a few of the pop songs of the moment. Many of them won't last three weeks. So we were trying to get good strong material. We were doing twelve songs. Out of twelve, we would have three or four sort of new songs that we felt would last. Then we put in some that were a little more country, but it was really a general mixture."

"Back then it was customary to go through the Top Ten," recalled Harlan Howard. "Owen Bradley loved to do that. In fact, I remember one day he and Patsy were in the office, and he was reading the Top Ten *Billboard,* and he asked her, 'You like this? You like that?' He assumed, and he was probably right, that if it was a good song, she could cover it just as successfully. After Patsy had the hit on 'I Fall to Pieces,' Hank and I got maybe fifty records by other people on the same song. Jim Reeves, Bobby Vinton—the hottest young pop singers. It was customary then to use hits as album cuts, especially if it was a pretty melody. That's what Patsy got to do after a while—getting other people's hits to give *her* version."

Patsy was hobbling around on crutches during a series of four session dates in August 1961 that gave Bradley enough material for the forthcoming LP. She was hurting. Her ribs were sore and bruised, which made breathing agony, and she had to use a constricting headband around her forehead to get relief from the constant headaches she suffered from her severe head injury. Still, she was just so grateful to God to be back, to be back singing, after having the shit kicked out of her, she would say.

She and Bradley poured over a selection of standards that would comprise album fill: Patsy would eventually come to refer to such pop album compositions as "any-which-way-you-want music." On the first day the pickings could have followed the fashion truism "Stick to the classics." They included the Cole Porter chestnut "True Love," from the 1956 Bing Crosby–Grace Kelly flick, *High Society,* which Elvis Presley had covered during his big foray into pop four years earlier; Patsy proved she could outcroon "the hoss."

Romantic and nostalgic, "San Antonio Rose" and "The Wayward Wind" were two of her favorite songs from her own repertoire. She concluded with a remake of "A Poor Man's Roses (Or a Rich Man's Gold)," which sounded like a pop song back in 1956 even when it was done country; on this version Patsy slowed the tempo while Bradley gave it the full-blown pop treatment with strings. Throughout the session, the Jordanaires' barely audible, spiritual-sounding fills counterpointed Patsy's vocal to make the smoothest of rides, a subtle multiphonic effect that sounded fresh and new at the time. Few realized that such effects would later degenerate into the equivalent of elevator music by the end of the decade.

The A Team included Martin and Harold Bradley, Moore and Harmon, and Pig Robbins on piano. Bradley kept a touch of country in the session with steel player Walter Haynes. Randy Hughes, who had an acoustic guitar strapped on, was along for the ride to make sure Patsy was happy. This time Bradley had something new for a Patsy Cline session.

He'd been using strings as part of Brenda's sound since her 1960 hit, "I'm Sorry"; now that Patsy was a designated country-pop artist, he was given the go-ahead by his bosses to hire string personnel from the Nashville Symphony for Patsy as well. On Brenda's dates he used a mini-orchestra of six to eight or more musicians. But for Patsy's first string outing, he started out a bit more modestly: two violins, viola and cello. Bill McElhiney, an alumnus of Bradley's band, scored all Bradley's string arrangements. Even the hillbilly in Patsy had to be tickled by the fancy fiddles; she thought they were pretty swishy. But when she heard their voices blending together with hers, she asked that her microphone and chair be placed next to the quartet. Though she normally stood while recording, this time Patsy had to be seated. The bruises on her face showed plainly since she couldn't wear makeup. She eased her self-consciousness about her scars by wise-cracking before the session.

Her work was a revelation. She'd obviously listened to all the stylists, yet came up with her own unique model on each of the standards she covered (though she couldn't resist a little Crosby-like humming on "True Love"). Her version of "San Antonio Rose" swings. At the slower tempos on the other songs, her diction sharpens and she takes risks with her phrasing, breaking away from the beat, breathing, sighing. It was a dramatic performance.

Her stamina was unearthly, the more so given her condition. She knocked off four songs in three hours. Bradley didn't have any quotas but he kept the sessions well organized; albums were made in just a few days, not the many months it takes today, and a single session cost

Apple Blossom Parade, 1957.
Collection of Donna Saville

Patsy and Charlie's wedding, 1957.
From right: Patsy's brother John (Sam), sister Sylvia, unknown woman,
Patsy, minister, Charlie, Charlie's brother Bill, and girlfriend Nancy.
Collection of Patsy Lillis Murphy

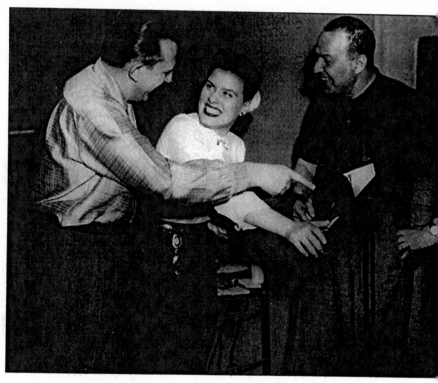

Owen Bradley, Patsy, and her A&R man, Paul Cohen, hamming it up in a post-"Walkin' After Midnight" session at the Quonset Hut, 1957.
Courtesy The Country Music Foundation

1957: Wearing the dress she wore for her winning appearance on Arthur Godfrey's "Talent Scouts," along with the stole Bill gave her and her favorite plastic high heels.
Courtesy The Country Music Foundation

At Carnegie Hall, 1961.
Collection of Betty Lacey

Backstage at Carnegie Hall
with Randy Hughes, 1961.
Collection of Betty Lacey

With Ernest Tubb (directly behind her) and the Texas Troubadours for a
radio broadcast, early 1960s.
Courtesy The Country Music Foundation

Patsy the homemaker.
A canned publicity
still taken in the dining
room of her "dream
house," circa 1962.
*Courtesy The Country
Music Foundation*

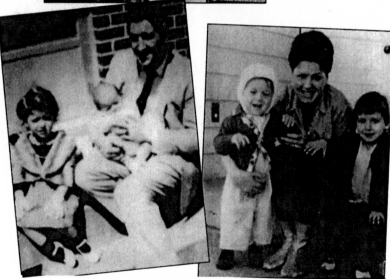

Charlie, Julie, and Randy.
Collection of Betty Lacey

Patsy and her children.
Collection of Betty Lacey

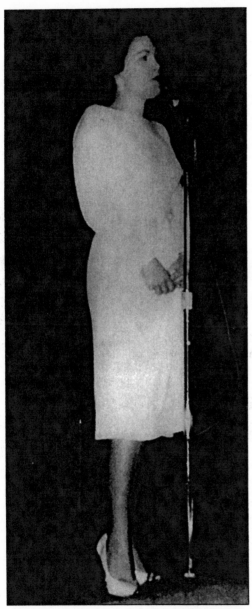

Patsy's final performance. Memorial Building,
Kansas City, Kansas, March 3, 1963.
Courtesy The Country Music Foundation

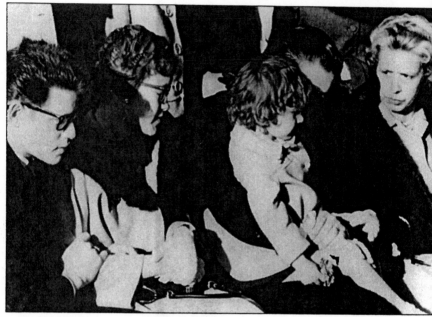

Graveside at Patsy's funeral, Winchester, Virginia. Left to right: Samuel Hensley; Sylvia Hensley; daughter Julia, age 4, seated on Charlie Dick's lap; Hilda Hensley.
AP/Wide World Photos

only about $2000 to produce. "If you've got eighteen, twenty people in the studio, you've got eighteen, twenty problems. You've got to get all that balanced out. That first song takes an hour or longer. Then after that, they sort of get a little easier, because you sort of know by then what you're in for that night. In those days, if I knew, for instance, if we were going to do ballads, I'd plan four ballads or something like that—do them all while we were set up for them."

Patsy rested four days, then returned to the studio for a session that would turn out to be devoted entirely to "Crazy." She had listened carefully to the demo, but Willie's peculiar phrasing and the kind of spoken singing that hillbillies called a "talker" left no clues as to how she would sing it. She was more than an interpreter. She had a genius for creating her own songs out of others' material. With "Crazy" she tried everything—even the talking style suggested in the demo. Finally, Bradley simply suggested, "Why don't you just do it *your* way, Patsy."

Patsy hurt. Literally and figuratively. It might have been the most dangerous moment of her recording career and, from an emotional standpoint, her life.

"With all the talking she did, she was really a close-mouthed person about a lot of details of her life," said Ray Walker. "I think she might not have liked her real self and those songs were a release. All of a sudden she was starting to do songs that reminded her of her. I think she listened to herself from a distance to those records for a while in the beginning. But then she finally caught on to herself. She started finding her life in those songs. And I believe she feared singing it because it sounded negative to her and she couldn't stand that. Like the difference between 'Walkin' After Midnight' and 'I Fall to Pieces.' I just know she thought about the fight she'd had with Charlie and the poverty and not getting any money from the record company and even losing her road money. She started finding some of her own pain in those songs and she started identifying with it."

"The demo was faster than what she wanted to do with it," remembered Gordon Stoker. "She couldn't get the feeling with the tempo that [Willie] did on it." Patsy tried modulating down, caressing the lyrics, but she couldn't sustain some of the notes because her ribs hurt her too badly to hold the breath. Bradley suggested she call it a night and return a couple of weeks later to lay down a single vocal track. He'd achieved a perfect performance from the musicians, and considered "Crazy" "one of the best tracks that I ever had anything to do with." Singers, back then, considered overdubbing a sign of weakness. But being the perfectionist she was, Patsy was probably grateful to Bradley for allowing her another shot at it, though she would certainly miss the excitement of having the hosses present.

Bradley explained: "Nowadays you do it line by line, and everybody forgets the overall. I don't think the public gives a damn. But back then it was a strange way to do it. Plus she felt she could put more energy into the song if she could do it with the musicians. Put an artist like Patsy Cline in a room with fifteen musicians, what's she going to do? She's got an audience and some people who are her peers; she's going to show them what she can do, okay? Put her in a room with an A&R person and an engineer, and it's not a contest. Who's she got to impress? She's got to imagine all that stuff, and it's a little different."

After three days, Patsy had rested sufficiently to return to the Quonset Hut for another marathon: five songs in four hours. This time the material was less demanding than the quirky "Crazy." Bradley had organized the session in favor of the country portion of the album, the title of which at that point was being promoted as *I Fall to Pieces* (but was released, on November 27, 1961, as *Patsy Cline Showcase*). The songs had been culled from 1950s country hit lists.

"Seven Lonely Days" was a cover of Bonnie Lou's 1953 version on King and probably was Patsy's pick. "I Love You So Much It Hurts" is simply a great country song; Patsy's recording was the seventh cover since Floyd Tillman's 1948 original. With lyrics that go to the guts and twist, it could easily have been one of Patsy's desperate phone calls to a friend in the middle of the night: "I love you so much it hurts me/ Darling, that's why I'm so blue/I'm so afraid to go to bed at night/ Afraid of losing you."

"Who Can I Count On?" (a 4 Star copyright) was a cover of the Cochran Brothers' 1956 version on Ekko. (Hank Cochran and Eddie Cochran, who had a "brother" act on the West Coast in the mid-1950s, were not actually related.) Patsy gave it a slightly mocking delivery in a "ha-ha" singing style, and Bradley seemed to be suggesting "the Cline Sisters" by double tracking Patsy's harmony against her lead vocal, à la Patti Page. "Have You Ever Been Lonely?" was a cover of a 1933 band version by Ted Lewis with the Paul Whiteman Orchestra. Harlan Howard–Buck Owens's "Foolin' Around" had been a big hit for Owens at the beginning of the year and was immediately covered by Kay Starr. Howard thought it was Starr's version that convinced Patsy she should put her stamp on it. She did it as a cha-cha, and playfully added a south-of-the-border touch she probably thought was sexy in the finale, in the form of a short, spoken throwaway.

Howard recalled: "We were up in Owen's office listening to the playbacks for the album. She was talking about 'Foolin' Around.' She said, 'Harlan, you sure are a slut. That's a *dirty* song, y'know?' She was laughing about it. She liked sexy jokes and slightly suggestive songs. I said, 'It's not dirty,' And she said, 'It's talking about getting laid!' And I said, 'It's not dirty; it's a fun song. People do cheat sometimes; either they cheat verbally or whatever, but it's just a fun song. Hell, it's already been a hit; people like it. I didn't hear from the Bible Belt or the Baptist ministry or anything.' "

The next day was another country day. Patsy laid down her version of "South of the Border (Down Mexico Way)," recorded by Gene Autry in 1939 and again in 1946, and by Frank Sinatra in 1953. Bradley put the 1956 hit version of "Walkin' After Midnight" to rest with a Nashville Sound treatment on which Patsy broke away from the trotting beat with jazz rhythms combined with a country twang. It remains the better-known version, both for the fact that it was included on her 1967 *Greatest Hits* album and that it was recorded in stereo. Hank Cochran's haunting "You're Stronger Than Me" was a song Patsy championed; Bradley didn't like it, and the two of them had a tiff over it. Ultimately he let her do it (as a shuffle), but cut it from the album. The Mel Tillis–penned "Strange" completed the material covered that day. Throughout the session, Patsy was more confident. Gone were the cowgirl stylings of the 4 Star years. Her diction, always clear but with a Virginia twang, sparkled. The Jordanaires' jazzy fills added to the sophistication.

Patsy came back and finished her work on "Crazy" two weeks after the initial attempt. She had a strong liking of the blues, and "Crazy," with all its space and repetition, was a wonderful vehicle for styling. A great reader of lyrics throws certain things away and pulls back on other lines to give the song power. Patsy was fascinated with phrasing. She didn't hit any bad notes—that part was child's play to her. Under Bradley's guidance, Willie's strange little song was transformed into midnight music. Harlan Howard was in the studio that day to hear how Patsy handled the transformation: "I think she actually sang better on 'Crazy' than she did on 'I Fall to Pieces.' I thought she had more confidence. Having that hit record will do it. I know it was the first time I ever heard anybody overdub their voice on a record. I don't know how I happened to be there, hanging out at the studio, but I do recall Owen and an engineer and Patsy went in there and they spent the afternoon and Patsy kept singing 'Crazy' over and over again. She was playing around with it.

"Owen—he thought she'd nailed it in the first take, and she probably did, but she kept saying, 'I can sing that better, hoss.' The song has so much space. 'I Fall to Pieces' you kind of have to sing on the beat, but 'Crazy'—singers love to sing that song because they can play around with it, style it. I sat in the control room for a couple of hours. Finally, she came in and said, 'I think that's it.' But it was nice of Owen to let her do that, even though he knew she'd already gotten it."

On October 16 Decca released "Crazy" back-to-back with "Who Can I Count On?" This time the rise to the top was swift and certain: it was an instant pop hit. If Patsy or her label feared that "I Fall to Pieces" was a fluke, "Crazy," which cracked the all-important New York market, proved otherwise. She had back-to-back smashes. The smooth, uptown sound of "Crazy" combined with Patsy's heart-torn delivery of the hurting lyric gave new definition to the lover-done-me-wrong genre. Whether she could admit it or not, Patsy had found her sound.

Two weeks later, *Billboard* announced its annual music awards at the Country Music Festival (the former Deejay Convention, in its smoothed-out incarnation). The 1961 version of old hoot 'n' holler was attended by three thousand representatives of the broadcasting and music industry who, as one operations manager put it, rejected "hayshakers, and clodhoppers and twangy, straw-in-the-teeth announcers and replace[d] them with announcers skilled in the King's English." Also wined and dined by the record industry sponsors were a contingent of powerful Southern politicos: Louisiana governor Jimmie Davis, the onetime Decca singing star, Tennessee senator Estes Kefauver, Tennessee governor Buford C. Ellington, former governor Frank Clement, Congressman Ross Bass and Nashville mayor Ben West were all on hand to lend their endorsement of the reborn country music.

The Cuban missile crisis, the building of the Berlin Wall and Kennedy's orders to resume nuclear testing while advising every "prudent family" to have a bomb shelter lent a solemn tone to the bacchanalia. "If we had a lot more singing in the world, we'd have a lot less fighting," said Governor Davis, while Senator Kefauver spoke of "a common denominator of music for the peoples of the world. If we can find this denominator, we have a chance of reaching freedom for everyone."

For the first time since 1952, Kitty Wells, the Queen of Country Music, was knocked off her pedestal. Patsy was voted "Favorite Female Artist" of the nation's country deejays. The rest of Patsy's gang cakewalked away with honors: Loretta Lynn was voted "Most Promising Female Artist"; Harlan Howard took ten awards including "Favorite Songwriter"; Owen Bradley was named "Country and Western Man of the Year" for his work with Patsy, Brenda Lee, Kitty Wells, Roy Drusky, Ernest Tubb and Bill Anderson.

For Patsy, it was the story of the prodigal daughter's welcome back home into the bosom of the family. She hobbled up to receive her award on crutches, her long, hard journey's scars tangible and real for the thousands who watched, many with tears in their eyes. Loretta Lynn recalled the day: "She had this little lace suit on that somebody had made for her—it was the same material as the curtains she had made for my house. It was aqua blue. Isn't it funny how things like that stand out in your mind? She already had two operations on her face and had more to go, 'cause her face was so bad. When it was all over she come back and she cried and hugged me and said, 'Now, little gal, next year you're goin' to get this.' "

On November 27, Decca released the *Patsy Cline Showcase* (including the countrypolitan version of "Walkin' After Midnight"). Country albums were still a relatively new concept, reserved only for the hottest artists, and rarely for girl singers. The cover featured a head shot of Patsy from the "Walkin' After Midnight" period. (The same album was issued posthumously as *Patsy Cline Showcase with the Jordanaires* with a different cover featuring a studio portrait taken sometime in 1962.) The liner notes were pure press agentry, glossing over the four-year blood, sweat and tears period of no airplay and $50 comeback trail gigs: " 'Walkin' After Midnight,' a song first sung by Patsy Cline on the Arthur Godfrey 'Talent Scout' [*sic*] TV program, put the young singer solidly on the musical map. 'Walkin' After Midnight' became an instantaneous and overwhelming record hit, and the girl from the Shenandoah Valley of Virginia proved that it was not luck alone that skyrocketed her to the top by following it up with hit, after hit, after hit—each one more exciting than the one before."

On the same day that *Showcase* was released, "Crazy" peaked at number 9 pop and number 1 country, while "I Fall to Pieces" was still getting heavy airplay. Meanwhile, Patsy, who started out wearing fringe and boots, who talked like a hillbilly and sang like a diva, was about to make her official debut at the sanctum sanctorum of "legitimate" music.

It was at the Country Music Festival that Opry management negotiated the first ever Opry package show to play at Carnegie Hall, on November 29, 1961. Country music was not unprecedented at Carnegie Hall. Ernest Tubb and several others acts had played there in 1947, and other hillbilly acts played in the clubs and theaters around Manhattan throughout the 1950s. But by 1961, everyone was talking about the Nashville Sound, and the composition of the package the Opry put together reflected the new, uptown emphasis.

The program was heavily weighted in favor of country crooners: Patsy, Jim Reeves, Marty Robbins, Faron Young and the Jordanaires.

The traditional acts included bluegrass virtuoso Bill Monroe, who, it was said, had a huge following among jazz aficionados in New York, Grandpa Jones, fiddler Tommy Jackson, Minnie Pearl and the Stoney Mountain Cloggers. Everyone was asked to donate his or her services for the exclusive one-nighter, a benefit for the Musicians' Aid Society, a fund to aid indigent musicians in retirement, mostly classical musicians from the orchestras around town.

Newspaper columnist Dorothy ("What's My Line?") Kilgallen couldn't resist exercising her acerbic brand of wordplay in the service of her avid distaste of hillbilly music. Prior to the event, Kilgallen took a jab at the coming appearance by the "hicks from the sticks" in her column in the New York *Journal-American,* taking her cue from a great *Variety* headline, "STICKS NIX HICK PIX," which a few years earlier proclaimed that country folks, large numbers of whom had migrated to the big cities, were no longer interested in seeing corny flicks of the Ma and Pa Kettle variety. But while the *Variety* headline was mostly just in fun, Kilgallen could be particularly caustic in her public dislike of what she perceived to be the primitive mode of expression of the Southern "po white," with its images of lynchings and gun racks stacked to the hilt with weaponry used to terrorize civil rights marchers and the Northerners who sympathized with them.

Nothing hacked Patsy off more than the kind of snobbery displayed by Kilgallen. The irony of the down-home Opry coming to the rescue of the highfalutin opera was not lost on Patsy, either. A few days before the New York date she fired her .22 right back at Kilgallen from a stage in Winston-Salem, North Carolina, stopping short of employing the "goddamns" and "son-of-a-bitches" that ordinarily came to her so quickly in such situations. Referring to Kilgallen as "the Wicked Witch of the East," she said, "[A]t least we ain't standing on New York street corners with itty-bitty cans in our hands, collecting coins to keep up the opera and symphonies."

WSM chartered a plane, dubbed the "Grand Ole Opry Liner," to convey the troupe to New York in style. Patsy's entourage included Charlie, Randy Hughes and Hilda, whom she wanted by her side as witness to yet another milestone. A WSM publicist drummed up the hoopla, staging a photo op for the wire services with Jack Benny standing in line as if to buy a ticket. The Opry performers were well aware of their position as ambassadors of country music and they donned their Sunday finest. Perhaps this is why, of all the performers, it was Minnie Pearl, the finishing school alumna who could get down with the hillbillies and who didn't pose any threats to the "women out there," who was elected the group's unofficial representative. It was

Cousin Minnie who was asked to come down to City Hall on behalf of the group to be presented with a key to the City of New York, not by Mayor Robert Wagner himself but his representative, who told the press, "We don't want to spread this business around that we're giving away individual keys to these people. If we do, then everybody who comes to New York will want individual keys. Someday we'll look up and there'll be five hundred Elks wanting golden keys."

From the outside, the old, brown building on West 57th Street hardly looked like the cultural palace Patsy had envisaged, not to mention the fact that the 2700-seat Carnegie Hall didn't hold as many folks as the former Pentecostal church that served as home to the Opry. Patsy was more impressed once she walked through the doors. The plush red interior of Carnegie Hall, recently redecorated, painted, polished and upholstered, was the ultimate in culture for the high and mighty: there was a gilded bar, burnished hand railings floating along thickly carpeted stairways and chandeliers. The dressing rooms had served Maria Callas, Leontyne Price, Lily Pons. "I guess they say that's the cream of the crop," Patsy later quipped.

The show was staged as the "Grand Ole Opry" in miniature, with performers making their usual fast-paced entrances and exits. Of all the artists on the program, she was the only one to have two bulleted records to her credit at the time. Still, girl singers were girl singers; Patsy was four acts from the closing act, preceding Marty Robbins, Minnie Pearl and Jim Reeves on the program. "Patsy was fairly new at the Opry, she was well thought of, but not the star," explained T. Tommy Cutrer, the veteran Opry announcer who emceed the event. But the *New York Times* reviewer didn't stay for Robbins and Reeves; he left after Patsy, noting only, "Patsy Cline, a modern popular singer, had a convincing way with 'heart songs,' the country cousin of the torch song."

Patsy wore a fitted dark blue lace shirtwaist, one of a handful out of the same pattern made by Hilda in different colors and fabrics. It was a new style she'd adopted as part of her crossover makeover. A single white orchid adorned the dress above her breast. Before she went onstage she put her crutches down to walk in her stiletto heels. She did a twenty-minute version of her show, including her hits, filler from the album and a few standards like "Lovesick Blues" and "Bill Bailey." "Patsy sang her butt off as only Patsy can do," recalled Cutrer. The virtually sold-out audience was on their feet throughout the night.

Three days later, the Carnegie Hall show was still on Patsy's mind when she appeared before a large, rambunctious Atlanta audience as a guest star on the "Dixie Jubilee" TV show. The crowd had just been warmed up by a hot-picking bluegrass group called the Sun Valley Boys, when Patsy strode onstage, and without further ado, launched into her signature: "Come On In."

Satisfied with the response she got, she relaxed and drawled in warm hillbilly accents about the recent New York gig. She couldn't have done better if Tennessee Ernie Ford had coached her: "We were awfully proud of being that fur up in high cotton." The emphasis betrayed the irony of Patsy's hard-won success—that she was afraid of being perceived as having sold out now that she had "gone pop." Going pop meant uptown, and Carnegie Hall was the epitome of uppity. It was chandeliers, fur coats, limousines and champagne. It was the Winchester Country Club. It was the Apple Blossom queen. Country was down-home and real. It was a good old cowgirl whose name the snooty town forefathers had omitted from the program book. It was a mother who sewed 1500 sequins on her daughter's costume one time until her fingers bled.

Country fans stood in line for hours to have an autograph and a picture of their favorite singer, and a true country singer waited until the very last fan went home satisfied. Patsy wanted to let the folks know that she was one of 'em; she didn't get above her raisin' because she was proud of who she was. And yes, she wore lamé and fur and spike heels, and the newspapers compared her to Marilyn Monroe and Gina Lollabrigida. She was Patsy Cline, and she would always be Patsy Cline, and she showed where she pledged her allegiance: "Ah love ya. This ain't like New York but it's uptown. You talk about a hen outta a coop—I really felt like one up there. I'm tellin' ya. But you know what? We made 'em show their true colors. We brought that country outta them if anybody did. They sittin' up there stompin' their feet and yellin' just like a bunch of hillbillies, just like we do. And I was real surprised. Carnegie Hall is real fabulous but, you know, it ain't as big as the 'Grand Ole Opry.' "

Patsy found her sense of humor through her lifelong crutch—her bravado—and she always found she was able to laugh at herself. She teased and cajoled the "dogies" that she never heard "such a swingin' beat in all her life," and yelled out, "Howdy, ever'body," as big as Kate Smith. "You havin' a good time? Well, let your hair down—we'll see what ya look like. We're havin' a ball."

In between the songs she led the audience through an anecdote, the punchline of which was to underscore the difference between "them" and "us," and to prove that she was still and always would be just Patsy, one of "us."

"Believe you me, it really did my ole heart good because little did I know who was sittin' in the audience, watchin' me, because if I had I wouldn't a been able to go on, I guarantee you. They had Jimmy Dean sittin' in the audience, and Jack Benny—I guess he come to see Tommy Jackson play the fiddle [laughter, beat, beat]. He was there, anyway.

"Above all, the most inspiring thing, the thing that excited me the most, was Princess Monassia, who is the sister of the king of Persia—the princess of Persia—was there in the first box seat on my right. And after the show was over she came to the fellow that was in charge of all the doin's, Dr. Brooks, of the musicians' union there in New York, and she told him, she said—well, I ain't got over it yet—she said, 'The girl that knocked me out—the whole acts were tremendous, but the most tremendous thing as far as I'm concerned on the show was the girl, the Cline girl.'

"Talk about! I was *all* shook up. They couldn't hold me. I said, 'Well, why didn't she tell *me*? We'd a had WSM's photographer there. I'd a took a picture of me and her and hung it on the wall!'"

By the end of 1961, girl singers and girl groups were staking claims on what was previously an all-boys club. Patsy represented the trend in country music. She was likened to "a female Ray Charles" by the British press, which put her in the same category as Aretha Franklin, Dinah Washington, Brenda Lee and Timi Yuro, all big overseas. In Europe, as in America, teenagers were turning the lights down and making out to "Crazy." Patsy was an anomaly: a country girl singer who went pop in spite of herself and never forgot her roots. Her country airplay was heavy throughout her pop years. She played the Opry faithfully for $25 a night even while concertizing at Carnegie Hall and, later, lip-synching on Dick Clark's "American Bandstand." But even after she hit, Nashville was slow to recognize the hipness of Patsy—which may explain the relatively low fees she received during her hit years.

Veteran deejay Hugh Cherry remembered: "We all knew that Patsy was a good singer but none of us ever dreamed she was as good as she was. Country music from the time that I went into it was traditionally a man's business. I think the reason we didn't attach the significance to Patsy we should have is that she was still one of the pioneers. I played a hell of a lot more Buck Owens at that time than Patsy, even though she was better than most of the pop singers."

Patsy was the only girl singer coming out of the country fold to hit the big time except for Brenda Lee, and Brenda had crossed over so thoroughly that, from her 1960 recording of "I'm Sorry" until the early 1970s, her country airplay died off entirely.

After "Pieces" hit in 1961, there was talk of Patsy going on an overseas tour. At that point, Brenda, whose career had eclipsed Patsy's, was the toast of Europe. "We talked about Europe," recalled Brenda. "I told her she needed to go over there, because that was another one of Owen's things: he felt like you should be known internationally, because when you are having hits over here, you could have them over there, and it would open up a whole new market. We recorded in six foreign languages back then and had hits in all those languages. He believed in that. I used to go over there and I played a lot of military bases, but I also played concerts and all kinds of stuff. She would ask me how was it, did people recognize your songs, was it fun to go over there and perform, how different was it from here and what have you. They would have loved her. She had a great personality—such a strong personality. They like that over there. They like honesty. They would have loved her and it's a shame she didn't get the chance to go over and plant some seeds on those grounds."

Patsy was a dervish. There was so much she wanted to do. Everywhere she sang, more and more frequently in the big venues she would point out the humorous irony of her hit "I Fall to Pieces" leading up to the punchline, "I just hope I don't try to live up to this 'Crazy' bit like I did the last one."

She would stand under a single spotlight on the torch songs, then turn around and coax and drive and yelp her sidemen through what she would describe as a "swingin' " version of "Bill Bailey," on which she seemed to stop just short of scatting. She always took a moment out to thank her fans for the concern and support she'd received right after the accident. It was the greatest revelation in her life to know that she was so dearly loved, and there was not a false note in her when she told them, "The greatest gift you could have given me was the encouragement you gave me right at the very time when I needed you the most; you came through with the flyingest colors. You'll never know just how happy you made this ole country gal."

While "Crazy" was in heavy rotation it dawned on her that where there were two hits there could be three, four, more. Now that she was up, she wanted to stay that way—for the sake of her kids: "It's all for them," she would say. She drove herself to make sure she lived up to her own expectations of a true star.

She put the word out in earnest to every writer she knew: bring me hits. Nashville was a small town. Everyone went to everyone else's sessions, and everyone socialized together, too. The atmosphere at Patsy's tiny, knick-knack-filled home in Madison, just thirty minutes from Music Row, was always a hospitable experience for the music folk, especially the writers, remembered Harlan Howard. When Patsy was at home, which was becoming increasingly rare, she luxuriated in the ordinary tasks of housewifery: mending, cleaning, cooking. A "party" was any gathering of two or more after a bottle had been broken out.

"I always knew if I wanted to go over there or call her, she'd have time for me," said Brenda Lee, who thought of Patsy as her big sister. "Once she got established, she had all these beautiful stage clothes, and I always wanted to try them on. They were huge on me, but she'd let me try 'em on anyway, and said things like, 'Now you look good in that; you need to go buy you one like it.' So I'd go over there and tell her whatever problems I was having, just like a big sister, boyfriend problems or whatever. She'd give me advice and she was great. I just loved her."

Said Harlan Howard: "We'd call each other up—'Patsy, I've got a couple of songs for you.' So you'd go over and she might be cooking something, and she'd take a little time out, break out a bottle, pour you a drink, and you'd play the demos and she'd pick through the songs—'I like this one. I don't like this one.' She'd give you her judgment. Nashville is so big now as far as the music business goes. Back then it was such a small town. There might have been, maximum, about a dozen writers really making a good living at it. There might have been a hundred singers. In fact, we didn't have any legitimate nightclubs where you could buy liquor by the drink, so that's why we had all these little secret places, places where you could bring your own bottle. It was actually kind of a backwards country town at that time, so we did a lot of hanging around each other's houses and partying."

On one such evening, Hank Cochran, who used to write his songs in his head in fifteen- or twenty-minute hops around town in his car, then hurry and write down the words, called Patsy to tell her he'd just finished writing a song; he hyped it to her like a used car salesman: "I've got it. It's a smash. It can't miss."

"Cut the B.S., hoss. Come on over and let's hear the goddamned masterpiece," was typical of Patsy's response. Cochran arrived at Hillhurst Avenue where Patsy cracked open a bottle and poured them each a tumblerful, as Cochran sang "She's Got You." Once she'd had a couple of drinks, Patsy would get sentimental. The two of them sat there and cried. "She just loved it," Cochran recalled. "We just sat there, singing it at each other over and over again. Then she called everybody and sang it to them over the phone, and said she was going to cut it."

Owen Bradley agreed it was a good song. On December 17 she went into the studio after dinner on a Sunday evening to cut just the one song. She was backed by the Jordanaires and most of the familiar faces on the A Team. Hank Garland at that point had been out of the studios since September 8, having suffered a severe head injury following a car accident. When he emerged after weeks in a coma, it was painfully clear that "Sugarfoot" Garland, whose explorations into jazz helped define the Nashville Sound, would never play a session date again.

Patsy spent three and a half hours working on "She's Got You" that evening. "Patsy didn't have to build herself up to a mood," said Ray Walker. "As soon as she got in front of a microphone, it was there. Whatever the song was, she was there. She was quite adaptable. There was no mystique about her in that way. She could come right from pitching hay, making soup, frying chicken, come into the studio and do just as good a job, because she adapted to what she was doing. She didn't have to work herself into a mood. She lived the words to the songs she sang, I can tell you that. Almost all the songs told her life story, and I think she fit herself into each one. Everyone of them were her. 'I've got these little things but she's got you'—that was her idea."

At the conclusion of the session, Patsy went home for two weeks of rest. There had been no time to recover fully from the head injury, let alone relax and enjoy her hits. She was in demand and the money was good. By the end of the year she was at a point of exhaustion from the relentless pace she'd set. She complained of being nervous ever since the accident and felt she never had enough time to spend with her family. The severe headaches continued; "Many times I have to leave a crowd and take a fifteen-minute break," she said.

According to Mae Axton, "She was exhausted. She went ahead and started touring even when she was in a cast, and all she did was go. Plus she was looking after everyone in her family. She missed having a home life. She was a very loving person toward her family and was just a homebody at heart."

Chapter Twenty

NINETEEN SIXTY-TWO was the year of the Cuban missile crisis. "The Beverly Hillbillies" was the top-rated TV series. Decca turned down an opportunity to sign the Beatles. And it was Patsy's best year. Two weeks after its release on January 10, "She's Got You" (backed by "Strange") was a smash hit—her third one in a row. Full-page ads cropped up in *Billboard, Cash Box* and the *Music Reporter*. She was touted as Decca's pop sensation. With a full schedule of personal appearances, she was determined to look her best ever. She approached her makeover into a sleek, singer-of-the-world look, with just as much willpower as she tackled everything else in her career.

Patsy never seemed to look the same. She could be a big, healthy farm girl, tired and fat, plain, bodacious, brassy and, toward the end of her life, coolly elegant. Some people say they never noticed her facial disfigurement. Others said when they talked to her, they tried hard not to stare at the scar. Her skin was flawlessly smooth except for parentheses framing her mouth from laughing. Her front tooth was chipped, from opening bobbie pins, she said.

In publicity stills from the "Crazy" period she looks far from her best: the scar is clearly visible under an unflattering helmet hairdo. But by the new year, no doubt with the aid of diet pills, she'd trimmed down to a record slenderness. She had an Audrey Hepburnish hairdo, bouffant on top and smooth at the sides. She had a simple but elegant new wardrobe obviously influenced by First Lady Jackie Kennedy. She started wearing hats, including the chic Jackie pillbox. Stiletto heels, flashy earrings and her trademark ruby red lips were a must. From the overweight, almost matronly appearance of just a year ago she'd been transformed into an orchidlike beauty.

Though she had some minor surgical fix-ups on her face, Patsy dreaded the idea of a hospital stay for the more extensive cosmetic surgery that had been urged. Instead, she resorted to thick applications of base and powder. She got her bangs cut and pulled them down to try to camouflage the scar. She fixed her eyebrows, which had been peeled away in the accident, by drawing in thin circumflexes so fashionable in the sixties, but which never seemed to go with the rest of her face. She used false lashes to play up her great dark flashing eyes and red lipstick on her greatest feature, her full sensuous Hensley lips.

"She was going to get it fixed, she was going to have some plastic surgery to take some of the scars away and to do some skin grafts, but she never did get that done," said June Carter. "She went on painting her face, trying to fix it, and I kept saying, 'Patsy, please go and take care of it now.' She'd say, 'Well, I've dealt with enough pain over this. I don't want to deal with any more pain right now.' So I helped her put her makeup on when we worked the road together, then at the "Grand Ole Opry" when she'd come in there when I was there. They taught me in New York how to take out those scars, and I taught her as best I could how to apply makeup a lot better and it helped a lot. But she was so conscious of it. Her face was so scarred."

"Patsy was not a beautiful woman," said Teddy Wilburn. "Her beauty probably came more from her voice than the actual features of her face. You know, she had the bulbous nose, she had beautiful lips. She had good qualities, but it was like they didn't all go together or something."

"I think she felt real insecure about her looks," observed Margie Bowes. "I don't think Patsy ever thought she was beautiful. But her teeth and her skin were beautiful, and her eyes were real pretty, even though they were so sad. I thought she was pretty, but I don't think Patsy thought she was. Patsy was real insecure in a lot of ways, she really was. And I think that's how she felt when she gave things away to people. Some people can love with all their hearts, but they can't show it unless they give you something. I think for her part of it was the need to be loved."

At what was the zenith of her career, Patsy joined "The Johnny Cash Show" as the group's mainstay vocalist. During the next fourteen months of her association with Cash (whom she might have first met when Cash guested on "Town & Country Jamboree" in 1956), she worked with Cash's "family" on fifteen or twenty different occasions, either one-nighters or ten-day tours with the likes of Don Gibson, George Jones, Carl Perkins, June Carter, Barbara Mandrell, Gordon Terry, Johnny Western and Cash's band, the Tennessee Three.

The Cash family stayed on the road an average of eighteen days out of the month and Patsy appeared with them mostly in the East, Midwest and Southwest. The venues were not huge—auditoriums or gymnasiums seating anywhere from one thousand to four thousand. Cash, heavy into pills, was perceived as a liability by bookers because of his unreliability. "You didn't dare gamble on those huge, huge buildings," offered Marshall Grant, bassist for the Tennessee Three.

Like most country stars, Cash carried a girl singer. The year before Patsy joined him, this was Rose Maddox. Maddox did not endear herself to the Cash entourage. She had "a lot of personal problems that made her pretty hard to live with on the road," recalled singer-songwriter Johnny Western, who worked with Cash from 1958 to 1966. "Her only son ran off and joined the Marines. It drove her absolutely crazy, it blew her mind and she was not herself." When Cash started looking for a new girl singer, Patsy Cline was the obvious first choice, and June Carter, whose relationship with Cash had already started at this point, backed him up. Compared to Maddox, Patsy was "a dream."

"You had to be part of that family to stay on the road as many days a year as we did, and Patsy was just perfect for it," said Western. "Not only did she have the name and the hit records and the stage presence and everything else, she was so much like us—one of the boys—that it was a dream to have her along. It was just a thing that flowed. She was our favorite."

It was likewise a dream for Patsy. Not only was she not given the girl singer treatment, she was regarded as a diva, billed second only to Cash, an association she felt enhanced her own status as a star vocalist. For despite his ravaged condition brought about by pill consumption, Patsy admired Cash for what he had achieved. He had a different image. He had appeared on "The Ed Sullivan Show" and "The Kate Smith Show." Even big stars did not attract the kind of attention Cash got. "People looked at him a little different in those days," said Western. "When it came to adulation, as far as the difference being on the road with him, and then going on the road with a standard Opry package, most of the Opry stars had their followings. But Cash was international. He was just humongous."

Patsy also liked Cash, more so than most of the country stars in Nashville, for the fact that he was considered something of a cowboy in Nashville. Just as she was always fighting to be more than just a girl singer, Cash, too, was considered an outsider because of his one-time affiliation with Memphis-based Sun Records and the fact that he chose to make his home in California instead of Nashville. One time in 1956, when "I Walk the Line" was a huge hit, Cash had a scheduled appointment to see Jim Denny about getting on the Opry. Denny made him wait outside his office for two hours. When the Opry manager finally admitted him, his first words were, "What makes you think you should be on the Opry?"

★   ★   ★

Patsy kicked off her association with "The Johnny Cash Show" beginning in the latter part of January 1962 with a two-week tour of the Midwest and Canada booked by Midwest promoter Hap Peebles, who had booked Patsy many times in the heartland of America. Besides Cash's band, the Tennessee Three (guitarist Luther Perkins, bassist Marshall Grant and drummer W. S. Holland), the other mainstays of the "family" were June Carter, Johnny Western and blue grass fiddler Gordon Terry. George Jones, Carl Perkins and thirteen-year-old Barbara Mandrell rounded out the entourage.

The show had two parts. Johnny Western opened with a twenty-minute singing act of his western-theme material (Western penned "The Ballad of Paladin"), then put his custom-made guitar down and took over as emcee for the rest of the evening. June Carter was doing a combination of comedy and singing her novelty songs and would join Cash onstage later in the program for a few songs and some repartee that centered around their two-and-a-half-year age difference. He would say, "I been listening to you on the 'Grand Ole Opry' since I was a little kid." The audience would get a big charge out of that, and her line would be, "Well, that's true, folks. I'm a little older than him, but by the time I got a hold of him, he had so many miles on him I never could catch up with him anyway."

Carl ("Blue Suede Shoes") Perkins came on about third in the program; Barbara Mandrell followed with her steel guitar and saxophone act; George Jones would close the first half. Patsy, billed second only to Cash himself, usually opened the second half right before Cash came on or one act away, that act most often being Gordon Terry. Every night, Western recalled, he brought her on with homage worthy of her star billing: "Ladies and gentlemen—the one and only—Patsy Cline."

"It was as glorioso an introduction as I could manage. She had arrived and she was at her zenith. She was one of the first country girls who had crossed over and her records were being played on pop stations all over the country. And I would say that onstage, really playing that to the hilt, the fact that she was something other than just another hillbilly girl singer. She was such a class act on that stage, it was very easy to do that, to make people believe that they were going to see the next best thing to the second coming of Christ."

Patsy wasn't the only star vocalist who didn't carry her own band in those days. During her period with Cash, neither Carl Perkins nor Jones nor Gibson had their own bands traveling with them, and so an augmented Johnny Cash band worked behind all the acts. Because the

Tennessee Three were backing everyone else on the show, the whole show was beginning to sound the same. By the time Cash took the stage, the audience had been listening to boom-chikka-boom-chikka all night. Cash gave Gordon Terry some extra money and let Terry put a couple of other pickers on the show—Glen Garrison and Roy Nichols, who came out of Bakersfield and played with Merle Haggard. Said Marshall Grant, "Luther would play acoustic guitar, and instead of doing the big slap thing that I did on all those records of John's, I just played a traditional upright, big doghouse bass. If one of the artists brought along a musician [as Jones sometimes did], then maybe he might come out and help out a little bit."

Patsy did about a half-hour of her A material. She was honed to perfection and she knew it; she was "pure dignity." At that point in her career a typical Cline performance was one without any extraneous jokes or patter. She came out under a solo spotlight. She stood in front of the microphone. She sang, and then disappeared, with the audience sitting there, frozen in their seats, as the house lights came up. She rarely did an encore. She didn't need to. Emotionally, both the performer and the audience were totally engaged. Women and teenage girls brought handkerchiefs to her shows. Patsy's "hillbilly with oomph" act had become an art of minimalism. Gone was the busy, "country music choreographer" of earlier years. She could take over just by her mere presence onstage.

"She had this ability to paralyze an audience," remembered Marshall Grant. "The only other person I seen who was like that was Hank Williams. He could walk out and just lay everybody flat. She would usually close the first set before intermission. Most times people would get up, go to the bathroom, go to the concession stand, whatever. When Patsy would walk off the stage and they would turn the lights on, everybody would stay in their seats. They couldn't believe that she was off the stage. It was, like, she'll be back in a minute. She was that dynamic."

Patsy opened with her good-time music, songs like "San Antonio Rose" and "Who Can I Count On?" Vocally she was equipped for the premicrophone era, so the mike became her only prop. "She used a hand mike there, so she would just walk a little bit from left to right onstage, kind of visit with the crowd type of thing," said Western. "She didn't move around like Dolly. Dolly is very animated onstage. Patsy would not stand in one place but by the same token she would make eye contact with people in the front row and kind of wave to the folks in the balcony. But there were no pop singer–type arm and hand gestures like Eddy Arnold when he's singing 'Make the World Go

Away,' and raising his left arm. Patsy didn't have those kinds of gestures."

She went all the way pop in terms of costume: long gowns or cocktail-length dresses, usually with a chiffon skirt, and spike heels. Glittery earrings were a must. And always, those red lips. Said Western, "She was elegant. Her great forte was the ballads, and a lot of people can't get by with that, but in auditorium shows you can. They'll listen to you sing one ballad after another. She was the best I ever saw, standing under a spotlight, just wringing that emotion out of people, to where you could hear a pin drop out there. While she was doing her show, her very favorite song of mine was 'She's Got You,' which she did in the same spot of the show every night. And I don't care who I was talking to in whatever dressing room, I would just start gravitating toward the stage. I never once was not at the side of the stage watching her sing that song.

"And that was one of these songs where she did this thing, sort of a stage mannerism, the only one she had, where she pressed her hands on her hips and smoothed out her dress. Her fingers were always spread, every time she did it, and they were almost in a little bit of an inward arch, to where her nails were not touching the dress, but she was smoothing the dress down with the palm of her hand and the inside of her fingers. I don't know if it was just to have something to do with her hands or what, but it was very sensuous and very pretty, and yet it looked right for what she was doing. And her fingers were always spread."

Cash's nightly introduction as "the fabulous Johnny Cash," after the album of the same name, certainly belied his condition. Cash was in bad shape. A lot of times the show had to be stretched to give him a break. He couldn't sing for more than an hour, if that. "He'd be lucky if he could sing for forty minutes," said Western. "His voice was very hoarse—you can even hear it on some of the recordings of that time. Many times I would have to go out there and say, 'Folks, Johnny really should not be out here tonight. The doctor would prefer that he was in the hospital, but rather than disappoint you he's going to come out here and give it all he's got.' Kind of lay the groundwork for the fact that you were not going to hear the Johnny Cash that you expected to hear from the best of his records. But he would get real dynamic on the stage and overcome the voice by stage mannerisms and pure animal magnetism, to the point where they'd still be screaming at the end of the night."

Cash then was entirely different than the present-day Cash-as-Patriarch, or Cash the Outlaw. He had a rock and roll act that reached its denouement when, ravaged and rail-thin, he would go into his "Elvis Presley impersonation." Johnny Western said, "My guitar usually stayed onstage all night. Therefore, when Johnny broke his guitar he would usually pick up mine. Marshall Grant can tell some pretty hairy stories about catching it in mid-air when Johnny did his Elvis thing. Throwing my guitar over his back violently like Presley did, the strap would break and the guitar would go sailing. Marshall just reached up from his bass one time—several times, actually—and caught it one-handed as it went by, like a missile going over his head."

On the January tour and on most of the other "Cash Show" tour dates that year, Patsy usually rode with Johnny Western, whom she already knew from the Nashville studio scene, and Gordon Terry. Terry and Western had driven from the West Coast, where they both lived, to Kansas City, the first stop on the tour, in Terry's white Cadillac four-door sedan. Johnny Cash and June Carter had already invited Patsy to ride with them. Her close friendship with June and her admiration for Cash, the artist, notwithstanding, she declined the offer. As bad as her own marital situation was at the time, their lives were even more of a mess. Cash's wife, Vivienne, was using Catholicism as a barrier to giving Cash a divorce, and June's then-husband, who was Rip Nix, was "one of those guys who never made it in the outside world, and was threatening to drag the Carter Family name through every mud hole in the state of Tennessee over the situation with her and Johnny," related Western.

Patsy was a big fan of all the acts, especially George Jones, whose mournful intensity made him one of the greatest pure country singers of all time. Jones had one of his greatest hits, "She Thinks I Still Care," at the time. His life and his art often seemed inextricably linked, and probably as a result, he was drunk most of the time on that tour. Under the influence, Jones could be particularly egregious, both to his fans and his fellow musicians. "George had that ability to go onstage even three-quarters smashed and do a great show, if you could get him out there," recalled Western. But whatever Patsy thought of Jones's personal habits as far as his drinking or not showing up for shows (he balked at one audience during the tour and refused to go on), his one saving grace was that he was sensitive enough when he sobered up to admit that he had done wrong. According to Grant, "George is the type of person, unlike John [Cash], who would apologize the next day. John would hide his head and go in the other direction and never get around to apologizing."

But no amount of apologizing would make Patsy overlook an incident that occurred early in the tour that must have rekindled memories of her own traumatic childhood. Every night of the tour, open invitations were extended after the show to party in Jones's camper, and that invitation included wholesome, thirteen-year-old Barbara Mandrell, who was making her first tour. The camper parties were raunchy affairs characterized by booze and uninhibited vulgarity and Patsy avoided them like the plague, and she evidently felt they were no place for a child like Barbara. When Patsy learned George had invited Barbara to one of these parties, she was livid. "It really made Patsy mad," said Western. Thereafter she appointed herself Barbara's "den mother."

"That little girl just can't stay in hotel after hotel on the road, one-nighters with a single room, with nobody to protect her and nobody to watch out for her," Patsy declared. "She's staying with me."

Barbara's father, Erbie Mandrell, usually traveled with his daughter but for the "Cash Show" he named Gordon Terry, who'd worked many dates with the Mandrell family band, as Barbara's chaperone. But after the camper incident, Patsy resolved not to let her young charge out of her sight. From then on, Mandrell, who worshipped her, called her "Miss Cline," until Patsy finally insisted she be less formal, at which point she started calling her "Miss Patsy."

Recalled Mandrell: "So here I am—and this is Patsy Cline, for heaven's sake—and I'm in her room. The first night it was not a room with two double beds. This is one bed. When I was a kid, I was all over that bed. In the middle of the night I heard her voice and she was kind of tapping me, saying, 'Barbara, Barbara,' trying to wake me up. And when she did she asked me to move over just a little. I'd been lying across the middle of the bed, all over her. When we would drive, she would sing. This didn't just happen once, it happened two or three times. She would start singing in the car. I don't know where that came from, but I don't sing unless I'm working or rehearsing. But when she would sing, it absolutely was as beautiful and as rich and as exquisite as it was recorded or onstage. God gave her such an instrument. It was so beautiful. Just sitting next to you, and here she was, singing. I remember being just stunned and thinking I wish she'd keep on singing forever.

"She was very motherly to me and very professional onstage, and she was also fun for me to be with; she would laugh a lot. I thought she was very strong and in control. Yes, there's never been a prettier female voice, and all that. But the qualities I admired, and I mean this in a complimentary way—she was also just as in charge as any man, you know? She wasn't some pretty little miss with a 'Don't bother me' attitude. And of course, I had her on a pedestal because she was Patsy Cline.

"I have this picture in my head, I don't know where it was, maybe

Des Moines, but the weather was cold and the sidewalks were icy, and we were coming out of a stage door, and she said to me, "Would you hold my arm and don't let me fall," because from the wreck she had bad pain and troubles with her hip, and she said it would be very dangerous if she fell.

"One day she was going to get her hair done and we were going to shop. Well, she got her hair done and she just hated it, I don't know how to say this in an immodest way, but I've always been pretty good with hair, even as a kid. When I was eleven or twelve I cut my mother's long hair into a short do and it was great, and I'd never cut hair in my life. I told her, 'Miss Cline, I could try to comb your hair.' You would think she might say something like, 'Oh, that's nice of you, honey, but it's okay.' But no, she didn't. She said, 'That would be great. Would you try?' So here I am, this little girl, combing her hair. And she loved it, so every day from then on I always combed her hair before the show.

"We were playing big auditoriums, and Johnny Cash was pleased. You talk about King Kong—every seat was sold out. What a show—I mean, Patsy Cline and George Jones and Johnny Cash. I was put on the show right in front of George Jones, and when we come off that first night he was using Johnny Cash's band, which was drums and bass and guitar. And he said, 'Boy, most of my records have steel guitar on them. It would be so great if you would play steel for me.' 'Cause he wanted me to kick them off and do a turnaround and an ending and stuff. I said, 'Sure, just give me the keys, I'd be glad to.' He said, 'You do your part of the show and when you come off they'll introduce me and I'll do one song and then I'll call you back out and ask you to play steel with me.' So I did that, too. From my very first tour as a little girl, my claim to fame was that I played steel guitar for George Jones and I slept with Patsy Cline."

In February, "She's Got You" rode up the charts to number 14, and the flip side, "Strange," got chart action as well. Patsy returned to Nashville just long enough to fit in another round of sessions. Because of the demand for personal appearances, she spent so little time at home she barely had time to unpack her bags before she was back out again. She now preferred to cut during the evenings, so she could spend as much time as possible with her kids. The frequent goodbyes were emotional. On the road she talked a lot about missing her "babies"—and "the old man."

Despite the run of hits, road money still accounted for a chunk of the savings Patsy was accumulating at this time and, with Randy's guidance, she had various investment accounts. And while she was getting the kind of pop airplay that few other Nashville acts, male or female, were getting, she wasn't getting the big money that pop stars commanded: $600 to $750 a day tops with Cash. Patsy had very few $1000 days in her whole career.

Still, $6000 for a ten-day tour made Patsy feel positively prosperous. She showered her bounty on family and helped financially strapped friends like Loretta Lynn with rent, clothes or groceries. She started socking away money to fund the next step in her vision of the perfect life: her dream home. She wanted to give little Julie and Randy the best. "They're all I'm working my butt off for," she often said.

Once the money started coming in, Charlie's leave of absence from his printing job developed into a permanent situation. Now that she spent so much time traveling, Patsy depended on him where the kids were concerned. He still accompanied her at times, "carrying her luggage and so forth," he said, but the benefits of his presence were often outweighed by the hassles. They would argue and bicker, eating away at each other with the usual assortment of loud, foul-mouthed verbal abuse. Patsy was always quite capable of standing up to anyone, male or female, who gave her a hard time, but she was wearying of the constant battling. She expressed a deep-seated disappointment not only in Charlie but in all men. "Most of them are sons-a-bitches," she remarked one night backstage at the Ryman.

"Patsy was tough enough to where Patsy could offend the abuser," said June Carter. "I mean, she was tough. But she was a marshmallow underneath all of it. But she had that thing just built around her soul that made it like iron, so she could carry on. I think she was outgrowing him, which was making it difficult for them to sustain. That was one of the problems. But they still loved each other enough to where they were still together."

Charlie very seldom would travel with Patsy when she was working with Cash. "She was strictly on her own," confirmed Marshall Grant. "Charlie was an alcoholic, and didn't treat Patsy very well, but Patsy was a tough, tough person. She had a vocabulary of four-letter words that put a lot of men down. Even though Charlie gave her a hard way to go, she took nothing off of nobody. I could never understand why the man had to be in the condition he was in every time I seen him, with a wife like Patsy, who could have been a very, very loving human being. But Charlie sort of forced her to be a hard person. If he had treated her with total respect and been a sober man it would have made Patsy a different type of person, even though she come from a pretty rough background. But she took care of him. Without her, I don't know what he would have done. I don't ever remember seeing the guy sober in those days."

Even during their worst days, when Patsy was out on the road, she and Charlie remained in contact every day by telephone. They were compelled to talk, if only to trade insults. Money had long been a sore point between them. Charlie tried to get what he felt was his share and she was forever hiding it from him or telling little white lies about how much she'd made. She was willing to make all the house payments and provide for the kids. She was willing to overlook all the problems because she could not be at home with the kids, and she felt guilty about it. "She wanted those children to have the things that she hadn't had, and she wanted that stability of a home, and she wanted it to be okay," explained June Carter.

But now that she'd finally arrived, Charlie mostly just wanted to party. "Charlie was hail-fellow-well-met," said Johnny Western. "He was a fun guy to be around, but that was Charlie's forte—being a fun guy, and somebody else had to pay the bills. Unfortunately, it was Patsy." She bitingly referred to him as "Mr. Cline." He displayed the one sign of weakness she could not bear. "I could have a lot of respect for Charlie if he just kept his job at the print shop," she told Western on a "Cash Show" tour stop in Albuquerque that summer. "I could have all the respect in the world for him. I realize that he cannot make the money that I make, but that's okay. I'll make the house payments and everything else. If only he would just buy his own damn cigarettes. Now he's quit everything and become Mr. Patsy Cline. I just hate it."

Recalled Faron Young: "Ole Charlie used to give her a bad time; then when she finally started making a little noise and doing something, it was funny to watch the tables turn. She'd start telling him what he could do, and what he had to do. She'd run him on errands and things. I used to play pool with Charlie and he could beat me. So we'd bet $15, $20, and I'd pay him. One night I beat him out of about $25, and he give me a check. Well, the check bounced. So the next time I was out with Patsy I give her the check and say, 'Patsy, here's this check your husband give me. I wonder if it's any good?' And she said, 'That son-of-a-bitch, I'm going to kill him.' She give me my $25 and she got him and said, 'You ever write a check again and don't pay your bills like you're supposed to I'm going to cut your balls off.'"

Compared to Charlie, Patsy thought Randy Hughes was more the type of man she should be married to, though he, too, in fact was an adulterer. She didn't understand business and she felt that having a good manager like Randy had been the main factor in her turnaround in 1961. When she was grateful, she was extravagantly so. A photo of herself inscribed to him illustrated her feelings: "Because of you, I am where I am today."

As the reality of her marriage to Charlie sank in and she realized she'd outgrown him, she backpedaled on her postaccident pledge to reform. Their sporadic affair continued, but whereas she originally felt she was in love with Randy, now it was "friendship and appreciation for what he was doing for her and his appreciation to her for how easy it was to manage her and how good she was, because she was such a great artist," said Mae Axton. For Patsy it was déjà vu; it wasn't the first time she'd expressed her gratitude this way. But Patsy was a patsy.

"You'd have to know Patsy," Axton said. "She was a very emotional sort of person. Randy had been really good to her as her manager. She'd get to appreciating somebody and liking them, and pretty soon if something disturbed her, her emotions went toward him. She would feel kind of guilty, but then she didn't think it was bad if she could make somebody happy. She had sometimes different thoughts than most of us."

"Charlie was on one drunk after another back then, and she was looking for love," said Billy Walker, whom Randy managed as well. "She needed a person that she could have confidence in at that time. She had those two small children and she'd almost gotten killed, and she couldn't rely on Charlie. She just needed someone else to help her, and so I think it just worked into a situation that they both were ashamed of."

Disillusioned by her unfulfilling experiences with romance, Patsy indulged in little road flings. There was an "admirer" on the West Coast who always saw to it that whenever Patsy was appearing in his part of the country there would be a white orchid in her dressing room. There was a club owner in Rapid City, South Dakota. There was a guy who played in Leon McAuliff's band, a good musician, but unattractive, with a pock-marked face. "She wanted to think that she was all right," said Axton. "She was afraid there was something wrong with herself."

"She never loved anybody, really loved anybody, but Charlie. But she was a very emotional person. It wasn't just Randy. There were several she thought she was in love with for a while, then it was over, and she wasn't in love anymore."

Charlie caught on to Patsy's infidelities but she was his "meal ticket," he sometimes declared during their public brawls. Patsy occasionally expressed bitterness about the double standard that made it okay for men but not okay for women, at least not the ones who wanted to keep their "reputation." Said Johnny Western: "I had an idea that had Charlie not broken that bond with her somewhere along the line, she was not basically the kind of person who was going to do that. Patsy would refer to 'Charlie and his girlfriend,' but she wasn't that much of a hypocrite because she had boyfriends, you know?"

Western continued: "We were riding on a very small airplane that Johnny had chartered to get us out of Louisiana for a date one time, and Patsy was riding with us, so in the plane was Johnny and June, Patsy and myself and the pilot. And Patsy was having all these problems with Charlie. And consequently she was having some little flings on the road. There's no other way to put it. June was trying to get Patsy to read the Bible on this little airplane way up in the sky, to get her act straightened up. She said, 'Patsy, honey, take my Bible and read this thing—it'll stop you from that runnin' and jumpin' and playin'.' That's the way June described those little affairs. Patsy's response was, 'June, you don't have to live with Charlie.' "

As with other men Patsy found sympathetic, Western was a good listener; she trusted him with her innermost secrets and longings. She wanted comfort, and during their many days on the road together during the last year of her life, they found solace not in bed but in their friendship. "I have always gotten along exceptionally well with women," Western offered. "I was toward the end of a very unhappy marriage, I needed somebody to talk to, and she was so unhappy with Charlie.

"She leveled with me. It was right on down the line. There were times when it got so intimate. I told her things about my relationship with my ex-wife that I never told anybody in the world, and consequently she told me things about Charlie and his peccadillos, and why she was so unhappy with him, that I felt at that time that she had not told anybody else either. But by the same token, Patsy really liked me and I don't think she wanted me to think badly of her by bringing up lovers that didn't need to be brought up. Because she just wasn't a tramp. She was looking for something out there. She was looking for affection. She certainly wasn't getting it at home. So she was doing these things and obviously it was something she needed at the moment.

"We were in Albuquerque, and she had always wanted to have a swimsuit that looked like a Miss America swimsuit, and she was a big girl, so she was afraid it wasn't going to look good on her. The afternoon of the show, which was in June of '62, she had gone downtown to a big department store in Albuquerque and had found a silver lamé stretch one-piece Miss America–type bathing suit. We were staying at the Travelodge on Sunset Boulevard in Albuquerque, and I was out at the pool, and she came out in that bathing suit. And she brought her camera. She said, 'Gee, I don't know whether this looks good on me or not but I just had to have it.' And honest to God, she looked terrific. She'd fixed up her hair and she had a little suntan oil on and it was a beautiful, sunshiny day in New Mexico. I ended up taking a couple of two, three pictures of her in that suit. One on the chaise lounge with one knee on the thing and one just a stand-up shot.

"We did the show. I think she felt good about that suit. She felt good all night long. After the show we went out and got a bite to eat and we came back. Probably at a quarter after twelve she knocked on my door and said, 'I can't sleep, I need somebody to talk to.' So I threw on my robe. She said, 'I can't close my door. Charlie or somebody may call and if it's an emergency call I gotta be here.' So I said, 'Fine,' and I locked my door and went over there and she was sitting on the edge of the bed and I was sitting in a chair not more than a knee's length away from her, and we started talking about things, you know.

"She said, 'I need somebody real bad. I think it could be you.' I said, 'Well, Patsy, I'm going through a really, really bad thing, as you know. My marriage is dissolving. Probably the last person in the world you need is me.' And she said, 'It's probably a good thing, because I'm right in the middle of my cycle and now is the time when I get pregnant, just as fast as Saturday is to Sunday. It's already happened to me once and I had to do something about it.' I did not ask for details. I gulped real hard about three times and tried to act real mature. She looked me dead in the eye when she said it. It kind of quelled any overpowering feelings that might have been going on at that time. It was an extremely intimate moment. We were in her room; there was nobody else who knew; I definitely needed somebody and she certainly did too, except we had this wonderful, fantastic friendship and it might have gone right down the toilet, you know?"

Chapter Twenty-One

*B*OYS, WE'RE COMING OFF a hit now. Let's let it *all* hang out. We're going to enjoy this session." Patsy was feeling good when she walked into Owen Bradley's studio the evening of February 12. "She's Got You," her first release of the year, was a smash hit, topping out at number 14 pop and number 1 country. She was on top and in demand. She joked and teased the musicians and the ever-present Jordanaires, and asked them about Elvis Presley: "What are y'all doin' with the hoss?"

Recalled Ray Walker: "That's what she called him—'the hoss.' One time we couldn't do a session that Owen had called us for and he used the Kerrs on it, and she said, 'Well, you turned me down for the hoss. The biggest hoss of all.' "

Patsy loved fancy cars and she drove to the session in an almost brand-new, white Cadillac with a sound system so fabulous she took Owen Bradley out to the parking lot to sit in the car while they listened to the sounds of one of her own performances coming out of the speakers.

As was customary on all her sessions, Randy Hughes sat in with the A Team for the first in a series of four sessions that would result in another album, released posthumously on August 6, 1963.

The material Bradley had organized that day was weighted in favor of Patsy's pop audience, with an emphasis on the torch songs her fans had come to expect of her. This time she would be covering established hits.

"You Made Me Love You (I Didn't Want to Do It)" was an old pop standard, the song she'd once sung for Jumbo Rinker on TV. Recorded by Al Jolson (1931) and the Harry James Orchestra (1941), and sung by the Andrews Sisters in the movie *Private Buckaroo* and by Doris Day in *Love Me or Leave Me,* it was Judy Garland's 1938 recording, from the movie *Broadway Melody of 1938,* in which Garland croons at a photo of Clark Gable, that really defined the song. Patsy had no hesitation going up against Garland on a torch song. In fact, she relished it. As Jimmy Dean observed, "She was cocky as hell about her ability. She knew she could sing and she loved to sing. She thoroughly enjoyed listening to herself, too."

"You Belong to Me" had been covered no less than seven times in 1952, including versions by Jo Stafford and Joni James, among Patsy's favorite female vocalists, as well as versions by artists as diverse as Patti Page, Dean Martin, Homer & Jethro, Eileen Barton and the Orioles.

Owen Bradley might have been responsible for bringing "Heartaches" to the session; the big band standard had been recorded by Guy Lombardo, Harry James and Ted Weems, with whom Bradley worked while he was in the service. "Your Cheatin' Heart," the encore number Patsy did on "Talent Scouts" five years earlier, had everyone's stamp on it; Patsy's version was followed later in 1962 by Ray Charles's recording.

The following evening was a two-song night: "That's My Desire" had been recorded in 1947 by Frankie Laine, and "Half as Much," the 1952 smash for Hank Williams on the country side and Rosemary Clooney on the pop side, had two other noteworthy covers: Dinah Washington (whom Patsy's idol, Kay Starr, considered one of her greatest influences) and Ray Charles, a rare R&B artist who also did country.

On the evening of February 15, Bradley added some sweetening beyond what the Jordanaires had been providing, in the form of a string quintet. He was slowly adding to the instrumentation on Patsy's sessions, in retrospect admitting how "chicken" he was about going too far pop and risk losing Patsy's country airplay. With the addition of the strings on Carl Belew's "Lonely Street," Bradley was once again trying to bridge the old separation between pop and country. "Lonely Street," the country classic that Donn Hecht claimed to have doctored, had a long cover history including, besides Belew's own 1957 4 Star cut, versions by Kitty Wells and Andy Williams. But it was most likely Don Gibson's 1960 version that influenced Patsy's decision to record the song.

Patsy was quite fond of Gibson, a gentle but troubled loner who was addicted to pills, and she absolutely loved his tear-stained singing. According to Gibson, "Patsy said that somebody had told her that she sounded like 'a female Don Gibson' and that was the greatest thrill she ever had. Of course, that made me really feel good."

She and Gibson got to know one another on a tour of California and the Northwest in the late fifties. At that point he had a hit on the self-penned "Oh Lonesome Me," and Patsy, who was hitless and depressed, and probably not earning more than $100 a day on the road, was opening for him. "That son-of-a-bitch can write," she would say about him. "We got to know each other pretty well on that trip," Gibson recalled. "She was a good person. She didn't take care of herself."

"She liked Don personally, as a lot of others did," said Jordanaire Gordon Stoker. "Don's a pretty good-looking cat, back in those days especially. And Patsy was always out for a good-looking man."

Patsy appeared on package shows with Gibson several times during 1962, including the "Cash Show," as well as a May 3 concert in Louisville for the Kentucky Derby that featured headliner Jimmy Dean, after Dean hit with "Big Bad John."

Though Patsy had also been dubbed "a female Eddy Arnold," her version of his 1948 smash hit, "Anytime," owed nothing to him. Same with "You Were Only Fooling (While I Was Falling in Love)," a 1948 hit for Kay Starr. She took Hank Williams's 1951 hit "I Can't Help It (If I'm Still in Love with You)" quite convincingly as a slow, bluesy lament. Patsy was no doubt unaware that the authorship of the song, which has long been attributed to Williams, was contested by her Winchester friend Johnny Anderson (who, besides playing piano behind Patsy as a member of the Kountry Krackers, also wrote songs).

"I wrote a couple of songs that made the *Billboard* charts, but nobody would believe it," Anderson related. "One of them I sent to Roy Acuff and Freddie Rose with the words and the recording I'd made. Same tune, same damn words, word-for-word: 'I Can't Help It if I'm Still in Love with You.' Hank Williams. They stole that. And that Elvis Presley done, 'Your Win Again.' Stole that slicker that hell. He sent the stuff back and said, "We can't use it.' And about six months after that, they came out. Didn't have a copyright or nothing, just tusted 'em. Just a dumb ol yokel."

Patsy went back out on the road for a week of personal appearances in Canada as well as her debut on Dick Clark's "American Bandstand" on February 22, on which she lip-synched her teen-pop "She's Got You." An appearance on TV's celebrated afternoon music showcase for American teenagers hosted by Dick Clark had apparently been under consideration the previous year, after "I Fall to Pieces," but was postponed because of the accident. (Clark's show, which debuted locally in Philadelphia in 1952, didn't go network until August 1957—which explains why Patsy wasn't invited to appear after "Walkin' After Midnight," since by then her first hit had fallen off the charts and she had no follow-up.)

On February 28, she was back in the Quonset Hut. This time, the theme was hurtin'.

"You're Stronger Than Me" was Hank Cochran's latest, written for Patsy, who'd apparently let it all hang out for him, more than once: "If you are sincere when you say you don't care/That our love is just a memory/If you can have fun with some other one/Darlin' you're stronger than me."

Harlan Howard claimed he wrote "When I Get Thru with You (You'll Love Me Too)" with Patsy in mind—"definitely": "You think you love Sue but when I get thru with you/You won't ever look at Sue again."

Rockabilly singer-songwriter Carl Perkins had just finished writing "So Wrong" while on the road with the Cash family the previous month when Patsy heard him sing it. She demanded he give it to her, which he was only too happy to do, since Patsy had the pop record sales and Perkins had already dropped off after 1956. "Imagine That," from the pen of Justin Tubb, Ernest's son, was not written specifically for Patsy, but when song plugger Buddy Killen heard it, he immediately thought of her and took it to her, and her reaction was enthusiastic: "Hot damn, that tears me up, hoss," she told him.

The single that resulted from that session made Harlan Howard and Justin Tubb the winners of that round. "When I Get Thru with You," backed by "Imagine That," was released on May 7. Two weeks later the single made its chart debut.

American country music has always found its audience in Canada, and in the early sixties there was a thriving market; Patsy made a number of swings throughout Canada. One memorable tour through the northeastern part of the country in the early spring of 1962 reunited Patsy with her former "Town & Country Jubilee" co-stars, Jimmy Dean and George Hamilton IV. Hamilton, by then, had gotten out of kiddie pop and was "born-again country." Dean had "Big Bad John," a three-million-seller (which featured basically the same A Team configuration as backup that played Patsy's countrypolitan sessions). By 1962, Dean and Patsy had patched up their earlier disagreement, wherein Dean felt Patsy had gotten "too big for her britches." Referring back to the time after "Walkin' After Midnight," when Patsy missed the pilot show for the 1957 version of "The Jimmy Dean Show," he offered: "What ticked me off was the fact that she was a little above coming back and doing the things that she had done before." Whatever—Dean conceded that Patsy was not "petty"; by the time they met in 1962, everything was, he said, "fine and dandy."

The story was often told that Dean and Patsy and Hamilton were sitting in the back seat of the car in a driving snowstorm, passing the bottle back and forth, when Patsy suddenly realized that the "college boy" wasn't drinking with them. After razzing him into joining them, she pronounced, "Now you're talking! Pass ole hoss here the damn bottle."

Dean's recollections of that tour were vivid: At their hotel Patsy spotted a Canadian Mountie in the lobby and took a shine to him and elbowed Dean, who didn't need to take any lessons in bawdiness from Patsy. His description of Patsy's verbiage was toned down: "She said she was ready for a chunk of him. That's all there was to it," he recalled demurely.

Though Patsy was the show headliner in most of the venues she played in 1962, she often traveled "on her own," with none of the phalanx of handlers that today's stars require to keep the fans at bay. Unpretentious and totally accessible, Patsy developed close friendships with several fans, including Ann Armstrong from Guelph, Canada: "We used to have house parties in those days. We used to all bring our records, food, drinks. We would dance and sing and act silly. When we first saw Patsy on Arthur Godfrey, we said, 'Gosh, would she be fun to have at one of our parties!' She seemed like the rest of our gang— funny, yet kind and thoughtful. So the next thing we heard, Patsy Cline was coming to Kitchener, about fifteen miles from here. And our radio station was giving away free tickets, so we decided we'd go. So it was me, my sister, sister-in-law, my neighbor. We all went to the show, and when it was half over I said to my niece, 'Let's go backstage and see if we can see Patsy Cline.' We went backstage, and this girl was standing there all by herself, on crutches, and I said, 'Excuse me, could you tell me where Patsy Cline is?' She said, 'Well, *I'm* Patsy Cline.'

"I had thought the girl on Arthur Godfrey was kind of stout, and this lady wasn't stout at all. So she took us backstage and then gave us pictures and autographed them. And then when it was over I said to Bootsie, 'Let's go back and see if she wants to go for something to eat.' So sure enough, she did. My niece had a pretty old car, so I said, 'This little car we got, maybe you might not like it.' She said, 'I don't care, as long as that little ole thing got four wheels on it, I'll go.' Then she took us to her room, threw the crutches on the bed and lifted up the pillow and said, 'Look what good-time Charlie gave me in case of fire.' It was a little red nightie.

"Restaurants were kind of scarce, the ones open after twelve. So we went to a little roadside place. We all sat there giggling away, laughing, talking. She ordered a steak and a side order of spaghetti—she was really hungry. They had a jukebox there and she said, 'Go over and see if they got Cline on that thing.' And I did, and sure enough, there she was, a record of hers. She thought it was great.

"We just kind of hit it off like real buddies. We talked mostly about our babies. It was always Julie and Randy, her mother and Charlie. You'd think we'd known each other for years. We went to a few of her concerts and once she said, 'The next time Charlie's coming, and I want all your husbands to come.' So we did that. They all seemed to get along great. Charlie was just one of the boys. One time my older children were in school and I was laying down with my little baby to get her to fall asleep. The phone started to ring. I slipped out of bed gently and I answered and it was Patsy. And I thought where the heck is she? She must be in Toronto or someplace nearby. But she was at home, and her and Charlie were wrapping records they were sending out. That was a great thrill. I never thought she'd call me."

Patsy always had a clear sense of her own style, and by 1962 she had broadened her definition of cowgirl couture. While she flat-out stated she was just "an ole country gal," her look was hardly hick. Her closet housed a leopard coat with a pillbox hat to match à la Jackie Kennedy, a silver fox stole, a full, street-length designer coat made in velvet, and any number of high, stiletto heels in colors and fabrics to match her ensembles. There was plenty of lamé. Patsy loved the glittery look. In New York for a photo session (that would produce the photo of her album *Sentimentally Yours,* released August 6, 1962), she got some badly needed lessons in makeup from the House of Max Factor, where she also ordered three wigs. Patsy thought wigs were cool. Two of them were close to her own shade of hair, but one was a totally incongruous, long, blond number. At a concert in Toronto where she was wearing the long tresses, she couldn't resist wisecracking to the audience, "How do you like my rug?"

Patsy's transformation into a glamorous singer of the world was noted by the other girl singers, who couldn't help but feel relieved that bombastic Patsy had finally smoothed out the rough edges. Singer Wanda Jackson, who at one time aspired to be a model, and her raucous, hard-driving rock and roll act notwithstanding, conducted herself as primly as a debutante offstage. She said she saw Patsy at a concert in Atlanta sometime in 1962. It was an all-female package show including, besides Patsy and herself, Martha Carson and possibly Jean Shepard. Patsy, she noted, was the headliner. "She had just come from New York, where she had a makeover, a new hairdo, long dresses, some wigs. I was tickled to see that because I had been working since around 1957 to change the image of the country singer. I got out of the cowboy boots and got the straight skirts with the fringe, long earrings, to try to put a little sex appeal into it. So I was glad to see she was really sharpening up, because we all need some professional help along the way, and she had gotten it and was real excited over it, too.

She told me whoever it was she had been with, and her makeup looked different that day.

"I probably commented on it, because I was happy to see her look the way I knew she could look. She had already lost some weight and was really excited about that, too. She didn't hide anything. See, I always was a lady. Onstage I was different. The way I was brought up, my father traveled with me until I was married, so that my reputation would be good. That was always important to me. I never used vulgar language, I never sat on anyone's lap, I couldn't lay my head on anyone's shoulder when I got tired. My daddy said that's not to be done.

"I think Patsy was a little more herself offstage than I was and wouldn't think anything about it. But my daddy said, don't ever sit in somebody's lap and don't ever have a cigarette in your hand, or a drink, and especially don't ever have your picture taken that way. If Patsy had that kind of background, she might have come across a little smoother. I just figured she was tomboyish, kind of rough around the edges. Rougher than I was."

Patsy's generosity to several girl singers in Nashville, particularly Dottie West and Loretta Lynn, was well known and was one of those things that, underneath all the rough edges, the cussin' and the "tell-it-like-it-is" old girlisms, endeared her to many in the Nashville music community. She was a patsy—a big softie. "She wasn't the kind to be jealous of another female singer," said Margie Bowes. "She had that much self-assurance. She was right there ready to help those girl singers up the ladder, and she did. Patsy could talk a little rough if the situation demanded, but Patsy was very warm-hearted, very big-hearted. If she liked you—and she either liked you or she didn't, and either way, you knew—she didn't know the meaning of the word 'no.' "

Dottie West first met Patsy backstage at the Opry right after "Pieces" hit. Dottie was green, and was an unabashed fan of Patsy's. (In the 1980s, inspired by Patsy, she went the cowgirl route and wore a holster and guns as part of her act.) When Dottie heard about Patsy's accident on the radio, she rushed to the site, then rode to the hospital in the ambulance with her, picking pieces of glass from the shattered windshield out of her hair.

The two singers were close. They shared the same dark emotional terrain inhabited by daughters who grow up without fathers. Dottie's father abandoned her family when she was a young teenager and she grew up, like Patsy, the hard way. After her hit records started bringing in some money, Patsy helped Dottie with rent, clothes, groceries. Sometimes she would take Dottie with her on the road for help with her wardrobe and makeup, dispensing advice like, "Find one person to sing to and sing to just that one," and "Now make each person out there think he or she is that one and cast a spell over them," and "If you can't do it with feeling, don't do it." Dottie later claimed, "Until I studied Patsy onstage, I just sang songs."

Patsy was equally generous to Loretta Lynn. "It was unreal," said Margie Bowes. "She gave her clothes, shoes, bags, guitars, you name it. I think it was her way of saying, 'I love you.' She couldn't just walk up and say, 'I love you,' but if she gave you something it made her feel good. She really gave Loretta a lot."

Patsy's love for Loretta was mutual, as Loretta made clear in her 1977 tribute album, *I Remember Patsy*. She claimed Patsy was "a woman's woman—she was the woman in my life who made me what I am today."

"We didn't live that far from each other. If she had a little problem, she'd send a taxi for me 'cause Doo [Mooney Lynn] took our car to work; he worked at a fillin' station and we did everything we could to stay alive. And I didn't call anybody but Patsy when I needed help. She'd say, 'Don't worry about it, little gal.' She always called me 'little gal.'"

Though Loretta never toured with Patsy, she had ample opportunity to study her mentor at the "Grand Ole Opry." In 1962 Loretta was booked for an unprecedented string of eighteen guest appearances by her manager, Doyle Wilburn, who tended to be very vocal about Loretta's talents, particularly when he was around other girl singers. A well-known story described a meeting of girl singers who were supposedly jealous about Loretta's bookings on the Opry and were getting together to do something about it. Nothing could be more calculated to work Patsy up into a state of righteous indignation.

"She didn't like many of the girl singers on the Opry anyway," claimed Harlan Howard. "I don't think she paid a lot of attention to women, period," Howard said. "I always thought she was a man's woman. She just enjoyed the company of men. She'd rather talk to musicians and songwriters than any of the girls on the Opry. In fact, probably the only run-in I ever saw her involved in was with other girl singers. It's amazing how in so many of the stories they tell about her they all say they were her best friend. I mean, Patsy was busy. I do recall her having a fondness for Loretta Lynn. She kinda liked Jan [Howard] and kinda liked Dottie West. She was out on the road a lot and so were they, so it wasn't like they spent a whole bunch of time together."

When Patsy decided that some of the girl singers had it in for her friend, she mounted a preemptive strike against them.

"I've been told a thousand times it wasn't true, but Patsy said it was," Loretta said. "Naturally I was cryin' and cryin'. She said, 'Don't worry about a thing, little gal. You and me is going to that meeting.' She bought me clothes to wear, an outfit like hers for me, 'cause she always bought whatever she got for herself for me in my favorite color, yellow, and she wore white, with the little boots. And we went. And there were no problems."

"I think she was filled with insecurities," said Margie Bowes. "We all were, because we were all trying to do our thing, but from what I know, it never happened, and I was supposed to have been there. I do know that disk jockeys used to try to bait you a little if you were a girl. They'd say, 'How do you feel about Wanda Jackson?' because she had a big hit, or 'Do you feel bad because you haven't had a number one yet?' I'd say, 'Do you know what? I'm glad to see women get in and get ahead, because all that does is open the door for me and I don't have to work quite as hard at it.' But you never heard them asking the men if they were jealous."

Patsy saw how green Loretta was and would get a big kick out of Loretta's attempts to walk around in high heels. But at the same time, her heart went out to her. She freely dispensed advice and pointers to her "little gal."

"Patsy knew she was a star," Loretta said. "She didn't have to say, 'I'm a star.' She knew it. And she let everyone know it as soon as she walked into a room. She demanded attention. She demanded respect. I would stand and watch her when she walked out on the stage, and she always seemed to say, 'I'm Patsy Cline,' like she was the president of the United States. She let the women know she was also a woman, don't mess with me, I'm not after your man, don't mess with mine. And I'm my own woman. She told me how to dress. She said, 'Now Loretta, when you go out onstage don't wear anything too low-cut. Leave something to the imagination. Not a lot, but some. Don't go out flauntin' things—it makes you look cheap. When you're walkin' onstage, let 'em know you're in charge. And always leave 'em wantin' more—don't ever do an encore.'

"About five minutes or so before she went on, she was just like me. She would say, 'I'm as nervous as a fox in a forest fire. I can't help it.' She didn't really want me to know it, because she was the star. And she didn't have nothing to get nervous about, but I learned, it's the stars who get nervous. The ones that ain't don't know that they can't sing and they don't get nervous.

"When she walked out there you noticed her, 'cause she knew what she was doin'. She'd do a slow song and it would get real quiet. It was like there was a hush over the audience. It would get real quiet and still. And I wondered what she had that did this. She demanded it, and when you demand it, you get it. I stood and watched the first time she went out and sung 'Crazy.' It was number one. She walked out and sung it and got three encores. No drums, nothing behind her. I couldn't understand it. That little girl walked out there and done that, and got three encores, and walks off with that head held real high, just like a walkin' horse—with pride."

Patsy often had to explain the facts of life to the coal miner's daughter from Butcher Holler, Kentucky. Once Patsy introduced her to a couple of adoring fans who turned out to be lesbians. Patsy invited them into her home, then called Loretta and asked her to stop by.

"I was real innocent about a lot of things, and she would tell me things I just didn't understand at the time. One day she called me and said, 'Hey, gal, come on over. I got something for you to see.' I said, 'Okay, but I ain't got no way to get there.' 'Taxi'll be there in a minute.' She got a taxi and when I got there she brought me a little pair of shoes like she always wore, little elastic gold shoes and silver booties. And she says to me, 'I have a friend here.' I says, 'A friend?' She says, 'Yeah, but this is a different kind of friend, and she's at my house today and I just wanted to tell you.' I think she wanted to teach me. See, this was a girl who was in love with her. I said, 'But she's a girl,' not really understandin'. But she told me. She took care of things like that. I said to her, 'Well, what are you goin' to do about it?' She said, 'Oh, Charlie, he's makin' a big deal about it. He's teasin' me and her too, and gettin' a big bang out of it, but she's lovin' every minute of it.' "

During the summer of 1962, Kathy Hughes helped Patsy find her "dream house." She'd fantasized about her perfect house ever since her hit records would allow her to entertain such thoughts, and discussed it with the Hugheses. The house, still under construction, was in a semi-rural area of Madison. It was a modest middle-class home by today's standards: a split-level, red brick house spacious enough for a family of four, not nearly as ostentatious as the gaudy Beverly Hillbilly residences of country music superstars like Webb Pierce, who had a swimming pool in the shape of a guitar. Her reaction, after sizing it up, was as instantaneous as when picking a song: "This is it." Randy Hughes helped work out the financing on the $30,000 price tag.

The house was her symbol of having arrived. She was like a kid with a new toy. She went into a delirium of decorating. This was her reward for all the hard work on the road, her legacy to her children. It is a point of pride among country folk that family are never turned away, and Patsy considered it an insult if friends passing through town spent the night in a motel or hotel. She intended to make her brand-new castle a bastion of hospitality.

She told friends as a child she'd seen a movie in which "some rich dame" sat in a bubble bath, sipping champagne. The bath was marble and the walls were sprinkled with "gold dust." That image influenced her tastes about the ultimate in luxury. She set about re-creating the image from her childhood, including the "gold dust," which was really only glitter in the wallpaper and linoleum. She called the master bathroom her "conversation piece," and it was always the first stop on the home tour when friends dropped in.

The house on Nella Drive reflected Patsy's idiosyncratic flair for combining luxury and kitsch. There was a fake magnolia tree made out of driftwood in the entranceway on which she fastened dozens of little fake songbirds. Patsy would scrub and wax the parquet floor herself, and if anyone scuffed it she would appear with a mop. The living room had a fireplace and a custom-made, pale green, three-piece sofa that was her pride and joy, and custom-made draperies to match. She had curtains made out of the same fabric for Loretta. There were separate bedrooms for the children; Julie's had a canopy bed with fluffy ruffles, the kind of thing that every little girl dreams about. The master bedroom was done in black, red and gold, which was considered very daring and very sexy. A big, walk-in closet held all her show clothes. Patsy dubbed the den her "music room." The walls held her albums and those of her friends, and her odd collections of stuff like salt and pepper shakers and trinkets that were souvenirs of her travels. The den had a mini-kitchen and a bar padded in leatherette, studded with "Patsy and Charlie," from which Charlie would hold forth like a pasha, reveling in his responsibilities as host. Patsy converted the basement into an office, from where she and Charlie handled correspondence to her fans and disk jockeys.

When the decorating was complete, she went from room to room with her camera, snapping pictures, holding the view finder on the diagonal to take in the panorama. Patsy got three of her old cowgirl outfits out of her closet and carefully draped them across the sea green sofa and snapped a picture, which she sent home for everyone to see, along with other pictures of her new home. "Now I won't be happy until I have one just like it for my mother," she would say.

Chapter Twenty-Two

*I*N MANY MINDS, the Hollywood Bowl was the West Coast equivalent of prestigious Carnegie Hall, conjuring images of palm trees and movie stars, the Los Angeles Philharmonic and the Hollywood sign against a movie-perfect backdrop of starlit sky. Directly on the heels of a sold-out Carnegie Hall performance (on which Patsy did not appear), "The Johnny Cash Show" was booked into the Bowl, Southern California's premiere venue.

The concert, on June 15, was billed as the kickoff event in a "Shower of Stars" tour that, after L.A., played dates in Arizona, Texas and New Mexico. Patsy, Don Gibson, Leroy ("Walk On By") Van Dyke, the Tennessee Three, Gordon Terry, Johnny Western and June Carter were booked for the tour, and the Bowl concert was augmented by a number of special guest stars, including the Carter Family, Faron Young, George Riddle, Walter Brennan, Stewart Hamblen and Gene Autry, for a total of forty-two people onstage that night.

Hilda sat in the audience to witness Patsy's triumph; Charlie was there, too, as was Randy Hughes. The manager was not able to get more than $750 for Patsy for the date, but thereafter he parlayed her Bowl experience into promotion aimed at beefing up her asking price to $1000: "the only solo girl vocalist in C&W to appear at Carnegie Hall *and* the Hollywood Bowl."

Cash was having one of his off days that night; his turn onstage was a brief one. Patsy did about twenty-five minutes of her A material. "It looked like a Who's Who out there," recalled Johnny Western, who emceed and stage managed that night. "George Jones disappeared on us and Faron Young got onstage and was supposed to do twelve minutes and he did nineteen, which threw the show way off, because he figured he may never play the Hollywood Bowl again, and with all those producers out there, he was going to give it his best shot and sell Faron Young, whether he ever worked another "Johnny Cash Show"—which he didn't. We gave a big award to Gene Autry; Stuart Hamblen had a broken leg and he hobbled out there and did 'This Ole House.' The place was star-studded."

From the Bowl, the musicians hit the road, stopping first in Stafford, Arizona, where five-year-old Tanya Tucker came backstage to sing for Cash, accompanied on guitar by one of George Jones's guys. Patsy's reunion with Don Gibson was mutually appreciated, though for most of the tour he "didn't know what planet he was on; he just floated," recalled Western.

"I was rooming with Gordon Terry on the tour and one night we were back at the motel and we get a knock on the door at two o'clock in the morning, and it was Don, looking like a tree full of wide-eyed owls. He wanted six Benzedrine tablets so he could go to sleep. They were chemically working in reverse on him. He had taken so many pills in his life that it was just like when Elvis took diet pills he got fat. Don Gibson had taken so many amphetamines that he would take a half dozen of them, which would kill a horse, ordinarily, and fall asleep."

As was customary for Patsy on her "Cash Show" runs, she rode with Gordon Terry and Johnny Western, who vividly recalled several thousand miles on the road with Patsy: "When she would ride with us she wore these jumpsuits, like flight suits, the kind a flier would wear, with a lot of zippers and stuff. She wore no makeup in the car whatsoever. She had her val pack with her show clothes and regular clothes, and three beautiful wigs that she carried on the road, in big wig boxes, that Max Factor had made for her, and she never once asked me or Gordon Terry to carry her luggage or wig boxes or anything else. Once in a while we would do that if we had an extra hand, but never once would she ask us or order anybody around or say, 'Get me a bell-boy,' or play Miss Big Star. Absolutely not.

"She was the greatest road buddy that anybody ever had. And also she was the greatest audience for a dirty joke that there ever was. She knew a million of them. I guess coming from the West Coast, Gordon and I had a bunch of jokes she had never heard out in Nashville, and she would laugh that real raucous laugh of hers. We would just regale each other with these stories. She had a mouth like a truck driver, and she wasn't afraid to use the words—we're talking everything from the big "F" to whichever way you cared to go. It was just jokes; it wasn't mean. But she would laugh until she had tears in her eyes, and you had to realize that Patsy, without the makeup and without the doodads, was not the prettiest girl who ever walked. She had a lot of rough edges and stuff. I think that's what endeared her to us. She had no ego whatsoever.

"She'd change clothes after a show and come out the stage door and be in her flight suit or whatever, and she'd stand out there and sign autographs, even in cold weather. She'd leave the hotel and throw a pair of sunglasses on and stash her stuff and then ride in this jumpsuit, which looked like a big, baggy uniform. And she was one person who could sleep sitting up in a car. She had done so much road traveling she could just throw her head back and fall asleep, which I could never do. I could catch a little cat nap or something but she could actually fall asleep in the car. From Los Angeles to Tucson was 500 miles, and many of these dates were four, five, six hours apart. She had that wonderful ability to be a great road buddy."

Patsy had nicknames for everybody: Cash was "J. R." George Jones was "Jones." Marshall Grant was "Grant." Luther Perkins, with whom she had a warm friendship, having invited him "home" to Winchester several times, had a poker-faced stage demeanor that belied a droll personality offstage, which Patsy adored. She called him "L. M." Don Gibson was always "Gibson."

"I never did look at Patsy as a big star because all of us were such good friends, and that's the way it was for everybody in those days," reflected Marshall Grant. "George Jones would come to my house and stay over the weekend and stay drunk the whole time. But instead of being artists, like they are today, we were all just big buddies. We'd travel together in the same car, or be together right in the same dressing room. If she was in the dressing room, she'd just run everybody out. She'd say, 'Get the goddamned hell out of here. I want to use this dressing room now.' And that's the way it worked. She was a class act who never really sought fame and fortune. Patsy never changed, from the first day I saw her until the day she died. She was always just Patsy.

"But her temper could flare in an instant, and she would tell you in an instant what she thought about the whole situation and use an awful lot of four-letter words. It would be anything that didn't go just exactly right; it didn't really matter. Something that somebody might say. A building that she might not like. A stage that she might not like. An audience that wasn't responding the way she wanted. A long trip. A promoter. I wouldn't say she was unbearable—I don't mean that at all. But she was the type of person who said whatever came across her mind and didn't hesitate for an instant."

After "She's Got You," Patsy scored five more pop-country hits in 1962, and while none of them were quite as successful as her first release of the year, she made respectable showings on the charts, though overall the action was slower. "When I Get Thru with You (You'll Love Me Too)" peaked at number 53 pop, number 10 country, following its release on May 7, and the flip side, "Imagine That," charted lower, at number 90 pop, number 21 country. On July 16 Decca released "So Wrong," which took longer to make its chart debut, on August 25, eventually peaking at number 85 pop, number 14 country. (The flip side, "You're Stronger Than Me," which Bradley recut with strings, didn't chart at all despite the Nashville Sound treatment.) "Heartaches," from her February sessions, was released on October 8 and made a number 73 showing on the pop charts. (There was no country action on Patsy's version of the old standard.) The flip side, "Why Can't He Be You," didn't get any chart action.

Filmdom beckoned Patsy once again in 1962, only it was a far cry from Hollywood. She traveled to De Land, Florida, supposedly to shoot sequences for what turned out to be, according to one of her "co-stars," Dottie West, "one of those stories you used to hear about a lot in country. The producer ran off with the money." The hillbilly hit parade type of musical also supposedly featured Sonny James and Webb Pierce.

One night during the summer of 1962, Dottie was on the receiving end of one of Patsy's desperate phone calls in the middle of the night. She and Charlie had been having a violent argument. Patsy's cousin, Punk Longley, claimed Patsy told him Charlie struck her and broke open the scar on her face. Patsy called the law and had him hauled off. West came over to her house to calm her down. After pouring them both a tumblerful, Patsy got out her two scrapbooks bulging with mementos of her career in the music business. She flipped through the book and reminisced, admired Elvis Presley's picture pasted on the back cover and suddenly turned the books over to her startled friend, with an unsettling explanation for why she was giving them to her: They wouldn't do her any good, she said. "I'll never live to see thirty."

Dottie was dumbfounded and figured Patsy was morose because of the fight with Charlie. When she got home she found a check for $75 tucked in between the pages with a note that explained, "I know you're having it hard and that you're not working. You can use this to pay the rent."

On September 5, Patsy returned to the Quonset Hut to bare her soul. "Your Kinda Love," a Roy Drusky–Alex Zenetis collaboration, told her story: "You say you love me, then you treat me like a stranger/I don't understand your kinda love/You say you need me and that makes it even stranger/No, I don't understand your kind of love."

Hank Cochran had two for Patsy that proved she was his muse. "Why Can't He Be You?" was originally titled "He's Not You," but when, the previous month, Elvis Presley came out with "She's Not You," he changed the title. Cochran's other contribution, the weary "When You Need a Laugh," played a cynical variation on the hurtin' theme: "Everybody says I'm crazy to let you treat me this way/But I can't explain, so what else can I say/At least I'm on your mind when you're laughing, somehow that breaks the fall/So when you need a laugh, give me a call." Wayne Walker's haunting "Leavin' on Your Mind," which, ironically, was to be her last single, rounded out the session.

Dottie West was relieved when Patsy's dire prediction passed unnoticed on September 8. Patsy celebrated her three decades with a big combination birthday party–housewarming party, at which Charlie was a source of embarrassment, getting drunk, mooning the guests and literally being the laughingstock of the party—giving added meaning to "When You Need a Laugh." Back in the Quonset Hut again on the tenth, she cut the up-tempo "Back in Baby's Arms," written by Bob Montgomery, a onetime singing partner of Buddy Holly's "Tra Le La Le La Triangle," a novelty song about a love triangle, written by Marijohn Wilkin, who sang occasional backup with the Jordanaires and penned "Waterloo," 'Long Black Veil" and a number of other hits. Patsy treated the slightly risqué subject tongue-in-cheek; no wonder—the lyrics were déjà vu: "I've got my life in such a mess and I don't know what to do/How can I live in this ole world and be in love with two?" The session closed with Harlan Howard's "That's How a Heartache Begins," which he'd written for a girl, not necessarily Patsy.

Bradley's earlier caution in the use of strings disappeared once it became clear that Patsy's records had found their niche. Like Brenda Lee, Patsy hit the pop market; unlike Brenda, she didn't lose her country audience in the process. Bradley used a six-piece string section as part of a lusher instrumental mix on this session and Patsy's remaining sessions. Bradley had finally ferreted out the "formula." Patsy's sound was set.

Following the September 1962 sessions, Patsy was booked for five straight weeks at Dan's Bar in Rapid City, South Dakota, and at the Frontier Hotel in Cheyenne, Wyoming, for the city's annual "Frontier Days" reenactment of the Wild, Wild West. The gigs were typical of the types of country dates she worked throughout her hit years. Dan's was a roadhouse-type environment, albeit a prosperous one. At that time Rapid City was a Cold War boom town. There was good money floating around and the city was teeming with union workers as a result of the government contracts to build Titan missile sites. A regional hot spot that seated five hundred people and featured such acts as Stonewall Jackson and Hank Locklin, Dan's was a big, military Quonset hut, 200 feet long and 100 feet across, with a huge dance floor frequented by patrons with thick wallets and a taste for country music.

Patsy worked two shows a night. There was a partition between the front bar and table area, where the stage was, and the dance floor was further back. Dan's patrons could either leave after the first show or move up front, to get closer to the bandstand, and pay a second admission. It was common for people to pay twice to hear Patsy, attired in a cocktail dress and high heels, sing to the cowboy crowd.

"Everybody there was a little rough-cut," recollected steel guitar player Sonny Deaton, who played behind her on that run. But Patsy ruled the roadhouse. As Deaton put it, "If she yelled 'crap,' they would all go out and holler, 'How much and what color?' " Patsy knew Deaton from Virginia and insisted he work the gig.

"They had a house band at Dan's that was supposed to back her, but they didn't have a steel guitar. She had known me back in the Virginia days. I used to be on television down in Roanoke every Saturday afternoon. The first night she played at Dan's, I got with her and talked to her. She remembered seeing me on TV and asked if I was still playing steel and I said I was. So she made arrangements there with the union in Rapid City for me to work with her on this gig, since I was in the military at the time and wasn't union. The union was wanting to put one of their guys in there. Actually, she was pretty straightforward about it with them, in not such nice terms. She basically said, 'If he don't play, I don't sing.' "

Patsy's act consisted of the kind of classic country songs and western swing material she had performed during her "Town & Country Jamboree" years, along with the heart songs from the Nashville tunesmiths that had made her the star attraction that she was. She typically opened with "Come On In" or "Jambalaya," getting the crowd to sing and clap along with her. Then she would lay them back with the ballads and some of her favorite Bob Wills material like "San Antonio Rose," "Home in San Antone" and "Faded Love." Patsy made love to the crowd as only Patsy could do.

"She could do any way she wanted to do, and have half of them crying," Deaton said. "It was great working with somebody like that. We never did do any rehearsing. The neat part about it was that everybody who was working in that little band knew her songs and knew the arrangements on them and everything clicked. They'd be giving her applause after a song and she'd just turn and holler the song and what key it was in, and everybody already knew the song and they'd just go right on."

Patsy had apparently played Dan's several times before the September 1962 run. Dan, the club owner, was one of Patsy's secrets, "a semi-rich rancher who couldn't help falling in love with Patsy," Deaton added. He was the only paramour Patsy admitted to, claimed Johnny Western: "We were in Lincoln, Nebraska, on a Hap Peebles tour and a guy from Rapid City, South Dakota, that owned a big club there that booked her two, three times a year came down to see her. It was very obvious from the minute he walked in backstage that they knew each other better than nightclub owner–singer. Then she told me about him. She said, 'I only see him a couple or two, three times a year, but he's really good to me and he really likes me.' She kind of left it like that. But it was very, very obvious, she just flat-out told me she had a fling with him every time she went up there. But it was not the kind of thing that she was leaving home for, and I'm pretty sure this guy was married, on top of that."

The packed houses and good money notwithstanding, Patsy was sad and homesick for much of the run. She kept to herself when she wasn't onstage. She talked a lot about her kids.

The affair with the club owner was "a one-way situation, one of those deals where he would love to be in love with her and she didn't care anything about it. She missed the old man a lot—that's what she called him—'my old man.' I think she wanted to get home. She'd get to having a few drinks and get kind of sad-looking, not to the point of crying, but just sad. She'd drink between acts and get a little high, so that by the second show she'd be ripe, but if you could lead her to the stage and get her to the microphone, she could do anything."

The 1962 annual Country Music Festival was held the weekend of November 9 and 10. The celebrants had a lot to whoop about. There were some seventy-three music publishers listed in the Nashville classified telephone directory, thirty-nine record firms and distributors and twenty-one recording studios. By the end of the year, Nashville-recorded singles were numbers one, two and four on *Billboard*'s Hot 100. From Doris Day to Fats Domino, it seemed that everyone was coming to Music City to cash in on the Nashville Sound. Everywhere, radio stations started making the switch from teen music to country, including the big metropolitan markets like Boston, Seattle, Philadelphia, Chicago and New York. Overall, the number of full-time country stations exploded in the sixties: from a mere 80 in 1961, to 208 in 1965, to 328 in 1967, to over 500 as the decade ended. A 1965 poll of ten major market stations that made the switch revealed that the trend to countrypolitan resulted in spectacular increases in market shares. Country music had more than simply survived the rock and roll juggernaut of the fifties; it had conquered the nation.

"The modern C&W station is, generally speaking, a tight ship," reported *Broadcasting* magazine. "The disk jockeys go by the record charts, there is a minimum of talk and the old 'friends-and-neighbors' approach appears to have gone the way of the Hupmobile, Tucker and Edsel."

One look around the Andrew Jackson Hotel confirmed that country music was big business. There was the usual press of singers and strummers sporting mail-order toupees and $300 hand-tooled cowboy boots. But like the darting fish that accompany whales, cleaning their mouths and grooming their crevices, there was a parallel world of big city operators cruising the hospitality suites and correspondents from the major media like *Time,* the *New York Times* and the *Wall Street Journal.* Within just a few years, Nashville had become Cashville. As Faron Young mused after a few scotches, "You got that dollar, you got America."

Patsy's sound defined the new country music and the "industry" it had spawned. She had her sixth hit running with the October 8 release of "Heartaches," and it didn't even chart country. No matter. Patsy reveled in her status as country's "Favorite Female Artist," as designated by *Billboard.* She strode into the flower-festooned banquet room of the Andrew Jackson Hotel for the big awards ceremony wearing the mantle of stardom with aplomb, fully prepared to acknowledge the tribute that was about to be paid her by the assembly of conventioneers anesthetized by Bloody Marys and screwdrivers that flowed like water at the Friday morning banquet, courtesy of the show's sponsors, Capitol, Columbia, Decca, Dot, RCA Victor and United Artists. Patsy wore gold brocade, gold spiked heels and, as if to flaunt her position in the new country music environment, a tiara.

The trade press had polled the nation's disk jockeys and the verdict was unanimous in giving her the nod as country music's leading lady. For the second year in a row she had dethroned the Queen of Country Music, Kitty Wells. Besides *Billboard's* official acknowledgment, Patsy took away honors for "Most Programmed C&W Female" and "Most Programmed Album of the Year" from *Cash Box;* "Star of the Year" and "Female Vocalist of the Year" for "Crazy" and "She's Got You" from the *Music Reporter;* and "Female Vocalist of the Year" for "Crazy" and "She's Got You" from *Music Vendor.* That night Patsy's gals celebrated along with her: Loretta Lynn came in fourth in the "Favorite Female Artist" balloting and Dottie West earned fifth place in the "Most Promising Female Artist" category.

Patsy's sweep meant more than engraved brass and wood memorabilia for the walls of her den. In the sixties, the booking of big-name talent in shower-of-stars types of packages was a major promotion for radio stations programming modern country Top 40. KBER San Antonio ran a half-dozen shows annually at the municipal auditorium. The average attendance was between 8000 and 10,000. WJJD Chicago, touted as "the largest gate for any unit C&W show ever held in North America," promoted shows in McCormick Place seating an average of 11,000 per show. WQIK Jacksonville, Florida, held two or three country music spectaculars a year in the city's coliseum seating up to 13,000. WBMD Baltimore turned away 3000 people after filling its 13,169-seat Civic Center for one "Country Jubilee" show.

While Patsy collected her awards, behind the scenes her manager was deal making, upping Patsy's ante to $1000 per show on dates not already booked. That weekend, in collaboration with talent agent Hubert Long, Randy negotiated what turned out to be the most lucrative run of her career, a thirty-five-day stint in Las Vegas.

In Patsy's mind, to play Vegas was to play the Monte Carlo of the West. Vegas conjured images of high rollers, twenty-four-hour casinos, the Rat Pack. Vegas was the ultimate gig for a country girl singer in the era of Elvis Presley, who worked on the fabled Las Vegas Strip along with the other big Vegas acts like Sinatra, Johnny Mathis, Liberace, Tom Jones and Ann-Margret. Patsy was compelled to play Vegas. At the same time, she was petrified of having to go up against *those* stellar show biz names: "I'm just an ole country gal," she fretted. "People won't like me there."

In 1962 it was still fairly unusual for a country act to play Vegas, which throughout the fifties had cultivated the big-name pop acts in an effort to turn into a sophisticated gambling center. Except for the annual Helldorado weekend where people grew beards, shot guns in the air and otherwise ran amok in a ritual regression into Vegas's frontier beginnings, country music was unheard of on the Strip. Country was relegated to a few downtown, off-the-beaten-track spots like the Show Boat and the Golden Nugget, which had been featuring hillbilly music as early as the forties, and the Mint Casino, which came along in the fifties. Patsy was booked into the Mint.

The Mint was the poor cousin of the far more glamorous Sahara (both were owned by the Del Webb Company). The Mint's most famous long-running act was the aging stripper Sally Rand, the fan dancer. The downtown casino had a parking lot as big as a football field and a spectacular, curving sign in the front that made you think you were entering someplace utterly fantastic; but the casino was more sign than building. There wasn't even a hotel to justify the sign. There was a twenty-four-hour buffet-style cafeteria and a small lounge that typically featured small revues.

With only ten days' notice before Patsy was to open, on November 23, Tompall Glaser and the Glaser Brothers were hired to do Patsy's backup vocals. It was Tompall's job to put the band together. Patsy let him know she wanted a steel player and a "classically oriented" pianist. On such short notice, there wasn't much of an array of pickers to choose from for such a long run so close to the holidays, and finding a piano player was "impossible." Tompall went to Printer's Alley one night and, as luck would have it, found some guys from Roy Orbison's band who were off because Orbison's wife was about to have a baby. Tompall hired guitarist Joey Lemmon, drummer Don Light and steel player Sonny Geno.

Patsy was jittery about the last-minute arrangements for what for her was such an important engagement. Pills didn't help her nerves. Once again, she'd been crash dieting in order to fit into the long, sleek, sequined, white and black gowns she'd gotten for her run. Patsy had one four-hour rehearsal with the band to run through her repertoire and she was upset about the lack of preparatory time she had. It wasn't enough time to run through the songs, let alone the dance steps she wanted to work into her act à la Ann-Margret.

She hired choreographer Gene Nash, who had given Eddy Arnold all his hand and arm gestures. In spite of everyone's advice to the contrary, she was convinced that she needed to give her act the Vegas treatment. Said Tompall: "She didn't need a lot of rehearsal. She really knew her stuff. It probably made her feel better but she didn't need it. She had the greatest voice I ever stood on the stage with, the greatest I think I ever heard. You can't tell now, with the way microphones are used, but her voice was strong and carried to the back of a room without a microphone, yet she could be gentle and tender with it. She had great control. And it just came out. She could be laughing, and it still had a tone that could make you cry."

Patsy had envisioned a capacious, Vegas-style showroom, with a big, curving stairway just like the movies, on which she would make her grand entrance—to a drumroll, just like Sophie Tucker.

The rehearsal was held at her house the week before she was to depart for Vegas. Patsy ran through the entrance Nash had coached her on, promenading downstairs as Don Light attempted the drumroll—to no avail. Light, who played snare drum on the Opry, couldn't manage a drumroll. "Patsy turned around and run upstairs crying. She was really emotional," recalled Tompall. "Charlie had to go up and get her to come back down and finish rehearsal. But that's what she wanted, that big entrance and a drumroll, so I had to let Don go then. He'd quit another job, so I had to pay him to stay home, and that's when I got Dewey Martin."

The Vegas money would be the best of Patsy's career: $1000 a day, clear of the other musicians, which made it possible for her to pay for her new home—later referring to it as "the house that Vegas bought." But the conditions of the stint were disillusioning at the very least. It was hardly the glamorous venue Patsy had imagined. The stage was so tiny the musicians were practically on top of one another, making a piano impossible. The "dressing rooms" were a joke.

"They wouldn't waste space on a dressing room if they could put a slot machine in there," offered Tompall. "Her only entrance was stumbling up two steps about a foot wide. They didn't have electric pianos then and there wasn't room on the stage out there for a piano. You got the drums up there and Patsy and the three vocalists doing backup, and we were hanging from the ceiling. We really thought we were going to Las Vegas, you know? And it was going to be this beautiful, big, wonderful place to work. And instead it was six forty-five-minute shows a night and a dressing room that was a closet. You couldn't bring in any more clothes than what you might change into that night. It had curtains instead of a door, so it was the dressing room, the curtain, and then the stage. I remember John Stewart, who used to be with the Kingston Trio, and Hoyt Axton would come by to see Patsy's act and jam in the dressing room, and the banjo was louder than any electric instrument we had on stage. It was not glamorous."

Regardless, Patsy's fans showed up, particularly on the weekends. It was an odd mix of people. "Patsy was like Cash—most people in Nashville didn't know how big they were," Tompall noted. "I wouldn't have believed it unless I'd played the show and seen the cross-section of the audience there. Patsy would draw. People would come in and stand in line for autographs from her. She'd have a lot of college students who were listening to pop music stations before rock and roll really took over the airwaves. By the same token the country fans just adopted her and took her in, more than they did Brenda. Brenda had trouble getting a country following, but Patsy just couldn't get rid of them. Maybe it's the way she talked or acted. I don't know why Brenda wasn't accepted. Maybe it's because she went pop first and the country fans just thought she'd abandoned them. That was something about Patsy, though—those country fans loved her. They wouldn't let go of her."

Patsy contracted the notorious Vegas throat, where a singer's larynx gets so dry it wears sores on the vocal chords and actually bleeds. She tried lip-synching along with a Silver Tone record player, as the band faked along. At one point, Willie Nelson showed up with then-wife Shirley, and he filled in for her for a couple of sets. "Who is this Hugh Nelson?" the manager demanded. "He's a terrible singer."

Patsy hated Vegas. She was depressed and homesick. She flat-out stated she would never work there again, even while Randy Hughes, who came and went periodically throughout her run and hovered around her protectively, was negotiating a return engagement at the more prestigious Sahara. Patsy felt that the decisions were out of her hands and it was driving her crazy. She said she felt "like a whore."

During her Christmas show she cried onstage and told the audience that Christmas was a time to be at home. She flew her mother, Charlie and the kids out to be with her. Hilda, expecting razzle-dazzle, dyed her hair blond. Patsy even offered to buy her Canadian friend Ann Armstrong and her husband tickets if they would come out and keep her company. "Las Vegas—so what!" she wrote on the back of a letter to Armstrong.

"I couldn't stand it," recalled Tompall. "Seven days a week. It seemed like you were going to die there forever, never really making a following, just playing to a bunch of gamblers, night after night. On Monday nights, you'd go to three, four o'clock in the morning. Those would be the people who would come in and just plunk down— they'd be so tired from looking at slot machines. I remember one night we were working, playing to one little old guy sitting there who said, 'When are ya goin' to bring on the heifer?' There's something demoralizing about that. But when she came out, he applauded her, and she sang to him. She did not let me continue with the joke, though. It was his joke and his alone. I did try. I think one night I said, 'Is the heifer ready yet?' She could look at you and just, like, cut you down to your knees. You knew she was pissed and you didn't want to pursue that anymore.

"She was terribly emotional. I don't think it was ever anything that anyone else wouldn't get emotional about; she just got more emotional about it. She would cry a lot. Her and Charlie fought a lot. They both had a great command of the language. She could cuss a blue streak, but somehow it didn't seem vulgar coming from her. I felt for her because of the condition she was in. She was trying to be a male singer as a female in a world that had only male singers. Kitty Wells was the only other one, and Loretta hadn't really arrived yet. And I think she over-fought for her rights because she had a lot of protective old boys around her, but it somehow ain't the same when somebody does it for you as when you do it for yourself."

Mae Axton kept an apartment in Vegas and Patsy was a frequent visitor: "She always had something she needed to talk about. She had bought this coat; it was a real pretty coat. At the time it was an awful lot of money. She paid $2500 for it. It wasn't fur; it was kind of like a velvety thing, black, a beautiful long coat. She said, 'Now, if anything happens to me, I want you to have this coat.' She turned to Charlie, who was there, and said, 'Charlie, I want you to remember that.' I said, 'Patsy, I don't even hear that.' Course the coat wouldn't fit me anyway; she was bigger than I was. She had a bunch of wigs and she said, 'And I want you to have my wigs.' She was just in that mood. She drank a little bit; both of them did. A little bit too much. She was a very emotional person. She really loved people; she loved her friends. She was very loyal, but very sentimental. Like the man who ran the Mint—he always gave her a gift, roses or something on stage, and the tears would just flow. And they weren't fake. She was just that way—very emotional."

When Donn Hecht showed up at the Mint one night during the end of the run to catch her act and say hello, their happy reunion ended in a "semi-morbid" state. Hecht met her in the "dressing room." Patsy was nursing the flu. She allowed him to pick her up from behind and crack her back as she crossed her arms in front. Then she started talking about another sore subject: Bill McCall. She said she was getting a lawyer to sue him for back royalties. She felt that people were "taking advantage of her royally."

Once she'd gotten the subject of McCall off her chest, she told him, "We owe each other a hell of a lot, Donn. I've got a little traveling to do and I gotta rest. I'm not feeling well. After I get this traveling done and I get back home, you prepare some songs. I don't give a shit what anyone says—you get the songs; we are going to do an album and we are going to have a number one album." Hecht said that Randy Hughes had vetoed the idea of Patsy doing Hecht's songs, since he wasn't a Nashville writer, and told him at one point, in reference to "Walkin' After Midnight," "That was an accident."

"Randy was pulling the strings and she knew it," Hecht said. The strings were getting her records that were before the public and that was what she was interested in. It was, 'I don't understand business, Donn, but that's the way it is. I spent a few years with nothin' happening and Randy is making some things happen, and that's the way it is.' "

That night in the dressing room, Patsy told Hecht that his song, "Cry Not for Me," a pure pop number she had recorded five years earlier, had special meaning for her: "Cry not for me, my love/When I am far away/There's nothing more to say/Cry not for me." "She kept reflecting on 'When I'm gone, that's the way I'd like to have people think about me,' " Hecht recalled. "In other words, 'Don't cry for me because that's bullshit'—that's what she would say—'bullshit.' "

It was clear that Patsy had a special love of her friend Hecht, another Nashville outsider. Randy, perhaps sensing this, interrupted their reunion. When Patsy suggested they all have dinner together, Randy was quick to smash the idea. Randy's possessiveness seemed to make Patsy angry, but even more surprising to Hecht was Patsy's submissiveness. She pretended to have second thoughts, saying she needed rest more than food.

Hecht accompanied them outside, forced himself to be gracious for Patsy's sake and gave her a hug and him a polite handshake. As they parted, Patsy yelled back at him, "Hoss, don't forget about the LP!"—which elicited an angry glare from Randy, "of the sort you would imagine from a father to a child, meaning, 'I told you not to do this.' "

Once his own anger waned, Hecht realized he felt sorry for Randy, for while the manager was obviously in love with her, it seemed to him she never confided in him enough that he knew what made her tick. "And what made her tick was her vocal communication with her audiences." She could be accommodating, even deferential, to Hughes or to any relationship that could serve to expand her career.

Not that Patsy was a user. "Singing for the folks" was an absolute necessity, as singing provided her with the ultimate gratification that no man could give her, and she indicated that she could be content to be "married to her music."

"I don't feel she ever came to terms with a man for a complete husband-wife relationship," said Hecht. "Possibly she could have if she would have gotten some therapy. But any time she needed to communicate something that was very intimate to her, it had to be done at arm's length."

Chapter Twenty-Three

If you've got leavin' on your mind,
Tell me now, get it over.

*I*T WOULD SEEM a cruel irony that the last single to be released during Patsy's lifetime was the prophetic "Leavin' On Your Mind," on January 7, 1963. Her first record of the year was another hit. "It's getting so that Cline can't follow Cline," she wisecracked.

Later that month, Patsy flew out to the West Coast with Charlie to tape a Cal Worthington production for KCOP, Los Angeles, then to hit the road with June Carter for a series of two-women shows in clubs in California. Johnny Western was at KCOP for the taping as well that day. It was the last time he saw Patsy, and she was hot under the collar.

"Charlie was with her, and he came into KCOP's studios with a sport coat and an open-throat shirt and he was wearing an ascot that day, looking every bit like he stepped out of the Polo Lounge at the Beverly Hills Hotel. He was over there, ordering these lighting guys to set this spotlight here and don't get too harsh there—telling these guys who were thirty-year veterans of the Hollywood scene how to light a television show for a little Nashville girl who came out to sing a couple of songs.

"She grabbed my arm and spun me around and said, 'Will you look at that? Mr. Cline is over there right now telling these Hollywood veterans how to do their job.' She was so angry. She said, 'Well, Mr. Cline'—that was her ultimate put-down of Charlie; she wouldn't say, 'Mr. Dick'; it was 'Mr. Cline,' which is what he had become—'Mr. Cline doesn't even know it but his ass is grass because he's just minutes away from having papers served on him because I am divorcing his ass.' Boom. It was a fit of exasperation. That 'Mr. Cline' thing really stung. I thought, 'Boy, she really is bitter; the shit has hit the fan this time.' I had to bite my lip because Charlie's standing fifteen feet away and he's a friend of mine, and yet I understood exactly where she was coming from, and I did not say a word."

"I had rented a car, and we were playing some little clubs up and down the coast, just the two of us," remembered June Carter. "We were leaving Oxnard, California, and she said to me, 'Please, June, would you let me drive. There's something I've got to tell you.'

"She told me many times she would die young, but this particular time she said, 'I want you to write all this down, because I'm going out soon, and I'm really going out fast and it's going to be tragic. I want you to tell my mother and Charlie, after I'm gone, what I want done. I want you to write it all down so that they'll know I'm not making all this up.'

"It was the only time I never said, 'Shut up, Patsy. I don't want to hear that kind of crap. I've just heard enough of that. I don't even want you to talk like that.' I remember thinking, 'Why am I not telling her to shut up?' At any rate, I wrote it down. I can still see myself, sitting in the dark, trying to write. I even pulled the cigarette lighter out and tried to make more light with that. She told me, 'I want my mother to raise my daughter and I want Charlie to raise the boy.' And then she said, 'I want to make sure that they bring my body home to my house. Just tell Charlie I want him to bring me home, and I want him to raise my son and my mother to raise my daughter.' That is what she told me."

The last sessions were held February 4, 5, 6 and 7. Bradley was preparing another album. Once again, he and Patsy chose songs that had proven popularity. It was a long way from the cowgirl good-time music of earlier years. "This sure is going to be an album of any kind of music you want," she quipped, suggesting she was not altogether happy with the pop direction her recording career was taking.

Day one: first up was "Faded Love," performed on the radio by Bob Wills in the late forties and subsequently recorded by Wills, the Wilburn Brothers, Ray Price, Patti Page, Floyd Cramer, George Jones, Leon McAuliff and Jackie DeShannon. "Someday (You'll Want Me to Want You)" also dated back some twenty years, having been recorded in 1946 by Gene Autry, then by Elton Britt and the Hoosier Hot Shots, Bob Eberly, the Mills Brothers, the Drifters, Eddy Arnold, Justin Tubb, Sam Cooke, Ricky Nelson and the Four Preps. "Love Letters in the Sand" went back to a 1931 recording by Ted Black, and was reprieved in 1952 by Mac Wiseman, but got its big revival when Pat Boone covered it in 1957.

The session started at 7 P.M. This time, Bradley unleashed a ten-piece string retinue, a small orchestra. The Jordanaires were again there to provide the aural cushion. They had just come off a Kitty Wells session earlier that day. "Now, boys, you been around that Kitty Wells—don't be too country now," Patsy joshed. Said Ray Walker, "She just loved Kitty Wells. She was just joking. But she would say things like, 'They're making me sing pop again.'"

"I'm going to sing it all in the same key," she told Bradley before it came time to do "Faded Love," which ordinarily asked the singer to change keys after two verses, since most singers don't have the range to sing it straight through in one key.

Recalled Bradley: "The way it had been written, it had too much range, went too high. So we sat down at the piano and worked out a way for her to do it all in one key; then we worked out that little ending, which she put a lot of heavy breath and emotion into, and it turned out to be part of the song."

Once the session was under way, Patsy's mood shifted and she started crying on every take. Bradley had to evict Charlie from the premises, not wishing to destroy the ambience. Patsy did four takes on "Faded Love" before the last version, on which at the end she paused and gasped for breath before singing, "lo-ove." It sent chills through the room. "That wasn't a breath—that was her weeping. They weren't just songs to her," said Ray Walker.

Day two: more classics. "Blue Moon of Kentucky" had been recorded in 1946 by Bill Monroe, in 1954 by Elvis Presley, who was then followed that year in versions by Bill Monroe again (who speeded up his version à la Elvis), the Stanley Brothers and Cliffie Stone & the Hepcats, and covered again in 1958 by Roberta Sherwood. "Always" was the Irving Berlin chestnut that dated back to the 1920s. Don Gibson had two versions of "Sweet Dreams"—the original in 1956 and a smoother version in 1960. Faron Young covered Gibson's original, MGM version to produce the first hit on it, in 1956. But it was Gibson's recordings that influenced her wanting to cut it.

According to Gordon Stoker, "She liked the song—she absolutely loved the song. Of course, Owen Bradley liked the song too, and that's really the reason it all came about."

It was an emotional date for everyone. Patsy stood close to the string section. "Evidently they really inspired her," recalled Bradley. "When she hit that first word, you could really feel it. She'd hit 'Sweet,' then swelled the thing. She didn't just sing the notes. She put so much feeling into it, and that made everybody else do the same. That's what I think you miss now, when everybody just lays down their track and you're going for technical perfection."

Day three's selections were both pop: "Does Your Heart Beat for Me?" was an oldie associated with bandleader Russ Morgan, a nephew of a Decca executive who'd once said to Bradley, "When are you going to get Patsy Cline to do a song from my nephew?"

"So I said, 'I don't know. We'll find one.' So when we got ready to do an album, we did 'Does Your Heart Beat for Me?' We did it not as a favor, even though we were trying to please our boss, but because at the time we felt that it was something that would be good for us. But they really loved Patsy in New York; they thought she was great."

Patsy finally got to record "Bill Bailey," the song that dated back to the Hensley family songfests. Patsy had always only done it at a rousing, bring-down-the-house tempo. Bradley suggested she try telling a different story by driving it in low gear; Patsy compromised. She did the first half as a mournful, guilt-ridden plea for forgiveness and the second half at her usual breakneck, scatting pace.

Day four was country music day, of the Nashville Sound variety. Harlan Howard had two in the offing, including one he'd demoed himself, "She Called Me Baby," a guy's song, reworked as "He Called Me Baby" for Patsy.

"She said, 'By God, Harlan, that *is* a dirty song.' I said, 'It's not dirty. It's a little sexy. If you think it's dirty, it's because you have a dirty mind.' We used to have these kinds of conversations, and she would laugh."

"You Took Him off My Hands" was another hot property for Howard—practically the same time Patsy was cutting it, Ray Price was off in another studio laying down his version (on which he later scored a number 11 country hit). "Crazy Arms" was a big hit for Price in 1956, the year Patsy first started singing it in her act. It was later covered by the Andrews Sisters, Webb Pierce and Damita Jo, before Patsy put her stamp on it. The final song of the session had a foreboding ring to it: "I'll Sail My Ship Alone," recorded by Moon Mullican in 1950, was aimed at Patsy's hard-core country fans.

Despite the "any which way you want" direction the sessions took, Patsy was thrilled with the results. The album, titled *The Patsy Cline Story*, was released June 17, 1963. Noted Harlan Howard: "It was probably the first really classy, expensive album cover. It had that gold, hazy, kind of mystical quality." There was a small party in Bradley's office at the completion of the final day of recording. After listening to the playbacks, Patsy went into Harry Silverstein's office next to Bradley's and came back with a 45 of "A Church, a Courtroom and Then Goodbye," obviously struck by the contrast between that and her latest efforts. "Well, here it is, folks, the first and the last," she said. Jan Howard, who was there, gasped at the implication. "Don't say that," she replied. "Oh, don't get upset. I just meant this is the first one and this is the most recent. Listen to the difference."

★   ★   ★

Two days after the final session, Patsy appeared at the Opry. She stopped Faron Young backstage and said, " 'Sheriff, why don't you come over to the house. I got some records I just recorded. I want you to hear them.'

"I said, 'What did you cut?' She said, 'I ain't tellin' you what I recorded until you come and see me. I ain't tellin' you nothin'.' I never did get over there. It wasn't long after that that she got killed. After that they came out with 'Sweet Dreams.' That was the song she'd done. I had a big number one hit on it in 1956. Even today when I go and sing it somewhere the younger kids in the crowd will come up to me and say, 'Boy, Mr. Young, you sure did a hell of a job on that Patsy Cline song.' "

At her last appearance on the Opry, Patsy, backed by the Jordanaires, sang "Bill Bailey" at the swinging tempo she preferred. After the show she told Ray Walker, "Hoss, you think I've been singing—just wait. I got some hellacious songs coming up." They purportedly included material by Nashville tunesmiths Felice and Boudleaux Bryant. Bradley claimed they were considering an album of Broadway songs, including "Can't Help Lovin' Dat Man of Mine," from *Show Boat*.

"We had just sung with her and she started to leave," Walker recalled. "She had a full-length black coat that someone had stolen from her. It took the insurance company a long time to replace the thing because it wasn't cheap. It had the beautiful, kind of bouffant, laid-back collar. When I say full-length, I mean full-length. It wasn't to the knees. It was a beautiful coat. So that night she was tickled to death. She said, 'Well, boys, I finally got my coat back.' We'd been visiting there and she was getting ready to leave. She hugged us and kissed us all. We knew she was going to be back in three or four weeks.

"Well, I, for some reason, followed her to the door as she was leaving. She put on that coat and I put it up on her shoulders for her and she headed toward the door. I said to her, 'Patsy, honey, you be careful. We love you. We love you a lot.' She had just gotten settled into that coat and she flipped that collar up and kind of looked over her shoulder and turned those flashing eyes at me and just held that collar and she said, 'Honey, I've had two bad ones. The third one will be a charm or it will kill me.' And she walked down those steps. And that's the last time we saw her."

Chapter Twenty-Four

*O*NCE PATSY started having hit records, Randy Hughes, for the first time in his life, started making big money. "Randy become a big shot then. In fact, you'd be lucky if he'd even talk to you then," said Faron Young, who remembered not so many years earlier when Randy was a mere sideman. "We were really good friends; we'd travel, bought some oil wells together, did different things. Once he got to managing her and made money, he bought a new Cadillac and a new home and all that shit—goddamn, he thought he was Colonel Tom Parker. The funny thing was how he changed. He became a big shot. Like, 'What the hell—you used to think you were the star. Now I'm the big shot.' That money changed him. He was going to break up with his old lady—I know that's what was fixin' to happen."

Randy always did want to fly. At one point he became fascinated with an experimental aircraft that was supposed to be a cross between an airplane and a helicopter. A number of country entertainers were finding that commercial plane schedules were unable to meet their personal appearance needs and were getting into flying—Faron Young and Roy Drusky, friends of Randy's, both piloted their own craft. In the summer of 1962, Randy took delivery on a yellow-winged, twin-engine Piper Comanche bearing the I.D. number 7000P, which he considered auspicious, seven being his lucky number. A few others thought it was a tin lizzie, or worse. Randy put in his flying time and got a license to fly VCR—visual flight rule, meaning he was not instrument rated. He used the plane mostly for scooter-putting around locally. His longest trip was a flight on which he took his wife and father-in-law to Omaha and back when Cowboy Copas was inducted into the Cowboy Hall of Fame. He'd never had a problem. He was confident. Besides, everyone said Randy was lucky.

But Faron Young had his doubts about Randy's piloting skills: "Randy bought that plane after I had an airplane. Randy was not a good pilot to start with. I let him fly in my plane and take off and land. I was teaching him some but I told him he had to take some lessons. And I always told him if you look ahead and see a bad storm, turn around and go back the way you came. But he was hardheaded."

After Randy got the plane, he would often shuttle Patsy around to dates himself, probably on at least a hundred different occasions. She trusted him. He was so dependable. "Patsy wasn't afraid of flying," said Young. "When we got on a little plane and it was jumping around, she'd laugh."

"Two weeks before that accident I was at her house, talking to her manager, Randy," said song plugger Al Gallico. "I said, 'Why don't you get rid of that plane. That's not even a plane. That's a nothing plane.' These little planes—I hate little planes. He said, 'Nah, I don't take chances; it's a good plane.' "

Patsy was booked solid throughout the latter half of February and into March. Her last dates during this period included Lima and Toledo, Ohio, on February 22 and 23, and New Orleans and Birmingham on March 2. After Birmingham, she was looking forward to two weeks off. Her next date wasn't until March 16, at the Baltimore Civic Center. Meanwhile, she had a lot of plans. She called her cousin Punk Longley, a CPA in Elkton, and told him once she got some rest, her life would be taking a new turn. Her friends claimed it was over with Charlie. She had outgrown him. Patsy told her cousin she'd even consulted with a lawyer.

"She was going to divorce him. See, when she was in that wreck, she had a scar that went from temple to temple. When she stayed with Ruth, Ruth said it would take her two, two and a half hours to put all the makeup on. She'd put on a layer, let it dry, put on another layer. Get it worked down so that the scar wouldn't show up so bad. She was on her way to Johns Hopkins Hospital to have plastic surgery on it when she got killed. She said that he hit her and broke the scar open. She brought charges against him for it. And that's what the judge got bent out of shape about. He told him, 'You come before me again for laying your hands on her, you're going to the penitentiary, young man.' That's the reason why when she got killed the only thing he really got was the Cadillac."

Patsy told Punk that on her trip home, she wanted him to prepare her taxes. "It's going to take you and a bunch of Philadelphia lawyers to sort this mess out," she joked. Even in the matter of costumes she was planning some changes—of a sort: "Nobody has been asking me to wear cowgirl clothes," she answered when queried by an interviewer about what happened to her old look. But after more people began asking her the same question, she claimed she ordered a new, western-style "layout from Hollywood."

Jack Wesley Call—"Cactus Jack"—was one of country's well-known Midwestern voices. Call had deejayed for KCKN-AM (now KFKF, one of very few stations in the country with an all-country format), before becoming program director for KANS-AM, an independent station that Call was instrumental in turning into an all-country format. After that, Call went on to KCMK-FM in January 1963. He had been on his new job only six weeks when he met his death in a car accident on his way to work during the morning drive-time. Disk jockeys were notoriously low-paid. Call was one of the luckier ones: he got something like $200 a week. But he didn't have insurance, and his widow and two young sons were left with a lot of hospital bills and very little else.

Country people are famous for coming to the aid of those in need. Guy Smith, a country deejay colleague of Call's, decided what was needed was a benefit concert with as many big names as he could get. Smith secured Memorial Building in Kansas City, and the next step was to contact Harry "Hap" Peebles, the biggest booker in the Midwest.

For over thirty years Peebles had booked everything from basketball to Broadway, and everyone from Elvis to the Beach Boys, from his Harry Peebles Agency office in Wichita (later, Kansas City). He was known to occasionally help down-on-their-luck artists by booking them on tours. But Peebles told Smith he would "get absolutely nowhere with the show because those people are not going to come anywhere and work for nothing." Smith proved him wrong, however. He called Billy Walker, who talked to the Opry acts, while Smith himself got George Jones and George Riddle to agree to the date, Sunday, March 3. Later, when Peebles saw what a big show it was going to be, he decided to jump on the bandwagon by volunteering his staff to handle the tickets and serving as emcee. Smith was happy to get any help he could from the well-known promoter and Peebles was able to plug his coming events during the concert.

Billy Walker and Randy Hughes were able to get a number of Opry folk to commit to doing the show: Roy Acuff, Ralph Emery, Cowboy Copas, Hawkshaw Hawkins, Wilma Lee, Stoney Cooper and up-and-comer Dottie West. Hughes had booked Walker on the same Ohio dates as Patsy and had flown them both there. After the last show, Walker told Patsy about the benefit and asked for her help. She'd never known Call, but when he told her what had happened, her response was positive: "Count me in, hoss." After all, she'd only just narrowly escaped death herself.

Late that night, Walker and Hughes stayed up late, drinking whisky and talking. Randy was candid about his affair with Patsy that night. It was over.

"They really tried to keep it from showing," Walker offered. "I never saw Randy drunk, but I seen him drink a lot. Both of us had a couple of drinks and we were talking. There was something said about the situation. He more or less intimated to me, 'Well, she's a wonderful woman, but I've got a wonderful family and I'm not letting anything interfere with that.' So just from the tone and the actions he betrayed that night, I'm pretty convinced it was over between them."

Randy flew Patsy and Charlie to Birmingham for her date there on Saturday, March 2. It was three sold-out shows on a package that included Tex Ritter, Charlie Rich, Jerry Lee Lewis and Flatt & Scruggs. Patsy closed the show.

Patsy was fighting the flu, but by the time she took the stage she was in fine fettle. She wore a simple, white, long-sleeved sheath dress that shimmered under the lights, a rhinestone broach pinned to her waist, dangly earrings and classic white high-heel pumps. "Any of you gals out there have any weight problems?" she put to the audience, which naturally erupted into howls of sympathy. "I been busy tryin' to lose weight," she drawled, "and this is the first time in a long time I've been able to wear white. I'm tellin' ya, don't it just look good?" Patsy proceeded to tick off the numbers, the result of her latest diet, including how much she had lost and her current weight.

Then, with tears in her eyes, she recalled the car crash that had almost claimed her life and told the crowd how grateful she was and how thankful that her life had been spared. After singing "Life's Railway to Heaven," she indicated that her life, too, had been like a mountain railway, a series of ups and downs. It took her accident to make her realize how precious life is.

After the show, she called her mother and sister, telling them she was sick and didn't feel like she could go any further. Her sister offered encouragement, adding, "You might as well go or you'll regret it."

She got only about three or four hours' sleep that night. Rising early, Randy got them back to Nashville by 8 A.M. Charlie got off the plane to make room for Cowboy Copas and Hawkshaw Hawkins. Their destination was Kansas City.

Billy Walker had purchased open airline tickets for everyone who was to appear in the benefit. His original plan was to fly over with Randy, Patsy and Copas on Sunday morning, while the others would fly by commercial airline. But on Saturday, Guy Smith called Walker to report there was a problem with the auditorium. Walker convinced Hawkins, who hated small planes, to take his place on Randy's plane. He took Hawkins's ticket and flew to Kansas City after the Opry on Saturday.

Harold Franklin Hawkins—"Hawk," as he was known by the country folks—stood six feet eight inches in his cowboy boots. He was enjoying something of a personal and professional renaissance. "The Hawk of the West Virginia Hills" was one of the country music traditionalists whose career flattened out when rock and roll came in. He played second-rate dives throughout the 1950s. Then he and Jean Shepard married in 1960 and at the age of forty-two he fathered his first child, Don Robin, named after Don Gibson and Marty Robbins. "I can't believe I waited forty-two years for my life to begin," he rhapsodized. Now Shepard was eight months' pregnant with their second child. That, and his recording of "Lonesome 7-7203," which debuted on the country charts earlier that week (and became a number 1 country hit after his death), boosted his ordinarily extroverted, happy-go-lucky personality clear into the stratosphere. The night before he left for Kansas City, he hugged and kissed his fifteen-month-old son. Early Sunday morning, before he took off with Randy, Patsy and Copas, he put his hand on Shepard's tummy and made a wish: "I hope this one's a boy, too."

Forty-nine-year-old Lloyd Estelle Copas was another stalwart of country music on the comeback trail. "Cope" was a popular entertainer of the late forties who had taken on the heroic persona of the cowboy, claiming to have grown up on a ranch near Muskogee, Oklahoma. It was a snow job for the publicity agents. Cope actually grew up in the hollows of Blue Creek, Ohio, the son of poor farmers who, during the dustbowl years, migrated in the wrong direction. He claimed to have worked with Leonard Slye, better known as Roy Rogers, when Rogers was part of the Sons of the Pioneers. In 1946 he hit big with "Filipino Baby" and enjoyed tremendous popularity until his career nosedived around the time Elvis hit. But, like Hawk, Cope's luck changed in 1960 with his recording of "Alabam," which clung to the country charts for thirty-four weeks before spilling over into the pop field. His rebound was considered a victory by country music traditionalists, one made all the sweeter by the fact that, far from being a sophisticated star, Copas was just a regular "slacks and shirt guy."

Cope's quiet demeanor betrayed a dry sense of humor and great capacity for telling stories. "He loved dogs better than any human being who ever lived," Kathy Hughes said. "Enough so he would stop at the side of a busy road on the way to make a date just to watch a dog." Copas's most recent album had been released only a month earlier with the ill-boded title *Beyond the Sunset*. It included songs dealing with life in the hereafter: "Family Reunion," "The Wreck on the Highway," "A Picture from Life's Other Side," and the tune that would become his posthumously released next single—"Goodbye Kisses."

Reports vary as to whether there were two or three shows that Sunday. Some accounts say there were shows at 2, 5:15 and 8:15 P.M. The 3000-plus-seat Memorial Building was filled to near capacity with fans who had paid $1.50 admission to hear Patsy, the headliner, and the other acts. Patsy's name appeared neither in the short press release that ran in the *Kansas City Star* nor in an advertisement Guy Smith bought in the same edition, but radio plugs for the benefit touted her as a last-minute addition.

Roy Acuff canceled his appearance at the last minute. Acuff's wife, Mildred supposedly had a "funny feeling" about the show and let him sleep in that morning. The understanding around Nashville, however, was that Acuff, "a real ladies' man," had been having an affair with a well-known Opry star's wife, who shot her husband twice with a .22 after a spat they'd had over her affair with the King of Country Music. There were no charges filed, but Acuff decided to cool his heels and disappear for a few days. Ralph Emery canceled too, staying at home to nurse the flu.

None of the acts brought their bands except for Wilma Lee and Stony Cooper, who were playing the area anyway with their band, the Clinch Mountain Clan. Guy Smith hired a local band to back Patsy and the others.

Before the show, in the dressing room she shared with Dottie West, Patsy, her eyes puffed with fatigue and flu, ironed her show clothes herself. She brought a red dress and the white one she wore in Birmingham and saved the white one for the last show.

That night Patsy was a star. She walked onstage, clutching a tissue in her hand, and launched into her hit songs, including "Leavin' on Your Mind." She held her finger to her right ear when she reached for the high notes, apologizing to the audience for not being at the top of her form. Even so, she "defied anyone to even vaguely remember who'd come on before her," West noted. Patsy was genuinely moved by the standing ovation and told them, "I love you all."

Ann Call, Cactus Jack's widow, waited backstage with her two sons, ages eight and eleven, to express her gratitude to all the acts who'd traveled to Kansas City to appear in the benefit. Call remembered in particular how beautiful Patsy looked that night despite her condition.

"She said she had been in a real bad accident and didn't know why the Lord had spared her life, because she'd seen me with my two little boys. I says, 'Patsy, it's for doing good, just like you're doing now.' She just smiled. It just kind of took her. She was such a beautiful person, not only on the outside but the inside too. She really had feeling for others. She had a beautiful white dress on. She showed me the scars on her face. She kind of wore her hair down in the front like maybe she was trying to cover up some of the scars. I said, 'They really don't show all that bad unless you're up close. It really hasn't taken from you at all.' "

At that, Patsy bent over and kissed Call's youngest boy. "She got that red lipstick on him and the only thing he could think of was getting it off. He didn't want no part of that."

After the Memorial Building cleared out, Hap Peebles' staff counted the receipts. Even with everybody donating their services, the benefit raised only $3000.

Guy Smith reserved rooms at the Town House Motor Hotel for all the acts to stay over that night. There was a reception for the artists, and Patsy and George Riddle sat on the sofa, talking about "nothing in particular," with Patsy mostly anxious to get back home to her kids. Little Randy had the flu, she had learned.

The plans were for Patsy, Copas and Billy Walker to fly back the next morning with Randy in the Comanche. But in the middle of the night, Walker got an emergency phone call: his father had suffered a heart attack. Walker had to get back to Nashville by the quickest means possible. Once again he called Hawk to explain his dilemma. Hawkins went to Walker's room, pulled out his airline ticket and said, "Here, kid, you take this. I'll fly back with Randy and them because I flew over with them and I trust him."

The next morning was one of those miserable Midwest days in the early spring—cold, rainy and foggy. Nearby Fairfax Municipal Airport was closed. Road-weary and impatient, Randy kept calling every hour for weather updates but it looked like they were stuck. The hours ticked slowly by, the ashtrays filled up and there was still no improvement in the weather.

Dottie West and her husband, Bill, had driven the sixteen hours to Kansas City and they were preparing to return to Nashville. Dottie offered to take Patsy with them. Patsy considered the proposal, went to her room to pack her bags, then emerged a few minutes later saying she'd changed her mind and would wait it out. They'd beat 'em home, she told her friend. This weather couldn't last forever.

"I'm really going to be worried about you flying in this weather," Dottie told her.

"Don't worry, hoss," she replied. "When it's my time to go, it's my time."

At 9:30 on Tuesday morning, Randy called the airport for weather information. Hawk called the Frontier Club in Independence, asking for the club owner, Raymond Scott. "Guy Smith had talked to Hawk and told him to give me a call," Scott recollected. "I was always booking singers on their way through town, giving them a night's work. I guess Hawk called the club from the airport, around 11 A.M., but if I'd a been there when he called, I would have told him to come on out and play that night. He wouldn't have been on that plane."

Patsy telephoned her mother. She seemed to be in good humor when she called, even cracked a joke or two—"just normal conversation.

"She told me, 'Thank goodness I don't have to work anymore 'til then'"—referring to her Baltimore Civic Auditorium date on March 16.

"Well, I'll get back to you," she told Hilda.

"She always ended a telephone call that way."

At 12:30 P.M., Patsy, Randy, Copas and Hawkins checked out of the Town House Motor Hotel, headed for the airport and boarded the little "shitbox," as some people referred to the plane. Hawkins sat up front with Randy, where he could stretch out. Patsy and Copas squeezed into the cramped back seats with their luggage. At 2:22, fifteen miles north of Butler, Missouri, and seventy miles south of Kansas City, there was contact with a plane registered as 7000P. Somewhere between Kansas City and Dyersburg, Tennessee, Randy landed and bought nineteen gallons of fuel. At 5 P.M. they landed, again in Dyersburg, Tennessee. Randy went off to call his wife to check on conditions in Nashville. The others went inside for a cup of coffee. Some stories suggested Kathy Hughes told her husband it was clear, that she could see "the moon and the stars." She denied she ever said such a thing.

"We had had horrendous weather here. All night long we had storms; all day long it had rained, simply because it was March. When Randy called the rain had stopped. There were no rains at that particular time. He asked me, 'What's the weather look like there?' and I told him, 'The rains have stopped; it looks like it's going to try to quit raining.' I never said anything about the sun shining. That has really haunted me. Perhaps just saying it had quit raining was all he needed to know. I don't know. I'll never know. I just told him what I would have normally, naturally said. He asked me if I would call and have the lights turned on at the airport so that he could land. Mother and I were having dinner at the time. As soon as we finished we got in the car, drove over to Cornelia Fort Air Field and sat there and waited."

Pilots call it "get-home-itus":

"I tried to get him to stay over because of the high winds on the way," said Dyersburg airport manager Bill Braese. "But Hughes said he was familiar with the area on the Nashville flight. He said he had already come from Kansas City and he was going ahead."

On Wednesday morning, Loretta Lynn had just finished making beds, washing dishes, ironing and putting away some of the show costumes Patsy had given her the day before she left town.

"I had gone over to her house and she give me all these clothes in a box, and I'm carrying them out, and she called out, 'Wait—you didn't kiss me goodbye.' I put the box down on the car and I go back and say, 'I'm sorry. I love you with all my heart and all my soul. I don't know what I'd do without you.' And I hugged her and kissed her. And she looked at me and said, 'Little gal, we're going to stick together 'til the day we die. It'll be you and me, all the way.' "

Loretta was daydreaming about the shopping trip they planned on taking the very day Patsy was back in town when the telephone jarred her out of her reverie. A friend's voice at the other end said, "Loretta, what are you doin'?"

"I just got through cleaning the house. I was thinking, 'Me and Patsy are going shopping today. She's buying me something for my front room. I'm so excited.' This friend of mine said, 'Loretta, you haven't listened to the news?' I said, 'Oh no. I fell asleep last night listening to the wind, and it was playing a tune.' Every time I listen to the wind and it plays a tune, something happens. I don't understand it. I don't know what it's going to be but it's going to be something. She said, 'Why haven't you listened to the news?' I said, 'Because me and Patsy's going shopping, and I wanted to be sure my house was clean.' She said, 'Honey, Patsy is dead.' I said, 'Oh no she ain't.' She said, 'She is.' I said, 'Oh no she ain't. I'm going shopping with her.' "

Mossie Miller of Route 1, Camden, Tennessee, ninety miles west of Nashville, told a newspaper reporter, "I heard something pop a little after seven. The dogs ran out. My wife heard a roar and a pop and then nothing."

Corn and cotton farmer Jeffrey Hollingsworth and his son Jeners were out early Wednesday morning. They had heard the news of the missing Opry stars on the radio. A Camden Civil Defense unit and the Highway Patrol had been out all night looking for the missing plane.

Hollingsworth and his son were scouting along a ridge line near a heavily wooded area known to locals as Fatty Bottom, when they looked down in the hollow and spotted the mangled remains of a yellow wing hanging in a tree. It was quiet, serenely so, in contrast to the chaos below.

"I almost had a nervous breakdown when I ran down and saw the bodies. I had to sit down on a log and then walk out to the road . . . 'til help came," the elder Hollingsworth said. His son ran to get the Highway Patrol. Trooper Troy Odle was the first to arrive: "I've never seen a wreck as bad."

Vertigo does strange things. In bad weather, unless a pilot is reading the instruments, the play of gravity on his body might tell him he is going up when he is actually headed straight down. A six-foot crater where the single-engine plane hit the hillside was filled with water, confirming that it was raining at the time of the crash. Only one large oak tree had been felled, leading to the official conclusion that, visibility reduced to zero, the pilot thought he was gaining altitude when he was actually nosediving at a speed estimated at 120 mph.

Clothes and personal effects were strewn over a 300-foot area like the pieces of the jigsaw puzzle that were found in the wreckage: a white belt with "Hawkshaw Hawkins" in gold letters; parts of a guitar; a silver expansion watch band; a soft gold slipper like one Patsy had been seen wearing at the airport in Dyersburg; a "Keep America Beautiful" plastic litter bag; a piece of paper with the hand-printed lyrics of a song that said, "Boo Hoo Hoo"; a hairbrush with a few of Patsy's hairs in it, and her favorite Zippo lighter, emblazoned with a Confederate flag that still miraculously played "Dixie"; a piece of skull with longish hair that could only have been a woman's.

Asked if he could account for the four passengers from the remains, a civil defense worker answered grimly, "There's not enough to count."

As news of the crash hit the airwaves over the next few days, the remote area swarmed with thousands of scavenging tourists. The site of the crash, above which the yellow wing still hung from the branches of a tree like an ominous banner, was only a few hundred feet from a gravel road that became so congested that many sightseers abandoned their cars along the way and trekked the half mile or mile afoot to gape at the scene. As many as twenty-five counties of Tennessee and several states were represented among the curious. Some were Opry fans. The throng included pregnant women, kids, senior citizens, lovers holding hands. They descended on the site like yellow jackets on a roadkill, hunting through the wreckage, picking up whatever they could find— it didn't matter: wiring, bolts, screws, pieces of metal. But the public had already been beaten to the site by some of the friends of the deceased, who'd been out scouring the area since the first bulletins of a missing aircraft hit the airwaves, and had already creamed the area for grisly souvenirs.

Jim McCoy was a night-shift deejay at WHPL, Winchester. He signed off the air at midnight on Tuesday and went home. The morning guy came on at 4:30 A.M., read the wire that awaited him and called McCoy at home. "You'd better come out to the station. Patsy Cline is missing." By 8 A.M. the crash was confirmed. There were no survivors. McCoy called Hilda at home. "She took it bad."

The *Winchester Evening Star* screamed the news in a front-page banner headline:

PATSY CLINE, 3 OTHERS KILLED IN PLANE CRASH

Hit records, awards, appearances on network television notwithstanding, her demise was, by far, the biggest press she'd ever received from the hometown newspaper. Even Harry Floyd Byrd's normally staid newspaper couldn't resist the opportunities for a bit of tabloid-style sensationalism: "A woman's red slip was hanging from a tree," the *Star* noted.

Patsy Lillis said: "I was standing in the living room combing my daughter's hair for school. I didn't have a telephone at the time. And the neighbor lady, her name was Mrs. White, she come over to my house. She said, 'You're wanted on the telephone.' So I told my daughter, 'Stay here. I'll be right back.' And I went over and it was my sister and she said, 'Have you had the radio on?' I said, 'No.' She said, 'Don't turn it on. I'll be right over.' And she come up, but before she got there, I turned the radio on. And it said there didn't seem to be any survivors. Right away I went to Hilda's as soon as I sent my daughter to school. Wasn't anyone there. I went back a couple of hours later and she was there. I went in, sat down and talked, then I went to the flower shop and got her some flowers with some musical notes on them. Her little girl, Julie, was there with her grandmother, and she had on a pair of little plastic high-heel mules, the slip-on kind that kids wore then. I said, 'Where'd you get those?' She said, 'Mommy got 'em for me in Legas.' Not Las Vegas, but Legas. It was sad."

Jumbo Rinker said: "When she died, I went over there to Mrs. Hensley's and cooked breakfast and everything for them. The phone rang and I answered it and it was Charlie and he said, 'That you, Jumbo?' I said, 'Yeah.' He was all upset, crying. Said, 'Can I depend on you for a favor?' 'Sure,' I says. 'I'm sending up a big spray of flowers. Cost me fifteen hundred bucks. They're roses. Want them to go on the coffin, and they've got to be refrigerated, cold and fresh for the service. Would you please pick them up, see that they're taken care of and see that they're delivered at the right time? Can you do that?' I said, 'Don't worry about it, Charlie. It'll all be taken care of.' So I did it. And when he come up for the funeral we were in the kitchen over at Mrs. Hensley's because I stayed to help out, cooking, seeing people and whatnot. Finally he said to me, 'I'm going to tell you something.' I said, 'What's that, Charlie?' He said, 'I used to hate your guts. But what you done for me, I'm sorry for the way I acted.' I said, 'Charlie, I understand.' He said, 'I'm telling you, I hated your guts. You were a thorn in my side, but I don't feel that way anymore.' "

A framed photograph of Patsy rested on top of the sealed bronze casket in the living room of her dream home. The "sitting up" ceremony of staying with the body through the night, before the burial, had begun. Hilda, Sylvia, John and Charlie's mother descended on the house on Nella Drive, joining Charlie, a lost boy-man, and her kids. Friends, Opry folk, record industry people, neighbors attended the twenty-four-hour vigil. It was a community affair, combining the sacred and the social, a paradoxical display of grief and hospitality meant to help the family and each other overcome the loss of sudden separation. Food and liquor were consumed, stories swapped, hugs exchanged, tears wiped and people who hadn't seen or spoken to each other for months or years were reunited in the festival of death.

June Carter had been on the road when she heard the news and she rushed back to Nashville to tell Charlie and Hilda what Patsy had told her. "I went over to the house to talk to Charlie and her mother both, but they were so upset, I don't know what they remembered of it," she recalled. "I kept the kids; I got everybody to bring different food and things in. I'd gone to all the other funerals but I stayed home with the kids when they had the service for Patsy."

Loretta Lynn helped hold the twenty-four-hour watch over at Patsy's, the most beautiful house in the world because that was where she had laughed, cried, cooked and just talked. Where she had intimate knowledge of the contents of her best friend's most intimate *closet*. She sat on the pale green sofa, one of Patsy's most beloved trophies, numb to the point of shivering, in a state of fear. "I kept thinking, 'What am I goin' to do? What am I goin' to do? I don't have nobody to take care of me. I don't have nobody to fight for me.' Everyone was in the kitchen and I went in the living room, because she had all her furniture made and everything looked so pretty and I went in and her couch was silk, with raised white flowers that were light green. It was so pretty. I was sitting down on the couch and looking at her picture on the coffin. And as I was sitting there, I got real cold and was thinking, 'Gee, it's cold in here,' but I was mad because everyone was in the kitchen talking as if 'Who cares?' That bothered me. It was about to kill me, and maybe I was taking it the wrong way, but it's the way I felt about it at the time. Then I just kind of heard her say, 'Well, turn up the damn heat!' And that's just the way Patsy would say it. I got up and turned up the heat before I realized she didn't say it, and sat back down and thought, 'My God— here I am listening to her *voice* and she's telling me what to do, and she's telling me to turn up the heat.' "

Nashville reeled. People said it was like the day Kennedy was shot. WSM quickly threw together an hour-long memorial program that aired the day after the crash. Ralph Emery, the WSM deejay who was considered a star maker, dedicated his entire all-night showcase to Patsy, Cope, Hawk and Randy. Emery, for whom Patsy, during her lifetime, "was not the best of guests," paused frequently to gain his composure as he talked about the careers of the artists. Tennessee governor Frank Clement issued an official statement: "The entertainment world suffers a great professional loss. Tennessee suffers a great personal loss. They were typical of the serious-minded, hardworking professional people dedicated to country music artistry." The Tennessee State Legislature offered a minute of silent prayer. Owen Bradley was quoted by the *Tennessean:* "Patsy Cline was one of the greatest voices in America—pop or country. There is no way to describe our feeling—our loss, personal and professional."

It was the first time a tragedy of such magnitude had brushed the lives of the close-knit music community in Nashville. The beat of Music City just lay there and bled, as the guitarists said, as everyone in the business of making music abandoned his or her routines and went to comfort the bereaved or the grief-stricken friends of the bereaved. In one unique moment, everyone was family, true family, the survivors shocked into a state of collective numbness.

A prayer service was held for Patsy on Thursday afternoon following the crash at Phillips-Robinson Funeral Home in Nashville, after which her remains were taken to Winchester for burial. Joint services for Copas and his son-in-law were held the following morning, and Hawkins's service was held that Friday afternoon. Jean Shepard had collapsed after hearing the news of the tragedy, and there was concern that she would lose her baby.

The services drew the largest crowd of mourners in Nashville history, as streets near the funeral home were blocked off and thousands jammed the environs of the funeral home, where loudspeakers had been set up to accommodate the crowd. Reverend Jay Alford, the Pentecostal preacher who'd witnessed Patsy getting it together with the Lord in the hospital, and like Billy Walker, saw her subsequent "slip" back into the old, sinful ways, said to the people, "We cannot possibly know the reasons why such tragedies occur, but I am sure that Almighty God in his wisdom and providence knows and understands."

The nightmare got worse. As the service was concluding, there was a commotion, as news filtered through the throng that Jack Anglin, the forty-six-year-old member of the singing duo Johnny and Jack, had been killed in a freak car accident on his way to Patsy's service. Anglin had just left a barber shop and was on his way to the prayer service when it happened. Wright and his wife, the regal Kitty Wells, were given the news as they exited the funeral home chapel. It was the final blow. There was a feeling that there was a jinx on the Opry.

On Saturday night following the services, the show went on, not quite as usual. Opry manager Ott Devine, whose job normally kept him behind the scenes, came out to the big, carbon WSM mike and read a tribute: "What do we say when we lose such friends? We can reflect upon their contributions to all of us through entertainment, their acts of charity and of love. We can think of the pleasure they brought to the lives of millions and take some comfort in knowing that they found fulfillment in the time allotted to them. We can share the sorrow of their families and appreciate the loss, not only to WSM and the "Grand Ole Opry" but also to their associates, to the music industry and especially to all of you . . . their friends. There is great significance that Patsy, Cope, Hawk and Randy were returning from a performance staged to help someone else when they lost their own lives. They will never be forgotten . . . Patsy, Cowboy Copas, Hawkshaw Hawkins, Jack Anglin and Randy Hughes never walked on this stage without a smile. They would want us to keep smiling . . . and to recall the happier occasions. I feel that I can speak for all of them when I say . . . let's continue in the tradition of the 'Grand Ole Opry.' "

Minnie Pearl wiped her tears, swallowed and ran out on the Ryman stage with her clarion call, "HOW-DEE." The other acts came on. The Jordanaires closed the tribute with an emotional rendition of "How Great Thou Art," as the rest of the cast joined in the hymn onstage, some of them openly weeping.

There was a famous wire service photo taken that night from the wings of June Carter gazing into the crowded fly space behind the stage, holding her face in her hands, crying.

It was bright and sunny and crisp the day Patsy was brought back to Winchester for burial. It was said to be the biggest thing to happen in Winchester after the Apple Blossom Parade.

The five-mile stretch of road between Jones Funeral Home and Shenandoah Memorial Park and even beyond was lined with people, three, four, five deep. The crowd was estimated to be upward of 25,000. They were standing on the roofs of nearby houses and barns, climbing walls, traipsing through backyards. They even buzzed overhead in small airplanes. Jones Funeral Home was filled to capacity and the broad sweep of lawn outside the funeral home was swarming with people, many of them fans from other parts of the country.

"We never did get inside," said Patsy's Aunt Nellie Patterson. "We sat on the steps, Frank and Harry and I. I remember Harry saying that if Patsy was living she would say, 'Just look at all these damn fools.' "

Cars were everywhere, some abandoned at the side of the road, as people gave up on finding parking spaces and hiked to get close as the funeral cortege wound its way to Shenandoah Memorial Park, on the south side of town. It was Patsy's last ride through the streets of Winchester. Senior citizens, children, residents, out-of-towners, her family, her friends, her enemies—they were all there with their cameras: movie cameras, expensive thirty-five-millimeter models and ten-dollar Brownies. The cemetery grounds were soggy and wet from the recent rain. There were banks of wreaths, a small fortune in flowers around the small tent that covered the grave, on which a small stone marker was later placed: "Virginia Dick 1932–1963."

As the solemn-faced Reverend Nathan Williamson, of the Valley Avenue Church of Christ, intoned the final words of the ritual over the casket, and a singer held the last bittersweet note of "Amazing Grace," the wave began.

Someone reached out and plucked one of the roses. A woman stepped forward and took another rose. Someone else snapped up a lily, a carnation, then another and another, and then as if on cue, the whole crowd pushed in, grabbing sprigs of flowers, plastic emblems, cards, whole bouquets and all the while there was no music, no drumroll, no brass band, no song, only the crisp clicking and popping of cameras recording the event.

Epilogue

The naming of streets after famous "personages" being something of a Winchester tradition, in 1986, the Winchester City Council met to vote on a referendum to have Pleasant Valley Road renamed Patsy Cline Boulevard. The vote, eleven against the measure, one in favor, came after months of heated debate. The views of the victorious opponents of the plan were characterized by one local resident in a newspaper story that appeared during the height of the controversy: "Ask anybody in this town and they'll tell you. Patsy Cline was nothin' but a whore."

It was perhaps serendipitous that the obscure little mountain hamlet of Gore would produce not one, but two, of this century's greatest female voices. While the Patsy Cline street-naming debate raged, a similar proposal was made to have the new elementary school right outside of town on Route 600 named after another famous person with ties to the area, the great American novelist, Willa Cather, who was born in Gore in 1873.

Cather was the grand-niece of the community's namesake, Sidney Sophia Cather Gore, a frontier woman and educator who lived along upper Back Creek, the same area given as Patsy's birthplace. After her husband died, Sidney Gore took in boarders in order to finance the education of youngsters from the poor families that lived along Back Creek. Later in life, Gore donated the money that built Hebron Baptist Church, where, many years later, Patsy sang in the church choir.

The year before Patsy's birth, Cather was profiled in *The New Yorker*. She had just been awarded an honorary doctorate from Princeton and had already received similar awards from the Universities of Michigan, Nebraska, Columbia and Yale, as well as the Pulitzer Prize. Of Cather it was said, "Her face, when she detects some affectation in another's words or actions, can lose every atom of warmth and become hostile and set. It is impossible to imagine her strong hands in a deprecatory gesture. The remarks, 'Oh well' and 'What does it matter?' have never, in all probability, passed her lips. She admires big careers and ambitious, strong characters, especially if they are the careers and characters of women. The most fortunate and most exciting of human beings, to her minds, is a singer with a pure, big voice and unerring musical tastes."

The proposal to name the school after Cather suffered a similar fate as the Patsy Cline Boulevard controversy. There was heated debate, but in the end it was considered inappropriate to name a "child-oriented building" after someone with "lesbian tendencies."

The idea of naming a street after Patsy Cline wasn't forgotten in Winchester, however. After the Willa Cather flap died down, the developer of the new Apple Blossom Corners Mall in Winchester decided to name the quarter-mile stretch of driveway between Pleasant Valley Road and the shopping center parking lot after Winchester's own—the Country Music Hall of Fame singer whose life inspired two Hollywood films, whose records continue to go platinum thirty years after her death, who has inspired virtually every major female country singer of a younger generation and whose face appears on a U.S. postage stamp. A sign was posted in the parking lot.

The only problem was the spelling: "NO EXIT TO PASTY CLINE BLVD."

Notes to Chapters and Sources

Unless otherwise noted, all interviews were conducted by the author during the period 1990-1994.

Introduction

The main sources were interviews with Johnny Anderson (5/24/91); Jim McCoy (3/5/91); Becky Miller (7/15/91); Pat Smallwood Miller (3/8/91); John Reid (5/21/91); Ralph "Jumbo" Rinker (3/7/91); Mary Klick Robinson (7/18/91); and Philip Whitney (5/21/91).

Other sources included: The Apple Annual, 1957; *Frederick County, Virginia: From the Frontier to the Future* (Donning, 1988), by Teresa Lazazzera and Rebecca Ebert; "Forty Years of Progress, 1917-1957" (Report by the Winchester Chamber of Commerce); *Winchester Evening Star*, 4/30/57, 5/1/57, 5/2/57, 5/4/57; "Facts & Figures About Winchester, Va.," 1951 (Report by the Winchester Chamber of Commerce); "Today in Frederick County and Winchester" and "The History of Frederick County," *Virginia and the Virginia County*, March 1950; Mr. Greeter Guidebook Directory for Winchester, Virginia, 1954; "Virginia—The State and the State of Mind," by Cabell Phillips, *New York Times*, 7/30/57.

Chapter 1

Important information was provided through interviews with Patsy's first cousin, Herman "Punk" Longley, Jr. (5/22/91 and 6/3/91), and her aunts, Marie Allanson (5/18/91 and 5/24/91) and Nellie Patterson (5/24/91). Other interviews included Carmel Longley (3/21/92); Randolph Mann (7/12/91); Hobby Robinson (7/15/91); Charles Spaid (3/8/91).

Chapter 2

Primary sources for this chapter included interviews with Marie Allanson; Mae Boren Axton (7/31/92); Owen Bradley (2/16/90); June Carter Cash (9/11/92); Robert Gaines, Sr. (5/21/91); Robert Getchell (7/13/91 and 1/21/94); Donn Hecht (6/15/92 and 6/22/92); Carmel Longley (3/21/92);

Punk Longley (5/22/91 and 6/3/91); Loretta Lynn (3/30/92); Pat Smallwood Miller (3/8/91); Patsy Montana (1/27/91); Nellie Patterson (5/24/91); Jumbo Rinker (3/7/91); Hobby Robinson (7/15/91); Bernard Schwartz (8/15/91 and 1/21/94); Charles Spaid (3/8/91); Ginny Trenary (9/27/91).

Other sources: "Hillbilly with Oomph," by Meredith S. Buel, *Washington Star* magazine, 3/18/56; "Patsy Montana and the Development of the Cowgirl Image," by Robert K. Oermann and Mary A. Bufwack, *Journal of Country Music*, vol. 8, no. 3; "Sweet Dreams," by Dorothy McGhee, *Washington Post Magazine*, 9/29/85.

Chapter 3

Interviews: Johnny Anderson (5/22/91, 5/24/91); Bud Armel (5/5/91); Jack Fretwell (5/20/91); Robert Gaines, Sr. (5/21/91); Punk Longley (5/22/91 and 6/3/91); Jim McCoy (3/5/91); Pat Smallwood Miller (3/8/91); John Reid (5/21/91); Jumbo Rinker (3/7/91); Charles Spaid (3/8/91); Philip Whitney (5/21/91).

Other sources: McGhee, "Sweet Dreams," *Washington Post Magazine*, 9/29/85; "Sweet Dreams," by Terri Higgins, *Winchester Evening Star*, 3/6/93; Buel, "Hillbilly with Oomph," *Washington Star Magazine*, 3/18/56; "She Was There for Patsy Cline," by Linda Gorton, *Winchester Evening Star*, 10/8/85.

Chapter 4

The primary sources for this chapter consisted of interviews with Wally Fowler (7/22/91 and 3/28/92). Walter Carter's excellent article, "Wally Fowler's Big Idea: The Origins of the Oak Ridge Boys," in *Journal of Country Music*, vol. 12, no. 1, 1987, provided detailed background on Fowler's performances at this time.

Other interviews and sources included Pete Kirby (10/21/91); "Spunky Patsy Top Performer," *Tennessean*, 11/11/62; "Official History of the Tennessee Centennial Exposition" (under the direction of Dudley and Baskette of the Committee on Publication, 1898); "Hillbilly Heaven," by Don Eddy, *American Magazine*, February 1952; "Country Music Is Big Business, and Nashville Is Its Detroit," *Newsweek*, 8/11/52; "Country Music, Nashville Style," by Richard Marek, *McCall's*, April 1961; "Nashville: Broadway of Country Music," by H. B. Teeter, *Coronet*, August 1952; "Sex, Sin, and Salvation," *Show*, February 1962; *Patsy Cline*, by Ellis Nassour (Tower Books, 1981).

Chapter 5

Interviews: Johnny Anderson (5/24/91); Bud Armel (5/5/91); Roy Deyton (5/19/91); Jim McCoy (3/5/91); Becky Miller (7/15/91); Pat Smallwood Miller (3/8/91).

Other sources: "The Queen of Country Music," by Geoff Lane, *Country Music*, December 1974; McGhee, "Sweet Dreams," *Washington Post Magazine*, 9/29/85; Nassour, *Patsy Cline* (Tower Books, 1981).

Chapter 6

The following articles by Joe Sasfy on Connie B. Gay and the Washington, D.C., music scene provided invaluable background for this and the following chapter: "When Fiddles Sang," *City Paper,* 8/15/86, and "The Hick from Lizard Lick," *Regardie's,* March 1987; writer and D.C. records discographer Jay Bruder provided background on Lillian Claiborne. Primary sources included interviews with Katherine Adelman (6/1/92); Johnny Anderson (5/24/91); Roy Clark (7/2/92); Wally Fowler (3/28/92); Durwood Haddock (8/24/91); Donn Hecht (6/22/92 and 6/29/92); Wade Holmes (7/28/92); James McCall (9/4/91); Leo Miller (8/5/92); Eddie Nesbitt (5/19/92); Don Pierce (11/13/91); Pete Pike (8/18/92); Marvin Rainwater (4/29/92); Cliffie Stone (11/12/91).

Other sources: "Lillian Claiborne: Her Art Is Lost to Us," by John B. Earnshaw, *Unicorn Times,* May 1975; Jonny Whiteside's notes for Rhino's reissue of Patsy Cline's first recordings, "Walkin' Dreams" (R2 70048); 4 Star Record Company, Inc., contract dated 9/30/54; Paul Kingsbury's notes for "The Patsy Cline Collection" (MCAD4-10421).

Chapter 7

Interviews: Marvin Carroll (7/24/91); Roy Clark (7/2/92); Jimmy Dean (5/19/92); Joli Jensen's interview with Connie B. Gay (4/20/80); Jumbo Rinker (3/7/91); Dale Turner (6/1/91).

Other sources: Sasfy, "When Fiddles Sang," *City Paper,* 8/15/86; "Country Boy Was Always Tuned In," by Hank Burchard, *Washington Post,* 2/18/71; "Our Respects to Connie Barriot Gay," *Broadcasting,* 2/2/59.

Chapter 8

Interviews: Owen Bradley (5/31/91 and 6/1/92); Roy Deyton (5/19/91); Milton Gabler (7/12/91 and 8/3/92); Al Gallico (8/19/91); Tompall Glaser (5/15/92); Goldie Hill (8/11/92); Wanda Jackson (9/16/92); Charlie Lamb (3/28/92); Leo Miller (8/5/92); John "Pete" O'Brien (5/28/92); Don Pierce (11/13/91); Janette Davis Musiello (5/26/92); Faron Young (7/9/92).

Other sources: "Cohen Sparks 22 Sessions," *Country Music Reporter,* 3/16/57; "The Decca Country Story," *Billboard,* 11/2/63; "The Emergence of Nashville as a Recording Center," by John Rumble, *Journal of Country Music,* vol. 7, no. 3, 1978; "It Happened Last Night: Hillbilly Lingo Now Needed to Schmooze on Broadway," by Earl Wilson, *New York Post,* 9/14/54; Nassour, *Patsy Cline* (Tower Books, 1981); "Turn the Cards Slowly" copyright Acuff-Rose/Opryland Music Group.

Chapter 9

Interviews: Johnny Anderson (5/24/91); Harold Bradley (3/25/92); Owen Bradley (2/16/90, 5/31/91, 6/1/92); Elizabeth Deyton (5/19/91); Milton Gabler; Donn Hecht (6/22/92); Pat Smallwood Miller (3/8/91); Kathy Southerland (7/24/92); Cliffie Stone (11/12/91); Gabe Tucker (10/26/92); Faron Young (7/9/92).

Other sources: Nassour, *Patsy Cline* (Tower Books, 1981); "Owen Bradley: The Way We Were," as told to Michael McCall, *Journal of Country Music,* vol. 12, no. 2, 1989; "Changing Methods, Changing Sounds: An Overview," by John Morthland, *Journal of Country Music,* vol. 12, no. 2, 1989; "Harold Bradley: The Dean Reflects on 40 Years in Nashville's Studios," by Rich Kienzle, *Coun-*

try Sounds, September 1986; "Patsy Cline's Recording Career," by Joli Jensen, *Journal of Country Music*, vol. 9, 1982; "Folk Talent & Tunes," by Bill Sachs, *Billboard*, 7/16/55; Kingsbury's notes to "The Patsy Cline Collection" (MCA); 4 Star Sales Company, correspondence, 7/20/55; "Hidin' Out" and "Honky-Tonk Merry-Go-Round" copyright Acuff-Rose/Opryland Music Group.

Chapter 10

Interviews: Harold Bradley (3/25/92); Owen Bradley (2/16/90); Marvin Carroll (7/24/91); Hugh Cherry (3/17/93); Jimmy Dean (5/19/92); Milton Delugg (6/2/92); Roy Deyton (5/19/91); Tompall Glaser (5/15/92); George Hamilton IV (5/11/92); Pat Smallwood Miller (3/8/91); Jumbo Rinker (3/7/91); Mary Klick Robinson (7/18/91); Gabe Tucker (10/26/92); Dale Turner (6/1/91).

Other sources: "Country DJs Carry Music to People," by Hugh Cherry, *Music City News*, October 1980; "Hillbilly Queens," *Country Song Roundup*, November 1955; "Folk Music Fireball," *Country Song Roundup*, September 1955; *Rock and Roll Is Here to Pay*, by Steve Chapple and Reebee Garofalo (Nelson-Hall, 1977); "Diskeries Score Anti-Pop Bias," *Billboard*, 3/3/56; "Country Stylist," by McCandlish Phillips, *New York Times*, 9/8/57; Buel, "Hillbilly with Oomph," *Washington Star Magazine*, 3/18/56; Sasfy, "When Fiddles Sang," *City Paper*, 8/15/86; "A Howling Hillbilly Success," *Life*, 4/30/56; "Hillbilly on a Pedestal," *Newsweek*, 5/14/56; "Elvis Presley: He can't be . . . but he is," *Look*, 8/7/56; "Diskeries in Race for R&R Country Talent," *Billboard*, 5/12/56; "Drop Petty Bickering," *Billboard*, 3/3/56; "Come On In," "Stop, Look and Listen," "I've Loved and Lost Again," "Dear God" copyright Acuff-Rose/Opryland Music Group.

Chapter 11

Interviews: Johnny Anderson (5/24/91); Mae Boren Axton (7/27/92); Owen Bradley (2/16/90); Jimmy Dean (5/19/92); Milton Delugg; Mel Dick (3/20/92); Billy Grammer (5/11/92); George Hamilton IV; Donn Hecht (6/15/92, 6/22/92); Don Helms (10/12/92); Patsy Lillis (11/30/92); Carmel Longley (3/21/92); Punk Longley (5/22/91 and 6/3/91); Becky Miller (7/15/91); Pat Smallwood Miller (3/8/91); Ray Rainwater (5/11/92); Jumbo Rinker (3/7/91); Mary Klick Robinson (7/18/91); Kathy Southerland; Johnny Western (1/18/93); Faron Young (7/9/92).

Other sources: Nassour, *Patsy Cline* (Tower Books, 1981); "I Remember Patsy Cline," by Donn Hecht, *Country Music*, October 1973; "D-J's Open Festival," *Country Music Reporter*, 11/10/56; "C-Music to Last," *Country Music Reporter*, 11/10/56; "1800 At DJ Festival Study Audience-Building Techniques; See Rosy Future for Country Music," *Country Music Reporter*, 11/24/56; 1985 interview with Charlie Dick by Rita Whitfield for WCTV (Nashville), "Wraparound"; "The Real Patsy Cline," Hallway Productions, Inc., 1985; "Walkin' After Midnight" copyright Acuff-Rose/Opryland Music Group.

Chapter 12

Interviews: Mae Boren Axton (7/31/92); Marvin Carroll (7/24/91); Janette Musciello Davis; Jimmy Dean (5/19/92); Milton Delugg; Al Gallico

(8/19/91); Billy Grammer (5/11/92); George Hamilton IV; Donn Hecht (6/15/92); Patsy Lillis (11/30/92); Punk Longley (5/22/91 and 6/3/91); Pat Smallwood Miller (3/8/91); Louis Nuneley (7/30/91); Marvin Rainwater (4/29/92); Ray Rainwater (5/11/92); Mary Klick Robinson (7/18/91); Dale Turner (6/1/91).

Other sources: Nassour, *Patsy Cline* (Tower Books, 1981); "Tops in Talent," *Winchester Evening Star*, 1/22/57; "There's Stardust on Patsy," by Sheila Gallagher, *Sunday Star TeleVue*, 3/9/57; "Cline, Torok Decca Leaders," *Music Reporter*, 4/13/57; "Music's Segregation Fades into Oblivion," *Music Reporter*, 9/28/57; "This Week's Best Buys," *Billboard*, 2/9/57 and 2/16/57; "Homespun Harmony; Hillbilly Music Sells," *Wall Street Journal*, 5/3/57; Sasfy, "When Fiddles Sang," *City Paper*, 8/15/86; "Town and Country Net Nabs CBS-TV Contract," *Country Music Reporter*, 3/16/57; "Our Respects to Connie Barriot Gay," *Broadcasting*, 2/2/59; Burchard, "Country Boy Was Always Tuned In," *Washington Post*, 2/18/71; "Patsy Cline Plans Recording," by Lula McDaniel, *Winchester Evening Star*, 4/4/57; Paul Kingsbury's notes for "The Patsy Cline Collection" (MCA); correspondence, Donn Hecht, 11/23/92; ad, *Music Reporter*, 3/16/57.

Chapter 13

Interviews: Johnny Anderson (5/24/91); Mae Boren Axton (7/31/92); Owen Bradley (2/16/90 and 5/31/91); June Carter Cash (9/11/92); Donn Hecht (6/15/92, 6/22/92, 10/11/92); Mary Lu Jeans (7/9/92); Patsy Lillis (11/30/92); Pat Smallwood Miller (3/8/91); Ray Rainwater (5/11/91); Jumbo Rinker (3/7/91); Wesley Tuttle (11/12/91); Faron Young (7/9/92).

Articles: McDaniel, "Patsy Cline Plans Recording," *Winchester Evening Star*, 4/4/57; Kienzle, "The Forgotten Hank Garland," *Journal of Country Music*, vol. 9, no. 3, 1983; correspondence, Donn Hecht, 6/22/92; ad, "Decca Records Country Tips," *Music Reporter*, 6/8/57; "A Stranger in My Arms," "Fingerprints" copyright Acuff-Rose/Opryland Music Group.

Chapter 14

Interviews: Mae Boren Axton (7/31/92); Mel Dick (3/20/92); Donn Hecht (6/15/92, 6/29/92); Brenda Lee (4/20/92); Patsy Lillis (11/30/92); Barbara Mandrell (1/14/93); Becky Miller (7/15/91); Pat Smallwood Miller (12/14/92); Hobby Robinson (7/15/91); Dale Turner (6/1/91); Faron Young (7/9/92).

Other sources: *A Satisfied Mind*, Porter Wagoner's biography by Steve Eng (Rutledge Hill, 1992); transcription of "Ozark Jubilee" of 8/10/57 collection courtesy Country Music Foundation; "Virginia Hensley Cline Wed to Charles Dick on Sunday," *Winchester Evening Star*, 9/16/57; Nassour, *Patsy Cline* (Tower Books, 1981); Higgins, "Sweet Dreams," *Winchester Evening Star*, 3/6/93; "Stop the World (and Let Me Off)," "If I Could See the World (Through the Eyes of a Child)" copyright Acuff-Rose/Opryland Music Group.

Chapter 15

Interviews: Johnny Anderson (5/24/91); Harold Bradley (3/25/92); Owen Bradley (5/31/91); Buzz Busby (7/24/92); Marvin Carroll (12/12/92); Floyd Cramer (6/9/92); Milton Gabler (12/14/92); George Hamilton IV; Patsy Lillis (11/30/92); Pat Smallwood Miller (12/14/93); Gordon Stoker (3/24/92,

12/15/92); Vernon Alderton Taylor (5/22/92); Ray Walker (3/24/92, 12/14/92).

Other sources: Nassour, *Patsy Cline* (Tower Books, 1981); "Cosse Assumes Handling Patsy Cline, Crescendos," *Music Reporter*, 1/13/58; "RCA's Sholes Puts 'Old' C&W in Crypt," *Billboard*, 11/26/58; Sasfy, "When Fiddles Sang," *City Paper*, 8/15/86; *Billboard*, 4/13/59.

Chapter 16

Interviews: Margie Bowes (3/26/92); Owen Bradley (5/31/91); June Carter Cash (9/11/92); Lightnin' Chance (6/15/92); Mel Dick (3/20/92); Dorothy Ethridge (7/12/92); Durwood Haddock (8/24/91); Kathy Hughes (1/9/93); Joyce Jackson (1/7/93); Buddy Killen (1/4/93); Rose Maddox interview by Jonny Whiteside, 1990; Marvin Rainwater (4/29/92); Dale Turner (6/1/91); Ray Walker (12/14/92); Johnny Western (1/18/93); Faron Young (7/9/92).

Other sources: Bob Allen's album notes for *Charline Arthur: Welcome to the Club*, Bear Family Records; Eng, *A Satisfied Mind* (Rutledge Hill, 1992); Paul Kingsbury's notes for "The Patsy Cline Collection" (MCA); "Creating the Nashville Sound: A Case Study in Commercial Culture Production," by Joli Jensen, degree dissertation for Doctor of Philosophy in Communications, University of Illinois, 1984.

Chapter 17

Interviews: Mae Boren Axton (7/31/92); Margie Bowes (3/26/92); Harold Bradley (3/25/92); Owen Bradley (5/31/91, 6/1/92); Hank Cochran (5/27/92); Floyd Cramer (6/9/92); Mel Dick (3/20/92); Donn Hecht (6/15/92, 10/11/92); Harlan Howard (3/27/92); Jan Howard (5/12/92); Kathy Hughes (1/9/93); Charlie Lamb (3/28/92); Patsy Lillis (11/30/92); Jim McCoy (3/5/91); Jean Shepard (3/27/92); Waylon "Stubby" Stubbyfield (5/15/92); Ray Walker (3/24/92); Teddy Wilburn (3/28/92); Rusty York (9/15/92); Faron Young (7/9/92).

Other sources: Nassour, *Patsy Cline* (Tower Books, 1981); "Change to C&W Boosts Audience, Profit," *Broadcasting*, 10/18/65; Marek, "Country Music, Nashville Style," *McCall's*, April 1961; Kienzle, "Harold Bradley: The Dean Reflects on 40 Years in Nashville's Studios," *Country Sounds*, September 1986; Kienzle, "The Forgotten Hank Garland," *Journal of Country Music*, vol. 9, no. 3, 1983; "Heartaches by the Score," by Robert Hilburn, *Los Angeles Times*, 6/14/92; correspondence, Donn Hecht, 6/15/92; Paul Kingsbury's album notes for "The Patsy Cline Collection" (MCA); "The Real Patsy Cline," Hallway Productions, Inc., 1989; *Willie: An Autobiography*, by Willie Nelson with Bud Shrake (Pocket Books, 1988); "Dakota Lil" copyright Sure-Fire Music Co., Inc.

Chapter 18

Interviews: Mae Boren Axton (7/31/92); Margie Bowes (3/26/92); Roy Deyton (5/19/91); Wally Fowler (3/28/92); Donn Hecht (10/11/92); Loretta Lynn (3/30/92); Pat Smallwood Miller (3/8/91); Billy Walker (2/16/93).

Other sources: Nassour, *Patsy Cline* (Tower Books, 1981). Will of Virginia Hensley Dick, dated 4/22/61, filed in the Probate Court for Davidson County, Tennessee, as part of a Dissent from Will motion filed by Charles A. Dick,

5/14/65; correspondence, Jim McCoy 7/7/61, courtesy the Handley Library Archives; "The Real Patsy Cline," Hallway Productions, Inc., 1989.

Chapter 19

Interviews: Ann Armstrong (1/17/93); Mae Boren Axton (2/24/93); Harold Bradley (3/25/92); Owen Bradley (2/16/90, 6/1/92); June Carter Cash (9/11/92); Hank Cochran; Harlan Howard (3/27/92); Kathy Hughes (1/9/93); Brenda Lee (4/20/92); Loretta Lynn (3/30/92); Willie Nelson (9/4/92); Gordon Stoker (3/24/92); Billy Walker; Ray Walker (3/24/92, 3/18/93).

Other Sources: "Car Smash Tied in with Hit Disc," *Disc*, 1962; "The girls are moving in," by Ren Grevatt, *Melody Maker*, 12/16/61; "WSM, CMA Hold Annual Events," *Billboard*, 11/6/61; *The Language of Show Biz* (Dramatic Publishing Co., Chicago); Nassour, *Patsy Cline* (Tower Books, 1981); "Staid Carnegie Set for Rural Assault," by Phil Sullivan, *Tennessean*, 11/29/61; " 'The Grand Ole Opry' Is Heard in a Program of Country Music," by Robert Shelton, *New York Times*, 11/30/61; Nelson, with Shrake, *Willie: An Autobiography* (Pocket Books, 1988); liner notes from *Patsy Cline Showcase* (DL 4202); "Dixie Jubilee" 12/2/61 broadcast transcription.

Chapter 20

Interviews: Ann Armstrong (1/17/93); Mae Boren Axton (2/24/93); Margie Bowes (3/26/92); June Carter Cash (9/11/92); Roy Deyton (5/19/91); Marshall Grant (3/5/93); Kathy Hughes (1/9/93); Barbara Mandrell; Pat Smallwood Miller (3/8/91); Billy Walker; Ray Walker (12/14/92); Johnny Western (1/18/93, 1/20/94); Teddy Wilburn; Faron Young (7/9/92).

Other sources: 1985 interview with Charlie Dick by Rita Whitfield for WCTV (Nashville), "Wraparound"; *Country: The Biggest Music in America*, by Nick Tosches, Stein and Day, 1977.

Chapter 21

Interviews: Johnny Anderson (5/24/91); Ann Armstrong (1/17/93); Margie Bowes (3/26/92); Jimmy Dean (5/19/92); George Hamilton IV; Donn Hecht (6/22/92); Joyce Jackson (1/7/93); Wanda Jackson (9/16/92); Buddy Killen (1/4/93); Loretta Lynn (3/30/92); Gordon Stoker, interviewed by Dale Vinicur 1992; Ray Walker (12/14/92).

Other sources: Nassour, *Patsy Cline* (Tower Books, 1981); "You're Stronger Than Me," "When I Get Thru with You (You'll Love Me Too)" copyright Tree Publishing Co., Inc.

Chapter 22

Interviews: Ann Armstrong (1/17/93); Mae Boren Axton (7/27/92); Owen Bradley (2/16/90); Sonny Deaton (2/20/93); Charlie Dick (6/1/91); Al Gallico (8/19/91); Don Gibson, interviewed by Dale Vinicur, 1992; Tompall Glaser (5/15/92); Marshall Grant (3/5/93); Donn Hecht (6/15/92, 6/29/92); Johnny Western (1/18/93); Bill Willard (11/29/92).

Other sources: Dottie West's quotes from Ellis Nassour's *Patsy Cline*; "Change to C&W Boosts Audience, Profit," *Broadcasting*, 10/18/65; "From Muskogee to Luckenbach: Country Music and the 'Southernization' of America," by James

C. Cobb, *Journal of Popular Culture*, Winter 1982; Paul Kingsbury's notes to "The Patsy Cline Collection" (MCA); correspondence, Donn Hecht, 6/16/92; "When You Need a Laugh" copyright Tree Publishing Co., Inc.; "Your Kinda Love" copyright Attain Music.

Chapter 23

Interviews: Johnny Western (1/18/93); June Carter Cash (9/11/92); Ray Walker (3/24/92, 3/18/93); Owen Bradley (2/16/90); Gordon Stoker interviewed by Dale Vinicur 1992; Harlan Howard (3/27/92); Faron Young (7/9/92).

Other sources: "Remembering Patsy," Hallway Productions, Inc., 1993; Paul Kingsbury, notes to "The Patsy Cline Collection" (MCA); "Leavin' on Your Mind" copyright Wayne Walker Music, Inc.

Chapter 24

Interviews: June Carter Cash (9/11/92); Al Gallico (8/19/91); Kathy Hughes (1/9/93) and as interviewed by Bill Anderson, "Yesteryears," The Nashville Network, 3/24/89; Patsy Lillis (11/30/92); Punk Longley (5/22/91 and 6/3/91); Loretta Lynn (3/30/92); Jim McCoy (3/5/91); Nellie Patterson (5/24/91); Jumbo Rinker (3/7/91); Jean Shepard interviewed by Bill Anderson, "Yesteryears," The Nashville Network, 3/24/89; Guy Smith (3/23/93); Billy Walker; Ann Call Wilson (3/23/93); Faron Young (1/6/93).

Other sources: Nassour, *Patsy Cline* (Tower Books, 1981); "Ohioana: A Lament for Ohio's Singing Cowboy," *Ohio Magazine*, October 1988; "Words of Cowboy Copas Had Prophetic Ring," by Frank Luppino, *Billboard*, 11/14/64; Higgins, "Sweet Dreams," *Winchester Evening Star*, 3/6/93; "4 Lost Lives Hurrying Home," by Phil Sullivan, *Tennessean*, 3/7/63; "Irony Tinges Opry Deaths," by Julie Hollabaugh, *Tennessean*, 3/7/63; "To Patsy with Love and Regret," by Brian Burnes, *Kansas City Star*, 3/2/93, and Brian Burnes's notes for the story; " '. . . Was Tops in Her Field, Only Way to Describe Her'," *Winchester Evening Star*, 3/6/63; "Dyersburg Airport Head Says Hughes Ignored Plea; Plane Crashed Hour Later," by Gerald Henry, *Tennessean*, 3/7/63; "Patsy Cline, 3 Others Killed in Plane Crash," *Winchester Evening Star*, 3/6/63; *Memories*, by Ralph Emery (MacMillan, 1992); "Disaster Stuns Country Greats," by Eugene Dietz, *Tennessean*, 3/7/63; "In Memoriam," *Music Reporter*, 3/23/63.

Epilogue

Sources: "Bittersweet Dreams" by Mike D'Orso, *Virginia Pilot & The Ledger Star*, 1/3/88; "Patsy Cline Gets a City Road," by Teresa Lazazzera, *Winchester Evening Star*, 12/10/87; "A Street Named for Patsy?" by Teresa Lazazzera, *Winchester Evening Star*, 2/27/86; "Fans Want 522 South for Patsy," by Terri Higgins, *Winchester Evening Star*, 11/8/86; "Many Years Later, Memorial to Patsy," by Terri Higgins, *Winchester Evening Star*, 2/10/87; "New School Named Indian Hollow," by Peter Krouse, *Winchester Evening Star*, 11/17/87; "Another Try for Patsy Cline Road," by Terri Higgins, *Winchester Evening Star*, 10/23/86.

This is a complete chronicle of Patsy Cline's recording career. Each session contains the following information (when available): date, time, personnel, Nashville Decca master numbers (assigned at the time of recording), New York Decca master numbers, song titles and composers, single releases, and album releases.

Patsy Cline's recordings have been reissued on more than a hundred different labels over the years and new albums continue to be released. The following list has been narrowed to include only the major releases. Included are all the original Decca, Vocalion, and Kapp (all presently owned by MCA) singles and albums, along with the current MCA product. The single numbers followed with (EP) refer to extended-play 45-rpm records that contain two songs per side. The album references include both the mono and stereo numbers plus the MCA reissue number when applicable. Also included are important collections on the RCA and Rhino labels. A list of singles and albums can be found at the end of the discography.

All sessions were produced by Owen Bradley and recorded at Bradley Film and Recording studios, Nashville, Tennessee, unless otherwise noted. Due to the unavailability of the 4 Star session sheets, session personnel through 1958 are not known for certain. Personnel listed are based on interviews with various session musicians and knowledge of musicians that were generally used during that era.

June 1, 1955; *Patsy Cline:* vocal; probably *Grady Martin:* electric guitar; *Harold Bradley:* acoustic guitar; *Don Helms:* steel guitar; *Bob Moore:* acoustic bass; *Tommy Jackson:* fiddle; *Farris Coursey:* drums; *Owen Bradley:* piano.

	HIDIN' OUT	Cor 61523	Rhn R2-70048
88219	[Eddie Miller– W. S. Stevenson]	Cor EC-81159(EP) De 25718	
	TURN THE CARDS SLOWLY	Cor 61523	MCA 1440;
88220	[Sammy Masters]	Cor EC-81159(EP)	MCA 4-10421; Rhn R2-70050

88221	A CHURCH, A COURTROOM, AND THEN GOODBYE [Eddie Miller– W. S. Stevenson]	Cor 61464 Cor ED-81159(EP)	MCA 4-10421; Rhn R2-70048
88222	HONKY-TONK MERRY-GO-ROUND [Frank Simon– Stan Gardner]	Cor 61464 Cor EC-81159(EP)	MCA 1463; MCA 4-10421; Rhn R2-70048

January 5, 1956; *Patsy Cline:* vocal; probably *Grady Martin:* electric guitar; *Harold Bradley:* acoustic guitar; *Don Helms:* steel guitar; *Bob Moore:* acoustic bass; *Tommy Jackson:* fiddle; *Farris Coursey:* drums; *Owen Bradley:* piano.

89149	I LOVE YOU HONEY [Eddie Miller]	Cor 61583	MCA 1463; MCA 4-10421; Rhn R2-70050
89150	COME ON IN (AND MAKE YOURSELF AT HOME) [V. F. Stewart]	Cor 61583	MCA 4-10421
89151	I CRIED ALL THE WAY TO THE ALTAR [B. Flournoy]		Rhn R2-70048
89152	I DON'T WANTA [E. Miller–W. S. Stevenson– Durwood Haddock]		MCA 4-10421

April 22, 1956; *Patsy Cline:* vocal; probably *Grady Martin:* electric guitar; *Harold Bradley:* acoustic guitar; *Don Helms:* steel guitar; *Bob Moore:* acoustic bass; *Tommy Jackson:* fiddle; *Farris Coursey:* drums; *Owen Bradley:* piano.

NA 9342 89855	STOP, LOOK AND LISTEN [George London– W. S. Stevenson]	De 29963	MCA 1440; MCA 4-10421; Rhn R2-70050
NA 9343 89856	I'VE LOVED AND LOST AGAIN [Eddie Miller]	De 29963	Vo VL-3753/ VL-73753/ MCA 738; MCA 1463; MCA 4-10421; Rhn R2-70048
NA 9344 89857	DEAR GOD [V. F. Stewart]	De 30794 De ED-2759(EP)	Rhn R2-70048
NA 9345 89858	HE WILL DO FOR YOU [V. F. Stewart]	De 30794 De ED-2759(EP)	Rhn R2-70048

November 8, 1956; *Patsy Cline:* vocal; probably *Grady Martin:* electric guitar; *Harold Bradley:* acoustic guitar; *Don Helms:* steel guitar; *Bob Moore:* acoustic bass; *Tommy Jackson:* fiddle; *Farris Coursey:* drums; *Owen Bradley:* piano.

NA 9539 101004	WALKIN' AFTER MIDNIGHT [Donn Hecht–Alan Block]	De 30221 MCA 60061	De 8611/ MCA 25200; MCA 12; MCA 4-10421; Rhn R2-70048
NA 9540 101005	THE HEART YOU BREAK MAY BE YOUR OWN [Tiny Colbert–Bob Geesling]		MCA 4-10421
NA 9541 101006	PICK ME UP ON YOUR WAY DOWN [Burton Levy– Glenn Reeves– Mae Boren Axton]	De 25732 MCA 60102	MCA 4-10421
NA 9542 101007	A POOR MAN'S ROSES (OR A RICH MAN'S GOLD) [Bob Hilliard– Milton Delugg]	De 30221	MCA 4-10421

April 24, 1957; probably Pythian Studio, New York, NY; *Patsy Cline:* vocal; unknown musicians and chorus.

102377	TODAY, TOMORROW AND FOREVER [Don Reid]	De 30339	MCA 1463; MCA 4-10421; Rhn R2-70049
102378	FINGERPRINTS [Donn Hecht– W. O. Fleener– W. S. Stevenson]	De ED-2542(EP)	De DL-8611/ MCA 25200; Vo VL-73872/ MCA 736; Rhn R2-70048
102379	A STRANGER IN MY ARMS [Charlotte White– Virginia Hensley– Mary Lu Jeans]	De 30406	Rhn R2-70048
102380	DON'T EVER LEAVE ME AGAIN [Lillian Claiborne– Virginia Hensley– James Crawford]		De DL-8611/ MCA 25200; Vo VL-73872/ MCA 736; MCA 1440; MCA 4-10421

April 25, 1957; probably Pythian Studio, New York, NY; *Patsy Cline:* vocal; unknown musicians; *Chorus:* Anita Kerr Singers [Anita Kerr; Dottie Dillard; Louis Nunley; Gil Wright].

	TRY AGAIN	De 30339	MCA 1463;
102381	[Bob Summers–Jerry Le Fors]		MCA 4-10421; Rhn R2-70048
	TOO MANY SECRETS	De 25738	De DL-8611/
102382	[Bobby Lile]		MCA 25200; Vo VL-73872/ MCA 736; MCA 1440; MCA 4-10421; Rhn R2-70050
	THEN YOU'LL KNOW	De 30504	De DL-8611/
102383	[Bobby Lile]		MCA 25200; Vo VL-73872/ MCA 736; MCA 4-10421; Rhn R2-70048
	THREE CIGARETTES IN AN ASHTRAY	De 30406 De ED-2542(EP)	De DL-8611/ MCA 25200;
102384	[Eddie Miller–W. S. Stevenson]		Vo VL-73872/ MCA 736; MCA 1440; MCA 4-10421; Rhn R2-70048

May 23, 1957; *Patsy Cline:* vocal; probably *Hank Garland:* electric guitar; *Grady Martin:* electric guitar; *Jack Shook:* acoustic guitar; *Harold Bradley:* electric bass; *Bob Moore:* acoustic bass; *Farris Coursey:* drums; *Owen Bradley:* piano; *Chorus:* Anita Kerr Singers [Anita Kerr; Dottie Dillard; Louis Nunley; Gil Wright].

NA 9829	THAT WONDERFUL	De ED-2542(EP)	De DL-8611/
102680	SOMEONE [Gertrude Berg]		MCA 25200; Vo VL-73872/ MCA 736; MCA 4-10421; Rhn R2-70049
NA 9830	IN CARE OF THE BLUES	De 25744	De DL-8611/
102681	[Eddie Miller–W. S. Stevenson]		MCA 25200; Vo VL-3753/ VL-73753/ MCA 738; MCA 1440; MCA 4-10421; Rhn R2-70050

NA 9831 102682	HUNGRY FOR LOVE [Eddie Miller–W. S. Stevenson]	De ED-2542(EP)	De DL-8611/ MCA 25200; Vo 73872/ MCA 736; MCA 4-10421; Rhn R2-70049
NA 9832 102683	I CAN'T FORGET [W. S. Stevenson– Carl Belew]		De DL-8611/ MCA 25200; Vo VL-73872/ MCA 736; MCA 4-10421; Rhn R2-70049
NA 9833 102684	I DON'T WANTA [Eddie Miller– W. S. Stevenson– Durwood Haddock]	De 30504	De DL-8611/ MCA 25200; Vo VL-73872/ MCA 736; Rhn R2-70050
NA 9834 102685	AIN'T NO WHEELS ON THIS SHIP (WE CAN'T ROLL) [W. D. Chandler– W. S. Stevenson]		De DL-8611/ MCA 25200; Vo VL-73872/ MCA 736; MCA 1440; Rhn R2-70050

December 13, 1957; *Patsy Cline:* vocal; probably *Hank Garland:* electric guitar; *Grady Martin:* electric guitar; *Bob Moore:* acoustic bass; *Farris Coursey:* drums; *Owen Bradley:* piano/organ; *Unknown:* vibes; *Chorus:* Anita Kerr Singers [Anita Kerr; Dottie Dillard; Louis Nunley; Gil Wright]

NA 10039 103878	STOP THE WORLD (AND LET ME OFF) [Carl Belew– W. S. Stevenson]	De 30542	Vo VL-3753/ VL-73753/ MCA 738; Rhn R2-70049
NA 10040 103879	WALKING DREAM [Hal Willis–Ginger Willis]	De 30542	Vo VL-3753/ VL-73753/ MCA 738; Rhn R2-70050
NA 10041 103880	CRY NOT FOR ME [Donn Hecht–Jack Moon]	De 30846	Rhn R2-70049
NA 10042 103881	IF I COULD SEE THE WORLD (THROUGH THE EYES OF A CHILD) [Sammy Masters– Richard Pope– Tex Satterwhite]	De 30746	Vo VL-3753/ VL-73753/ MCA 738; MCA 1440; MCA 4-10421; Rhn R2-70049

February 13, 1958; *Patsy Cline:* vocal; probably *Hank Garland:* electric guitar; *Grady Martin:* electric guitar/electric bass/banjo; *Bob Moore:* acoustic bass; *Buddy Harmon:* drums; *Floyd Cramer:* piano; *Unknown:* horns; *Chorus:* Anita Kerr Singers [Anita Kerr; Dottie Dillard; Louis Nunley; Gil Wright].

NA 10122 104577	JUST OUT OF REACH [V. F. Stewart]	De 30746	Vo VL-3753/ VL-73753/ MCA 738; MCA 1440; MCA 4-10421; Rhn R2-70049
NA 10123 104578	I CAN SEE AN ANGEL [Kay Adelman]	De 30706	MCA 1463; MCA 4-10421; Rhn R2-70049
NA 10124 104582	COME ON IN (AND MAKE YOURSELF AT HOME) [V. F. Stewart]	De 30659	
NA 10125 104579	LET THE TEARDROPS FALL [C. C. Beam–C. L. Jiles– W. S. Stevenson]	De 30659	MCA 1463; MCA 4-10421; Rhn R2-70050
NA 10126 104580	NEVER NO MORE [Rita Ross–Alan Block]	De 30706	MCA 1440; MCA 4-10421; Rhn R2-70050
NA 10127 104581	IF ONLY I COULD STAY ASLEEP [Ethel Bassey– Wayland Chandler]		MCA 1463; MCA 4-10421; Rhn R2-70049

January 8, 1959 [5 P.M.–8:30 P.M.]; *Patsy Cline:* vocal; *Hank Garland:* electric guitar; *Grady Martin:* electric guitar; *Harold Bradley:* 6-string electric bass; *Bob Moore:* acoustic bass; *Buddy Harmon:* drums; *Floyd Cramer:* piano; *Chorus:* The Jordanaires [Gordon Stoker; Hoyt Hawkins; Neal Matthews, Jr.; Ray Walker].

NA 10554 106452	I'M MOVING ALONG [Johnny Starr]	De ED-2768 (EP) De ED-2802 (EP)	De DL-4586/ DL-74586; MCA 1463; MCA 4-10421; Rhn R2-70050
NA 10555 106453	I'M BLUE AGAIN [C. C. Beam–C. L. Jiles– W. S. Stevenson]	De 30929 De ED-2768 (EP)	De DL-4586/ DL-74586; MCA 1463; MCA 4-10421; Rhn R2-70049

NA 10556	LOVE LOVE LOVE ME	De 25724	De DL-4586/
106454	HONEY DO	De ED-2768 (EP)	DL-74586
	[C. C. Beam–C. L. Jiles–		MCA 1463;
	W. S. Stevenson]		MCA 4-10421;
			Rhn R2-70050

January 9, 1959 [2 P.M.–5 P.M.]; *Patsy Cline:* vocal; *Hank Garland:* electric guitar; *Grady Martin:* electric guitar; *Harold Bradley:* 6-string electric bass; *Bob Moore:* acoustic bass; *Farris Coursey:* drums; *Floyd Cramer:* piano; *Chorus:* The Jordanaires [Gordon Stoker; Hoyt Hawkins; Neal Matthews, Jr.; Ray Walker].

NA 10557	YES, I UNDERSTAND	De 30846	Vo VL-3753/
106455	[C. C. Beam–		VL-73753/
	W. S. Stevenson–		MCA 738;
	C. L. Jiles]		MCA 4-10421;
			Rhn R2-70049
NA 10558	GOTTA LOT OF RHYTHM	De 30929	MCA 1463
106456	IN MY SOUL		MCA 4-10421;
	[Barbara Vaughn–W. S. Stevenson]		Rhn R2-70050

July 3, 1959 [12:30 P.M.–3:30 P.M.]; *Patsy Cline:* vocal; *Hank Garland:* electric guitar; *Grady Martin:* electric guitar; *Bob Moore:* acoustic bass; *Buddy Harmon:* drums; *Floyd Cramer:* piano; *Chorus:* The Jordanaires [Gordon Stoker; Hoyt Hawkins; Neal Matthews, Jr.; Ray Walker].

NA 10789	LIFE'S RAILWAY TO HEAVEN	De ED-2759 (EP)	Vo VL-3753/
107844	[Arr. by W. S. Stevenson]		VL-73753/
			MCA 738;
			MCA 4-10421;
			Rhn R2-70049
NA 10790	JUST A CLOSER WALK	De ED-2759 (EP)	Vo VL-3753/
107845	WITH THEE		VL-73753/
	[Arr. by W. S. Stevenson]		MCA 738;
			MCA 4-10421;
			Rhn R2-70049

January 27, 1960; *Pasty Cline:* vocal; *Hank Garland:* electric guitar; *Grady Martin:* electric guitar/fiddle; *Jimmy Day:* steel guitar; *Harold Bradley:* 6-string electric bass; *Bob Moore:* acoustic bass; *Buddy Harmon:* drums; *Floyd Cramer:* piano.

NA 10964	LOVESICK BLUES	De 31061	De DL-4586/
108693	[Irving Mills–Cliff Friend]	De ED-2703 (EP)	DL-74586;
			MCA 4-10421
NA 10965	HOW CAN I FACE	De 31061	Vo VL-3753/
108694	TOMORROW?	De ED-2768 (EP)	VL-73753/
	[C. C. Beam–C. L. Jiles–		MCA 738;
	W. S. Stevenson]		MCA 4-10421

NA 10966 108695	THERE HE GOES [Eddie Miller–Durwood Haddock–W. S. Stevenson]	De 31128 De ED-2703 (EP)	De DL-4586/ DL-74586; MCA 4-10421
NA 10967 108696	CRAZY DREAMS [C. C. Beam–C. L. Jiles–W. S. Stevenson]	De 31128	De DL-4586/ DL-74586; MCA 4-10421

November 16, 1960 [2:30 P.M.–5:30 P.M.]; *Patsy Cline:* vocal; *Hank Garland:* electric guitar; *Randy Hughes:* acoustic guitar; *Ben Keith:* steel guitar; *Harold Bradley:* 6-string electric bass; *Bob Moore:* acoustic bass; *Doug Kirkham:* drums; *Hargus "Pig" Robbins:* piano: *Chorus:* The Jordanaires [Gordon Stoker; Hoyt Hawkins; Neal Matthews, Jr.; Ray Walker].

NA 11314 109887	I FALL TO PIECES [Hank Cochran–Harlan Howard]	De 31205 De ED-2703 (EP) MCA 60062	De DL-4202/ DL-74202/ MCA 87; De DXB-176/ DXSB-7176/ MCA 2-4038; De DL-4854/ DL-74584/ MCA 12; MCA 6149; MCA 4-10421; RCA AHL1-4127
NA 11315 109888	SHOES [Hank Cochran–Velma Smith]	De 25694	De DL-4586/ DL-74586; MCA 1440; MCA 4-10421
NA 11316 109889	LOVIN' IN VAIN [Freddie Hart]	De 31205 De ED-2703 (EP)	De DL-4586/ DL-74586; MCA 25019; MCA 4-10421

August 17, 1961 [2 P.M.–6 P.M.]; *Patsy Cline:* vocal; *Grady Martin:* electric guitar; *Randy Hughes:* acoustic guitar; *Walter Haynes:* steel guitar; *Harold Bradley:* 6-string electric guitar; *Bob Moore:* acoustic bass; *Buddy Harmon:* drums; *Hargus "Pig" Robbins:* piano; *Violins:* Brenton Banks; George Binkley III; Lillian Hunt; Suzanne Parker; *Viola:* Cecil Brower; *Cello:* Byron Bach; *Chorus:* The Jordanaires [Gordon Stoker; Hoyt Hawkins; Neal Matthews, Jr.; Ray Walker]; Arranged by Bill McElhiney.

NA 11659 111030	TRUE LOVE [Cole Porter]	De 25724	De DL-4202/ DL-74202/ MCA 87; De DXB-176/

			DXSB-7176/ MCA 2-4038; MCA 4-10421
NA 11660 111031	SAN ANTONIO ROSE [Bob Wills]	De 25673	De DL-4202/ DL-74202/ MCA 87; De DXB-176/ DXSB-7176/ MCA 2-4038; MCA 4-10421
NA 11661 111032	THE WAYWARD WIND [Stan Lebowsky– Herb Newman]	De 25747 De ED-2719(EP)	De DL-4202/ DL-74202/ MCA 87; De DXB-176/ DXSB-7176/ MCA 2-4038; MCA 4-10421
NA 11662 111033	A POOR MAN'S ROSES (OR A RICH MAN'S GOLD) [Bob Hilliard– Milton Delugg]		De DL-4202/ DL-74202/ MCA 87; De DXB-176/ DXSB-7176/ MCA 2-4038; MCA 1440; MCA 4-10421; Rhn R2-70048

August 21, 1961 [7:15 P.M.–11:15 P.M.]; *Patsy Cline:* vocal; *Grady Martin:* electric guitar; *Randy Hughes:* acoustic guitar; *Walter Haynes:* steel guitar; *Harold Bradley:* 6-string electric bass; *Bob Moore:* acoustic bass; *Buddy Harmon:* drums; *Floyd Cramer:* piano/organ; *Chorus:* The Jordanaires [Gordon Stoker; Hoyt Hawkins; Neal Matthews, Jr.; Ray Walker].

NA 11671 111037	CRAZY [Willie Nelson]	De 31317 De ED-2707 (EP) MCA 60063	De DL-4202/ DL-74202/ MCA 87; De DXB-176/ DXSB-7176/ MCA 2-4038; De DL-4854/ DL-74854/ MCA 12; MCA 6149; MCA 25019; MCA 4-10421; RCA AHL1-4127

August 24, 1961 [1:45 P.M.–5:45 P.M.]; *Patsy Cline:* vocal; *Grady Martin:* electric guitar; *Randy Hughes:* acoustic guitar; *Walter Haynes:* steel guitar; *Harold Bradley:* 6-string electric bass; *Bob Moore:* acoustic bass; *Buddy Harmon:* drums; *Hargus "Pig" Robbins:* piano; *Floyd Cramer:* organ; *Chorus:* The Jordanaires [Gordon Stoker; Hoyt Hawkins; Neal Matthews, Jr.; Ray Walker].

NA 11672	WHO CAN I COUNT ON?	De 31317	De DL-4508/
111048	[Sammy Masters]	De ED-2707 (EP)	DL-74508/
			MCA 224;
			MCA 4-10421
NA 11673	SEVEN LONELY DAYS	De 25686	De DL-4202/
111049	[Earl Shuman–		DL-74202/
	Alden Shuman–		MCA 87;
	Marshall Brown]		De DXB-176/
			DXSB-7176/
			MCA 2-4038;
			MCA 4-10421
NA 11674	I LOVE YOU SO MUCH	De 25686	De DL-4202/
111050	IT HURTS	De ED-2719 (EP)	DL-74202/
	[Floyd Tillman]		MCA 87;
			De DXB-176/
			DXSB-7176/
			MCA 2-4038;
			MCA 25019;
			MCA 4-10421
NA 11675	FOOLIN' 'ROUND	De 25707	De DL-4202/
111051	[Harlan Howard–	ED-2707 (EP)	DL-74202/
	Buck Owens]		MCA 87;
			De DXB-176/
			DXSB-7176/
			MCA 2-4038;
			MCA 4-10421
NA 11676	HAVE YOU EVER BEEN	De 25718	De DL-4202/
111052	LONELY (HAVE YOU EVER		DL-74202/
	BEEN BLUE)?		MCA 87;
	[Peter DeRose–George Brown]		MCA 4-10421

August 25, 1961 [2:30 P.M.–6:30 P.M.]; *Patsy Cline:* vocal; *Grady Martin:* electric guitar; *Randy Hughes:* acoustic guitar; *Walter Haynes:* steel guitar; *Harold Bradley:* 6-string electric bass; *Bob Moore:* acoustic bass; *Buddy Harmon:* drums; *Hargus "Pig" Robbins:* piano; *Floyd Cramer:* organ; *Chorus:* The Jordanaires [Gordon Stoker; Hoyt Hawkins; Neal Matthews, Jr.; Ray Walker].

NA 11681	SOUTH OF THE BORDER	De 25673	De DL-4202/
11057	(DOWN MEXICO WAY)	De ED-2707 (EP)	DL-74202/
	[Michael Carr–	MCA 60061	MCA 87;
	Jimmy Kennedy]		De DXB-176/

			DXSB-7176/ MCA 2-4038; MCA 4-10421
NA 11682 111058	WALKIN' AFTER MIDNIGHT [Donn Hecht–Alan Block]		De DL-4202/ DL-74202/ MCA 87; De DXB-176/ DXSB-7176/ MCA 2-4038; De DL-4854/ DL-74854/ MCA 12; MCA 5319/ MCA 1467; MCA 4-10421
NA 11683 111059	STRANGE [Mel Tillis–Fred Burch]	De 31354 De ED-2719 (EP)	De DL-4282/ DL-74282/ MCA 90; De DXB-176/ DXSB-7176/ MCA 2-4038; De DL-4854/ DL-74854/ MCA 12; MCA 4-10421
NA 11684 111060	YOU'RE STRONGER THAN ME [Hank Cochran–Jimmy Key]		De DXB-176/ DXSB-7176/ MCA 2-4038; De DL-4854/ DL-74854/ MCA 12; MCA 4-10421

December 17, 1961 [7:10 P.M.–10:40 P.M.]; *Patsy Cline:* vocal; *Grady Martin:* electric guitar; *Randy Hughes:* acoustic guitar; *Walter Haynes:* steel guitar; *Harold Bradley:* 6-string electric bass; *Bob Moore:* acoustic bass; *Buddy Harmon:* drums; *Floyd Cramer:* piano; *Bill Pursell:* organ; *Chorus:* The Jordanaires [Gordon Stoker; Hoyt Hawkins; Neal Matthews, Jr.; Ray Walker].

| NA 11832
111504 | SHE'S GOT YOU
[Hank Cochran] | De 31354
De ED-2719 (EP) | De DL-4282/
DL-74282/
MCA 90;
De DXB-176/
DXSB-7176/
MCA 2-4038;
De DL-4854/
DL-74854/ |

MCA 12;
MCA 6149;
MCA 4-10421;
RCA AHL1-4127

February 12, 1962 [7:15 P.M.–10:45 P.M.]; *Patsy Cline:* vocal; *Grady Martin:* electric guitar; *Ray Edenton:* rhythm guitar; *Randy Hughes:* acoustic guitar; *Walter Haynes:* steel guitar; *Harold Bradley:* 6-string electric bass; *Bob Moore:* acoustic bass; *Buddy Harmon:* drums; *Floyd Cramer:* piano; *Bill Pursell:* organ; *Chorus:* The Jordanaires [Gordon Stoker; Hoyt Hawkins; Neal Matthews, Jr.; Ray Walker].

NA 11905	YOU MADE ME LOVE YOU	De 25738	De DL-4282/
111781	(I DIDN'T WANT TO DO IT)		DL-74282/
	[Joe McCarthy–James V. Monaco]		MCA 90;
			MCA 4-10421
NA 11906	YOU BELONG TO ME		De DL-4282/
111782	[Pee Wee King–		DL-74282/
	Redd Stewart–		MCA 90;
	Chilton Price]		De DXB-176/
			DXSB-7176/
			MCA 2-4038;
			MCA 4-10421
NA 11907	HEARTACHES	De 31429	De DL-4282/
111783	[Al Hoffman–John Klenner]	De ED-2729(EP)	DL-74282/
			MCA 90;
			De DXB-176/
			DXSB-7176/
			MCA 2-4038;
			MCA 4-10421
NA 11908	YOUR CHEATIN' HEART	De 31754	De DL-4282/
111784	[Hank Williams]	De ED-2729(EP)	DL-74282/
		MCA 60063	MCA 90;
			De DXB-176/
			DXSB-7176/
			MCA 2-4038;
			MCA 4-10421

February 13, 1962 [7:15 P.M.–10:45 P.M.]; *Patsy Cline:* vocal; *Grady Martin:* electric guitar; *Ray Edenton:* rhythm guitar; *Randy Hughes:* acoustic guitar; *Walter Haynes:* steel guitar; *Harold Bradley:* 6-string electric bass; *Bob Moore:* acoustic bass; *Buddy Harmon:* drums; *Charlie McCoy:* harmonica; *Floyd Cramer:* piano; *Bill Pursell:* organ; *Chorus:* The Jordanaires [Gordon Stoker; Hoyt Hawkins; Neal Matthews, Jr.; Ray Walker].

NA 11909	THAT'S MY DESIRE	De 25707	De DL-4282/
111800	[Helmy Kresa–		DL-74282/
	Carroll Loveday]		MCA 90;
			MCA 4-10421

NA 11910	HALF AS MUCH	De 25694	De DL-4282/
111801	[Curley Williams]	De ED-2757(EP)	DL-74282/
			MCA 90;
			MCA 4-10421

February 15, 1962 [7:15 P.M.–11:45 P.M.]; *Patsy Cline:* vocal; *Grady Martin:* electric guitar; *Ray Edenton:* rhythm guitar; *Randy Hughes:* acoustic guitar; *Walter Haynes:* steel guitar; *Harold Bradley:* 6-string electric bass; *Bob Moore:* acoustic bass; *Buddy Harmon:* drums; *Charlie McCoy:* harmonica; *Floyd Cramer:* piano; *Bill Pursell:* organ; *Violins:* Brenton Banks; Cecil Brower; Solie Fott; Lillian Hunt; Verne Richardson; *Chorus:* The Jordanaires [Gordon Stoker; Hoyt Hawkins; Neal Matthews, Jr.; Ray Walker]; Arranged by Bill Justis.

NA 11911	LONELY STREET	De 25699	De DL-4282/
111802	[Carl Belew–	De ED-2757(EP)	DL-74282/
	W. S. Stevenson–		MCA 90;
	Kenny Sowder]		MCA 4-10421

NA 11912	ANYTIME	De 25744	De DL-4282/
111803	[Herbert "Happy" Lawson]		DL-74282
			MCA 90;
			MCA 4-10421

NA 11913	YOU WERE ONLY FOOLING	De 25699	De DL-4282/
111804	(WHILE I WAS FALLING		DL-74282/
	IN LOVE)		MCA 90;
	[Larry Fotine–Billy Faber–		MCA 4-10421
	Fred Meadows]		

NA 11914	I CAN'T HELP IT (IF I'M	De 31754	De DL-4282/
111805	STILL IN LOVE WITH YOU)		DL-74282/
	[Hank Williams]		MCA 90;
			MCA 4-10421

February 28, 1962 [7:15 P.M.–11:15 P.M.]; *Patsy Cline:* vocal; *Grady Martin:* electric guitar; *Ray Edenton:* rhythm guitar; *Randy Hughes:* acoustic guitar; *Harold Bradley:* 6-string electric bass; *Joe Zinkan:* acoustic bass; *Buddy Harmon:* drums; *Floyd Cramer:* piano; *Violins:* Brenton Banks; Cecil Brower; Lillian Hunt; Verne Richardson; *Violas:* Howard Carpenter; Ed Tarpley; *Cello:* Byron Bach; *Chorus:* The Jordanaires [Gordon Stoker; Hoyt Hawkins; Neal Matthews, Jr.; Ray Walker]; Arranged by Bill McElhiney.

NA 11928	YOU'RE STRONGER	De 31406	MCA 25019;
111889	THAN ME	De ED-2729(EP)	MCA 4-10421
	[Hank Cochran–		
	Jimmy Key]		

NA 11929	WHEN I GET THRU WITH	De 31377	De DL-4508/
111890	YOU (YOU'LL LOVE ME TOO)		DL-74508/
	[Harlan Howard]		MCA 224;
			MCA 4-10421

NA 11930	IMAGINE THAT	De 31377	De DXB-176/
111891	[Justin Tubb]		DXSB-7176/
			MCA 2-4038;
			MCA 25019;
			MCA 4-10421

NA 11931	SO WRONG	De 31406	De DXB-176/
111892	[Carl Perkins–Danny Dill–	De ED-2729(EP)	DXSB-7176/
	Mel Tillis]		MCA 2-4038;
			De DL-4854/
			DL-74854/
			MCA 12;
			MCA 5319/1467;
			MCA 25019;
			MCA 4-10421

September 5, 1962 [2 P.M.–6 P.M.]; *Patsy Cline:* vocal; *Grady Martin:* electric guitar; *Ray Edenton:* rhythm guitar; *Randy Hughes:* acoustic guitar; *Harold Bradley:* 6-string electric bass; *Bob Moore:* acoustic bass; *Buddy Harmon:* drums; *Hargus "Pig" Robbins:* piano; *Rita Faye Wilson:* autoharp; *Violins:* Cecil Brower; Solie Fott; Nancy Hearn; Lillian Hunt; *Violas:* Verne Richardson; Howard Carpenter; *Cello:* Byron Bach; *Chorus:* The Jordanaires [Gordon Stoker; Hoyt Hawkins; Neal Matthews, Jr.; Ray Walker]; Arranged by Bill McElhiney.

NA 12192	WHY CAN'T HE BE YOU?	De 31429	De DXB-176/
112595	[Hank Cochran]		DXSB-7176/
			MCA 2-4038;
			De DL-4854/
			DL-74854/
			MCA 12;
			MCA 5319/1467;
			MCA 4-10421

NA 12193	YOUR KINDA LOVE	De 31588	De DL-4508/
112596	[Roy Drusky]		DL-74508/
			MCA 224;
			MCA 25019;
			MCA 4-10421

NA 12194	WHEN YOU NEED A LAUGH	De 31552	De DL-4508/
112597	[Hank Cochran]	De ED-2770(EP)	DL-74508/
			MCA 224;
			MCA 25019;
			MCA 4-10421

NA 12195	LEAVIN' ON YOUR MIND	De 31455	De DXB-176/
112598	[Wayne Walker–	De ED-2757(EP)	DXSB-7176/
	Webb Pierce]		MCA 2-4038;
			De DL-4854/

DL-74854/
MCA 12;
MCA 5319/1467;
MCA 25019;
MCA 4-10421

September 10, 1962 [2P.M.–5P.M.]; *Patsy Cline:* vocal; *Grady Martin:* electric guitar; *Ray Edenton:* rhythm guitar; *Randy Hughes:* acoustic guitar; *Harold Bradley:* 6-string bass; *Bob Moore:* acoustic bass; *Buddy Harmon:* drums; *Hargus "Pig" Robbins:* piano; *Bill Pursell:* organ; *Violins:* Brenton Banks; Cecil Brower; Solie Fott; Lillian Hunt; Verne Richardson; Michael Semanitzky; *Chorus:* The Jordanaires [Gordon Stoker; Hoyt Hawkins; Neal Matthews, Jr.; Ray Walker]; Millie Kirkham; Arranged by Bill Justis.

NA 12196	BACK IN BABY'S ARMS	De 31483	De DXB-176/
112628	[Bob Montgomery]		DXSB-7176/
			MCA 2-4038;
			De DL-4854/
			DL-74854/
			MCA 12;
			MCA 5319/1467
			MCA 4-10421
NA 12197	TRA LE LA LE LA TRIANGLE	De 31455	De DXB-176/
112629	[Marijohn Wilkin–	De ED-2757(EP)	DXSB-7176/
	Fred Burch]		MCA 2-4038;
			MCA 4-10421
NA 12198	THAT'S HOW A HEARTACHE	De 31616	De DL-4586/
112630	BEGINS	De ED-2802(EP)	DL-74586;
	[Harlan Howard]		MCA 25019;
			MCA 4-10421

February 4, 1963 [7P.M.–10P.M.]; *Patsy Cline:* vocal; *Grady Martin:* electric guitar; *Ray Edenton:* rhythm guitar; *Randy Hughes:* acoustic guitar; *Harold Bradley:* 6-string electric bass; *Bob Moore:* acoustic bass; *Buddy Harmon:* drums; *Floyd Cramer:* piano; *Violins:* Brenton Banks; George Binkley III; Solie Fott; Lillian Hunt; Martin Katahn; *Violas:* Howard Carpenter; Cecil Brower; *Cellos:* Byron Bach; Gary Williams; *Chorus:* The Jordanaires [Gordon Stoker; Hoyt Hawkins; Neal Matthews, Jr.; Ray Walker]; Arranged by Bill McElhiney.

NA 12359	FADED LOVE	De 31522	De DL-4508/
113131	[John Wills–Bob Wills]	De ED-2770(EP)	DL-74508/
			MCA 224;
			De DL-4854/
			DL-74854/
			MCA 12;
			MCA 4-10421

NA 12360 113132	SOMEDAY (YOU'LL WANT ME TO WANT YOU) [Jimmie Hodges]	De 31588 De ED-2770(EP)	De DL-4508/ DL-74508/ MCA 224; MCA 25199; MCA 4-10421
NA 12361 113133	LOVE LETTERS IN THE SAND [J. Fred Coots– Nick Kenny– Charles Kenny]	De 31616 De ED-2802(EP)	De DL-4586/ DL-74586; MCA 25199; MCA 4-10421

February 5, 1963 [7P.M.–10P.M]; *Patsy Cline:* vocal; *Grady Martin:* electric guitar; *Ray Edenton:* rhythm guitar; *Randy Hughes:* acoustic guitar; *Harold Bradley:* 6-string electric bass; *Bob Moore:* acoustic bass; *Buddy Harmon:* drums; *Floyd Cramer:* piano; *Bill Pursell:* vibes; *Violins:* Brenton Banks; George Binkley III; Solie Fott; Lillian Hunt; Wilda Tinsley; *Violas:* Howard Carpenter; Cecil Brower; *Cellos:* Byron Bach; Gary Williams; *Chorus:* The Jordanaires [Gordon Stoker; Hoyt Hawkins; Neal Matthews, Jr.; Ray Walker]; Arranged by Bill McElhiney.

NA 12362 113134	BLUE MOON OF KENTUCKY [Bill Monroe]	De 31522	De DL-4508/ DL-74508/ MCA 224; MCA 25199; MCA 4-10421
NA 12363 113135	SWEET DREAMS [Don Gibson]	De 31483 MCA 52684	De DXB-176/ DXSB-7176/ MCA 2-4038; De DL-4854/ DL-74854/ MCA 12; MCA 6149; MCA 25199; MCA 4-10421; RCA AHL1-4127
NA 12364 113136	ALWAYS [Irving Berlin]	De 25732 De ED-2794(EP)	De DL-4508/ DL-74508/ MCA 224; MCA 25199; MCA 4-10421

February 6, 1963 [7P.M.–10P.M.]; *Patsy Cline:* vocal; *Grady Martin:* electric guitar; *Ray Edenton:* rhythm guitar; *Randy Hughes:* acoustic guitar; *Harold Bradley:* 6-string electric bass; *Bob Moore:* acoustic bass; *Buddy Harmon:* drums; *Floyd Cramer:* piano; *Violins:* Brenton Banks; George Binkley III; Solie Fott; Lillian Hunt; Wilda Tinsley; *Violas:* Howard Carpenter; Cecil Brower; *Cellos:* Byron Bach; Gary Williams; *Chorus:* The Jordanaires [Gordon Stoker; Hoyt Hawkins; Neal Matthews, Jr.; Ray Walker]; Arranged by Bill McElhiney.

NA 12365	DOES YOUR HEART	De 25712	De DL-4508/
113154	BEAT FOR ME	De ED-2794(EP)	DL-74508/
	[Russ Morgan–		MCA 224;
	Arnold Johnson–		MCA 25199;
	Mitchell Parrish]		MCA 4-10421

NA 12366	BILL BAILEY, WON'T YOU	De 31671	De DL-4586/
113155	PLEASE COME HOME		DL-74586
	[Hughie Cannon]		MCA 25199;
			MCA 4-10421

February 7, 1963 [7P.M.–10P.M.]; *Patsy Cline:* vocal; *Grady Martin:* electric guitar; *Ray Edenton:* rhythm guitar; *Randy Hughes:* acoustic guitar; *Wayne Moss:* 6-string electric bass; *Bob Moore:* acoustic bass; *Buddy Harmon:* drums; *Floyd Cramer:* piano; *Violins:* Brenton Banks; George Binkley III; Solie Fott; Lillian Hunt; Martin Katahn; Mildred Oonk; Verne Richardson; *Viola:* Howard Carpenter; *Cellos:* Byron Bach; Gary Williams; *Chorus:* The Jordanaires [Gordon Stoker; Hoyt Hawkins; Neal Matthews, Jr.; Ray Walker]; Arranged by Bill McElhiney.

NA 12371	HE CALLED ME BABY	De 31671	De DL-4586/
113160	[Harlan Howard]	De ED-2802(EP)	DL-74586;
		MCA 60062	MCA 25019;
			MCA 25199;
			MCA 4-10421

NA 12372	CRAZY ARMS	De 25747	De DL-4508/
113161	[Chuck Seals–Ray Price]	De ED-2794(EP)	DL-74508/
		MCA 60102	MCA 224;
			MCA 25199;
			MCA 4-10421

NA 12373	YOU TOOK HIM OFF	De 25712	De DL-4508/
113162	MY HANDS	De ED-2794(EP)	DL-74508/
	[Harlan Howard–		MCA 224;
	Wynn Stewart–		MCA 25019;
	Skeets McDonald]		MCA 25199;
			MCA 4-10421

NA 12374	I'LL SAIL MY SHIP ALONE	De 31552	De DL-4508/
113163	[Henry Bernard–	De ED-2770(EP)	DL-74508/
	Henry Thurston–		MCA 224;
	Lois Mann–Morry Burns]		MCA 4-10421

Date unknown: Ryman Auditorium, Nashville, TN; Recorded during one of Wally Fowler's "All-Night Gospel Sing"; *Patsy Cline:* vocal; unknown pianist and chorus.

	JUST A CLOSER WALK WITH	Ka K-659	Ka KL-1445/
	THEE [traditional]		KS-3445;
			MCA 4-10421

Singles

Highest Billboard Chart Position				
Country	*Pop*	*Release Date*	*Record Label & Number*	*Song Titles (A Side/B Side)*
—	—	07/20/55	Coral 61464	A Church, a Courtroom, and Then Goodbye/ Honky-Tonk Merry-Go-Round
—	—	11/05/55	Coral 61523	Hidin' Out/Turn the Cards Slowly
—	—	02/05/56	Coral 61583	I Love You, Honey/Come On In
—	—	07/08/56	Decca 29963	I've Loved and Lost Again/Stop, Look and Listen
02/14	12	02/11/57	Decca 30221	Walkin' After Midnight/A Poor Man's Roses (Or a Rich Man's Gold)
—	—	05/27/57	Decca 30339	Today, Tomorrow and Forever/Try Again
—	—	08/12/57	Decca 30406	Three Cigarettes in an Ashtray/A Stranger in My Arms
—	—	11/18/57	Decca 30504	I Don't Wanta/Then You'll Know
—	—	01/13/58	Decca 30542	Stop the World (And Let Me Off)/Walking Dream
—	—	06/02/58	Decca 30659	Come On In/Let the Teardrops Fall
—	—	08/18/58	Decca 30706	I Can See an Angel/Never No More
—	—	09/09/58	Decca 30746	If I Could See the World (Through the Eyes of a Child)/Just Out of Reach (Of My Two Open Arms)
—	—	12/15/58	Decca 30794	Dear God/He Will Do for You
—	—	02/23/59	Decca 30846	Yes, I Understand/Cry Not for Me
—	—	07/20/59	Decca 30929	Gotta Lot of Rhythm in My Soul/I'm Blue Again
—	—	03/07/60	Decca 31061	Lovesick Blues/How Can I Face Tomorrow?

—	—	08/01/60	Decca 31128	Crazy Dreams/There He Goes
01	12	01/30/61	Decca 31205	I Fall to Pieces/Lovin' in Vain
02	09/99	10/16/61	Decca 31317	Crazy/Who Can I Count On?
01	14/97	01/10/62	Decca 31354	She's Got You/Strange
10/21	53/90	05/07/62	Decca 31377	When I Get Thru With You (You'll Love Me Too)/Imagine That
14	85	07/16/62	Decca 31406	So Wrong/You're Stronger Than Me
—	73	10/08/62	Decca 31429	Heartaches/Why Can't He Be You?
08	83	01/07/63	Decca 31455	Leavin' on Your Mind/Tra Le La Le La Triangle
05	44	04/15/63	Decca 31483	Sweet Dreams (of You)/Back in Baby's Arms
07	96	08/05/63	Decca 31522	Faded Love/Blue Moon of Kentucky
47	—	10/28/63	Decca 31552	When You Need a Laugh/I'll Sail My Ship Alone
—	—	02/20/64	Decca 31588	Your Kinda Love/Someday You'll Want Me to Want You
—	—	04/27/64	Decca 31616	That's How a Heartache Begins/Love Letters in the Sand
23	—	09/14/64	Decca 31671	He Called Me Baby/Bill Bailey, Won't You Please Come Home
—	—	02/10/65	Kapp K-659	Just a Closer Walk with Thee (Part 1)/(Part 2)
—	—	03/15/65	Decca 31754	Your Cheatin' Heart/I Can't Help It (If I'm Still in Love with You)
—	—	07/06/65	Decca 25673	South of the Border (Down Mexico Way)/San Antonio Rose
—	—	11/08/65	Decca 25686	I Love You So Much It Hurts/Seven Lonely Days
—	—	03/28/66	Decca 25694	Shoes/Half as Much
—	—	07/18/66	Decca 25699	You Were Only Foolin' (While I Was Falling in Love)/Lonely Street
—	—	12/12/66	Decca 25707	That's My Desire/Foolin' 'Round

—	—	03/20/67	Decca 25712	You Took Him off My Hands/Does Your Heart Beat for Me?
—	—	07/24/67	Decca 25718	Hidin' Out/Have You Ever Been Lonely (Have You Ever Been Blue)?
—	—	12/04/67	Decca 25724	True Love/Love, Love, Love Me Honey Do
—	—	04/29/68	Decca 25732	Always/Pick Me Up on Your Way Down
—	—	08/05/68	Decca 25738	You Made Me Love You (I Didn't Want to Do It)/Too Many Secrets
73	—	11/11/68	Decca 25744	Anytime/In Care of the Blues
—	—	03/10/69	Decca 25747	Crazy Arms/The Wayward Wind
—	—	05/14/73	MCA 60063	Crazy/Your Cheatin' Heart
—	—	06/25/73	MCA 60062	I Fall to Pieces/He Called Me Baby
—	—	08/06/73	MCA 60102	Crazy Arms/Pick Me Up on Your Way Down
—	—	10/15/73	MCA 60061	Walkin' After Midnight/South of the Border (Down Mexico Way)
98	—	03/??/78	4-Star 1033	Life's Railway to Heaven/If I Could See the World (Through the Eyes of a Child)
18	—	08/01/80	MCA 41303	Always/I'll Sail My Ship Alone
61	—	11/??/80	MCA 51038	I Fall to Pieces/True Love
05	—	10/??/81	RCA 12346	Have You Ever Been Lonely (Have You Ever Been Blue)? [duet with Jim Reeves]/Welcome to My World [Jim Reeves solo]
54	—	05/??/82	MCA 52052	I Fall to Pieces [duet with Jim Reeves]/So Wrong
—	—	10/??/85	MCA 52684	Sweet Dreams/Blue Moon of Kentucky

Extended-Plays

CORAL
| 08/05/57 | EC 81159 | *Songs By Patsy Cline* |

DECCA
08/05/57	ED 2542	*Patsy Cline*
08/14/61	ED 2703	*Patsy Cline*
01/29/62	ED 2707	*Patsy Cline*
04/30/62	ED 2719	*She's Got You*
09/24/62	ED 2729	*So Wrong—You're Stronger Than Me*
05/20/63	ED 2757	*Leavin' on Your Mind*
06/10/63	ED 2759	*Dear God*
02/10/64	ED 2768	*How Can I Face Tomorrow?*
11/09/64	ED 2770	*Someday You'll Want Me to Want You*
03/29/65	ED 2794	*Always*
10/11/65	ED 2802	*Love Letters in the Sand*

Albums

DECCA (& REISSUED MCA)

Release Year	Title and Number	
1957	*Patsy Cline*	DL-8611/MCA 25200
1961	*Patsy Cline Showcase*	DL-4202/DL-74202/MCA 87
1962	*Sentimentally Yours*	DL-4282/DL-74282/MCA 90
1963	*The Patsy Cline Story*	DXB-176/DXSB-7176/MCA 2-4038
1964	*A Portrait of Patsy Cline*	DL-4508/DL-74508/MCA 224
1964	*That's How a Heartache Begins*	DL-4586/DL-74586
1967	*Patsy Cline's Greatest Hits*	DL-4854/DL-74854/MCA 12

[This album was reissued again by MCA in 1988 as *12 Greatest Hits* using the same album number. All selections are the same except for "Walkin' After Midnight." On the original release, the 1961 recording was used. On this reissue, the 1956 recording replaced it.]

VOCALION (& REISSUED MCA)

Release Year	Title and Number	
1965	*Here's Patsy Cline*	VL-3753/VL-73753/MCA 738
1969	*Country Great*	VL-73872/MCA 736

KAPP

Release Year	Title and Number	
1965	*Buddies*	KL-1445/KS-1445 [various artists]

MCA

Release Year	Title and Number	
1980	*Always*	MCA 3263/MCA 27069

[New instrumentation and chorus added to original vocal tracks]

1982	*Remembering*	MCA 5319/MCA 1467

[Includes the "duet" song "I Fall to Pieces" by Jim Reeves & Patsy Cline, plus five Cline songs and four Reeves songs]

1986	*Stop, Look & Listen*	MCA 1440
1985	*Today, Tomorrow & Forever*	MCA 1463
1985	*Sweet Dreams* [soundtrack]	MCA 6149

[Eight out of twelve songs have new instrumentation added to original vocal tracks]

1986	*Songwriters Tribute*	MCA 25019
1988	*The Last Sessions*	MCA 25199
1988	*Live at the Opry*	MCA 42142
1989	*Live, Volume 2*	MCA 42284
1991	*The Patsy Cline Collection*	MCA 4-10421

RCA

Release Year	Title and Number	
1981	*Greatest Hits*	AHL1-4127

[Includes the "duet" version of "Have You Ever Been Lonely (Have You Ever Been Blue)?" by Reeves & Cline, plus four songs by Cline and five by Reeves]

RHINO

Release Year	Title and Number	
1989	*Walkin' Dreams: Her First Recordings, Volume 1*	R2-70048
1989	*Hungry for Love: Her First Recordings, Volume 2*	R2-70049
1989	*The Rockin' Side: Her First Recordings, Volume 3*	R2-70050

About the Compiler

Don Roy is a Nashville-based freelance music historian who has spent the past fourteen years studying the career of Patsy Cline. Other discographies that Roy has compiled include those for Marty Robbins, Brenda Lee, Webb Pierce, Johnny Horton, and Tanya Tucker. He is currently a contributing discographer/researcher for the Germany-based Bear Family Records.

Printed in the United States
59832LVS00001B/17

9 780306 808869